GESTALT VOICES

FRONTIERS IN PSYCHOTHERAPY SERIES
Edward Tick, *Series Editor*

Gestalt Voices

Edited by
Edward W.L. Smith

ABLEX PUBLISHING CORPORATION
NORWOOD, NEW JERSEY

Second Printing 1994

Copyright © 1992 by Ablex Publishing Corporation

Printed in the United States of America

Library of Congress Cataloging-in-Publication Data

Gestalt voices / edited by Edward W.L. Smith.
       p.   cm. -- (Frontiers in psychotherapy series)
   Includes bibliographical references and index.
   ISBN 0-89391-802-4 (cloth). -- ISBN 0-89391-803-2 (paper)
   1. Gestalt therapy.   2. Gestalt therapists.   3. I. Smith, Edward W.L.,
  1942–   . II. Series.
   RC489.G4G86   1991   91-37392
   661.89'143--dc20   CIP

Ablex Publishing Corporation
355 Chestnut Street
Norwood, New Jersey 07648

To the editors who have nurured *Voices:*
Tom Leland
John Warkentin
Vin Rosenthal
E. Mark Stern
Edward Tick

Also by Edward W.L. Smith:

The Growing Edge of Gestalt Therapy (ed.) (1976, 1977)

The Body in Psychotherapy (1985)

Sexual Aliveness (1987)

Not Just Pumping Iron: On the Psychology of Lifting Weights (1989)

Gestalt Therapy emphasizes not that we live for the moment, but that we live in the moment; not that we meet our needs immediately, but that we are present for ourselves in the environment.

Joseph Zinker

TABLE OF CONTENTS

II. Gestalt Practice

Acknowledgments

I had fun editing this book. Part of the fun was my interaction with a number of encouraging people.

When I first conceived of *Gestalt Voices* I mentioned my idea to a long-time colleague, Ann McKain. Her immediate and forceful response was "Neat Idea!" With that, I was on my way.

Tony Fey, at that time my office administrator, had a similar reaction. Time and time again, he reminded me that he thought this book was a good idea.

Early in my plans I contacted Mark Stern, then Editor of *Voices*, to get his opinion. His support was immediate. He offered several useful suggestions, and presented my idea to the Executive Council of the American Academy of Psychotherapists. The Council issued a formal statement of encouragement to me.

I discussed *Gestalt Voices* with two other colleagues, Earl Brown, then President of the Academy, and Bernhard Kempler, then a member of the Academy's Executive Council. They too, were very supportive of my project.

During the article selection phase, another colleague, Bob Timms, supplied me with several back issues of *Voices* which I was missing, and discussed the selection process with me.

Joe Wysong, editor of *The Gestalt Journal*, added his enthusiasm, and upon seeing the table of contents, opined that this volume would be a worthwhile contribution to the Gestalt community.

Ed Tick, current editor of *Voices*, has been of immense help. He has encouraged me to continue when I have grown tired.

Finally, I thank Bob Weitz, editor of *Psychotherapy in Private Practice* for the idea of including some of the cartoons which have appeared in *Voices*.

So, to all of you I am grateful. And, to all of the authors: I thank you for your permission to include your articles.

Preface

Several months ago I was studying some early Gestalt therapy articles in preparation for teaching my part of the didactic portion of a nine-month professional training program in Gestalt therapy. Some of the articles were ones I had read before, others were new discoveries for me. In both cases, as I read I felt exhilarated. When I re-read the articles I had read months or even years before, I found nuggets which I had forgotten. I also found nuggets which I had overlooked on the previous reading or readings, nuggets which I could now recognize in light of the months or years of additional clinical experience and life experience which I had had. Some of the old articles which I had never read before were teeming with rich material.

Wanting to find more of these treasures, I thought of *Voices* as a possible hunting ground. Having subscribed to *Voices* since its second year of existence and having served on the editorial board for ten years, I recalled that there had been some good Gestalt therapy articles throughout the years, contained therein. I wanted to go back through the issues and find those good articles, and perhaps find some I had not recognized during my first reading.

Next, I thought about the reason for *Voices'* even being. The oral tradition allows for interpretation, embellishment, and distortion of the story with each telling. The written word, on the other hand, gives a permanent account of a story at some particular fixed time and place. So, the written word serves as still frames in the ongoing, constantly evolving story which is as a moving picture. These still frames allow for detailed study, and for repeated study. Such study can preserve two important things which may be lost in the ongoing story. First, a sense of history, a sense of the evolution of the material, is allowed. Second, the continued presence of still valid and viable material which otherwise might be forgotten, is provided. So I believed that the Gestalt therapy articles published in *Voices* over the past 22 years could provide a perspective on the history of Gestalt therapy and a continued reminder of some material which is as valid and viable today as it was when it was first put in print. This second point is to resist the forces in our field which assume that new is better, that validity is another word for novelty, and that good psychotherapy is ruled by the same fickle market as the "Top 40."

But *Voices* is already a printed form. Why reprint selections in book form? I have four reasons. First, it is a question of sharp focus. Although there are many Gestalt therapy articles in *Voices*, they are ensconced in a matrix of material much broader. By pulling them out of that broader matrix and putting them together under one cover, a new form is created. This new form offers a convenience to the searcher for Gestalt material.

I want to show, under this one cover, the specific contribution of *Voices* to the Gestalt therapy literature. This is the second reason for the book.

Any printed form has a limited distribution. So, my third reason for this book is to reach an additional audience by virtue of the marketing possibilities of a new book. I intend for this book to be seen by professional and serious nonprofessional readers who may never read the professional journal *Voices*, and perhaps have never even heard of it.

My fourth reason is a subtle one having to do with the difference between a journal, published periodically, and a book, published once. Because of their sharing in periodical publication, journals have similarity with magazines. As such, journals have a slightly lower status than books. Books are more lasting, at least in our way of thinking about them. Journals, which are to be kept, are often put in indexed boxes, or even bound, and thus made book-like. So, again, my wish for book form.

In keeping with the meaning of the title of the journal, *Voices,* I decided on the title for the present book, *Gestalt Voices.* May the following voices of Gestalt therapy be heard anew!

Edward W.L. Smith, Ph.D.
Atlanta, Georgia
Winter, 1990

Introduction

The American Academy of Psychotherapists and Gestalt therapy have been on intimate terms for most of their lives. The public appearance of Gestalt therapy and the founding of the Academy's journal, *Voices*, both occurred in the 1960s. Although Perls, Hefferline, and Goodman published *Gestalt Therapy: Excitement and Growth in the Human Personality* in 1951, it received little notice, and the proliferation of Gestalt therapy literature did not begin until the 1960s. By the mid-1960s there were a few articles, some published in *Voices*. But the explosion occurred in the late 1960s and the first half of the following decade. In 1969 Perls published *In and Out the Garbage Pail, Gestalt Therapy Verbatim*, and a new edition of a hitherto obscure book *Ego, Hunger, and Aggression* (written in South Africa and published in 1947). During the next seven years no fewer than 23 books appeared with a Gestalt therapy theme. Included were works by Downing, Fagan and Shepherd, Greenwald, Kempler, Latner, Naranjo, the Polsters, Rhyne, Simkin, the Stevens, and my first book, as well as two more by Perls. While all of this prolific writing was taking place, a sizable number of the Gestalt therapy articles were brought into print through *Voices*. *Voices* has continued to be a major forum for articles on various facets of Gestalt Therapy—theory, philosophy, training, technique and practice, and history—as well as personal views and reflections of therapists who identify their orientation as Gestalt. To date there are over 140 such articles within the covers of *Voices*.

The intimacy between the Academy and Gestalt therapy has also been manifest in ways other than literary. From the early days of the Academy, its membership has reflected the growth of the number of Gestalt therapists in the United States. This is demonstrated by the fact that in a recent directory of AAP, 30 percent of the 798 members indicate Gestalt therapy as one of their theoretical orientations. This is probably a deflated figure. Some of the therapists who list their orientations as "eclectic," "humanistic," or "phenomenological" may well include Gestalt therapy under those rubrics. So, I believe it is safe to say that about one-third of the members of AAP have been influenced in their orientation by Gestalt therapy.

Many of the luminaries of Gestalt therapy have been quite prominent in their participation in the Academy meetings, including both Fritz and Laura Perls. Through such participation, AAP has been a major vehicle for disseminating Gestalt therapy to the professional community. (AAP holds two national meetings per year. The Summer Workshop is a members only meeting, but the Fall Institute and Conference are open to nonmembers and often draw heavily for their registration from the local professional communities as they convene at various locations throughout the United States. There are also regional meetings which invite nonmember participation.)

In addition to the publication of articles, *Voices* has furthered the exposure of Gestalt therapy by running announcements of training workshops, advertisements for books, and the listing of tapes from the AAP tape library. Beginning with Vol. 1, No. 1 of *Voices* in the fall of 1965 there was the following tape listing:

#16 Naomi
This is a demonstration session, recorded at a recent AAP Workshop, of the Gestalt approach to dream analysis and interpretation. The therapist is Dr. Fritz Perls working with a young woman and interacting with the group present.

Note that the description was of "the Gestalt approach to dream analysis and interpretation." Apparently word had not gotten around that Gestalt dream work, according to Perls, was nonanalytic and noninterpretive. In that same listing of tapes there is a second, designated as #18 and titled "Gestalt-Expressive Therapy." This is by Gene Sagan. The tapes continued to be listed for several years, with additions being made by Fritz Perls, Laura Perls, and Jim Simkin.

Several Gestalt therapy books have been reviewed in *Voices*. Included are Clements' review of Perls' *Ego, Hunger, and Aggression* (Vol. 3, No. 3, Fall 1967), Sonia and Ed Nevis' review of Fagan and Shepherd's *Gestalt Therapy Now* (Vol. 7, No. 1, Spring 1971), Banks' review of Hatcher and Himelstein's *The Handbook of Gestalt Therapy* (Vol. 14, No. 2, Summer 1978), Benjamin Adams' review of Feder and Ronall's *Beyond the Hot Seat* (Vol. 16, No. 4, Winter 1981), Arbuckle's review of Rainwater's *You're in Charge: A Guide to Becoming Your Own Therapist* (Vol. 17, No. 4, Winter 1982), and Harman's review of my book, *The Body in Psychotherapy* (Vol. 23, No. 2, Summer 1987). In addition to these reviews, Fagan and Shepherd's book, Gaines' *Fritz Perls Here and Now*, and Simkin's *Mini-Lectures in Gestalt Therapy* were grandly announced in *Voices* in half-page or full-page advertisements.

Several announcements for Gestalt therapy training workshops and programs have appeared in *Voices* over the years. Some of these announcements were repeated in several issues. The Gestalt Institute of Cleveland, Michael Conant's Institute for Bioenergetics and Gestalt, Esalen Institute, Eric Marcus, Jim Simkin, and the Western Institute for Group and Family Therapy have all placed such listings.

It seems clear that Gestalt therapy and AAP have a considerable area of overlap. They share some common ground. It is the literary expression of this common ground which I wish to present and highlight in *Gestalt Voices*.

I want to describe my process of choosing the material for *Gestalt Voices*. My first step was to screen for all material relating to Gestalt therapy. So I perused *Voices* from Vol. 1, No. 1 to the present, noting the following:

1. Articles by authors whom I know to be Gestalt therapists or whom I know were Gestalt therapists at the time the articles were written.
2. Articles by authors who identified themselves as Gestalt therapists.
3. Articles in which any aspect of Gestalt therapy was discussed.
4. Reviews of Gestalt therapy books.
5. Listing of Gestalt therapy tapes in the AAP tape library.
6. Advertisements for Gestalt therapy books, training programs, and workshops.

Through this first step I informed myself that there was ample material for a book. I then photocopied the material for convenience. This act of data reduction yielded a two-and-one-half-inch stack of photocopies from a 30-inch stack of *Voices* raw data.

The second step was to eliminate dated materials. In keeping with this criterion, I decided only to mention in this introduction the reviews of Gestalt therapy books, Gestalt therapy tapes, and advertising for Gestalt therapy books, workshops, and training programs. (The exception is the review of Gaines' *Fritz Perls: Here and Now*.)

My third step, and the one requiring the most in terms of editorial judgment, was my selection of which articles to include in *Gestalt Voices* from the pool of over 140 articles. Basically, I excluded articles which had nothing *substantial* to say about Gestalt therapy, even though in some cases the authors are recognized as Gestalt therapists, or were self-identified as such. In addition, I did include some articles which were written by Gestalt therapists, and although they may not contain substantial Gestalt therapy information, give a flavor of the Gestalt perspective. Through this editorial process I arrived at what I judged to be the best of the Gestalt therapy material published in 25 years of *Voices*.

As I looked at the articles chosen, I found I could cluster them into six categories: Theory, Practice, Training, Views, and Reflections by Gestalt

Therapists, Criticisms of Gestalt Therapy and Rejoinders, and Appreciations to the Pioneers of Gestalt Therapy. The appreciations are probably not of great interest at this point, so in consultation with Joe Wysong I deleted those, with one exception. Because of its clarity and profound message I included Fagan's "The Importance of Fritz Perls Having Been."

For several years *Voices* ran cartoons in each issue. That was unique, as far as I am aware, in professional psychotherapy journals. I chose a number of these cartoons which are particularly relevant to Gestalt therapy, and have sprinkled them about in *Gestalt Voices*. I see them as another aspect of what *Voices* has offered, a touch of graphic humor to lighten where too much heaviness might otherwise prevail.

In a back issue of *The Gestalt Journal* (Spring 1984, Vol. 7, No. 1) Isadore From urged "a restoring of Gestalt therapy to its proper place in the mainstream of psychotherapy." He observed that many of the Gestalt therapists, familiar only with the techniques, have moved on to other "technique-ful" systems, remaining ignorant of the richness of Gestalt therapy. I resonate with From's observation. I, too, wish to see Gestalt therapy more broadly recognized as a rich wellspring. The Gestalt approach embodies a particular existential philosophy (with a Taoist-Zen flavor), and an organismic theory of personality and psychopathology, as well as a body of therapeutic techniques. To know only the techniques is to be a technician, at best. To know the rich philosophical and theoretical underpinnings of the techniques is to embrace a profound "way" of understanding. It is to this end, and to the restoring of Gestalt therapy to its proper place in the mainstream of psychotherapy that I dedicate *Gestalt Voices*.

Part I
Gestalt Theory

Chapter 1

Concepts and Misconceptions of Gestalt Therapy*

LAURA PERLS

In Goethe's *Faust*, Mephistopheles says to an eager disciple:

Denn eben wo Begriffe fehlen,
Da stellt ein Wort zur rechten Zeit sich ein.
(For, whenever there's a lack of concepts,
There at the proper time a word comes handy).

The Devil takes a hand in every human endeavor, not only in philosophy and theology. I see him at work in politics and education, in science and art, and particularly in our own field, the teaching and practice of psychotherapy, busily supplying not only words but ready-made formulas, techniques and gimmicks, a whole quick-change bag of tricks to whoever is needy, ignorant and credulous enough, and willing to pay.

The Devil is the master of short-cut, pretentious, seductive and deceiving, promising, coaxing, and relentlessly bullying. His tools are simplification, manipulation, and distortion.

Let us proceed now from myth to facts. At a meeting of the New York Institute for Gestalt Therapy, I put the question: What is your answer if

---

* This article was originally presented as an address given at the European Association for Transactional Analysis in Seefeld/Austria in July 1977.

somebody asks you: "What is Gestalt therapy?" Our Vice President, Richard Kitzler, who likes to play the Devil's advocate, mumbled under his breath: "The hot seat and the empty chair." Of course, like Mephisto, he said it tongue in cheek. But the naive and impatient disciple takes it at face value; he will always take the part for the whole.

The style that Fritz Perls developed in demonstration workshops for professionals during the last few years of his life has become widely known through films and video tapes of those workshops and through *Gestalt Therapy Verbatim* (1969), the transcripts of these tapes. The dramatization of dreams and fantasies is a beautiful demonstration method, particularly in workshops with professionals who have already had their personal analysis or therapy, and are themselves experienced in working with people. But it is only *one* aspect of the infinite possibilities in the Gestalt approach. It is not useful in working with very disturbed people and not usable at all with the real schizophrenic or paranoid patient. Fritz Perls knew this very well and simply by-passed workshop participants where he sensed the schizoid or paranoid disturbance.

Unfortunately, this workshop approach has become widely accepted as the essence of Gestalt therapy and applied by ever growing numbers of therapists to whomever they are working with. Thus, Gestalt theory is reduced to a purely *technical* modality which, because of its obvious limitations, then is combined with any other technical modality that happens to be available in the psychotherapeutic armamentarium. So we get sensitivity training *and* Gestalt, body awareness *and* Gestalt, Bioenergetics *and* Gestalt, art and dance therapies *and* Gestalt, Transcendental Meditation *and* Gestalt, Transactional Analysis *and* Gestalt, and something or other *and* Gestalt ad infinitum.

All these combinations show that the basic concepts of Gestalt therapy are either misunderstood or simply not known. Gestalt therapy is neither a particular technique nor a collection of specific techniques. Thus, it is not an encounter or confrontation method with a structured sequence of directions, demands and challenges. It is also not a dramatic-expressive method aimed primarily at the discharge of tension. Tension is energy, and energy is too costly a commodity to be simply discharged; it must be made available for making the necessary or desirable changes. The task of therapy is to develop sufficient support for the reorganization and rechanneling of energy.

The basic concepts of Gestalt therapy are philosophical and aesthetic rather than technical. Gestalt therapy is an existential-phenomenological approach and as such it is experiential and experimental. Its emphasis on the Here and Now does not imply—as is often assumed—that past and future are unimportant or non-existent for Gestalt therapy. On the contrary, the past is ever present in our total life experience, our memories, nostalgia, or resentment, and particularly in our habits and hang-ups, in all the unfinished business, the fixed gestalten. The future is present in our preparations and beginnings, in expectation and hope, or dread and despair.

Why do we call our approach *Gestalt* therapy? "Gestalt" is a holistic concept (*ein Ganzheitsbergriff*). A gestalt is a structured entity that is more than, or different from, its parts. It is the foreground figure that stands out from its ground, it "exists." The term "Gestalt" entered the psychological vocabulary through the work of Wolfgang Koehler who applied principles derived from field theory to problems of perception. Gestalt *psychology* was developed further by Max Wertheimer, Gelb and Goldstein, Koffka and Lewin and their colleagues and students. For the development of Gestalt *therapy* the work of Wertheimer, Goldstein and Lewin became particularly important. Anybody who wants fully to understand Gestalt therapy would do well to study Wertheimer on productive thinking, Lewin on the incomplete gestalt and the crucial importance of interest for gestalt formation, and Kurt Goldstein on the organism as an indivisible totality.

Goldstein's organismic approach links up with Wilhelm Reich's theory of organismic self-regulation to become in Gestalt therapy the postulate of the awareness continuum, the freely ongoing gestalt-formation, where whatever is of greatest interest and importance for the survival and development of the individual or social organism will become figure, will come into the foreground where it can be fully experienced and responsibly dealt with.

But Reich's most essential contribution to the development of Gestalt therapy is his recognition of the identity of muscular tensions and character formation. The character armor, epitomized in the obsessional character, is a fixed gestalt which becomes a block in the ongoing gestalt formation. The practical focus on body awareness, however, became part of Gestalt therapy not through Reich, but through my lifelong experience with eurythmics and modern dance, my early study of the work of Ludwig Klages "Ausdrucksbewegung und Gestaltungskraft" (expressive movement and creativity), and my awareness of Alexander and Feldenkrais methods long before the development of Bioenergetics and other body therapies. Working with breathing, posture, coordination, voice, sensitivity, and mobility became part of my therapeutic style already in the 1930's when we still called ourselves psychoanalysts.

The gradual shift from the psychoanalytical to a gestalt orientation is documented in *Ego, Hunger and Aggression* (Perls, 1969), published first in 1942. I contributed to it two chapters that are predominantly gestaltist: "The Dummy Complex," which is the *fixed gestalt* that prevents change, and "The Meaning of Insomnia," which is the *incomplete gestalt*, the unfinished situation which does not let us sleep. In *Ego, Hunger and Aggression* we changed from the historical-archeological Freudian viewpoint to the existential-experiential, from piecemeal association psychology to a holistic approach, from the purely verbal to the organismic, from interpretation to direct awareness in the Here and Now, from transference to actual contact, from the concept of the Ego as a substance *having* boundaries to a concept of it as the very boundary phenomenon itself, *being* the actual *contact function* of identification and alienation. All these concepts, then still tentative, often confused and confusing, developed during the next ten years into a more organized coherent theory which was published as *Gestalt Therapy: Excitement and Growth in the Human Personality* (Perls, Goodman, & Hefferline, 1951). This is the basic book that I still consider indispensable for a full understanding of Gestalt therapy.

However, at the risk of repeating what some of you have heard before, but what seems generally not well understood, I want to confine myself to a few concepts which are interconnected and—for me—essential for the theory *and* practice of Gestalt therapy: the concepts of boundary, contact, and support.

Contact is the recognition of, and the coping with the *other*, the different, the new, the strange. It is not a state that we are in or out of (which would correspond more to the states of confluence or isolation), but an activity: I *make* contact on the boundary between me and the other. The boundary is where we touch and at the same time experience separateness. It is where the excitement is, the interest, concern, and curiosity or fear and hostility, where previously unaware or diffused experience comes into focus, into the foreground as a clear gestalt. The freely ongoing gestalt formation is identical with the process of growth, the creative development of self and relationship. If this continuum is interrupted by outside interference or blocked by the fixed gestalten of rigid character formation or of obsessional thoughts and activities, no strong new gestalt can emerge. The boundary experience becomes blurred and even wiped out by the fixed and incomplete gestalten. Excitement changes into anxiety and dread or indifference and boredom. The faculties of differentiation and discrimination are disowned and projected; attitudes, ideas, and principles of other people are misappropriated and introjected; energy that might be available for direct and creative action is deflected into dummy activities or retroflected in self-interference, self-reproaches, self-pity, and self-destruction. (For a more detailed phenomenology of introjection, projection, deflection and retroflexion, I recommend Erving and Miriam Polster's book *Gestalt Therapy Integrated* (1973).)

How does a gestalt therapist cope with this pandemonium of neurotic and psychotic pathology that we are faced with every day? Our aim is the awareness continuum, the freely flowing ongoing gestalt formation, which can go on only when excitement and interest can be maintained. Contact can be relevant and creative only to the extent that support for it is available. By support I mean only to the smallest degree the care and assurance that I as the therapist provide through my availability and interest, but the self-support that the patient (or the therapist, for that matter!) either relies on or is lacking. Support starts with primary physiology like breathing, circulation, and digestion, continues with the development of the cortex, the growing of teeth, upright posture, coordination, sensitivity and mobility, language and its uses, habits and customs, even and particularly the hang-ups which were formed as support at the time of their formation. All the experience and learning that has been *fully assimilated and integrated* builds up a person's background, which gives meaning to the emerging gestalten and thus supports a certain way of living *on the boundary with* excitement. Whatever is not assimilated either gets lost or remains an introject.

The integrated personality has *style*, a unified way of expression and communication. He or she may not conform to what is regarded as "well adjusted," socially useful and desirable, or even healthy. He will be called "eccentric" or "irresponsible," "queer," "crazy," or "criminal," he may be an anarchist, a painter or poet, a homosexual or a hobo. But the person who has *style* does not come for therapy, at least not voluntarily. The people who want and need therapy are the ones who are stuck with their anxiety, their dissatisfaction, their inadequacies in work and relationships, their unhappiness. They lack support for the kind of contact that would be necessary or desirable and adequate to the situation they find themselves in.

Now any lack of essential support is experienced as anxiety. Usually anxiety is equaled with insufficient oxygen, but the reduction and even suspension of breathing and with it a reduction of excitement and interest may already be a reaction formation to a potentially dangerous situation (playing possum) or to the demand for "self-control." There is a whole scale of malcoordinations of support and contact functions ranging from occasional unease, awkwardness and embarrassment to chronic anxiety and panic. We have not enough time to go into the whole phenomenology of these malcoordinations. I only want to emphasize one point: awkwardness and embarrassment are potentially creative states, the temporary lack of balance we experience at the growing edge where we have one foot on familiar and one foot on unfamiliar ground, the very boundary experience itself. If we have mobility and allow ourselves to wobble, we can maintain the excitement, ignore and even forget the awkwardness, gain *new* ground and with it more support. We can see this graceful awkwardness in every small child before it becomes socialized and constrained by the civilized demand to "keep it cool." I know from my own experience how difficult it is to rid ourselves of the introjects that we have remained encumbered with through most of our lives. At this point, I feel nearly always a little awkward and embarrassed. Right now I feel a bit uneasy not exactly knowing who I am talking to and rather talking *at* you. But I also know that I'll survive it. I have learned to live with *uncertainty without anxiety*.

How we do facilitate this development of more elastic support functions in our *patients* depends on the support we have in ourselves and our awareness of what is available in our clients. A good therapist does not use techniques, he applies himself in and to a situation with whatever knowledge, skills, and total life experience have become integrated into his own background and whatever awareness he has at any given moment. Thus, I would speak of *styles* of therapy rather than techniques. Nearly any technical modality is applicable within the framework of Gestalt therapy, if it is existential, experiential, and experimental only to the degree that support can be mobilized, e.g., if the patient is already or can be made aware of what and how he is doing now and willing to experiment with expansions or alternatives. So we start with the obvious, with what is immediately available to the awareness of therapist as well as client, and we proceed from there in small steps which are immediately experienced and thus are more easily assimilable. This is a time-consuming process which sometimes is misunderstood by people who are out for easy excitement and magical results. But miracles are a result not only of intuition, but of timing. I feel suspicious of the miracle worker and am weary of the instant breakthrough. More often than not, it results in a negative therapeutic reaction, a relapse or even a psychotic break. It shows a lack of respect for the patient's existential predicament, not accepting him as he is at this moment, but manipulating him quickly to where we think he should be. It does not contribute to the development of his awareness and his autonomy, nor does it contribute to the growth of the therapist.

REFERENCES

Perls, F., Hefferline, R.F., & Goodman, P. *Gestalt therapy: Excitement and growth in the human personality.* New York: Dell Publishing Co., Inc., 1951.

Perls F. *Gestalt therapy verbatim.* Lafayette, CA: Real People Press, 1969.

Perls, F. *Ego, hunger, and aggression.* New York: Random House, 1969.

Polster, E., & M. *Gestalt therapy integrated.* New York: Brunner/Mazel, 1973.

Comment

Edward W.L. Smith

Several years ago Fritz Perls spoke out strongly against the attempted short-cuts, the promises of instant cure, the gimmicks, and the use of techniques, copied yet not understood. He was keenly aware and appreciative of the growth process.

As the Gestalt approach has become more widely known, or perhaps more accurately, as it has become more widely "heard of," it has been identified usually as a technical skill. It is the techniques which are recognized and borrowed, for the most part. As I travel about doing presentations on the Gestalt approach, I frequently surprise my audience by doing things which they identify as "belonging" to Bioenergetics, or to T.A., or to Psychomotor, or to P.E.T., or to some therapy system of which I have never even heard. And then when I talk of the philosophy and theory of personality functioning of the Gestalt approach they are often inspired, going back to their own work feeling some renewal of enthusiasm born of a rich perspective on the process of growth. I enjoy providing a training experience which demonstrates the powerful use of therapy procedures and creation of nonce techniques, out of a well-developed and solid cognitive framework.

One of the masters from whom I have learned and been inspired is Laura Perls. And as I read this present manuscript I learned, and even more importantly, I was inspired. Her style is concise and very clear. Being so, the profundity of what she says can be missed by a quick reading. This manuscript could be read and pondered repeatedly with profit by most of us. Laura has lived a long and full life. She knows much.

Chapter 2

Acting Out vs. Acting Through: An Interview With Frederick Perls, M.D., Ph.D.

COOPER C. CLEMENTS

Fritz: Before you ask questions I want to say something about "acting out" in general. This term, acting out, takes me back to the time when I was a psychoanalyst, and where Acting Out was a bad thing. Freud's rigid demand was, "You should not act out, but remember instead." In his preoccupation with the past, Freud said people should remember instead of acting out. But his idea, in my opinion, was that they should be aware and have enough distance from this way of living so that they could work on it. They should be, in Freudian terms, more conscious of what they were doing. In a way, Freud's idea was correct. He believed that people lived certain neurotic attitudes and by living them and acting them out, they escaped treatment. Now in Gestalt Therapy when we talk about "acting out" we do not mean living out but "Be an actor." We have a script in the form of a dream or a fantasy. We see that the dream (or fantasy) is a story, a drama, and we act it out again in therapy to make us more aware of what we are, of what is available.

Cooper: And this is acting out the role in the therapy situation.

Fritz: Exactly. So the trouble lies partly on a semantic level. The acting out idea of Freud should say, "Be aware that you act out a role." But instead a taboo was presented by Freud as, "You should not act out because it is a bad thing." Now in Freudian therapy you don't bring this into the therapy, and so maybe the prohibition makes sense.

Cooper: In Gestalt Therapy you are aiming for conscious awareness of the acted out roles?

Fritz: Exactly. The difference between us and Freud is that he stressed remembering and we stress being aware. We stress the difference between *deliberate acting* and being unaware of living in a certain way. The latter is living a part of life's script and doing it compulsively, without knowing that it is a pathological way of living. I want to emphasize that in Freudian terminology Acting Out is a dirty word. And many things are then covered as "acting out" and a taboo is put on things which might just as well be a genuine expression of the personality. Freud's idea was that everything is predetermined and whatever happens is just a repetition of something that happened before. In other words, this Freudian analysis does not leave room for creative living because if everything happened before, it's an automatic repetition. Again this might often be the case so far as the Freudian type of acting out is concerned.

Cooper: So we want to look ahead to what is authentic living, in addition to the process of getting out of the neurosis.

Fritz: My opinion is this: Any unfinished situation, any incomplete action, will come to the surface and will be or wants to be completed. Now much of what Freud called "the repetition compulsion" (compulsive repetitiveness) is the unfinished situation. Freud thought this is just maybe a habit formation, a petrified way of living. And I maintain it's just the other way around. These compulsive repetitions, the living out of something in a very similar way, are our attempts (futile attempts in most cases) to solve the situation. This is because very often something is left out in this acting out; there is something one is not yet aware of.

Cooper: This would bring in the avoiding part. There's always some avoiding.

Fritz: Yes, yes.

Cooper: It's a crucial element. And then you try to get at this particularly in dream work and body language work?

Fritz: I don't try to get to this. The organism gets to this, and whether it gets to this in the form of acting out or dreaming out—alright poetrying out—it is just a matter of chance the way this person expresses himself. To talk in old-fashioned words, the extrovert would rather live it out and the introvert would make a poor piece of poetry out of it. But in both cases it points to some arresting in one's development by avoiding taking a certain step, taking a certain risk.

Cooper: So you would relate it to the general thing of a person trying to experience and express himself?

Fritz: Look, consider a cat which plays and climbs up a curtain and uses its claws. When the cat is young it cannot avoid using the claws. Claw-using is unfinished business for the young cat; so it does not "act out" at this moment clawing you. Now if a grown-up cat would always use the claws, would act out the claw bit, then something is missing in its development. The moment that it learns to walk without using the claw, then the differentiation has taken place.

Cooper: So you're looking at the development of the individual and his needs for completion, rather than focusing on a prohibition or taboo.

Fritz: Yes. Now let's take an example of a human being learning to do something, say typing. When I've learned to type well and formed the Gestalt by practice, then I'm free to attend to the content and not the mechanics of typing. But if my typing is still faulty, like doing an *m* for an *n*, then a lot of effort must still be invested in the unfinished situation. The whole acting out bit of Freud is something similar. We are repeating a certain unfinished situation. For example, we always get disappointed in the same friend or we are always being sucked in by certain personalities. All this is because we avoid something in the relationship that would lead to a closure, to an understanding of that person, or to the ability to "let go" if this is not the right person. Sure psychoanalysts probably think in the same terms. They would say we have to cure, we have to work through that complex. But the complex is not worked through in the form of coming to closure but only in retracing the event to some so-called trauma, some happening in childhood. This is something quite different from completing the person.

Cooper: And picking up on what's happening here and now.

Fritz: And working on what's here and now and what's missing in that person.

Cooper: I wonder if you would like to relate acting out to the four layers of therapy and neurosis that you were talking about in the group this morning. You described the role-playing layer as first, then the implosive layer leading to the impasse, then the explosive layer, and finally authentic living. Would you see acting out as related to the third layer, the explosive one?

Fritz: Yes, that's very interesting. We are "acting out" in the first layer in playing out roles but this is definitely not in the Freudian sense of thinking that this is an unfinished situation that is bad. We are acting out the patient in the therapy situation so eventually an explosion can be achieved. The acting out in the Freudian sense, the incomplete situation without awareness, is the *blocking* of the explosion.

Cooper: I am thinking of the four areas of explosion you've mentioned in this third layer: explosions into sexual love, into anger, into joy, and into grief. The anger and the sexual love are the ones that get the most attention and that is where the therapists get most concerned with social consequences.

Fritz: I would say Freud is very much in favor of living out, acting out, the grief. He's done beautiful work on the mourning labor. I don't see much of him ever written about the acting out of joy. He, Wilhelm Reich, Adler, and many others have written a lot about anger and they are completely off the mark by having real semantic confusion. Sometimes they talk about aggression, then sadism or cruelty, then anger, then hostility.

Cooper: Hostility seems to be popular these days.

Fritz: Yes, and they never make clear what is going on. These are completely different forms of functioning. A salesman can be aggressive, having initiative, without being hostile.

Cooper: His assertion could also be quite appropriate.

Fritz: I want to give you my favorite example. If I swallow my food, forcing the food down on the basis of greediness, and I am not aggressive toward the food (do not try to destroy the food), then I might get stomach trouble and also develop a certain amount of "introjective tendency" instead of understanding assimilation.

Cooper: In Gestalt the aggression is a necessary part of the assimilation process.

Fritz: In Gestalt? In nature! The supermarket made us forget that we kill in order to survive. Every being kills in order to survive. Only the human being kills out of greed more than he needs. He kills out of habit formation.

Cooper: We've been talking mainly, I think, about acting out in terms of working through the process with the person in the therapy situation. Many times when the acting out taboo comes up, it's that the patient is doing something outside the therapy situation. He is acting out sexually or aggressively in ways that the therapist gets concerned about. The therapist feels the person may not be contributing to his development by this behavior.

Fritz: Okay, I'll give you an example of mine. When I was in analysis, I had no relationship to that guy. He hardly ever spoke in therapy. Five minutes before the therapy hour was finished, he scratched the floor as a signal that the hour was over. He believed in completely passive therapy. Now I noticed what he cherished. He called me an Omar Khayyam when listening to my adventures. So all I did during the time I was in analysis with him was go out for more and more adventures so as to be able to tell him something. I acted out, and the acting out was to please him. He never discussed this with me.

Cooper: So you were trying to have something to report.

Fritz: Sure and this happens with other therapists. The whole thing is so silly, the acting out bit. Just as silly as psychoanalysis itself among Gestalt therapists. The acting out, the compulsion! Come rain, come shine, the person goes every day to the same place for an hour whether he is depressed or happy, whether he wants to go or not, he goes. What rigid compulsion, rigid acting out that is! And then the hour must not be one minute less or one minute more than fifty, notwithstanding the fact that most of the people don't say a real thing except for the last two minutes. Suddenly then they have something urgent to say so as to torture the therapist, to prolong and put him into a quandry on how he can finish up and get his ten-minute rest. Have you not seen that?

Cooper: Yes, and I've done it myself.

Fritz: That's crap and being compulsive, the 50 minutes. Look at our workshop advantage. Sometimes we work 20 minutes with a person, sometimes an hour and a half. This whole individual therapy crap is completely obsolete. It's a fossilized survivor of the Freudian period when they thought psychoanalysis was a means to cure people.

Cooper: So you see this general term of acting out as a taboo that Freud got started.

Fritz: Not only that. I go a step further. Consider the deep phobia of Freud who was a very, very sick man; what was he acting out? He was acting out the business of not going out, *not* acting out. Such pain he had to cross the street, what pain to talk to any person. He was so embarrassed and so self-conscious. However, in a true deep meaning of Freud, I think he was saying be careful of acting out as a means of avoiding, bring your real problems to this place of therapy, this is better. Notwithstanding this, I'm very suspicious whether the taboo of acting out is not just as much a rationalization of Freud's phobia.

Cooper: How would you relate the acting out taboo to different cultural mores and settings? Like in one setting they may allow more sexual freedom and more aggressive expression.

Fritz: Freud never meant this by acting out. Freud meant by acting out that some type of pathological behavior is slipping out and is executed as a piece of living, instead of as a piece of discussion on the couch. What you are talking about is freedom of action, a full awareness that this is permissible and that is not permissible. This is fine to an extent but has nothing to do with the specific thing Freud meant by acting out. If you go that far, then the only way to live would be not to do a thing.

Cooper: So you want to look more in terms of the process going on in the person and how much awareness he has of what he's doing.

Fritz: Yes, as well as what awareness he has of what he's not doing.

Cooper: What he's avoiding.

Fritz: Yes.

Cooper: And that would be the basis for differentiating between role playing in these earlier layers of neurosis and authentic living?

Fritz: Yes, yes. It is to say that somebody cannot see himself as a grownup. He has to have parents; hanging on to a real mother, a dead mother, a psychoanalytical mother, anything not to let go.

Cooper: This is related to what you call the Dummy Complex in your book *Ego, Hunger, and Aggression*, isn't it?

Fritz: Yes. Hanging on to the idea that one is a child, and this is Freudian acting out—one repeats what has happened before, investigates what has happened before, and it is part of keeping the patient in an infantile state. Now acting out in a good sense means letting go, let the dead bury the dead, let the parents be the parents. The other man does so and so but I am a free agent, a free agent on my own. I don't relate to this guy out of a fixation; I relate to him because I want to and to the degree that I feel relatedness.

Cooper: A here and now experience with the person.

Fritz: Yes, Yes.

Cooper: Could you relate acting out to the balance concept in Gestalt, the figure-ground balance of the person you are working with?

Fritz: Yes, in this acting out material (the repetition of something), one of the polarities is always hidden. Let's take the basic acting out. What do we act out as our usual moral or self-improvement system? The topdog-underdog system. You know this game. We are aware of the inefficient underdog part in ourselves, but we are not aware of the character of the top part in ourselves. Our own righteous behavior, we take that for granted. And thus the balance between the submissive behavior and the bullying behavior, between the aggressive and the frightened, cannot be achieved. Let's go back to Freudian terms. He would say there is not a strong ego because the patient is all superego. What Freud misses is that there is an infra-ego balancing of the superego. What do you call acting out there? If I torture myself, sure then I am acting out. But where is the exact point of where you put in that the acting out is bad? Just because you are naughty and don't bring your therapist these things?

(Pause)

Fritz: I feel this is good to take a new look at acting out and what some of the confusion has been. This is the bloody thing always when somebody creates a wrong notion. This wrong notion is then accepted as a reality where there should be nothing. And then the whole world has to start to refute and fight the nonsense. Look what it did to Wilhelm Reich to take the libido as something real instead of as just a conceptual whim of Freud. He went completely off his rocker. Are there some questions you'd like to ask?

Cooper: I know in groups I've been in with you, you usually say you take no responsibility for an individual's behavior outside the group situation. Would that be your view of the patient's behavior outside the therapy situation, that it's up to him?

Fritz: Exactly. I'm responsible only for myself. If you decide to go crazy, it's your business. If I am a responsible therapist I invest my skilled knowledge into working with you.

Cooper: If he wants to bring this into the therapy situation and work, then you're there to work with him?

Fritz: Yes. I don't have a compulsion to win or be the Almighty or the best therapist in the world. Anyone not willing to limit his responsibility to himself is beset with the need to be omnipotent. This is a distorted view of the self and of one's potential.

Cooper: He's expecting more of himself than he can really deliver.

Fritz: Sure.

Cooper: I wonder if we can relate acting out some more to the different layers: role-playing, implosive, explosive, authentic. The first or role-playing layer is obviously related; we see all kinds of behavior which could be labelled acting out.

Fritz: Sure.

Cooper: What about the second layer, the implosive one? What would you see happening there?

Fritz: What is happening is not acting out. There is fear of being, a basic contraction or freezing. This is the equivalent with what Freud sensed as the death instinct. But it is not an instinct for death; if anything, it is the opposite. As you see when it's worked out to the explosion, it's very much being alive! Look at my hand. If I keep an exact balance of extensor and contractor muscles, I can get an extremely rigid claw which can't move. A very rigid position. Yet there is a double amount of energy here, two parts of myself trying to take control and in exact balance. This is life still; it is catatonic.

Cooper: You don't have any figure-ground shifting.

Fritz: Exactly. This is the impasse—being stuck—neither acting out nor not acting out. The slightest acting out here, a slight trembling, is the beginning of dissolution of the implosive layer.

Cooper: How about the third layer, the explosive one? Here you mention explosions into sexual love, anger, joy, grief.

Fritz: These are explosions from the center of the personality which is the soul, also called the center of emotion. This brings the ability to feel and live again.

Cooper: It starts coming out in strong form at that point?

Fritz: Not necessarily strong. In some cases there are extreme explosions at this point. In other forms there is just a slight trembling. Explosions can be like those in your auto engine, not that noticeable. The thing is that the contractions are beginning to work again. The implosive layer is kind of like hibernating. A hibernating animal freezes up, contracts. It's not dead, it preserves life. And then it finally begins to vibrate again.

Cooper: Do people get to the explosive layer, then back up to the implosive layer before they get going with authentic living?

Fritz: Yes. Sometimes you find that only a certain segment is freed by explosion, and then the energy is freed in the total personality. The person becomes more alive. He then is able to cope with other of the feeling levels better. The one emotion easiest to reach is usually grief because it is, in most cases, socially acceptable. The explosion into love is often difficult. The hardest for the neurotic is the explosion into joy.

Cooper: Could you talk about the way you work with say anger and sexual love in therapy, the kinds of limits you put on?

Fritz: I don't put any limits on any explosion, including fucking! It doesn't really come to fucking, but there are no taboos in my kind of therapy. You can at least fuck in fantasy and aggress against a pillow.

Cooper: Here in the workshop one time you had people fighting with just their feet. Wasn't this a way to limit what they could do to each other?

Fritz: No, no, the leg thing came about because some of the people had no legs. Legs are very important for self-support. I suggested they move further apart as they began to use their legs so they would not accidentally hit the genitals or something. There are small precautions. But in the extreme, I've very nearly been killed quite a few times. But if you don't want to take the risk, don't be a therapist.

Cooper: In a group situation you have some support from the group to help control explosions.

Fritz: What do you mean "control explosions?" We don't want to control explosions!

Cooper: Okay. Prevent injury, shall I say?

Fritz: These injuries are not true explosions. True explosions I've seen are usually like those into joy where people dance around. Exceptions are real psychotic cases, a psychotic episode when somebody really wants to kill. Instead of exploding into impotence and realizing the impotence of impotence, they try to avoid impotence by killing. Killing is always a sign of impotence.

Cooper: So you just take your chances?

Fritz: EXACTLY!

Chapter 3

A Trialogue between Laura Perls, Richard Kitzler, and E. Mark Stern

EDITOR'S INTRODUCTION:

> Don't just do something; stand there.
>
> BUDDHA

For Laura, remaining on the frontier is all that truly counts. Here she continues to get into more profound contact—those "contact boundaries" which give Gestalt Therapy its energy and zest. Laura Perls has through the years steadfastly maintained the relevance of the fundamental principles of Gestalt Therapy. Her thesis is that one should be less enthralled with novelty than loyal to the process of mastication and digestion of these fundamental principles of Gestalt Therapy.

The following conversations highlight the mind and vision of Laura Perls. Enjoy and chew well.

E.M.S.

E. Mark Stern: What I would like to ask at the very beginning is something about the history of the New York Institute for Gestalt Therapy.

Laura Perls: The idea started with Fritz. I said at the time, "If you start an Institute it will be our baby and I won't be in it; I won't have anything to do with it." I was overworked at the time, spending one day a week in Philadelphia, and working the other five or six days here in New York. The children were still at home. And then there was the addition of a granddaughter. It was just too much to handle, resulting in my becoming very ill at the time. I developed a tumor and had to have a hysterectomy. This was all in 1952.

Richard Kitzler: Isn't it true, that a large part of the seeds for what came to be called the Institute arose out of the therapy group you were leading?

LP: The group you refer to started in 1949 while Fritz was in Los Angeles. He had been there for almost a year and a half. We thought at the time that we would move to Los Angeles or to some other West Coast location. When I visited him there in the summer, I found myself rather disgusted with the whole atmosphere in Los Angeles, I didn't want to live there and we both came back to New York. It was then he wanted to start the Institute. The group you refer to included several figures who were to figure prominently in Gestalt Therapy. Among them were Paul Goodman, Paul Weisz, Elliott Shapiro, and two documentary photographers. This all took place between 1949 and 1951. The group itself was ongoing.

I was in Los Angeles only in July and August 1950. Fritz came back to New York later and started working with Paul Goodman as editor on *Gestalt Therapy: Excitement and Growth in the Human Personality* (Perls et al., 1951). It was Paul who got the members of the group to run courses at the Institute.

Interestingly, they had all been in individual therapy with me and the group was formed from this source. At the time most of my patients were artists and writers.

Elliott Shapiro taught a course on his use of Gestalt methods with his classroom of schizophrenic children at Kings County Hospital. In 1952 Fritz gave a course of lectures at the Institute. Forty people showed up, so I agreed to take half of them for the ongoing practicum group.

EMS: In 1951 the book *Gestalt Therapy* had just been published. There would have been a tremendous amount of new interest in Gestalt Therapy?

LP: It wasn't a tremendous amount. The interest came mostly from individuals who today would be called "fringe" people. At the time Paul Goodman and Paul Weisz were still on the fringe, that is, they were not accepted in any way. Paul Weisz was well known as a biologist and biochemist, while Paul Goodman had some reputation as a writer and teacher. As a writer he was ignored by the establishment. His early books were published privately or by very small presses and were appreciated by only a small circle. It was only with *Growing Up Absurd* (1960) that he managed to get his name associated with Random House.

RK: Laura, in the address you gave at the 25th anniversary of the Institute, you said, "Without Paul Goodman, I don't think there would be a Gestalt Therapy." Could you elaborate on that?

LP: Without him there wouldn't have been any *theory* of Gestalt Therapy. There would be Gestalt Therapy or what people call Gestalt Therapy but there wouldn't be a coherent theory. Paul was my patient and was subsequently hired by Fritz actually as an editor. Fritz was working at the time with Ralph Hefferline, who did some experiments with his classes at

Teachers College in Columbia University. Yes, Paul was an essential figure in the theoretical development of Gestalt Therapy.

EMS: Do you remember how it got to be called Gestalt Therapy?

LP: I was against calling it Gestalt Therapy because I was a Gestalt psychologist and I knew that the Gestalt psychologists would be up in arms, a prediction which has fulfilled itself to this day. As an aside, Doctor Michael Wertheimer, the son of Max Wertheimer, with whom I studied in Frankfurt, has recently asserted that Gestalt Therapy comes entirely out of Gestalt psychology. I'm not sure, but he must have made some contact with Gestalt therapists on the West Coast.

RK: Wertheimer was not living at the time Gestalt Therapy got its initial thrust.

LP: No, he died in 1943. We came to America in 1946.

EMS: Kurt Goldstein was living at that time.

LP: He was very interested in our development and we always sent him our publications.

RK: You also worked with Adhémar Gelb.

LP: He was the sponsor for my dissertation. He was a wonderful teacher but a terrible dissertation advisor.

RK: What was the title of your doctoral dissertation?

LP: It was in the field of color contrasts and color constancy, which at the time was being investigated by many researchers (Jaensch, David Katz, and others).

RK: What was Fritz's orientation?

LP: His was mostly psychoanalytic.

RK: He worked with the wounded veterans at the Kurt Goldstein Center in Frankfurt, didn't he?

LP: That's where I met him—in a course being given by Gelb. Actually, it was through Gelb that I switched from law school and moved into psychology. I had originally planned to go into juvenile court work. It was just after the First World War, and there were no woman lawyers at the time save a few pioneering girls studying law.

EMS: What was Schilder's role here in Gestalt Therapy?

LP: He died before any of our developments took place.

EMS: Karen Horney was helpful to you, wasn't she?

LP: Karen Horney actually sponsored our immigration into the United States. Fritz had been a patient of hers in Berlin before she emigrated.

EMS: Was there a sustained relationship with her once you arrived in America?

LP: No, not at all. There was the beginning of a relationship with the William Alanson White Institute which broke away from Horney. Clara Thompson took a shine to Fritz and wanted him to join the faculty as a training analyst. At the time they only took M.D.'s. They wanted him to go back to medical school and take another degree here. He was over 50 and at that time in life you don't go back to school anymore.

EMS: Otto Fenichel did go back to medical school on the West Coast and died during his training.

LP: Fenichel had been my supervisor in Berlin but sadly I didn't learn anything from him. You learn from Fenichel when you read him. He didn't say a word for the several months—almost a year—he was supervising me.

EMS: This all brings up your relationship to psychoanalysis and psychoanalytic theory.

LP: Remember, I was a Gestalt psychologist before I got into psychoanalysis. Fritz was an analyst before he got into Gestalt psychology. Sometimes it set up quite an insoluble conflict. I sometimes said I felt like Pavlov's double-conditioned dog who fell asleep in the middle of the experiment.

Then we started psychoanalytic practice. I began my analytic training and analysis in Frankfurt, first with Clara Happel. When she moved to Hamburg I worked with Carl Landauer who was a wonderful analyst, who was later murdered by the Nazis. Clara Happel moved to Detroit, but died soon after of a brain tumor.

RK: Did you learn anything from them?

LP: I learned a lot in Frankfurt, especially through my own analysis which was a comparatively free one. Landauer was a friend of Sandor Ferenczi and Georg Groddek, both of whom were already among the more avant-garde people at the time. Landauer started the Frankfurt Psychoanalytic Institute with Frieda Fromm-Reichmann and Carl Meng. I met Fromm-Reichmann a few times later in this country and was surprised that she remembered me so clearly, since I had been a student at the time and hardly opened my mouth.

EMS: Then when you went to South Africa you started a psychoanalytic institute?

LP: We did, but we were then sabotaged by somebody who had been active in getting us to come there. He turned out to be a little bit paranoid and subsequently disowned us as well as the young Institute.

EMS: There were other roots too, were there not? Phenomenological origins?

LP: Quite right. We were reading Heidegger and Scheler in our Kurt Goldstein seminars. Actually Scheler was supposed to come to Frankfurt as a professor of philosophy and he had given his initial lecture already before the vacation just before he died. Paul Tillich was brought in as his substitute. I studied with Tillich for two years. Tillich and Martin Buber, who was another teacher of mine in Frankfurt, had more influence on me than any psychologists or psychoanalysts. I was impressed by the way they respected people.

EMS: Your roots are really exciting, which I sense you hold in exquisite balance: a reverence for people and a healthy respect for their psychological dynamics. But tell me, how does your psychoanalytic grounding get involved in your practice of Gestalt Therapy?

LP: It got involved in the way in which I somehow transcended it.

EMS: That's a profound way of putting it.

RK: Paul Goodman felt that psychoanalysis could be taken as a ground on which to stand and grow. As the architect of a theory of Gestalt Therapy he used it so and then went on to Reich and finally through Reich to Gestalt. He felt that Gestalt Therapy evolved from Charcot to Freud to Reich and to us.

LP: The first deviation from Freudian theory can be found in *Ego, Hunger, and Aggression* (Perls, 1947), which was actually written by Fritz as a revision of psychoanalysis. At the time we came to this country we were still calling ourselves psychoanalysts.

RK: You not only wrote the chapter on The Dummy Complex but also initiated the theory of dental aggression. To my mind this theory is one of the absolute grounds of Gestalt Therapy. I believe it evolved out of your observations on infants' nursing.

LP: Fritz expanded my research, that had already started in Berlin, into a paper on oral resistance, which laid the ground for the chapters on mental metabolism in *Ego, Hunger and Aggression*.

RK: It's too easy to lose all that in the razzle-dazzle of the human potential movement. As you, Laura, have said so many times, the theory of dental aggression can be summed up as follows: Things take time. Chewing takes time. Therapy takes time.

LP: It takes time and aware activity.

EMS: Do you tend to see the human potential movement as it was flourishing in the late fifties and sixties as a kind of necessary and/or destructive detour from the foundations of Gestalt Therapy?

LP: To a great extent, I think, destructive. In the sixties Fritz got caught up in what was going on on the West Coast. It was a kind of anti-intellectual anything-goes, *laissez-faire* atmosphere. In some ways it suited Fritz because he was basically not a scholar but was very intuitive, that is, intuitively insightful. He was neither a scholar nor a true theoretician.

RK: He was rather vain about that. He said to me once that he had no referential knowledge. It came across as a boast but I suspect that underneath it all there was a nagging feeling that he ought to have had a more intellectual base. He was exactly on the other side of the same coin Goodman was on. Paul Goodman provided the philosophic base for this revolution and he provided a format for the community. As far as I know, Paul never changed a single word of the theoretical base of Gestalt Therapy, whereas Fritz renounced it totally.

LP: Fritz never understood it fully in the first place.

RK: He termed it his own oral underdevelopment.

LP: During his next-to-last visit here, the one before he came back sick, Fritz said to me, "You know, I wish I had understood Goldstein better."

RK: What did you take that to mean, Laura?

LP: I took it to mean that he had not fully understood the organismic theory on which Gestalt Therapy is based. The theory is, of course, essential to Gestalt applications. Fritz did not have the philosophic background to understand. Incidentally, Goldstein was a cousin of Ernest Cassirer.

RK: Fritz claimed he was influenced by Cassirer's book but I doubt he ever really got its essence.

LP: Fritz was always very quickly impressed by something that said something new and then, having gotten the essence of it, he couldn't be bothered with details.

*   *   *

EMS: In both of your eyes, did you feel that the human potential movement represented an unfortunate detour, which resulted in the loss of intellectual forebears?

RK: We held on here in New York. We sort of hunkered down with a bastion out in Cleveland and just manned the barricades against all attempts to reduce Gestalt Therapy to a cult.

LP: I think it is very unfortunate that Fritz's Gestalt Therapy Verbatim (1969) has gotten around the most. It has been translated into many languages. Yet it is nothing else but transcripts from workshops, demonstrating (very impressively) one particular psychodramatic approach that was congenial and comfortable for Fritz in his declining years. He just couldn't be bothered with keeping to a frame of reference. Yet this book is being taken by many as the bible of Gestalt Therapy.

RK: Because it's easy to do; you don't have to chew!

EMS: Speaking of roots, once when I was in conversation with Ted Aidman and Fritz, I remember Fritz's speaking of how he'd discovered LSD as the only therapy which suited him at that time. This was several years before his death.

RK: He told me the same thing in Cleveland, how he had first discovered LSD and had his first "trip." "I think I finally made peace with my father." He was 63 years old.

LP: He later took a lot of LSD. He took it regularly for a couple of years and for a while he really went completely schizzy.

RK: In 1955–1956, when Allison Montague, who was a psychiatrist, was his patient, they had just come out with Thorazine and those other drugs. Monty was telling Fritz about it and his response was, "Ah! You have something new? Something good?" And Monty gave him a prescription. Which is something interesting and charming and inspirational in an odd way.

LP: Fritz was very impatient and always looked for shortcuts.

EMS: I wonder if shortcuts have in some way given Gestalt Therapy a reputation for having less regard for the personal history of the individual?

LP: The history of any person is, according to Gestalt Therapy, visible and audible and feelable in the present moment of the patient. We start there. Of course when you work with what symptoms are there, history does come up. It's not important to dig into these symptoms in order to begin to make historical interpretations about them. This is in contrast to the psychoanalytic method.

RK: But I think I know where Mark is coming from. There is a leaning in some people who do not fully integrate their learning who are most likely to tend to put the "here and now" label on behavior as a guise to hide their own lack of diagnostic and therapeutic expertise; they thus manage to avoid a great deal of the hard work. The notion of the here and now is connected with a scientific conception of the gestalt, as Laura says.

LP: The here and now is the integration of the disintegration of all the previous history.

EMS: Where I'm coming from, it sometimes seems to me to have something to do with an American characteristic which is both fortunate and unfortunate, that is, a desire to renounce the notion of any personal history. "I am where I am and I start here." Gestalt Therapy, did, after all, develop in American soil.

RK: I think that may be past. We are now more involved in a battle between the experiential vs. the structural. It sometimes represents itself in a bureaucratic battle which develops in all dynamic organizations including the American Academy of Psychotherapists and the New York Institute for Gestalt Therapy.

EMS: Could you talk a little more about that?

RK: Every organization ultimately dulls the charismatic call that quickened it. Integral to this process is bureaucracy as the organization wraps itself in the corruption of respectability. Everyone wants to belong. But to what? The cutting edge is precisely in the area of fear and trembling, faith, deviancy. Either we press on to the next resistance or again we succumb to the secondary process which manifests itself in yearning for the security of authority, mega-bucks, being good, replacing freedom with bread. Committees proliferate, specious democracy becomes a rigid norm, the very life that warmed the organization is strangled in the process. This is facism and, I am persuaded, intentional. I see this pseudo-debate going on now in the Academy, which I take to be extreme unction. At the Gestalt Institute we are already at the graveside. There can be no growth without the destruction of the novel in the process of contact in the here and now. Then differences and surprises are appreciated. But this process requires aggression. Paul Goodman felt that the bureaucratization of the prophetic was not necessary; all that is required is the faith to aggress. But I think the price is too high: loneliness, constant attacks and carping, political infighting, unenjoyable gossip, misunderstood yet one more time. Most important, sublime indifference to the importunings and blandishments of the flatterers. I think a dose of healthy contempt for mankind is indicated here. The choices are contempt or hemlock.

The experimental emphasis, which more closely resembles the cutting edge of Gestalt, indicates that when an organization gets overstructuralized, one must move, restructuring history in the here and now. This is what we see happening within a unifying concept of contact. For example, we have always attracted homosexuals, artists, and others who are on the fringe.

Ignoring the fringe creates a throwback to what people crave from authority. Then one is stuck all over again. Then it becomes a failure of aggression at the cutting edge of an organization itself due to shock and anxiety about a group of people standing on their own two feet, facing the unknown.

Now what does this say about the notion of history? It is simply that you—as you are right now—have integrated everything that you have learned. This is what manifests itself in the way Laura works with a patient, who then goes on to learn about it academically after it is first experienced.

We have routinely brought our patients to their own cutting edge so that they ultimately become our trainees. The more one cries for rigid structure or structured history at the beginning, the more the person or the organization may find itself suffering from a failure of healthy aggression.

I think you want to know a bit about how we proceed in the New York Institute for Gestalt Therapy. It is a non-profit membership organization interested in furthering professional involvement with all of the many aspects of Gestalt Therapy. The Institute does not grant degrees or accreditation. Workshops, Seminars, and Practica are approved by the Institute and are given autonomously by each of the individual instructors. Requirements for admission and the establishment of fees are at the discretion of the instructor. Interestingly enough, we're getting fewer and fewer new candidates.

EMS: There is either a proliferation of training facilities or else psychotherapy as such is becoming less and less a career people train for.

RK: The market is now quite saturated. We'd hoped that education would have taken over where psychotherapy had left off. But of course that's completely hopeless.

* * *

EMS: Laura, what are the goals of Gestalt Therapy as you see them?

LP: Ongoing gestalt formation. What is of greatest interest to individuals, to groups, to couples, to families, to social movements advances into the foreground where it can be clearly experienced and dealt with. Once resolved, these interests can move into the background which then leaves the foreground free again for the next challenge—the next gestalt.

EMS: Now, if we had to make that real clear to a high-school student, what language would we put it in?

LP: I would first make clear what the word gestalt means. Gestalt is actually a philosophic, aesthetic concept. In Germany an art school is called *Eine Hochschule für Gestaltung*, and actually *Gestaltung therapie* would be the much better term, because the term "Gestaltung" describes a process— and not a fixed gestalt. And fixed gestalten are precisely what we don't want in the therapy or in the theory.

EMS: You want a constant field of openness with a hint of some missing element which could make for a sense of completion. The point Gestalt Therapy makes is that there must never be total completion or closure.

LP: Closure is always temporary. If I aim for a complete closure, such closure is usually premature and very narrow.

EMS: But the promise of closure creates hope. I gather it's the quality of this hope which really counts in therapy.

LP: The notion of openness creates hope.

RK: Or closure creates the openness. I understand Laura to mean that contact leads to abstraction—that you see what is available for your growth so that you go on to the next most pressing thing.

LP: Actually, we have an obligation to see that Gestalt Therapy doesn't become a fixed gestalt.

RK: It has. In explaining Gestalt, one would have to go beyond mere words to such factors as body language and posture. It can be seen in the way a person grounds him or herself. People need to experience what Laura is putting in words.

EMS: Whether one looks to the body or to one's images, one should be aware that the task is to avoid being fixated. In your language being grounded means being supported by what one has assimilated. That creates openness.

RK: Otherwise we're eternally into what we call the conflict of objects.

LP: It's the relationship between figure and ground. This constitutes meaning.

EMS: With all the renewed interest in psychoanalytic object-relations theory, one can note according to that theory, that the appearance and/or disappearance of objects introduces a definition of the self in search of its coming together, whereas within the Gestalt frame of reference, the self is taken for granted and is represented in the many wholes.

RK: The object-relations theorists have tried to bridge the split—mind/body—without doing it and now one winds up with all kinds of contortions, codes, turgid prose. *Gestalt Therapy* is an entire book based on denying all such splits in the first place and instead talking about the interaction and the contact at the boundary between organism and environment.

* * *

EMS: I noted that the late Ernest Becker called attention to your work in one of his volumes: "As Laura Perls so vividly puts it, man is suspended between these two poles. One pole gives him a feeling of overwhelming importance and the other gives him a feeling of fear and frustration." The original quote is from *Gestalt Therapy Now* (Fagan & Shepherd, 1971).

LP: To elaborate, the neurotic is really the person who is afraid to cope with the process of dying and therefore he can't live. Being aware of one's own mortality is actually an incentive to being alive. I became aware of that when I was about 24 and I went to the funeral of a young friend who had suddenly died at age 26 from some kind of infection. At the time there was no penicillin or anything like that. It was very shocking and I came away from the cemetery and suddenly everything looked very bright and cheerful and I felt very energetic and I couldn't explain it and I told my analyst the next day. I said at the time that it struck me that if we weren't aware of the fact that we would die we would probably live like the cow—that the zest and the drive toward creation is for human beings allied with the awareness of dying. And my analyst said at the time, "Now your analysis is finished."

* * *

EMS: Laura, how do you feel about some of the mergers of schools such as Gestalt Therapy/Transactional Analysis and Gestalt Therapy/Psychoanalysis?

LP: In the framework of Gestalt any technique is applicable so long as it is existential and experiential, and experimental only to the degree that support for the experiment can be mobilized.

EMS: But Transactional Analysis is hardly an existential approach; it is a highly mechanized approach to the person.

LP: The life scripts that they talk about are fixed gestalten, and to make a new gestalt, a new script, is again a fixed gestalt.

RK: I've heard you say in the past, Laura, that if a practitioner of a school of thought has integrated his or her approach with his or her experience, a variety of technical approaches can be used.

LP: I would rather talk about styles than about techniques. One develops one's style out of one's background and experience.

EMS: So that style really focuses on the individual whereas technique focuses on a formula or somebody's fixed gestalt.

LP: And style is comprehensive.

EMS: Within the relationship is a cogent understanding. I think we're now opening up some understanding of how Gestalt begins to deal with the phenomenon of transference.

LP: What is transferred is not father-mother-child relationship but what is transferred are certain fixed behavior patterns which at the time when they were acquired were acquired not as resistance but as assistance for something. It's part of the development and then it becomes automatic. This implies a *fixed gestalt* of which one is not consciously aware. What we do in Gestalt Therapy is to de-automatize these fixed gestalten and thus make the patient aware of them as sources of energy which form a new basis of activity.

RK: Precisely. The therapist is not the mother or the father but is in fact somebody new offering the possibility of an experiment. And when you say "You're treating me like you treat your father," you're really saying that you're distorting the possibility of a ripened experiment. But this requires faith as well as staying at the cutting edge. it also requires "chewing" the obstacles so that one resists an immediate return to rigid structure. Rigidity in the form of anything fixed, whether they be so-called mental health or rigid goals, become extrinsic comparisons which denigrate the self and make one less than what one came with.

LP: It makes me think of Paul Goodman's definition of faith: "According to faith, a next step is possible."

RK: It is a foolish optimism.

EMS: I gather what you mean is that when one embraces foolish optimism, the next step is possible. Laura, I recall that at the American Academy of Psychotherapists' annual Conference in 1980 you talked to me about your notion of a sense of transcendent faith.

LP: It is difficult to talk about.

RK: But isn't it connected directly to your experience of coming from the cemetery when your friend had just died? Suddenly in contact, one is one with the universe.

LP: Any step in development is a transcendence of what there was before. Also, I think, in transcending it, one gives up something.

RK: I think Mark is sort of grinding an ax here from his own interest in religion.

EMS: Well, maybe not. Andras Angyal used to talk about the fact that as the individual sees a further gestalt, or becomes a part of a superindividual construct, s/he becomes a participant in an enlarged or enlarging gestalt, this gestalt consists of the person and an other or others. This further means becoming involved in a sense of the Thou as a result of a donation of oneself. What then follows is that vital relationship with the enlarged community or cosmos. This is what Angyal meant by superindividuality.

RK: For me it is more comfortable to think of it as faith than religion.

LP: You may have a prejudice with the concept of religion. Try not to identify religion with any kind of church setting. Religion can also be seen as a holistic concept.

EMS: It reminds me of our conversation. You spoke about the gestalt as having transpersonal consequences.

LP: It's something that's going on all the time. The ongoing gestalt formation is precisely that, transcending one state by the next one. When I go out in the woods or in the park and I see a tree that has been standing there for over a hundred years and it will probably still be there when I am gone, I know that just by my seeing it I am part of it.

RK: The other side of that, though, in another person, would be a rage within him or her to destroy that tree.

EMS: I plant trees on some property we own and I cut trees down for firewood. I love cutting up trees for our wood stove just as much as I love planting new trees. I think of the rage as helping me transform various life forms—seedlings to trees—dead wood to live fires which help warm our house.

RK: Laura, you would differentiate rage and destruction, wouldn't you?

LP: "Rage, rage, against the coming of the night." Destroying does not mean annihilating. It is rather a process of destructuring or deautomatizing the old structures.

EMS: From a Gestalt Therapy frame of reference I gather that without destructuring there can be no field? There would be no new gestalt formation.

LP: My experiences in transcending gestalten have mostly happened after either a great shock or exhaustion. They may also occur when I'm sick. When I am well, I am perhaps too well organized and structured. An example comes to mind. When I was struck with a high fever I wrote what I thought was a nonsense poem. More important, it made a lot of sense after my recovery. However, when I first completed it I didn't know that it represented a transcending leap. Another time, shortly after my arrival in South Africa, I took a stroll up the hill and I had to walk past a herd of cattle. I was wearing a red jacket and I was somewhat afraid of the consequences. Nevertheless I continued my hike in a somewhat upset state. Soon I arrived in the woods where I stopped to take a short rest. In fact, I had made a long detour in order to avoid these cattle, and I was sitting there in the woods on a fallen tree breathing in the stillness of the air. I honestly don't know how I got down again, but I soon realized that I must have walked straight through the herd of cattle as if I were a cow myself. I can't really describe the essence of the experience.

RK: You've described it very well. And you seemed to experience it as you were recounting it. Along the same note, I once heard you talk about managing embarrassment. As I recall it, you spoke of an incident where you were so embarrassed that the only thing you could do was to walk right into it and grow with it. Do you recall what I'm talking about?

LP: Well, not quite. But I think I realized pretty early and it's really part of my whole approach in therapy and in the training of therapists that embarrassment is the boundary state *par excellence*. There you are with one foot in what you know, and one foot in what you don't know. If you can accept your embarrassment then you'll begin to make contact with the "different," the other. As you go with the experience your boundary expands. If, on the other hand, you try to avoid acknowledging your embarrassment and present a well-structured front, you'll stay within your self-set boundaries, resulting in a feeling of safety and security. But at what a price!

RK: You notice I ask Laura about her embarrassment and she tells me about mine.

LP: At this point I don't feel embarrassed.

EMS: On the subject of being ill, I've just come through a very severe attack of diverticulitis which was not at all pleasant. Nevertheless I find that in your remarks about destructuring I find a new place for the torturesome pain. What I sense in my intestinal functioning is sometimes the need to de-structure. Psychosomatic medicine would do well to appreciate destructuring tactics as a need to introduce a newer self. Illness, in this context, isn't therefore simply related to some unresolved conflict but may represent an absolute desire to de-structure in order to find new boundaries—a cutting edge. I always find that I'm very changed after a bout of physical illness. It becomes a sort of pregnancy and birth.

LP: The full experience of illness is a part of the life instinct and it shouldn't be confused with the death instinct.

RK: You're talking about a new integration at a further level that is more profound.

LP: That's what I meant when I said that something must always be given up in order to achieve the next level.

RK: It's the same experience as knowing that the pregnant person dies and yet bears new life. Is this something new for you?

EMS: New in the sense that it helps me accept my today, which may be a little less filled with "manic" energy. I like the idea that Gestalt Therapy stresses meaning at all times. As Laura has said before, ultimately the interpretation is what the patient makes, but in order to be effective it has to have meaning. It's as if the patient is making the interpretation on the "boundary."

RK: We Gestalt therapists would say that the patient is creating new figures and relating them to his or her grounds. Both are the same thing.

LP: T.S. Eliot in the *Four Quarters:* "Anything less than the emergence of new beings...Costing not less than everything."

* * *

RK: Laura, I remember your saying that Gestalt Therapy has transcended its name. My sense is that you're part of this transcendence.

LP: At this point I seem to have made an impact on a lot of therapists who had formerly been mainly influenced by Fritz and by "Fritzers"—there is a fundamental difference between them. My solid application of Gestalt Theory to Gestalt Therapy practice is being taken seriously now. And I have an increasing clientele in Europe.

RK: Would you say, Laura, that this influence reflects both your capacity to reinterpret "Fritz" into Dr. Perls again? What I mean by that is what Fritz was *really* about in contrast to all this folderol. In addition, I know that you're developing into a deepening of your insights. Does that make sense?

LP: The next development for me is really more and more withdrawing. I'm 76 years old.

RK: So what?

LP: When Fritz died he was 76 and a very old man. He looked as if he was in his eighties.

RK: Laura, you can't get away with that. Withdrawing to what? You're certainly talking about a new integration, not a withdrawal.

LP: Right now I am on the boundary again. A couple of days ago there was an article in *The New York Times* differentiating being elderly from being old. I had never really felt elderly. In truth, I felt middle-aged until about a year or so ago. But now it's coming and coming rather fast. I realize that I'm getting very slow in a lot of things. I can't really learn anything new, except for momentary breakthroughs of my own. if I don't write it down immediately or share it with somebody, it all gets lost again.

EMS: Two minutes ago you were talking about having an increasing clientele all over Europe.

LP: I was scheduled to give a workshop in Frankfurt. I had thought that there would be an audience of between 30 and 40 people. Surprisingly there were between five and six hundred people, requiring us to move to a large auditorium. More recently I'm getting invitations to give lectures and workshops from universities.

RK: Laura, doesn't that mean that what you don't remember isn't worth remembering now at your point? I'd relax and enjoy what my brain does.

LP: I remember the earlier experiences much better than later ones. Now I forget something from one moment to another. I also wish that I could withdraw from the amount of traveling I do. It all becomes so familiar that it's simply becoming vulgar.

RK: You're not trying to catch up to Fritz, are you?

LP: No. I have developed a reputation personally at this point, in what I consider a more serious way than he had. Fritz maintained a reputation for putting on what amounted to a fantastic show. His promoters actually called it a showcase. I loathed such theatrics.

RK: Getting back to your failing memory, don't you feel that your next step has been simply not recalling that which is not worth remembering?

LP: That's right.

RK: So, isn't it something to feel the freedom of your new stance rather than experiencing it as constriction?

LP: I agree but I do get into trouble these days with my daughter. You know, younger people can't really understand the forgetfulness of old people. A further example was my granddaughter's three-month stay with me last year. During that time she talked to me as if I were an absolute nincompoop.

EMS: It's fascinating to me that you go back to Germany and further that you're pleased at being taken seriously there after having been an exile from the then-developing Nazi onslaught. Do you go back to redeem something?

RK: Laura, you never really felt that you were an exile. They—the Germans—were the exiles till they came to their senses again.

LP: Well, actually they lost everything there in the 30 years after the war and it's only the last 10–12 years that they have started to catch up.

RK: What Mark is trying to say is that you are going back to your roots. But you in fact never really left Germany. The evidence of that is this increasing acceptance; and you enjoy being there, walking in the mountains. . . .

LP: I accept it more and more. And I still have some old friends in my home town, Pforzheim, which is on the north rim of the Black Forest. It's very nice there and I have some old friends who don't know at all what I'm doing here and they have no idea what it implies, but there are artistic and literary roots which I hold in common with them.

RK: And you're better able there to treasure your alone moments than you are here?

LP: Yes, and to indulge in all kinds of things that I have very little time for here, like reading Auden. This summer in Pforzheim I read the whole collected poems; I also re-read *The Magic Mountain* by Thomas Mann.

RK: Did you meet Auden?

LP: Yes. I didn't really know him well, but I met him several times. I met Christopher Isherwood in Los Angeles.

EMS: Auden also went back to his roots.

LP: He went back to Oxford again. Actually, he had property in Bavaria.

RK: So you met him through Isherwood. How about Stephen Spender?

LP: I met Auden through Daniel Rosenblatt, who knew him. I met Stephen Spender through a translation I did of one of his poems. He had given a reading here at the Young Men's Hebrew Association and I showed him a translation I did and he thought that it was marvelous. I said, "When one translates you, however it comes out it comes out Rilke." He was so influenced by Rilke that the German translation reads like Rilke.

RK: How wonderfully into the background formal psychology and therapy recede.

LP: I have to remind you that I was a musician and a writer long before I was anything else.

RK: Why did you move away from these other enterprises?

LP: We became Socialists after World War I. I was about 15 years old and wanted to do something that was socially useful. So I thought I would go into juvenile court work, which was something very new at the time. In fact, few women had entered the legal profession. There was a significant segment of the German community who were at a socially aware stage of development that was not achieved here in the United States until the 1950's and 1960's.

RK: The battle is still being waged by women for a real piece of the pie. Certainly in the Gestalt Therapy movement women have had a significant role from the earliest stages.

LP: For the first time in my professional practice I have an all-women's group. This has never happened to me before. I've usually had all men in my groups. And in South Africa my individual patients were mostly men. The women went to Fritz and the men came to me.

RK: How do you think of Fritz now?

LP: I find that I think of Fritz much more as he was when he was younger.

RK: I still have trouble seeing him with that beard he had in his last years.

LP: Well, I can see him that way, but that's not the Fritz I was with. In the last years we really no longer lived together, we just visited occasionally.

RK: When I asked you how you saw Fritz, I was speaking more of dreams and visions. You know, those moments of clarity which get expressed in a sense of presence.

LP: Fritz had moments of clarity which were just fantastic. Unfortunately, he used to dim this clarity with a lot of bullshit which he eventually got tired of. In the end he was silent to a great extent. Working mainly with dreams in the end allowed him to keep himself away from the personal relationship with the trainee or client altogether. In fact, he fell back to an early ambition—wanting to be in the theater and to be a theater director.

EMS: It's kind of fascinating tracing the kind of man Fritz was and seeing him in contrast to another great—Jacob Moreno, the father of psychodrama. One of Moreno's first fantasies was of being a god. In the first volume of *Psychodrama* (volume two was never published) Moreno speaks of pretending to be God. Getting on a ladder, he saw himself as superdirector of a world drama.

LP: He was even more grandiose than Fritz. Fritz wanted to be a theater director.

RK: Laura, the way in which you have developed certainly related to the ways in which you were when you were with Fritz.

LP: The way in which I am now is still developing, as it has done for many years for these past 12 years of my life I have been on my own. I feel sad as I look at Fritz now and note how he developed—or didn't develop. Sadly, Fritz could not take any sort of criticism.

RK: I recall a meeting we were having in your apartment. Fritz said to you, "Laura, you are the only person who can make me explain myself." That seems to me to sum up some of the "why's" of the separation. He simply couldn't take it in.

LP: Fritz was afraid of me. He couldn't stay with me because I had become separate. When I met Fritz I was 21 years old and a virgin and a little girl from a small town, a student who knew nothing. He was 33 and he was a doctor and he was very brilliant but actually not doing anything with it, just what people in Germany call Geistscheissen—what he called elephant shit. But he was very impressive. He had also been in the war and through terrible things and was, in a way, when I met him, a kind of desperate cynic, but he did eventually become a *mensch*.

REFERENCES

Fagan, J., & Shepherd, I. *Gestalt therapy now*. New York: Harper & Row, 1971.

Perls, F. *Ego, hunger, and aggression*. New York: Vintage Books, 1947.

Perls, F. *Gestalt therapy verbatim*. Lafayette, CA: Real People Press, 1969.

Perls, F., Hefferline, R.F., & Goodman, P. *Gestalt therapy: Excitement and Growth in the human personality*. New York: Julian Press, 1947.

Chapter 4

Self-Support, Wholeness, and Gestalt Therapy

STEPHAN A. TOBIN

"**T**ime's up," I said. Jim hesitated a moment, then slowly got up. I also stood. Instead of moving toward the door, Jim looked at me. Then he smiled, walked over to me, and hugged me rather stiffly. He then stepped back and said, "I've been thinking of going to Colorado for awhile." He looked at me searchingly and I felt uncomfortable. I imagined he was waiting for me to give my opinion about his going to Colorado. "Are you asking me if I think you should go?"

"Yeah, I guess I am."

"Jim, it doesn't matter to me if you go to Colorado or not."

"Yeah, well...you know, I don't think I *really* want to go to Colorado at all. I feel more like going to the beach right now." Another searching look.

"I don't care if you go to the beach either."

A disappointed look now. He backed away, said he had to be going. He wasn't through yet, though.

"You know, I just about decided to stop screwing around. I have been thinking about going back to college, maybe medical school."

"Look Jim, I really don't give a damn what you do; it just doesn't make any difference to me if you go to Colorado, medical school, or Disneyland. You're still trying to get me to approve of your decisions, to support...."

33

"Yeah, yeah, you're right," he interrupted. "Well, guess I'll be going." He again started edging towards the door. "Oh, look, I hate to ask you, but I'm broke and don't have enough gas to get home. Could you lend me a buck?"

This dialogue is from a recent session with a young man I have been seeing in group therapy and infrequent individual sessions for about a year. He had a great deal of previous therapy before coming to me, about ten years of analysis and analytically-oriented therapy. Despite all the "insight" he has obtained, he still regards himself as "sick" and leads a chaotic, unrewarding existence. Instead of making his own decisions and supporting himself emotionally, he continually attempts to manipulate others into taking responsibility for his life.

Although the analysts could make a convincing case for unresolved oedipal conflicts within Jim, I feel that such an explanation is irrelevant to Jim's major problems, which are existential. Underlying his continual need for validation from others are feelings of incompleteness, of being split-up into many parts, and inadequacy.

I believe that the desperate search outside oneself for self-esteem gratifications seen in Jim is also the major symptom of our culture, affecting the successful and well-functioning as well as the failures and "mentally ill." The basic feeling of worthlessness found in most people much of the time is, I believe, the motivating force behind the politician's striving for power, the businessman's dishonest practices, the black militant's hatred of "whitey," and the welfare recipient's attempts to cheat a humiliating, infantilizing Establishment.

As Fritz Perls has pointed out (Perls, 1965), any system of therapy that does not result in the patient's being able to provide his own validation as a human being is incomplete. The purpose of this paper is to discuss certain features of this ubiquitous problem of our times. I shall discuss its phenomenology, its causes, how it is maintained in our culture, and how the ability to validate onself can be attained in therapy.

THE PHENOMENOLOGY OF INCOMPLETENESS

The emotional state of one who needs to manipulate others into validating him can best be described as a feeling of incompleteness. I find that when I myself am unable to provide my own self-esteem supports I feel empty, worthless, tense, and vaguely dissatisfied. I am partially unaware of what is going on around me, and have fleeting, scattered thoughts about things I "should do." I sense that I am *missing* something and feel I must search outside myself for it. In the past I attempted to fill myself up with material objects, with praise from others, or by doing work I imagined would bring me prestige or power. Even major achievements, however, only made me feel worthwhile for a very brief time, and then I usually became depressed.

This pattern I have noticed in my own life has been reported to me by many other people. For example, a physician I know imagined that he would feel complete when he had established a successful practice. After eleven years of college and specialized medical training, and another four years of building up his practice, he had achieved his dream. He had "arrived," but, as you may have already guessed, his achievement left him feeling empty and despairing.

A 65-year-old patient of mine had come to me after 15 years of analytically oriented therapy. She had hung on to unsatisfactory relationships with her therapist and her husband because she felt basically worthless and empty, and believed that someday they would give her what they had previously been withholding. She would then, she imagined, feel complete and whole. When I spoke with the ex-therapist I learned of his part in this neurotic relationship: as he spoke of her, his pessimism and despair and his opinion that she could never stand on her own came through his technical description of her "case."

Jim, the patient I described earlier, is luckier than the physician and the elderly patient, for he is dealing with this existential problem while still young. If he were unfortunate enough to be "well-adjusted" to our psychotic society, he would probably have started on the same path as the physician, only to realize years later that what he was searching for all that time was something that only he could give himself.

CULTURAL CAUSES OF INCOMPLETENESS AND OTHERSUPPORT

1. *The view that man is basically evil.* Because of the Judeo-Christian concept of original sin and the continuing influence of Puritanism, most people in our culture have an underlying attitude that man is innately bad. This attitude is revealed in the way we regard being itself: a person is worthless just existing; he must *do* something to be worthwhile. This attitude is also revealed in the great emphasis we place upon "self-control" and in our glorification of the mind and ignoring of the body. This lack of trust of man's free use of his body, with all its drives and functions, is related to a second aspect of American culture, its pervasive authoritarianism.

2. *Authoritarianism in major institutions.* The family, the school, the armed forces, the athletic team, the business, and almost all other major institutions in our culture are structured in an authoritarian fashion. The infant is viewed as an impulse-ridden, megalomanic little monster who would destroy everything in sight when frustrated had he the power to do

so. Therefore, the child is supposed to need a great deal of "socialization" before he can be trusted to make any decisions on his own. In contrast, as Lee points out (Lee, 1959), the Navajo Indians see the child as having complete autonomy. An adult never speaks for a child or forces an idea or an act on him. Personal autonomy and freedom are so much a part of the Navajo culture that their language does not even contain words of ownership or coercion. An adult will speak of "going with" a child someplace, not "taking" him, and of "the child I live with" rather than "my child."

In most of the Western institutions mentioned above, the individual, whether he be an adult or a child, is treated in a dictatorial, authoritarian manner. Workers must punch time clocks because their bosses are certain they would not come in or leave on time were they not treated like irresponsible idiots. The whole system of grading in our schools is predicated on the notion that people will not want to learn anything unless they are forced to.

Our institutional dictators—parents, team coaches, teachers, etc.— dole out the rewards as well as punishments. Since a member of American culture has lost all feeling of intrinsic self-worth by the time he is three years old, he is dependent on his dictators to validate him as a worthwhile human being for the rest of his life. To be approved or loved he must accomplish or achieve something.

3. *Thinking, achievement, and future-orientation.* In order to gratify himself fully in any situation, a person must be totally *in* the situation cognitively, emotionally, and sensorily. Unfortunately, however, most people tend to be only partially in the here-and-now, and partially in the there-and-then. That is, instead of attending fully to the situation at hand, they are partially aware of it and are thinking about the past or the future. There are a number of reasons for this inability to exist in the present.

First, a normal person in our culture is never to rest on his laurels. He is supposed to present himself with a new goal immediately after one is reached. To like oneself just for being human and alive is simply un-American. Thus, since the new goal can exist only in the individual's fantasy about the future, he must tear part of himself away from the present and put this part into the future.

Second, the complexity of our culture makes it virtually impossible to stay in the here-and-now. I find that I must remind myself of things I "should" do in the future or I forget them, e.g., people to call, letters to write, a loaf of bread to pick up on my way home. While reminding myself of these chores, however, I am not really involved in the present and thus am not getting complete fulfillment from the current stimulus situation.

Third, we are continually making comparisons between what is immediately present to us and something that is present in fantasy, e.g., an ideal.

4. *Playing comparison games.* In order to evaluate someone, one must use a standard. The standard can be an absolute one existing in the evaluator's mind, or it can be another person; in either case, the individual to be evaluated is placed on a scale and compared with the standard.

Making comparisons is so much a part of our culture that it is almost impossible for most people to talk without continually using words such as "better than," "worse than," "bigger," "older," etc. As soon as a person is born in the United States he becomes involved in comparisons, i.e., adults evaluate him with respect to his weight, his looks, which parent he most resembles, etc. As he grows older he is placed in a great many situations in which he is in competitive and comparative relationships with others. Unless he is extremely lucky, his approval events are likely to be few in number. This is particularly true in school, for there are only a limited number of "winners" allowed. Even the extremely bright and "well-behaved" child is apt to feel anxious and incomplete much of the time, for there is always the possibility that some other competitor will get a higher grade on the next test. The child's top dog[1] usually plays a major role in preventing him from feeling good about his achievements by torturing him with catastrophic expectations about failure if he does not continue to drive himself.

As the child gets older, the competition for self-esteem rewards becomes greater and the things he must do to get approval become more complicated and difficult. No longer does he get praised for doing things like brushing his teeth and taking out the trash. He has to play ball well, be popular with girls, be "tactful" (i.e., dishonest and indirect), and not antagonize authorities while presenting a facade of self-assertiveness and aggressiveness. Even if he involves himself in a creative activity, he is not left to his own devices, but must seek approval from others for his creations.

By the time he reaches adulthood, he is almost totally unable to provide any of his own self-esteem rewards, for he now has a rigid, authoritarian, irrational top dog. The top dog is insatiable and he can never attain a feeling of self-worth that lasts more than a brief period of time. If he manages to achieve excellency (e.g., all grades of 'A' except one 'B' in school), his top dog is likely to say "That's pretty good but what about that 'B'?" If he achieves perfection (e.g., all 'A's), the top dog says "Good, now keep up the good work and get the same grades next semester." If, however, he then repeats his success (all 'A's the next semester), the top dog says "That's not so great, getting good grades is easy for you."

---

[1] The top dog is a Gestalt Therapy concept; it is the self-righteous, demanding, perfectionistic part of the person. While similar to the concepts of conscience and superego, it is closest to Berne's concept of Parent (Berne, 1964).

Many persons assume incorrectly that making comparisons is a universal trait and that man can never be satisfied with what he is. In many "primitive" cultures the individual is valued for being himself, a unique part of the universe, and is not compared to anyone or anything else. The Trobriand Islanders, for example, do not even have comparatives or superlatives in their language. Words equivalent to "better," "worse," "the most," and "younger" just do not exist (Lee, 1959).

The Hopi Indians, another supposedly primitive people, regard each person, animal, plant, and inanimate object as unique and as having an essential place in the universe. The idea of splitting people up into abstract attributes and then placing them on a scale to compare them would seem ridiculous and shameful to a Hopi. Anglo-American school teachers who have attempted to teach Hopi children have found that a Hopi child feels humiliated when he is singled out and praised in the classroom (Lee, 1959).

5. *Duplicity in interpersonal relationships.* Another custom of our culture that leads to incompleteness and low self-esteem is the ritual of attempting to get others to gratify one's need for self-esteem without asking for it directly. This is done by tricking the other into praising one or approving of a decision that has already been made. One technique I find college students using on me is to ask questions in class instead of stating their own opinions. If I answer their "questions" the way they want, they feel pleased because I "agreed" with them. If I don't answer the way they want, they are safe because they haven't committed themselves to an opinion.

The drawback with this technique (as with all indirect methods of trying to raise one's self-esteem) is that it's simply difficult to get what one wants when the other person does not know what's being requested. In addition, when two people are playing this game with each other at the same time, it is generally impossible for either one to get anything, for they're not really listening to each other. When their attempts to get support from the other are frustrated, the duplicity game is likely to degenerate into the blame game.

6. *Blame games and incompleteness.* I have found that the blame game starts when A makes an indirect request for a self-esteem present, and B fails to meet the request. A then feels hurt and worthless, blames B, and then B feels worthless. B then attacks back and, by this time, both parties are deliberately attacking each other's most vulnerable spots. This game is played endlessly by married couples. For example:

WIFE: "Do you like the dinner tonight, dear?" (Translation: tell me I'm a good cook, i.e., a worthwhile person.)

HUSBAND: (He either thinks she wants to know about the dinner or really knows what she wants but is feeling resentful because of an esteem-attack he got from her recently.) "No, I don't care for it."

WIFE: "Well!! That's a *rotten* thing to say after I spent hours cooking. You're *always* criticizing me, nothing I ever do is good enough for you." (Translation: I'm hurt, but I won't give you the satisfaction of knowing that because I think you'll gloat. Instead, I'll get *you!*)

HUSBAND: "Nag, nag, nag. If you spent as much time cooking as you say you do, your food wouldn't taste like you got it from the neighbor's garbage pails. Or maybe you do spend that much time, but you're too stupid to put a decent meal on the table." (Translation: I feel guilty and resentful because I also see myself as a critical grouch.)

And so they're off on another endless cycle of brutal, cutting attacks on each other's self-worth. What makes this type of game so difficult to stop is that they are unaware of their wishes, feelings, and intentions.

UNAWARENESS AND INCOMPLETENESS

To summarize, self-esteem is intimately related to awareness of the here-and-now. Unfortunately, however, most Americans spend most of their time fantasizing about the past or the future. They do not make use of their own resources. They don't trust their eyes and ears, their sense of touch, and the kinesthetic sensations from their own bodies that would tell them what they are feeling. Without sensory awareness, they are unable to express themselves and get what they want from the world. This inability to use one's own resources for self-fulfillment makes it necessary to look outside for these resources.

As an example of what I mean about awareness and completeness, I shall discuss something that happened to me when I first started teaching at San Fernando Valley State College about a year ago. After a class in which I had discussed and criticized the scientific and cultural assumptions underlying contemporary psychology, I noticed I was feeling tense and anxious. The class had been very exciting to me, and, as I was driving back to my office, I was having fantasy conversations with a few students who had argued with me in class. I noticed that I was constricting my breathing; when I deepened it, I became aware that I had been suppressing the excited joy that had been aroused in class. I stopped my fantasies at this point and began singing at the top of my lungs. Not only did I fully enjoy myself, but my anxiety left me. I also experienced a sense of wonder at my own potential for achieving a deep sense of fulfillment in life. Without awareness of my physical sensations, I would have continued to feel tense.

I also became aware that I had prevented myself from expressing my joy in the classroom by telling myself it would be unseemly for a professor to show too much excitement. Like most people, I had accepted my top dog's prohibition about expressing excitement without really examining this prohibition. This relative unawareness of the absurdity of the top-dog's threats and "shoulds" is characteristic of most people with whom I have contact, and is another barrier to achieving a feeling of wholeness.

I have also found, however, that most people are even less aware of their under dogs.[2] They usually have little sense of the under dog as a sub-self that is *actively* sabotaging, making excuses, and generally conning their top dogs. They describe themselves as "lazy," not being aware just how much active effort the under dog is putting into creating what superficially appears to be inertness.

I have an idea that people have less awareness of the under dog than they do of the top dog because the former tends to be less verbal. Many of the dogmatic, dictatorial, and persecutory aspects of the top dog are introjected by persons from their parents when they are very young and had a limited vocabulary. Since language helps to create one's picture of "reality," the top dog *seems* to have a more accurate and well-defined picture of the world. The child, however, rebels even without having words to express his rebellion, e.g., the two-year-old who refuses to eat but can't tell his parents why.

Finally, most people have experienced feelings of wholeness so infrequently that they are unaware that incompleteness is not the natural state of man.

THE ATTAINMENT OF WHOLENESS IN THERAPY

In order to create a climate in which a patient can achieve a sense of wholeness and the ability to provide his own support, the therapist should be able to support himself or at least be aware of how he is incomplete. Without awareness of his own incompleteness, therapists are apt to become involved in a variety of mutual manipulation games with patients.

For example, therapists who view themselves as "healers" of sick persons tend to be vulnerable to patients who play the sick role as a way of manipulating the environment. These patients never really want to "get well" even though they pretend to put complete faith in the "doctor."

The therapist who needs to have his patients admire him, agree with him, and ape him is easily trapped by the person who plays the "good patient." The "good patient" picks up the therapist's jargon very quickly. He is particularly obvious in group therapy, where he plays the role of assistant therapist. If the therapist happens to stress honesty and self-

---

[2] The under dog is, in Gestalt Therapy, the guilty, "bad," rebellious part of the person. It rebels however, in subtle, indirect ways against the top dog's demands, saying, e.g.,, "I can't do it, I'm too sick" (rather than "I won't"). It is similar to Berne's concept of Child (Berne, 1964).

expression, the patient gets the idea that the quickest way to get the magical goodies the therapist has hidden is to play bad patient. So he becomes nasty, obstinate, and argumentative. If the therapist does not approve of his change in behavior, he will revert back to playing good patient. In neither role is he doing what he wants; he is doing what he thinks the therapist wants.

The therapist who does not *need* anything from his patients realizes the patient is just as autonomous as he is and therefore is just as responsible for his behavior. Not needing anything, he sets the patient free. He is only responsible to himself, not the patient. In a very fundamental sense, he doesn't care *about* the patient, although he may care *for* him. He responds to the patient as he is right there in front of him, not as the patient says he is outside the office or as he intends to be in the future.

I feel that the self-esteem problem is fundamental to the entire progress of therapy, that the lack of wholeness and of an intrinsic feeling of worthlessness is the real "ultimate symptom" (to use Helmut Kaiser's phrase) of Western man. Consequently, I focus much of my therapeutic effort on communicating to patients that "I don't care." Eventually the patient may come to the awesome realization that neither I nor anyone else has any magical goodies for him, no fountain of chicken soup, no giant penis, no immortality pills.

PHENOMENOLOGY OF WHOLENESS

I shall conclude this paper with a brief discussion of how I experience wholeness on the infrequent occasions that I do.

I am sensorially aware of the present; I see, hear, smell, touch, and feel without the intrusion of thoughts. I use thinking only when a conflict is experienced and for the purpose of considering various alternatives for resolving the conflict. I know when I have found the best solution: my feeling of completeness returns.

I am aware that, as Steve Tobin, I am alone in the universe. I am not *lonely*, but realize the inevitability of my death in a much more profound way than I do when I am feeling incomplete. (In fact, I would say that I don't really believe I shall die when I am feeling split, even though I "knew" it intellectually.) I realize that no one is more of an expert about what is right for me than I myself am. I also realize that I don't need power, prestige, love, or lots of money: these things will not make me feel any more worthwhile as a person.

Paradoxically, I feel a sense of community, of being a part of the entire universe. Since I am not observing myself, I have no sense of "I" as separate from the universe. I have a sense of the unity of the universe, but see myself as neither more nor less important than any other part of the universe. This feeling of no sense of self seems to contradict the feeling of aloneness I described in the preceding paragraph, but I do not experience any contradiction when I feel whole.

Freedom is a very important part of the experience for me. I realize that I had innumerable invisible, enslaving bonds between myself and others that I have broken, at least for the time being. I am also free in the sense that I know I can make my own decisions, that I am not enslaved to the past, to expectations of the future, or to any other person.

I also feel very much alive and am in touch with all my emotions. Sometimes these are painful, sometimes they are joyful but, whatever the emotions, I have no need to avoid them. Experiencing "pleasure" is unimportant to me, and I find myself becoming annoyed at anyone attempting to attenuate my painful feelings by comforting me.

Finally, and most importantly, I find I can really become involved with people in a non-defensive way. Since *I don't need* anything from them I can risk asking directly for *what I want* from them, even though refusal might hurt me. I find I can really see people at these times, instead of viewing them as potential enemies or as potential ass-wipers.

REFERENCES

Berne, E. *Games people play*. New York: Grove Press, 1964.
Lee, D. *Freedom and culture*. Spectrum Books, 1959.
Perls, F.S. Gestalt therapy and human potentialities. *Esalen Paper No. 1*. Esalen Institute, Big Sur, 1965 (mimeograph).

Chapter 5

Dreams: Contact and Contact Boundaries

E. MARK STERN AND DON LATHROP

INTERVIEW ISADORE FROM

E. MARK STERN: Isadore, why don't you just start off from where you're at.

ISADORE FROM: You wanted me to share a few ideas about the use of dreams in gestalt therapy. I suppose I can start by giving a general idea. In Gestalt therapy, as I see it, the central concern of the serious Gestalt therapist with his client is what we call the contact boundary and, importantly, disturbances at the boundary. Disturbances, as they're clearly outlined in *Gestalt Therapy* by Perls, Hefferline, and Goodman, particularly in the second volume, are projection, introjection, retroflection, and confluence.

For the most part, how we have tended to deal with dreams is, Perls points out in *Gestalt Therapy Verbatim*, almost exclusively, I think, as if they were projections and, as I think he puts it, projections of the unwanted parts of the client's or patient's self. This seems to me useful but inadequate. What it fails to recognize or perhaps doesn't recognize enough is that a dream is importantly a retroflection. By that we mean that which is intended for the environment but is somehow turned back toward the self or the organism. How that is done and why this is done becomes important in therapy. To regard dreams only as a projection of the self is to ignore the contact of the patient and the therapist. Because he tended to ignore this contact is why I think Perls so frequently used the empty seat—which ignores the actual contact of the therapist and the patient. So I'm considering, what if we consider the patient's or client's dream as a retroflection which was somehow intended for the therapist? We might find some interesting therapeutic matter, also something which tells us something about the contact of the patient with the therapist, not just of the patient with himself.

The second concern of Perls, or of his way of dealing with dreams, was something he called an "existential message," which I've regarded, in Gestalt therapy, as an unfortunate phrase, for once again it calls for the therapist to interpret the patient's dream, which in Gestalt therapy we would want to discourage. In dealing with the dream and in considering it possibly, not necessarily, as a retroflection, I'd interject that sleeping is the optimum condition for retroflecting, because the only contact the dreamer has with the environment is by his breathing. This, of course, goes on whether or not he is sleeping; all other contact is given up. That's where I got the notion that perhaps it might be useful, when a patient reports a dream to the therapist, to consider this as an unawares attempt to undo a retroflected message for and to the therapist. That's about as much as I want to say right now.

EMS: I'm not clear as you talk right now, Isadore, about how what you're saying becomes clinically applicable. Can you give an example of what you mean?

IF: If I think of the context of the dream or of the dreamer, the dreams that interest me in therapy are particularly the dreams of the night before or the night after the therapy session, and what may have been withheld, perhaps even thought about but not said, may somehow be used in the dream. The patient, of course, realizes that the next day he has, or the day before he had, a session with this therapist. I'm trying to think of an example right now.

I see a patient and that night he has a dream. This patient happens to be a psychiatrist. He dreams of his office, which in the dream is very messy—something which, when he tells me this, seems to be highly improbable as the one thing I know is that ordinarily he would not be messy at all. My question to him as I remember it was "How am I messy?" He then tells me with some hesitation that I usually dressed messily and that was disturbing to him. My next question to him was "What stopped you from telling me this?" He then said something to the effect that he was very angry with me.

Given the small example which I just told you, then we have the subject of anger, but first the difficulty of getting angry at the therapist. That can then—at that point—be usefully and contactfully worked through, and then I could get to the subject of what makes it difficult in other situations for this particular patient to get angry, what does he mean by getting angry. What it turned out he meant was almost murderous, so of course he had to restrain his anger and do anything he could not to make me angry. That's what anger turned out to mean to him. Now we got to this much more quickly by this so-called retroflective dream which I assume—I cannot know—was prepared for me. Is that any clearer to you?

EMS: Don, are you any clearer than I am?

DONALD LATHROP: I'm not sure how clear I am. As I understand it, you're dealing with what, in my language, I would call a transference dream and I don't get far beyond that.

IF: Why do you call that a transference dream? Transference is not necessarily something from the present situation, mainly of the patient with the therapist, but usually is something which deals with infantile material that is now being transferred to the therapist. Isn't that what we really mean by transference?

DL: If that's what we mean then for me both the dream and the way of working with it are certainly dealing with the transference.

IF: Not at first. In Gestalt therapy we would first more importantly deal in the present context with the therapist. Now I certainly do not deny that there is also transference material but this would be a way of vividly revealing the transferential material as presently contactful or noncontactful.

EMS: Isadore, as I hear you talking about the reality of the contact with the therapist. . .

IF: The actual contact.

EMS: Yes, the actual contact. I still go back to Don's original point. Aren't we really dealing with transference or going back to early relationships contrasted with a present reality?

Doesn't the dream itself create some distance between the two, or symbolize the therapist in a way which makes him or her less accessible and less involved with the present life of the patient? From my understanding of a classical analytic approach the messiness might represent and symbolize a hell of a lot of primary process material. More importantly—whether or not we agree on terminology—how do you, Isadore, get the patient beyond the confusion in the relationships, perhaps to a relationship this patient is having with the world and other significant figures.

IF: Well, there would not be much of a step. What am *I* doing that makes it difficult for my patient to express this directly to me? Contained in that may also be a projection. But first I would be quite willing to attend to the criticism, anger, which has emerged in the dream, either acknowledge or deny that I do what the patient suggests, and then say "Where else do you experience this?" That way we would get to other material.

DL: That's in the dream work but not in the dream. Let's go back for a moment to your view of the dream. You said that Perls regarded the dream as a statement of the unwanted parts of the ego, I assume, and that you are adding to that the dream as a communication. . .

IF: A disturbed or retroflected communication.

DL: May I ask why disturbed?

IF: By disturbed I mean that the contact of patient and therapist has somehow been disturbed. How is it that the patient could not or would not say to the therapist what he now says to himself in the dream?

DL: How do you differentiate in your own mind between the dream that attempts to communicate and the dream that represents unwanted material?

IF: I don't think you have to differentiate that because they're not necessarily two different dreams but may be the same dream and even the same material.

DL: I see.

IF: What interests me about this as a Gestalt therapist is that it would be odd for us to ignore not only the context of dreaming but the fact that the dream is now being told to this particular therapist, and that is how I would bring it to what we call the present, and that certainly our client or patient is aware of that; and that he will be telling the dream to this therapist we have a right to consider might make a difference in what he dreamed about. What I didn't say because I didn't think of it is that I think it's very important in Gestalt therapy, and may be useful for other orientations, that the patient, who produces the dream, may at first be unable to realize that this is his production.

EMS: His production or reduction? I didn't quite hear you clearly.

IF: Production.

EMS: He produces. I seem to be having a little trouble getting the sense of what you're saying, so I assume that my slip may be an important one. For me, it sounds reductive. I get a feeling of a kind of narrow, uninteresting, non-mythologically-rich dream.

IF: I think that what you're saying, Mark, is that because it's nonmythological it's not interesting.

EMS: I'm perhaps saying the way it's seen as not being interesting. I'm perfectly willing to understand a dream as the relationship between therapist and patient.

IF: I would prefer the word "contact."

EMS: Contact. I'm also willing to expand on that and see the dream as going beyond the therapist and into areas of contact with self which I think the therapist has to see by standing apart from, and I think it's an easy trap to see oneself as therapist in every dream the patient produces while in therapy and I can't help but wonder how therapeutically valid such a view is.

IF: I think I can agree with you there Mark, and the way I can put it is, I think in the dream the patient may be telling the therapist what to do next or what is now available for therapy, but again, that is still a retroflection as he dreams it. He may not be aware of it, and I can see that he was in his dream attempting to be his own therapist, and is now requesting his therapist to take over, and is instructing him what is now available for therapy.

DL: One of the difficulties I have with Gestalt theory and techniques is illustrated by your contention that the ego produces the dream. I don't believe there's any evidence whatsoever that the ego produces the dream.

IF: Well, certainly our patient produces the dream.

DL: Something in the individual produces the dream.

IF: What is that something?

DL: Whatever it is, it's not the ego.

IF: Well, can I enable our patient to assume that he produced the dream and not something else?

DL: We each identify with our ego. That's who we think ourselves to be, and Gestalt psychology tends to put the ego in the center of the personality— again—where it doesn't belong.

EMS: Or we might talk about the unborn parts of the person as not necessarily being attached to the ego. I would include the non-ego aspects of the person under the aegis of the unconscious. Without the notion of the unconscious, where does an egoless sense of relationship go? If you're simply saying. . .

IF: I would prefer you leave the word "simply" off.

EMS: OK. I'll leave it off. But without the unconscious where do you go? Or, better yet, without those undisclosed parts of the person, where do you see the direction heading?

IF: In this case, why don't you call it unawareness or without awareness?

DL: That's fine, as long as you don't attribute to the patient the power to produce his or her own dreams. That doesn't conform with observation. You can't tell yourself what you're going to dream; you can't create your dream. You can have a dream—you can experience one—but you can't create it. The best you can do is to have some input into some of the images in the dream. You can direct the feeling of the dream but as for creating the images—that can't be done by the ego.

IF: How does the unconscious produce these images and whose unconscious is it? Are you speaking of the patient's?

DL: I don't like the concept of the unconscious either. I'm just saying that it's not the ego that produces the dream.

IF: It is my patient who produces the dream and, unawares, he is also producing it for the therapy, in the context of producing the dream while in therapy. This is consistent with the way Freud dealt with dreams.

DL: I absolutely agree.

IF: Also, Don, I do not intend this as a theory of dreams. That would be pretentious. Now Freud indeed produced a theory of dreams from which we all have learned a great deal, but in dealing with the manifest content of the dream—which, interesting enough, in the actual dreams which Freud discusses is almost all that he talks about or refers to—he rarely refers to the latent content of the dream in his writings—whether or not he did otherwise in his work I do not know. He was very much concerned with the events of the day before.

DL: Right.

IF: I simply bring this to somewhat more concentrated areas, to events of the day before, with one's therapist. And I'm not suggesting this as the *only* way of dealing with dreams, but as one way. I think you can see it might have some usefulness with the contact of the patient and the therapist. That is not its only use.

   This might have been neglected, dealing with the dream as only projection of unwanted parts of the self, you neglect the contact of the patient and therapist and the very context that the patient is in, the therapy, as he is reporting the dream, and he knows this.

EMS: As you talk about the unwanted parts of the self coming through in dreams, maybe I could clarify my other questions. What about the overly wanted parts of self?

IF: I think we could consider that too. What I was trying to do was suggesting that with many Gestalt therapists, this is the only way to deal with dreams and I think not sufficiently. Is that clear to you, Mark? I agree with you, it might be quite useful and interesting to also consider overwanted parts, exaggerated parts.

EMS: I hadn't thought of exaggerated parts but I understand what you're saying.

IF: Over-valued. I can tell you one of the problems I've had in using dreams of my clients in this way is that it makes it difficult for the therapist in that our patients are indeed often very perceptive.

EMS: Going back to the dream that you cited about the doctor who was, in the dream, very messy when in fact in his waking life he was not. I wonder how each of us would have handled that dream, imagining to ourselves what the patient looks like, what he talks about other than through his dreams. I don't know if you want to have a go at that, Don?

DL: I'm a little reluctant because it's clear to me that what Isadore says is perfectly valid. Everyone knows that the patient's dream is in relation to their therapy and therapist and furthermore it is demonstrable that patients dream in the metaphor of their therapist, that is, that Gestalt patients dream Gestalt dreams, Freudian patients dream Freudian dreams, etc. It seems to me we would not get very far taking the material and putting it into a different context. Obviously if that were my patient he would be dreaming the kind of dreams that correspond to my conceptual system. That's the way it works.

EMS: That's what T.S. Eliot says anyway. "I can make you dream what dreams I want you to." I'm not convinced of that being the case.

IF: Don, aren't you now saying—and I agree with you—that the patients dream pretty much what their therapists expect from them?

DL: I didn't quite say that. I said they dream in the metaphor of the therapist.

IF: But how do they do this? It's because of their contact with that particular therapist, isn't it?

DL: Positively. I think that that relationship is invested with a tremendous amount of energy which is called transference by some people. Call it anything you want, but it's a high-energy relationship.

EMS: I've had patients who've come to see me and probably after seeing me have brought me dreams they've continued to dream throughout their lives and which they've brought to other therapists and other magic men—have dreamed the same dreams with me and continue to dream them with other therapists.

        I would like to have a go at the dream from my vantage point.

DL: Go ahead.

EMS: OK. I see the messiness as a possible diabolic message. The word diabolic comes from *diabolo*—which is everything flown around, strewn around, and I see it as his desire to re-negotiate pretty much everything in his reality. Now obviously he might have picked the diabolic, i.e., messiness, up from me if he were coming in to my office—and even picked it up as a positive factor now in his desire to completely re-order or non-order. That's where I am right now just hearing the dream.

DL: I definitely see the dream as a statement of potential, as a statement of what may be, therefore that maybe this individual may need to move toward less orderliness, toward more chaos or whatever you want to call it.

IF: Or what he fears would be chaos. That's what came out in the discussion of the dream.

        One thing. When we keep talking about transference. it certainly is a phenomenon which Freud discovered. But I think that we vary as to how we use it. It would be absurd for me to deny that there is such a thing. But isn't transference also what we in Gestalt therapy mean in emphasizing this awful phrase "here and now"? Freud also meant that, because in this phenomenon of transference *again* something is occurring that occurred much earlier. But the important thing, and what makes it available for therapy, is that it is being done in a distorted way perhaps, but *again;* and in Gestalt therapy we would say that that's what "here and now" means, and by concentrating on the contact of the patient and therapist, which you two have indeed pointed out, you are also dealing with the transference. In some sense we would ordinarily avoid interpretation; we would be dealing with it somehow differently, that is, not with interpretation.

DL: And again in talking about that dream and in talking about dealing with transference, that depends entirely on the patient, hopefully, rather than on the therapist, that is, it is determined by the stage of the treatment and by the degree to which the individual can use insight as a tool to grow. So the interpretation of the transference is by no means desirable in any therapy with certain individuals.

IF: I think I meant something slightly different. I wonder if we couldn't consider that what Gestalt therapists are trying to do without always knowing it, is to resolve the transference as it develops.

DL: Right. Positively.

IF: What I'm proposing here is probably a way of regulating the transference. Ideally it would happen in every session but in fact doesn't. One would attempt to dissolve the transference in every session. It's not an absurd ideal.

EMS: I'm going to have to call time. I'd like to suggest that we sum it up.

IF: Well, after talking to both of you, I think how I would now put it as a Gestalt therapist—and perhaps this would be useful to other therapies—is that to consider our patient's dream as a possible unawares retroflection, which is one of the disturbances at the contact boundary, might be a way of attempting to dissolve transference as it develops. Now I leave it to you.

EMS: I'm concerned about what you mean by dissolving transference since I've never been very sure of transference although I think I am some of the time. I don't know what you mean by dissolving it and I wonder if you'd take the few remaining moments on it.

IF: We must not leave out of the word "transference" that what Freud meant by that is transference neurosis (neurosis, which is left off), then you have to do something about it. That I think is what Freud meant by transference, that the development of, in a sense, a new neurosis instead of the old one, and that he called transference neurosis. A complete analysis would mean dissolving that transference neurosis.

EMS: Don, do you have any final comments?

DL: The central issue to me is that the dream is a communication and I'm satisfied that Isadore is seeing the dream as a communication, both of the dreamer and with important persons in the environment which certainly includes the therapist.

IF: And as a Gestalt therapist I would add: and that is now being told to *this* therapist.

DL: Right.

IF: Alright, Mark, why don't you finish?

EMS: I'm also concerned about what the dream says about the relationship be-tween the patient and the therapist. Except that I'm not always sure that there aren't more important preoccupations going on. Sullivan talks about the dream of the schizophrenic and preschizophrenic as a first stage in the dissolution of what we might call ego or personality. I get a feeling as I hear you that there is a therapist being addressed. Nevertheless, there may be the more important or more vital areas of *self* being aroused, and in this vein the therapist may simply be a stand-in for the patient's shadow, and I wouldn't want to forget this as I looked at a dream or in effect—as I see it—shared a dream with the patient. Again this may be a 90° angle from your point of view in which the relationship is demonstrable in the dream material.

IF: Mark, I have to interrupt. I do not use the word "relationship"—that is Sullivanian. I use the word "contact with." There is a difference.

Chapter 6

Gestalt Therapy is Permission to be Creative: A Sermon in Praise of the Use of Experiment in Gestalt Therapy

JOSEPH C. ZINKER

If Fritz were alive today he would be disappointed to see multitudes of little people parroting his work as if it were the last word in psychotherapy. What many of us didn't have the courage to learn from him was his sense of inventiveness, his way of creating dramatic learning in the human situation. For Fritz, the "hot seat" or the "top dog-under dog" were momentary insights to be explored then moved aside so that other experiments and notions could take their place. Like all great artists he was nourished by the process of his own creative juices. Once a painting is finished it carries little cathexis because the next one is more timely and exciting. If Gestalt therapy is to survive it must stand for this kind of integrating growth process, this kind of creative generosity; it must keep intertwining new discoveries about our musculature, our archetypal origins, our primal screams into its original discoveries. If we, the teachers of the craft, forget this basic principal of creative experimentation, of evolving novel concepts out of our own sense of daring, of being unabashedly bold, then Gestalt therapy will die with the rest of the contemporary therapeutic fads. Fritz gave us a personal model of outrageous inventiveness.

Gestalt therapy is really permission to be creative. Our basic methodological tool is the experiment. The experiment moves to the heart of resistance, it changes and transforms rigidity into an elastic support system for the person. The experiment is a behavioristic approach of moving into novel functioning. It may be used to help the person reach his blind polarities, his "shadow," or to exaggerate his crazy behavior. The experiment does not have to be heavy, serious, or even precisely fitting—it can be theatrical, hilarious, crazy, transcendent, metaphysical, humorous. The experiment gives us permission to be priest, whore, faggot, holy man, wise witch, magician, and all the things,beings and notions hidden within us. Experiments don't have to grow out of concepts—experiments may move from simply playfulness into profound conceptual revelations.

In one group I worked with, a simple Christmas carol was transformed into what felt like a Bachian choral work. Its immediate impact was not even clearly appreciated by the therapist-participants but somehow they knew that they created something beautiful and transcendent of their own personal limitations. Gestalt therapy is permission to be exuberant, to have grandness, to play with the nicest possibilities for ourselves within our short lives. Experiment is powerfully effective in groups because it is supported by the varied creativeness of a total community. No one person gets depleted and everyone is nourished. Gestalt therapy is not the routine repetition of stale prayers of sundown. For me it stands for all that is in front of me, for all that promises completeness of experiencing, for the things to come which are awesome, frightening, tearful, moving, unfamiliar, archetypal, growthful. For me it means the full embrace of life —the savouring of all its subtle tastes.

Chapter 7

Chicken Soup Is Poison

ROBERT W. RESNICK

In order to make chicken soup, you have to kill a chicken. Although not particularly leading to self-actualization for the chicken, this sacrifices the bird to a greater cause—being helpful. Combined with onions, greens, carrots, water and seasoning, the resulting elixir is ready for its role as a helper. The giving of chicken soup is an attempt to "help" the other—to do for him, to make him feel better. The chubby, sponge-like

"TELL ME THE DREAM FIRST, THEN YOU CAN HAVE THE CHICKEN SOUP."

Figure 1.

matzo ball, not unlike the unconscious, lies 90% below the surface of the soup. By the time the unaware gourmet has had enough of this brew, the soup around the submerged matzo ball has cooled and, like a dead submarine, it spews forth its fatty oil slick. CAUTION: Chicken soup is likely to be as fatal to the recipient as it was to the contributing poultry. Now don't run around like a submarine with its head cut off—there is an antidote.

Many therapists see themselves as members of the "helping profession" engaged in the "helping relationship." Beware! Such people are dangerous. If successful, they kill the humanness in their patients by preventing their growth. This insidious process is somehow worse realizing such therapists typically want the reverse. They want their patients to grow, to live and to be, and they guarantee the antithesis with their "help." The distinction between true support and "help" is clear: *To do for the other what he is capable of doing for himself insures his not becoming aware that he can stand on his own two feet.* The difficulty is in judging whether or not the person is potentially capable of doing or being himself. This depends on your own convictions about human beings and possibly your own need to be "helpful." If you are convinced (sucked in) that the person is as helpless, as impotent and as incompetent as he plays then you are "helpful."

Gestalt therapy has as a basic goal the substituting of self-supports for environmental supports. Perls talks about the therapeutic impasse—what the Russians call the "sick point." Typically people experience confusion, helplessness and nothingness at such a point. Their usual attempts to manipulate their environment for support by playing deaf-dumb, by misunderstanding, by crying, by demanding, by playing crazy, by pleading, etc., are not working. If the therapist (or anyone else) walks into the manipulation by trying to be "helpful" he successfully keeps the other an infant. In order to achieve integration and to potentiate growth, the patient must "do his own dirty work." Perls, in a more poetic mood, states that the essence of Gestalt therapy is allowing (by frustrating) the patient to discover that he can "wipe his own ass." He illustrates this point by talking about the human embryo in utero. Here, the organism does nothing for himself. He is completely dependent on environmental supports. Sustenance, warmth and oxygen are all provided by the mother. At birth, the child enters his first impasse: He can breathe for himself or he can die. Throughout development the neonate becomes more and more able to crawl on his own four limbs. At birth he cannot stand by himself. Soon, if allowed, he stands autonomously. Carry a baby around all the time and he may never learn to walk. His muscles may atrophy and he may even lose the possibility of ever walking by himself. In western cultures mothers are "helpful" and their babies walk, on the average, almost a year later

than children in some other cultures where the child is allowed to experiment, to make mistakes, to grow, to be. Children who get others to satisfy
their needs with baby-talk never need to learn to speak. As long as they
have someone helping them—taking responsibility for communicating
their needs to the world—they never need speech. Without their "helpers"
they are like a Robisperre without his Baby Snooks. Initially, they may
scream and cry for others to support them. Eventually, they will learn to
communicate directly themselves or die.

No one can be completely without some environmental supports nor is
it easy for me to conceive of wanting to be in such a position. There is a
great difference in getting from the environment that which I cannot do
for myself and conning others into doing what I can do for myself. Most of
us to varying degrees are under the illusion that "we can't." Typically I
have found that "I can't" really means, "I won't." I won't take the risks
involved. To want the environment to help, to comfort, to support, even
when I can rely solely on my own self-supports entails taking the risk of
asking for such help. I take the responsibility of asking for help rather
than manipulating the other into offering what he believes I am incapable
of generating for myself. Even the manipulation can be self-supporting if
I am aware that *is* what I am doing. Such awareness allows me the choice
and freedom to do this or to do otherwise. I am then still me—not relin-
quishing my autonomy, my power, unless *I* want to do so.

People coming to therapy usually want something. Often they ask for
"help" and what they want from therapy is a way to change the consequences of their behavior without changing their behavior themselves.
They state that they eat spicy foods and get heartburn. "Can't you do
something about my heartburn since I am sure I can't stop eating spicy
foods. Stop the heartburn or at least help me find out 'why' my eating
spicy foods gives me heartburn." (They are under the illusion that the only
possible way for them to change *what* they are doing is to find out *why*
they are doing it.) Their cop-outs vary. The unconscious, although diminishing in popularity, probably still gets the most blame. Parents are always
popular as are wives, husbands, social systems, economic systems, world
situations and the "soup-man" (or Superman, depending on how you see
your therapist). As long as they attribute responsibility for *their* behavior
to another person or concept *they* remain powerless. More exactly they
are *giving* their power/autonomy/humanness to the other person or concept. Their implicit therapeutic request is: Let's you and he (or it) fight.
The therapist, if he is unaware, willing or both, is pitted against the free-
floating unconscious or whatever via the patient's manipulation while the
latter drools over the flow of chicken soup and is never sated. Slow down
or, noodles forbid, stop the soup, and the patient tries that much harder
to unclog his lifeline. When the help is not forthcoming and the patient

has not yet discovered his own ability to give himself his own chicken soup, he then encounters his impasse. If the therapist successfully frustrates the patient's attempts to manipulate, the impasse is pregnant with growth. If the therapist is "helpful," he assures the patient's remaining impotent and up comes the oil slick from the murky depths of the soup. Even when a person breaks through his own shackles as often happens in encounter groups, sensitivity groups, nude groups, marathon groups and drug groups, he typically has great difficulty in integrating his behaviour and experience into his everyday life. I am convinced that his freedom to be was given to him by the situation, the group, the leader, fatigue or drugs. Chicken soup comes in many flavors.[1]

The most popular way patients avoid standing on their own two feet is by looking for reasons. Simkin calls this the "why merry-go-round." (I'm sure you're all familiar with the tune.) The patient hops on the "why merry-go-round" and plays thirty-two bars of "why, why, why does this happen to me?" After finding the reason, he hops off the merry-go-round only to find that nothing has changed. He crawls back on his outside horse looking for the brass-ringed "why"—spends more time, effort and money so that this time his new reason is elevated to the status of an insight. Stumbling off his horse, brass ring in hand, he finds nothing has changed. Some people have been on this carousel of "therapy" for five, ten or twenty years. Many of those who got off the merry-go-round have changed their tune. The first eight bars go something like: "So now I know all the reasons and I'm still miserable." Indeed, if you allow them, they'll delight in relating their insights interminably (Excedrin headache No. 2002). It's as if the purpose of therapy is to find out "why." I'm convinced the purpose of therapy is change behavior, experience or both. Behavior *is* caused and knowing the whys has nothing to do with change.

The most popular way therapists help their patients to avoid standing on their own is to first deny that they have the blueprints and answers the patient is asking for. (Of course, the therapist doesn't believe this.) This done, the therapist "helps" the patient with the content of his problems (e.g., he manipulates the patient into discovering for himself what the therapist knew all the time). Even if I assume (and I do not) that the therapist is better equipped to make decisions than the patient himself, I am convinced that this leaves the patient no better off than when he started. If anything, he is a worse cripple. The lyrics of his problem change over the months and years but the melody lingers on and on and on. The process

---

[1] With this statement I in no way wish to condemn encounter groups, etc. I feel they can play an extremely important role in potentiating human growth by allowing people to experience possibilities. This, however, is not enough. It is only a beginning. The work then is to find out how (not why) I prevent myself from enjoying my possibilities.

by which he stops himself from fuller functioning continues as long as he deals with the content of his problem to the exclusion of the process. Blaming his parents *for making him weak or insecure* is not his problem. . . *HIS BLAMING IS.* What he is doing is making his parents responsible for who he is *now*. *How* he is doing this is by playing "victim" and blaming them. *Why* he is doing this is irrelevant to changing and if pursued guarantees his staying stuck. Is it any wonder he remains "weak and insecure." Only when he becomes aware of *his* blaming his parents for who he is *now*, does he have a chance to grow. When he is in touch with *his* "responseability"—his ability to respond—he enters a world of possibilities, choices and freedom. As long as he blames the other, he remains impotent.

The making of chicken soup is a fine, old art with many variations. However, one thing remains unchanged: In order to make chicken soup you have to kill the chicken.

Chapter 8

Beginning the Therapy

JOSEPH C. ZINKER

Your letter about *Beginnings* reached me here in London where I am about to start a two day Gestalt workshop with members of the Humanistic Psychology group. I am therefore writing you a reply on my feelings and style of beginning a group especially in the present context.

The first thing that happens in me just before the beginning of a group is pure excitement. This excitement may begin several days before I meet with the group and reaches a peak in the first hour of the actual group meeting. As everyone seems to be doing "groups" ("T-Groups," etc.) these days, I would like to specify part of the formal process that goes on in my head before the group actually meets:

THEORETICAL ORIENTATION

My first decision, although this is almost automatic, relates to the kind of theoretical orientation which is most comfortable for me and which I feel will be most useful with the particular group. Although Gestalt Therapy within the group setting is usually of the "hot seat" type (i.e., Perls), for me the Gestalt orientation in a group deals with the integration of principles dealing with body work, awareness, experiment, etc., and group process as a whole. Experiments may be invested by the group for the whole group as part of a particular problem that may develop at the time.

58

WHO ARE THE GROUP MEMBERS?

I use the energy that builds up within me to investigate the participants of my group. In the kind of group I am doing here in London, some people get together and find the person they want to work with so that I have little initial power in "composing" the group. Nevertheless I still want to know who they are, what their professional affiliation is, how sophisticated (or experienced) they are working in groups, what idiosyncrasies some of the group members have, if there are any psychotics floating around, and what the group would like from me.

GOALS OF THE GROUP

I always feel more comfortable when I know ahead of time what the general purpose of the group is. I have learned my lessons: Not very long ago I was asked by the administrator of a psychiatric hospital in the middle west to spend a day with a group of psychiatrists for the purpose of illustrating how a Gestalt therapist works. I agreed to do so and assumed that the group members were aware of this particular plan. After working with them for about six very painful and distressing hours, I discovered that no one in the group (the administrator was not there) ever heard of me or Gestalt Therapy or the general reason for my presence. After the air was cleared, we spent two very useful hours learning from each other and about Gestalt principles.

With respect to the London group, I think they want to gain individual insights (i.e., "personal growth") within my theoretical framework, circumscribed within the time limits of two days. A follow-up workshop will be done by my colleague, John Adams, a month later.

COMMUNICATION OF GROUND RULES

At the very outset of a workshop, I like to let the group know the general "design" of our work and communicate the general ground rules within which we will operate. The group has the freedom, of course, to discuss these principles and to question their validity. Here are some of the statements I will communicate to my group here:

1. Priority on here and now experiencing
2. Do it, don't talk about it

3. Make statements out of your questions
4. Talk directly to someone
5. Take ownership of your statements
6. Pay attention to your physical experience
7. Don't apologize for your feelings and needs
8. "Listen" to the other's feeling, don't interpret it away

Ground rules are especially important when a group is time limited; if there is no time limitation, these rules grow out of the therapist's interventions and become implicit in the workings of the membership. As we work together, the sense of being close and helping each other and experimenting with new modes of being free human beings moves beyond such formal qualities yet they are necessary in the beginning.

THE PLEASURE OF CLOSENESS

What is most exciting to me in the very beginning is the prospect of "working" well together, the prospect of becoming free enough to really move into new realms of functioning, the prospect of having real and authentic encounters, the prospect of opening closed persons, the prospect of creating a uniquely loving community—a mutually supportive group of people who will not be the same people when they leave. These possibilities I can feel in the very beginning and they energize me to deal with the "nitty-gritty" stuff in the here and now.

As I am writing this, I am really getting excited about working with these people in a country I have never been to, thousands of miles away from home. I suppose that home is a place where I can experience this kind of closeness to others.

Chapter 9

The Compleat Psychotherapist as Artist: Gestalt Perspectives on the Organic Integration of Six Selves

ROBERT A. HALL

I *believe that psychotherapy in its highest form is a creative art of facilitating human growth and healing.* This occurs when therapists are able to employ their *personal, unanalyzable creative force.* They allow this force to integrate certain *essential elements* into ever unique configurations. These emerging gestalts have living authenticity and novelty. This stems from the continual innovative, creative, organically flowing integration of the elements.

Since the concepts of Gestalt therapy strongly focus upon the integrative aspects of organismic flow, I believe they offer useful perspectives from which to view any psychotherapeutic artist. The theory and philosophy of Gestalt may also, to a greater extent than some other disciplines, support a therapist in taking the risk of allowing their moves to be the expression of their own inner flow.

THE ESSENTIAL ELEMENTS:
THE "SIX SELVES" OF THE PSYCHOTHERAPIST

I have derived six categories which seem to describe and encompass the full range of those ways that psychotherapists move with clients which can be construed as fostering growth and healing. They are proposed to constitute the *essential elements* which, when coordinated by "something more," result in psychotherapeutic art. They are fairly distinct, with some overlap. Two or more may be found together in one communication. The examples used are mostly illustrative of what occurs in Gestalt therapy. However, examples from other orientations that fit into at least the first three categories can readily be found; with some exploration, instances of inadvertent appearance of the last three categories can be found in therapy of any orientation.

1. The Experiencing Self

Therapists engage their clients with their experiencing selves when they merely express what they are experiencing. This is the sharing of awareness of what is noticed—what is heard, what is seen, what is felt—in response to what the other person does. The simple and accurate reflecting back to another person how he or she is experienced can be a very valuable gift. It provides people a way of knowing what their impact is on another person. It can accentuate their awareness of what they are experiencing and what they are doing.

Examples
"I notice your voice sounds weak and breaking when you speak to her."
"Did you notice what you are doing with your hands? I feel pushed away."
"I feel sad (angry, frightened, excited) when you do that."

2. The Imagining Self

Therapists express their imagining self when they communicate their *thinking about* the client. This includes recognizing and labelling, guessing, analyzing, predicting, explaining, and all other cognitions that go beyond direct experiencing but are based on current or past experiencings of the client; the client's own expressed imaginings, memories, or fantasies; or the therapist's projections of himself. Such communications can touch off profound experiential reverberations and provide sharpened focus for further work. This category considerably overlaps with the following one, since expressing cognitive communications may be used as technique. This is especially true when they are offered as "interpretations." In Gestalt they tend to be clearly identified as what they clearly are—just one person's imaginings about another.

Examples

"When you say you feel tightness in your throat, I imagine you are choking off a scream."

"I wonder if you stop yourself from expressing anger now by assuming that he would act like your father did when you expressed anger."

"I imagine that, to you, being self-sufficient means to cut yourself off."

"Maybe you also hate your mother."

3. The Technician Self

Therapists use their technician self when they employ devices intended to propel the therapeutic process. These may enhance awareness or insight, assimilating, taking responsibility for one's self, exploring contact (ego) boundaries, finding self-support. This device-using self tends to bear most distinctly the stamp and flavor of therapists' theoretical orientation. The techniques tend to be imitative of those used by the leaders of their schools. They are the "bag of tricks," most prone to artificial repetition rather than artful use and creative innovation. They may be very valid and effective when integrated into an organically artistic whole process.

The techniques of Gestalt therapy tend to be action-experience oriented devices. They are among those most prone to unartful abuse.

Examples

"Put your depression out here and talk to it."

"Be the desert in your dream. What does your desert have to say?"

"Your dream has no ending. I suggest you end it now."

"Are you willing to see what happens *when* you tell a few people in the group, 'I don't know how to get close to you'?"

A man is bent over, weakly expressing his anger to his oppressively experienced boss. My cotherapist moves around and lays on his back. He repeatedly tells her to get off, which she does only when he begins to yell this angrily. He resumes the imagined encounter with the boss with angry vitality. The next day he finally makes legitimate demands of his boss, who agrees! His severe insomnia and headaches are gone for the first time in years.

"See what happens when you say that louder."

4. The Other-Nourishing Self

Therapists use their other-nourishing self when they give from themselves to their client. They may do so by expressing genuine support, appreciation, affection, understanding, sympathy, or respect. They may do some favor as they would for any other friend. This is a legitimate part of any real human interaction. It is considered forbidden in some schools. For example, in classic psychoanalysis it is usually seen as a "counter-transference problem," but frequently occurs inadvertently *and* therapeutically, I believe. It may in fact be untherapeutic when the therapist becomes such an ardent "helper" that the client is robbed of opportunities to find his own support, and dependence on the therapist is encouraged. Chicken soup may be poisonous. However, nourishing expression by the therapist can be growth enhancing when it provides necessary support for risky experimentation. It also may be a part of the prerequisite process of developing trust in the therapist.

Examples
"I appreciate your sharing your sadness with me. This is a gift."
"I like your taking the risks you took today."
"I wish you would go farther with that."
"I feel warmth and closeness with you now."
"I admire your frankness."
The therapist takes time to find an unlisted telephone number the client wants.
The therapist offers to drop the client off on his way home.
The therapist touches or holds a sobbing, shaking client having a profound experience.
The therapist holds a client who desires and fears such contact, and is willing to see what will happen.

5. The Self-Nourishing Self

Therapists give expression to their self-nourishing self when they take care of themselves. They stay aware of and respond to their own human needs. Such actions are also avoided by some schools of psychotherapy. They seem to believe that a human being called therapist should be there pretending to have no needs except to be paid money and that this is consonant with therapeutic process. Existentially-oriented approaches support the therapists' being the only thing they can *really* be, human and real people with a wide range of needs of their own to be attended to. Therapists need to take in and to express. They need to know how they are experienced, to express their sadness, anger, affection. To attempt to exclude or hide this in the therapeutic relationship is false artifice. In openly engaging their own life-supporting behavior as part of the therapeutic process, they provide for their own existence. They also often give the gift of modeling self-support to clients who need to learn to take better care of themselves. Further, this may put clients in touch with particular neglected needs of their own. When I take care of myself, in or out of therapy, this usually is also best for others.

Examples

A therapist tells the client with whom he is working in a group that he experiences her as shoving people away. When she responds by denying that she needs anyone (of which he had not "accused" her), he feels and freely expresses anger. This catalyzes her sudden open release of previously covert anger. She then becomes aware of sadness. Later, this leads into experiments through which she gets some real sense that perhaps she could feel independent and self-supporting without rebuffing people and feeling sadly alone.

I felt dull and "out of touch" at the begining of a group. I went around and made some contact with 6 or 7 people. This enlivened me. I then felt ready and worked with several people. I had passed by one man, telling him I was unwilling to deal then with some contact barriers I felt with him. After working with the others, I expressed my need then to tell him that he seemed to be looking at me with hurt and anger. He acknowledged and further expressed these feelings. He then got in touch with his murderous rage towards his father and was willing to powerfully experience and express it. This in turn facilitated his releasing his very powerful loving feelings for his father which he said he had never before allowed himself to accept.

6. The Fellow-Traveler Self

Therapists' sharing personal information about themselves I call using the fellow-traveler self. This includes revealing private information, feelings, events, fears, needs, humor, sorrows, joys, pains, successes, failures. It may be done on request or spontaneously. To do so compulsively or despite real willingness is an artifice. Some willingness to do so is an appropriate matching of the enormous willingness for openness that therapists receive from clients. It may lubricate the therapeutic process by putting clients in touch with similar experiences. It may enhance the client's willingness to risk exposure. It may serve as an antidote to the clients' feeling alienated in their own "bad" feelings or "shameful" history. It may intercept or neutralize clients' tendency to become ambivalently and heavily dependent on their therapists. At the very minimum it is part of having the experience of a real and open human relationship, something which many clients seeking psychotherapy seldom have had and sorely need.

Examples

I was in a training group with Jim Simkin 3 years ago. He spoke of having had a big problem with insomnia, "until I decided that insomnia was nothing to lose sleep over!" Previously, I occasionally had this "problem," got "uptight" over my "insomnia," and took sleeping pills. I haven't taken one since. I now conceive of my not going to sleep as indication that my organism needs to do something else. I let that happen, and usually go to sleep much more quickly than when I took pills. I don't think I ever let him know. Thanks, Jim.

An ex-minister therapist tells his client, an ex-minister who is holding back expression of anger, that he has personal knowledge of how "we ministers carry a lot of anger around." The client felt more in contact with the therapist, whom he began to see as empathic and less likely to be a potential critic of the anger which he was then willing to more fully express.

I shared with a client having problems with my father similar to his, and how he had put me in touch again with my own anger and frustrated affectionate feelings. This facilitated his further work.

SIX SELVES, ONE SELF

Artfulness rests upon *how* the artist integrates his materials into the production or performance. Artfulness in psychotherapy depends on *how* the therapist uses these six aspects of himself, his working materials.

During the course of the evolution of any work of art there are innumerable points of juncture, places where one thing is done (or happens) out of many possibilities. The painter puts a certain mixture of a certain pigment in a certain spot; the psychotherapist engages the client with a certain mixture of his six selves at a certain moment. The crucial question is how these "juncture events" happen artfully, how they occur in the specific way they do when they are part of an artful process.

Artful juncture events can only be the manifestation of a "personal, unanalyzable creative force." This force is the expression of the organic integrity, the wholeness of being, the unique living configuration, the *gestalt* that is each artist. Since it already is, the artist cannot *make* the force express itself. He or she can only *let it happen* when he trusts and follows his organismic flow.

As illustration, I will refer to Jim Simkin's work with a passive woman.* There is an especially beautiful juncture point which occurs after the client reexperiences being tied to a post as a child.

---

* Simkin, James. Mary: A session with a Passive Patient. In *Gestalt Therapy Now*, J. Fagan & I.L. Shepherd, Eds. New York: Harper and Row, 1970.

M: [Long pause, voice controlled.] Now, I'm back here in this room, but I'm still a little girl all tied.

T: Right.

M: I'm closed in—alone.

T: [softly] Now I want you to talk to your little girl—to tell your little girl that she knows exactly how to untie herself and how to open up, and I care too much for that little girl to do anything that would interfere with her doing it for herself.

Jim's move clearly has a profound effect on her. She goes on to mobilize her own power to "untie" herself. She opens her senses, makes contact with the people there, moves, breathes, asserts herself, laughs excitedly, enjoys her powers. Jim's particular response seems to lubricate a *real* discovery—an experienced differentiation between herself now and as a child. Jim might have responded in many other ways. He might have experienced and expressed anger. He might have "gone into his computer" and interpretively offered some imaginings about how she got support from her parents by being helpless. Acting as technician, he might have tried to propel her into experiment of his design, perhaps that she tell individuals in the group that she was closed in and alone with them. What he *did* do was express tender caring he felt, caring too great to allow himself to rob her of a chance to discover her self-supportive potential; he nourished by gently challenging her to find her own way out. This was a creative artistic stroke. I believe this was made possible by Jim's being aware and willing to express what *he* felt, *he* wanted, and *he* believed at that moment. His move has the flavor of authenticity. I believe he let himself "happen" without any self-conscious attempt to contrive the "right" move. Throughout this session he seemed to trust his own flow, his own "unanalyzable creative force" and allowed this to interact with his client's flow to yield self-realizing creative events for both.

This, or any other example of artistic psychotherapy, is an unreproducible unique event. We cannot even hope to reproduce an artistic effort of our own, let alone those of the ones who have taught and inspired us. When we attempt to imitate, we only stultify our creative process. Our only chance is to trust and let the wholeness of our authentic one self unfold as an ever novel realization of our six therapeutic selves.

Chapter 10

Exploring Contact Boundaries

JOHN B.P. SHAFFER

T wo schools of psychotherapy that have received increasing attention during the past decade are Paradigmatic and Gestalt psychotherapy. While each school has shown a minimum of interest in the other, I—by virtue of the supervisors and therapists who have had the most influence on me—have been strongly attracted to both. There are some striking parallels between the two approaches that have not yet been written about, and each has had an effect on the work that I do with patients; yet in other ways the two techniques are curiously incompatible. This paper is written in an attempt to note some of the similarities and differences between the two approaches and to put "my own house" in order. A firmly entrenched eclecticism prevents me from formally defining myself as an adherent to either school, and my goal for myself is to arrive at a point of integration wherein I experience my therapeutic interventions less as a derivation from one theoretical model or another (be it classical-analytic, Paradigmatic, experiential, or Gestalt) and more as an emanation from my own unique and centered style of relating to a patient (a point of integration that both Paradigmatic and Gestalt theory conceptualize as a consolidation —or "assimilation"—of introjects).

Paradigmatic therapy was founded by Marie Coleman Nelson, and it was through my personal contact with Mrs. Nelson, in seminars and in personal supervision, that I first became acquainted with Paradigmatic theory. It is along the methodological parameter of interpretation that she departs from traditional analytic procedure; her finding that certain kinds of patients—particularly borderline and narcissistic ones—could not meaningfully absorb, or learn from, classical types of interpretation led to experimentation on her part wherein she attempted to embody within her own behavior, via various roles of "paradigms," some of the patient's characteristic attitudes. For example, rather than pointing out and talking *about* a patient's obsessionalism, she might become obsessively involved in his obsessive-compulsive world, to the point of asking him to describe his daily routine in even *more* detail. The therapist's obsessionalism here can be seen as having two related objectives: (1) it can help to create an initial atmosphere in which the patient's style of being-in-the-world is not challenged, thereby enabling him to feel accepted and safe, and (2) it can help him to gradually become uncomfortable with, and openly critical of, the therapist's nit-picking and constricted approach to life. The fact that it is the patient who now points out to the therapist the latter's obsessional pattern, as opposed to the reverse process, has distinct advantages: it directs the patient's energies outward, it makes him an active criticizer (as opposed to the passive recipient of what he may well experience as the therapist's criticism), and it gives the therapist an important clue as to the patient's readiness to abandon some of his obsessive defenses. The obsessional paradigm, like many other Paradigmatic stances, can be viewed as a kind of "joining" of the resistance. A distinct advantage of any resistance-joining strategy is that it permits the patient to prod the therapist into movement rather than vice-versa; such a reversal can be particularly important for the obsessive patient, since he will now find an outside focus for his hitherto narcissistically-directed energies, whereas the therapist's *interpretation* of his obsessive needs too often repeats the patient's previous experiences with his parents in which he was found to be insufficiently good, smart, healthy, etc.

An especially useful paradigm involves the therapist's keeping his distance from the highly withdrawn patient, whose autism is often a response to parents whom he perceived as highly intrusive and over-stimulating. The therapist's paradigm of distance is designed to reassure the patient that he can safely keep *his* distance until he is ready to relinquish it. In response to the autistically-relating, albeit talkative patient (who speaks to the therapist as he might into a taperecorder and who seems to experience the other's comments or questions as an intrusion), the therapist might remain silent for entire sessions. As the patient becomes readier for contact, he often will project his own needs for separateness onto the therapist and begin to complain about the latter's aloofness. Hence the therapist is kept accurately informed as to the patient's desire for more contact; the fact that it is left to the patient to decide at what point to initiate contact often helps to enhance the latter's sense of mastery in the treatment situation and to lessen his feelings of vulnerability.

Mirroring of the patient is generally helpful in the case of highly narcissistic patients who tend to feel most liked by people who *are most like* (i.e.

resemble) them. In s me cases the therapist, much like the mother who communicates with her very young infant by cooing and babbling, might find himself imitating some of the patient's characteristic speech patterns. Not all of the therapist's paradigms need involve a mirroring of the patient; indeed, some can involve a demonstration of certain healthy ego attitudes —e.g., decisiveness, enlightened self-interest, etc.—that are notably lacking in the patient.

I can think of three specific instances in my own work where my conscious attempt to "go along" with the patient's characterology proved useful. In the first I intentionally read the philosophy books recommended by an extremely schizoid and intellectualized patient; the ensuing intellectual dialogue clearly strengthened our relationship. In the second instance my intentional use of passive-anal imagery with a latent homosexual man ("You got a bug up your ass?!") helped him to find the treatment much more meaningful. The third instance involved an extremely schizoid young man from whom I purposely kept my distance, since he had given several clues that he might break off treatment were I to make active efforts at contact. He has very slowly moved from treating me as a mechanical ear to viewing me as a potentially-giving breast, as when he recently made an overt request of me for the very first time (that I refer him to a psychiatrist who would be willing to prescribe tranquilizers for him). I have in general found resistance-joining strategies beneficial when it comes to highly negativistic patients, particularly adolescents. Here any direct opposition to their unrealistic plans—or even mildly questioning remarks— on my part frequently stimulates intense opposition on theirs. On the other hand, my apparent acceptance of the adolescent's plan (e.g., to marry impulsively), partly because it is so different from the parent's response, often frightens him into a beginning acknowledgment that he has *some* reservations about it. Now his negativism—his need to find fault—can bounce off and challenge my paradigm of acquiescence. Similarly, where the adolescent denies personal difficulties and sees himself as forced into treatment by his family, my willingness to accept this view of his life and to relate to him around any material that he brings up—be it sports, hobbies, dating, etc.—often creates an atmosphere in which he is eventually able to introduce problematic material.

On the surface, Paradigmatic interventions, which encourage occasional role-playing on the part of the therapist, seem antithetical to the spirit of Gestalt therapy, which emphasizes straightforwardness and non-manipulativeness in the therapist. Another apparent difference lies in Gestalt therapy's conceptual heritage, which is rooted more in existential-phenomenological psychology than in psychoanalysis. Yet Fritz Perls' emphasis on moving away from interpretation of, and talking *about,* emotional issues toward a here-and-now *experiencing* of them has much in common with Nelson's insistence on the utilization of paradigms to recreate and to make emotionally vivid within the therapist-patient interaction those emotional dilemmas that plague the patient. Indeed, both Perls and Nelson are suggesting that the therapist purposely highlight, exaggerate, and intensify (or, in the language of Gestalt theory, render more "figure") certain facets of the patient's characteristic attitudes and behavior. In this respect both models have a shared parent in Moreno's psychodrama, since each introduces a highly theatrical metaphor into the therapeutic transaction. A point-of-difference between the two models involves the question of which party to the therapeutic transaction gets to be the "actor": the Gestalt therapist adopts the role of a stage-director who instructs the patient-actor to intentionally mirror or exaggerate some of his own characteristic behaviors and introjects, whereas the Paradigmatic therapist is both director and actor—he silently directs himself to "act out" certain behaviors or roles vis a vis his patient. Hence in Paradigmatic therapy it is the therapist who mirrors, in Gestalt therapy it is the patient; in Paradigmatic therapy the theatrical metaphor is introduced unbeknownst to the patient, in Gestalt therapy it is introduced explicitly.

Both techniques pay explicit attention to the role played by toxic introjects in the patient's dynamics, but their contrasting ways of working with this introject are pertinent: Perls, when he had noted the patient's self-critical ruminations and "self-torture games," instructed the latter to go to the empty chair and "to play" the criticizing (or introjected) part of himself, addressing his disparagement to the hot-seat (representing himself). If the patient were to become consciously aware of the similarity between the criticizer and his actual parent—e.g. his mother—Perls might then encourage him to speak to himself as his mother once did, then instruct the patient to return to the hot-seat, to answer his mother, then shift back to the empty chair, etc.—all in an attempt to put him in touch with these two aspects of his psychic self and their deadlocked struggle vis a vis each other. Nelson, at a crucial point, would instead attempt to embody the introject herself, hoping that her belittling remarks to the patient will release autistically-directed, aggressive energies (against the "mother inside") onto herself, providing the patient an opportunity to "spit up" his introject (whom he can now perceive in an externalized form, via the therapist) and to direct his anger in more appropriate, less masochistic ways. Thus, the kind of dialogue that the Gestalt therapist encourages the patient to have with himself the Paradigmatic therapist prefers to place directly within the therapist-patient interchange. Either way—whether through the empty chair, or through the therapist's paradigm—the patient is encouraged to *externalize* or *re-project* the once-internalized introject. In this sense both techniques are focused on a similar goal—i.e., to enable the person to "own" his introject and to thereby experience himself as the *criticizing*, as well as the criticized, party. Hence when Gestalt therapists encourage reversals wherein the patient is directed to find fault with the therapist rather than to worry about whether the latter is finding fault with him, they are explicitly encouraging the patient to do what Nelson *indirectly* fosters through her resistance-mirroring paradigms (i.e. at some point the patient will hopefully complain about her excessive silences, her obsessive concerns with detail, etc.)

What are the implications of the differences inherent in the two methods? A consistent difference lies in the fact that the Paradigmatic therapist presents his "role" behaviors as though he is playing "straight," whereas the Gestalt therapist makes clear to the patient that the latter will at times be asked to either play significant people in his life or to exaggerate particular aspects of his own behavior. Obviously there will be certain advantages (and certain disadvantages) to either approach. I will attempt to briefly dramatize—in Gestalt-therapy-fashion—my inner debate as to these respective advantages:

Perls Introject: Marie, how can you expect the patient to get better when you are repeating the same role-playing shit that his mother and father foisted on him in the first place?!

Nelson Introject: But I don't confuse my role with my real feelings, unlike his parents. Besides, my role-playing is in the patient's interest, not in mine—it is designed to make him free of me, not to bind him to me. If a patient says that he now sees, in retrospect, that some of my previous behavior was probably a bit "put on" or exaggerated, I don't challenge or dispute him on this point.

Perls Introject: Perhaps—but I still think of a Paradigmatic maneuver as manipulating, and "playing games" with the patient. I am straight with him; if we are about to play a "gestalt-therapy game" I make this clear to him.

Nelson Introject: But in so doing you might, because of the obvious artificiality of the situation, minimize the mastery that he can gain from a more direct and life-like confrontation; after all, when he tells me off as I play the bitchy, seductive mother he has introjected —really shouts me down, no-holds-barred—he is having a reconstructive experience that cannot be matched by his telling off his mother-in-the-empty-chair.

Perls Introject: You assume much too much responsibility for the patient when you decide whom to "play" and when; I simply facilitate a situation in which the patient can find his way to a dialogue with the various parts of himself, without benefit of my expert interpretations.

Nelson Introject: But it is still you who takes responsibility for setting up the stage directions that he is supposed to follow.

Perls Introject: The patient is always free to resist my instructions, to tell me
                      that I am barking up the wrong tree.
Nelson Introject: Just as mine is free to react to my Paradigmatic behavior in any
                      way he chooses.

My recent experience in a supervision group led by a Perls-trained
Gestaltist, Isadore From, has reduced what I experienced as the distance
between the Paradigmatic and Gestalt models, thereby providing an integrative force around the "split" revealed in the dialogue above. By
enabling me to become more aware of my tendency to over-introject and
by insisting that I make explicit any disagreement that I had with him,
From helped me to "own" whatever I had chosen to incorporate from either
model. His interest in learning more about Paradigmatic techniques (which
helped *me* to become the teacher as well) also helped the models to seem
less foreign to each other—Dad was at least willing to acknowledge Mom's
existence! His disagreements with Perls and his discarding of those aspects
of the latter's technique (e.g., the empty chair) that were incompatible
with his own style helped provide a model (or unintentional paradigm)
for comfortably assimilating aspects of a technique that are congenial to
one's own style and rejecting those aspects that are not. And, by challenging the usefulness of a dichotomy wherein a therapist's behavior is seen as
either "straight" or "phoney" (or "real" versus "Paradigmatic"), From
helped to make the issue of straightforwardness a less loaded one for me.
He presented his idea in Gestalt terms, stating that the "figure" that one
presents as a therapist is different from the "figure" one presents as a friend
—e.g., we might often find ourselves more willing to do a favor for a
friend than for a patient. In Gestalt therapy terms, then, there is no "true"
or absolute self that functions independent of the context—or "ground"—
in which it finds itself.

From's consistent emphasis on "What will be most *contactful* for this
patient now?" bears a strong resemblance to Nelson's recommendation
that the therapist find a way of *engaging* the patient (particularly the
highly resistant patient) in such a way as to render treatment emotionally
meaningful. The Paradigmatic therapist's notion of engagement is very
close to the Gestalt therapist's concept of contact, and it was his wish to
offer more immediate contact between the patient and himself that led
From to discard the empty-chair approach. Now the Gestalt therapist and
the patient were engaged in a direct, on-going dialogue, a procedure that
also renders Paradigmatic and Gestalt approaches less dissimilar. Differences, of course, remain. What From typically promotes as a contactful
interaction differs from what Nelson is likely to promote. Each selects a
kind of contact or engagement that is more in keeping with his or her theo-

retical orientation. From, for example, will direct the patient, as Nelson never does, to intentionally exaggerate certain aspects of his own behavior. He is less likely than she to be intentionally critical and/or seductive and he is more frequently willing to share with the patient how he experiences him.

A basic point of contact between the two approaches lies in their approach to the patient's resistance; both Paradigmatic and Gestalt techniques actively support and/or join resistances. The Paradigmaticist joins resistances in ways that I indicated earlier. The Gestaltist acknowledges and legitimizes resistances in several distinct ways: (1) his theoretical grounding in an existential-humanistic orientation leads to a direct emphasis on "letting the patient be" and on relating to him as he "is" rather than as he "should be," (2) he might ask the patient to intentionally exaggerate a resistance—e.g., to have a fantasy in which he withdraws from the therapy-session to as distant a place as he wants to go, (3) he will remind the patient that the latter is free to say No to the various exercises and games that are suggested to him, and (4) the patient is repeatedly reassured that he is under no pressure from the therapist to stop or eliminate those of his contact-avoiding behaviors that the latter points out to him. It is around this point of accepting resistances that the two approaches become most closely "joined" in my thinking; whether it is via the Gestalt therapist's saying that it is all right to withdraw through fantasy or via the Paradigmatic therapist's silently accepting the patient's need to exclude him, both approaches disarm the patient by reminding him that he has a "right" to his pathology. To the extent to which these are mere maneuvers to "get" the patient to change, they lose their force; to the extent to which they are designed to provide an atmosphere that is congenial to growth, and to the development of feelings of safety wherein the patient can begin to *choose* to change, they can prove very powerful indeed. Nelson makes an important contribution in reminding us that what is a congenial atmosphere for one kind of patient may well fail to be congenial for another. For example, the paranoid person is likely to be threatened by an excessively benevolent atmosphere, since the absence of any apparent threat will render him all the more vigilant; instead, the kind of atmosphere that is likely to prove more comfortable for him would be one in which the therapist is somewhat forceful and challenging.

Throughout this paper I have taken the position that the therapist's adoption of one technique as opposed to the other is pretty much a matter of theoretical background and personal style, that neither one seems inherently superior to the other, and that it would seem possible for both to be assimilated into an eclectic orientation. However, it can be argued that Gestalt techniques have distinct limitations in the case of strongly unmotivated patients (like the hostile adolescent who sees himself as attending therapy only at his family's insistence), since the Gestalt approach tends to assume an overt complaint and/or some willingness to cooperate in an exploration of his verbal and non-verbal behavior on the part of the patient. Paradigmatic approaches, because they make no such assumptions and thereby allow the therapist to be as lackadaisical, as tangential, and as "crazy" as the patient, can in this sense be viewed as more versatile. Yet the effective Gestalt therapist who makes his *contactfulness* with the patient his very first order-of-business would probably find a way of relating that permitted the extremely guarded or resistant patient to deny his pathology, to discuss seemingly innocuous and irrelevant matters, and to refuse to focus his attention on his own behavior in the session.

Gestalt theory states that an exploration of similarities and differences constitutes a fundamental means of defining "contact boundaries." I feel somewhat fulfilled in the goal that I set myself at the outset of this paper, and sense that I have taken an important step in "laying to rest" the various and introjected "ghosts," both Paradigmatic and Gestalt, roaming within. They are in more comfortable contact with one another. Now it is time for contact with the outside world: I invite the interested reader to respond.

REFERENCES

Nelson, M.C. (Ed.). *Roles and paradigms in psychotherapy.* New York: Grune & Stratton, 1968.
Perls, F.S. *Gestalt therapy verbatim.* New York: Bantam, 1971.

Chapter 11

Dreamwork As Theatre

JOSEPH C. ZINKER

T *raditionally, the "analysis" of dreams* has been the province of psycho-therapists working individually with their fantasy-musing patients. With the advent of the "sensitivity training, T-Group, Gestalt Basic Encounter Group" movement in this country, the dream has moved into public domain; the dreamer is now sharing his experiences with his encounter group. And the great Gestalt therapist who made important innovations in this area was Fritz Perls.

DREAM WORK IN GESTALT THERAPY

Perls was a phenomenological behaviorist. He believed that the primary datum of the therapeutic process is the person's own experiencing, his own body movements, visceral and sensory awarenesses. All therapeutic encounters are anchored in these basic experiences. He also believed—and beautifully demonstrated—that in order to "understand" one's dream, one must not merely get in touch with its imagery and conceptual meaning, but also *act it out*. The dream must be lived out muscularly and in the living present in order for the patient to take full ownership of it, including the projections therein. Accordingly, Perls asked his dreamers to act out every person, object, and event in their dreams. He encouraged the person to carry on dialogues between these various parts, thereby letting the dreamer get in touch with the significance of his own imagery as a self-teaching process rather than as an interpretive-conceptual-rational deductive process. There are no interpretations, no arguments about the "on target" insights of the therapist since the dreamer becomes the architect of his own dream work. The therapist merely creates a situation wherein the patient can become more clearly aware of his present appearance, movement, sensation, voice, tensions, and polarities within the experiment of the acted out dream. The assumption is that behavior modification can take place more rapidly when the dream work itself includes muscular and sensory activity rather than mere discoursive activity. Behavior modification takes place in the total organism rather than in its cerebral cortex.

Perls was no group therapist. He did not pay attention to group process nor did he really deal with problems between group members. He worked with individuals in the group in front of the group, so to speak. He was a master demonstrator and this was consistent also with respect to working dreams. The patient acted out his dream in front of the group and the group enjoyed the master's work, identified with the dreamer's progress, gasped and laughed and supported and attacked the man in the "hot seat"; the rest of the group never quite directly participated in the person's dream-acting to get something they could directly benefit from.

Yet Perls did think of the dream in theatrical language. He spoke of the "characters" on the "stage" of the person's existence. He had the dreamer "play" the different "parts" in his "production." But the emphasis began and ended with the expanding awareness of the individual.

DREAM AS GROUP EXPERIENCE

Several years ago while working with a group of therapists in Chicago, it occurred to me that an individual's dream could be used to benefit the whole group; that once the individual "played out" his own dream and came in touch with himself in it, the whole group would take parts in the drama and actively participate in it. Thus, if the dream contained a run-down house, a crippled boy, his parents, and a station wagon, members of the group would pick roles which would seem relevant to their own lives. One person chooses to be the crippled boy. He tells the group how he often feels impotent with strong women and that this role would help him deal with his problem. Another person chooses the role of the domineering mother, still another, the run-down house, and so on. The dreamer helps the group understand his characters and the therapist facilitates the production of the dream as a dramatic acting experience for the whole group.

Here is an example of a vignette from the above dream played by only two of the characters neither of whom told the original dream.* The "crippled boy" is acted by John, a 40 year old man. He has a sad face and curved-in shoulders, appears to have rather shallow breathing so it is not surprising when he suggests that he play a son suffering from emphysema. Myra, a middle-aged woman who pouts a lot, volunteers to play the "domineering mother" and several members of the group smile and nod approvingly.

The vignette begins with introductions a la Perls. The man speaks first: "I am a crippled boy and I can't breathe and this is my existence..." The woman answers: "I am a domineering mother. I keep my boy crippled and this is my existence..." (Her face changes, tears welling up in her eyes. She tells the group about her relationship with an older son. They go on...)

Boy:	All my life I have needed you to take care of me but now I'm beginning to feel your suffocation...I mean my suffocation. I feel that you are choking me to death.
Mother:	When you were very young, you were sickly and I have tried to protect you from unnecessary discomfort...
Boy:	(Interrupting) Yes, and by the time I was seven I was afraid to go to school by myself and I would vomit when I got there...
Therapist:	John, how do you feel in your stomach right now?
Boy:	All right, but I still feel like she is choking me.
Therapist:	(to mother) Myra, put your hands on his neck and squeeze a bit...let him get in touch with the suffocation.
Mother:	(follows directions) I only want to take care of you...
Boy:	(tearing her hands away and coughing) Then get off my back! Let me live! (He looks as though he has suddenly taken his first full breath this evening.)
Member of the Group:	She doesn't hear you.
Boy:	(hollering very loudly) Get off my back, let me breathe, let me live my own life! (panting deeply)
Another Group Member:	I want to play alter ego for Myra. (to boy) If I let you be, let you go, will you hate me all my life?
Mother:	(completing statement) If I could only feel that you will love me when you leave, it wouldn't be so difficult...
Boy:	I need you to help me leave and I will always love you, but differently ...as a man, a strong man, not a cripple.

(The pair embrace spontaneously and Myra cries because she realizes that she will have a talk with her son who flunked out of college and came home six months ago...)

---

* Part of the originally reported dream by a male member of the group was: "...I see my mother approaching and I feel strangely uncomfortable in my chest..."

Everyone becomes involved. People exchange roles, play alter-egos for each other and try out different interpretations of the dream's content. Finally the group takes ownership of the dream by spontaneously introducing variations in its process and modifying the outcome of the action.

Everyone is enlivened and in process of understanding a part of himself. Each person in the group becomes an active creator of the life of a character, shaping it, moving in and out of it, experimenting with his behavior more freely within the make-believe context of the production.

The dreamer, the original creator of the "play," is not lost in the process; he can watch the drama or the nightmare or the fulfillment of a wish take concrete shape in front of him. He can move in and change the action. He can take over one of the roles and demonstrate it in detail. He can experiment with different outcomes: the crippled boy can become transformed into superman or a sadistic torturer or a self-righteous rabbi.

How does one identify with anything in another person's dream? There is no dream with which a person can't identify simply because it is the dream of another human being. Everyone had a mother and father figure, everyone has experienced changes in his body, everyone has felt helpless sometime in his life. Where there are no obvious identifications, there are archetypal ones: our evilness, animal nature, godliness, deadness, maleness, femaleness, needs for transcendence, for mothering can come to the foreground by getting in touch with another person's dream or with some special portion of it.

In the process, the group works as a cohesive team because everyone has a stake in the development of the drama. Everyone wants to be a good actor and acting well is a rehearsal for living well, for practicing to become a whole person.

SIGNIFICANCE OF INNOVATION

Is this modification of the Perls dream technique significant or is it merely a new "gimmick" to use with groups? I believe that the dream-theater technique is significant for the following reasons:

1. Gestalt therapy developed basically as an individual therapy. In the context of groups, it has often been a form of demonstration and teaching rather than a group process therapy in which the group creates its own integrity and its own individual and interactional changes. The dream-as-theater technique is one example of the transition of an individual therapeutic experience into a growth experience for the total group. It is one way in which basic Gestalt assumptions about the primacy of the phenomenological experience, the notion of non-inter-

pretation and the concept of learning by doing can be used in groups as whole, self-determining social entities.

2. This technique uses all the creative resources in the group, not merely the patient's or the therapist's.

3. The technique has economy; it offers more effective behavioral modification of a larger number of persons within a given period of time.

4. Watching a person working with himself is fascinating but can become deadly and boring unless one is watching a great master. Besides, most of us join groups because no matter how hesitant we may be we want to "get into the action" and experience active behavioral change in ourselves. This kind of work makes such participation possible.

ONE MORE COMMENT

No skillful therapist uses a particular method as a stereotyped repetitive formula. He takes ownership of parts of it and rejects aspects that don't fit his experiencing. He experiments with it and modifies it to his liking and to his particular style of working. The particular methodology acquires his working characteristics; his depth or shallowness, his discipline or "gimmickry," his awareness or dullness, his liveliness or cautiousness, his spontaneity or conservatism, his expansiveness or stinginess, his creativity or constriction. The dream as theater is an expansive notion. It is one other way we can enliven our work with groups.

REFERENCES

Perls, F.S. *Gestalt therapy verbatim.* Lafayette, CA: Real People Press, 1969.
Perls, F.S., Hefferline, R.F., & Goodman, P. *Gestalt therapy.* New York: Julian Press, 1951.

Chapter 12

Right Hemispheric Brain Function As It Relates to Gestalt, Phenomenology, and Small Systems

JOSEPH C. ZINKER

Laura:

Creative experience takes place in a nourishing environment: at least it helps. You have been, and continue being, a supportive presence for me. As I get older, I learn to appreciate old friends and the special ways each has been generous with me. May you continue enjoying life, love, and work for many years to come.

In recent years attention has been drawn increasingly to Right Hemispheric brain functions as distinguished from Left Hemispheric thinking (abbreviated as R-H and L-H). The contrasts are dramatic.

The left hemisphere is verbal, the right sensory. Analytic thinking belongs to the left hemisphere, synthetic (putting things together) to the right. The left brain creates the symbolic and the right craves the concrete.

The right loves what is, as it is. The left gorges itself with theoretical abstractions, and the right lingers with analogies, metaphors, associations. How the left loves order! How it appreciates linear sequence! Its temporal segmental nature is balanced by the wide-angle lens, the vast, full dimensionality of the right. As my friend Sonia Nevis might say, "This part of the brain appreciates the 'fat moments in life.'" Other contrasting dimensions are listed in the table below (Edwards, 1979, p. 40; Zinker, 1978, p. 60):

LEFT HEMISPHERE (L-H)	RIGHT HEMISPHERE (R-H)
Rational: Judgmental, Interpretive	Dreamlike; Paleological; Accepting of the "isness" of things, events
Digital (using numbers in counting)	Spatial: The space between things, not necessarily the things themselves; Spaces between parts of a whole
Logical	Intuitive
Linear—thinking in terms of linking ideas or events leading to specific outcomes	Holistic—seeing (or hearing) whole things at once—experiencing whole gestalten
Naming of things (remembering by naming)	Seeing things: Remembering faces—recognizing visually—recognizing configurations
Product; Purpose; Content	Process

Although we use both hemispheres all the time, I like to think that Gestalt Therapy work is grounded in R-H functions. The therapist is asked to see and to hear what is there first and foremost. The therapist practices (like the art student) *to see*, to love seeing, suspending judgment, evaluation, and interpretation. Thus, the emphasis is on primary sensory input linked to the client (or client system), rather than interpretation originating in the therapist's left brain.

Many therapeutic interventions are reports of R-H experiences: "When you spoke to me about your resentment, your face turned pink, you moved closer to me. . . I felt as if your voice came to life. . . . " Such interventions, although sounding benign, are often powerful and may have a profoundly affirming effect on the client.

When we teach therapists, we wish for them the real curiosity which springs from a childlike seeing and hearing of the actual. It is only much later that we teach the student about the complex interventions, the naming of *themes*, the development of *experiments*, the building of intentions, i.e., what we expect might—or will—happen as a result of our interventions. Thoughtful laying out of *themes*, experiments and potential (hypothesized) results is related to the shifting from R-H functions of being to the L-H functions of creating order out of the myriad of fascinating inputs. Singing the praises of R-H function without the appreciation of L-H capacity for order, elegance, and analysis is to naively reinforce a simplistic notion of humankind. However, to *emphasize* R-H functioning in the work of *Gestalt Therapy* may be very helpful—especially to the student.

The experienced Gestalt therapist is always in process; he/she travels on the crossroads of the corpus callosum cells between the two great hemispheres. Like a graceful dancer, s/he never gets caught in a lopsided position.

PHENOMENOLOGY

Phenomenology is the study of *what is* in the experience—the isness itself, its nature, its color, its texture, its sound, its movement. Here, too, the student must rely on R-H experience. We are not asking for meanings. Strictly speaking, we leave that to the existential philosopher. The phenomenologist says: "This is what I feel when I am alone," and the existentialist explains: "Aloneness is part of our life dilemma. . . aloneness is part of our freedom and part of our fright."

Phenomenology teaches us to appreciate the experience of our process (R-H), and existentialism helps us evaluate the implications of these observations (L-H). To jump into the L-H analysis without a respectful appraisal of what is, is to be ungrounded, flying up in a colorful balloon of "beautiful" words (L-H)—to fly by the seat of our pants, rather than to ascend out of concrete experience (R-H). On the other hand, to stay only with the phenomenological is to get lost in the mire, the complexity of moment-to-moment experience, without making sense of it, forming a clear Gestalt. R-H functioning by itself is psychological anarchy.

SMALL SYSTEMS

Gestalt therapists are increasingly interested in working with small systems like couples and families. Some of us try to do individual therapy with each person in the system, rather than with the system as a separate and real entity, a distinctive gestalt. Gestalt Therapy and systems-oriented work are first cousins. Both emphasize that the whole is different from the sum of parts; both emphasize seeing the phenomenon in the present (although systems theorists are also interested in the more-or-less lasting qualities of couple, family, and group structures.) There is also the similarity of interest in boundaries. For example, the couple is not a "clinging" husband and an "independent" wife, but a complex structure, a system, a gestalt, a metaphor. It is two bounded individuals enclosed in a larger bounded entity, and their relationship, their system, is defined by the nature of their changing boundaries, the changing quality of contacts along those boundaries, and the way they take in and relate to the world outside themselves.

This special entity is separate and distinctly different from putting two persons together. The Gestalt therapist learns to relate to this new whole, this third entity, this metaphor. The change of emphasis from the intrapsychic, dialectic world to the world of the Gestalt-System is dramatic. It requires that the therapist look at the couple with different eyes, the vision of the Right Hemisphere.

R-H seeing and listening brings attention to the Gestalt-System. The emphasis with the couple, for example, is not on who is right or sick (L-H), but on how they get together to make things happen or to interrupt contact between them. The emphasis is not on what goes on inside each, but on what goes on in the space between them. The emphasis is not on who caused what, but how the dance was choreographed by the complementary talents of the couple as a team. The emphasis is not on pushing them toward a specific outcome, but on enticing them to become curious about their own process. The emphasis is not on the content of each experience, but on the total melodic composition they create.

Because most of us are so dominated by L-H thinking, we fall into the trap of taking sides, looking for causes and effects, suggesting—often prematurely—practical solutions to complex interactive processes. Emphasis on R-H functioning in such sessions helps the Gestalt therapist remind him/herself where his/her interventions should come from, guiding him/her in the development of process. Process and patience lead inevitably to the couple's or family's realization of its own integrity, wisdom, talents, and sense of direction: When the therapist takes time to emphasize R-H function for the small system, the system can move on to clearer formed awareness and conceptualizations which result in solidly grounded actions.

Gestalt, phenomenological, and systems approaches are united, are bound together by our capacity to be sensory, synthetic, concrete, improvisational, in the moment, dreamlike, spatial, intuitive, holistic, and process oriented. Here is where we must start in order to *see* what is before us. When we add L-H talents to this marvelous capacity of seeing unique wholes, we can become more articulate, clear, and aware of our intentions as Gestalt therapists.

REFERENCES

Edwards, B. *Drawing on the right side of the brain.* Los Angeles: J.P. Tarcher, 1979.

Zinker, J. *Creative process in Gestalt Therapy.* New York: Vintage Books, 1978.

Chapter 13

A Talk with Laura Perls about the Therapist and the Artist

NIJOLE KUDIRKA

INTRODUCTION: *The development of Gestalt Therapy in general and Laura's thinking in particular have been intimately intertwined with various artistic disciplines. My personal involvement with the visual arts prompted my interest in Laura's experiences with art. I know that my experience as an artist has greatly influenced my work as a therapist, and so I wanted to hear if this was the general case. From this a discussion evolved about the importance of Laura's experiences in the arts in her growth as a therapist, as well as its general importance in the developing of therapeutic knowledge and skills.*

N.K.

Nijole Kudirka: I know you have always been very interested in the arts, and I'd like to talk about how this interest developed and how it has influenced your work in Gestalt Therapy.

Laura Perls: I have been interested in the arts from early childhood on, and my interest in the arts was predominant long before I became interested in psychology or philosophy.

NK: So your first love was for the arts?

LP: Sure, and my friends all were, or have become, artists. I started to play the piano when I was five. My mother was a good pianist, and I heard good piano playing and all the classical music from the cradle on. I wanted to play and I started when I was five, with my mother teaching me, and when I was seven I got a real piano teacher. She was very good. I think I learned more from her than with a later teacher who was better known.

NK: Did you think of going into music professionally?

LP: That was really the idea; I didn't think of anything else. I was becoming a great pianist. In a way, I was already that when I was fourteen, fifteen, sixteen.

NK: Then what happened?

LP: When I was sixteen I had what they call a "nervous breakdown," but I was simply going on strike somehow, being very confused, and in love with somebody who was much older. My family got wise to it and cut it off. For a few months I got into what they called a sanatorium—a kind of convalescent home run by an Adlerian psychologist. There, for the first time, I heard the name Freud, and I read *The Analysis of Dreams* and then *Psychopathology of Everyday Life*. And so I became somewhat interested in that. After that time, I went to law school, because at that time we were all left-oriented, and one had to do good or something that is socially useful.

NK: Somewhere in there the thought of being a concert pianist changed for you.

LP: That was not useful enough socially. Of course, that idea I would debate today. The arts are as useful and as necessary as anything else, but at the time the general attitude was that art had to take a back seat.

NK: Did you feel torn or conflicted about this choice?

LP: Actually no, I was getting into political thought at the time and some kind of feminist thing, too. I was among the first women who went to law school, and I thought of getting into juvenile court work. It was all new at the time, after the First World War, in the twenties. The whole political orientation at the time went socialist.

NK: So your music went into the background.

LP: Yes, it went into the background, but at the same time I still took piano lessons, from a very famous teacher and pianist, Fritz Malata, a Czech pianist. I started right from scratch again learning a new technique, a new approach to the piano. At first I was very desperate. I didn't play well at all at first, but somehow it later jelled with what I had already learned, and then when I was eighteen, nineteen, twenty, I was really a professional at the piano, but I stopped the lessons then because I got involved in psychology.

NK: These are two such different kinds of experiences: being involved in art and being involved in almost any other intellectual discipline.

LP: Oh God, there were many more things which somehow did not go together. Then I started in psychology with Gelb and Goldstein, where I met Fritz. That was in 1926, and we started an affair in 1927.

NK: In terms of the arts, music was the discipline that you were the most professional at and knew most about.

LP: It was something that I grew up with. I knew the whole classical literature, all the symphonies, which I had played four hands with my mother, long before I ever heard an orchestra. I grew up in a small town where we didn't have an orchestra, and one would come once or twice a month.

NK: You also said that in addition to the music you developed other interests in the arts.

LP: I want to a classical gymnasium. There were no girls' gymnasiums at the time, so I went to a boys' gymnasium. The first year I was the only girl there. Later on, another girl came in, with whom I have remained friends.

NK: So in the gymnasium you began to develop more excitement and interest in literature.

LP: In literature, I was very good in languages, in Greek and Latin and French. English is the only language I never studied. I read all the modern literature, the classical and the modern literature. I don't think there is anything in German literature from the Middle Ages to the modern ones that I haven't read.

NK: Did you find reading classical literature more fun and more interesting than reading psychological literature?

LP: I never found the psychological literature terribly interesting, but actually, Gestalt literature didn't exist then, though it was being written at the time. When Wertheimer did his lectures on productive thinking for instance, and Kurt Goldstein was conceiving and talking about his organismic concept. At the time Goldstein—together with Gelb—was doing small articles on brain-injured people and how they reintegrated what they have, and how they read and develop compensations.

NK: You also said that somewhere along the line you developed an interest in modern dance.

LP: I did modern dance since I was eight. I started with Delkraus; that was already before the First World War. I was nine when the war broke out. Then our teacher, who was a dancer from Stuttgart, was taken into the army, and for a few years I stopped. But when I was thirteen, fourteen, I started with the Lowelin system, which was connected with Rudolf Steiner and the Steiner schools. I found out later that what they actually did were to a great extent Yoga and Zen techniques. I have kept up this interest all my life. Actually, in South Africa, there was one of the Lowelin people, and we worked twice a week in my garden. I wanted Fritz to join us. He thought at the time that it was girls' stuff, and it was boring, and he took up ice dancing and later flying. Later on, just a couple of years before he died, when he had become more aware of body awareness and the role it was playing in Esalen, he said, "You never taught me anything." I said, "Of course not, you didn't want to learn it."

NK: You said that during your lifetime you had a lot of artist friends, and that you cared about them a great deal. How would you compare your artist friends with your psychologist or therapist friends? Do you feel there are any differences?

LP: It has become progressively more disappointing. You know, the first people who were in psychology, and in new approaches in psychoanalysis, were interesting people. Somebody like Goldstein was an absolute genius. Gelb in a way was a famous teacher. He was not reliable, and as an advisor he just conked out somehow, and I didn't do well with him. People who got interested in psychology at one time were all, in a way, artists. There were not such great differences. They were artists. Fritz was also more of an artist than a scientist. Actually, I was more of a scholar than Fritz. Fritz was very insightful and very intuitive. He had a kind of mathematical brain that I don't have. I was not good in mathematics. He was excellent in mathematics. At that time, psychology, and particularly psychotherapy, became an art and not really a science in spite of all the attempts to make it a science. The people who really did it well, they were really artists.

NK: What's your feeling about what has happened currently in the field?

LP: I think in America psychology has become academized, and people who were, or are, training with us, have become too specialized too early and don't have a broader humanistic background at all. Only very few of them have it. The ones who do still, in some way, become outstanding.

NK: So your feeling is that someone with a broader humanistic and artistic background is potentially a better therapist?

LP: That's right. They can also work with a great diversity of people. I think a lot of what is now called pathological, and even psychotic, is to a great extent what people do not understand and have no approach to.

NK: Focusing on the arts, I'd like to hear more about how you feel that knowledge and experience in the arts adds to one's being a therapist. What kinds of things it can bring in.

LP: I have always been reading a lot of poetry and also writing poetry. I once had a girl in therapy. Actually, it's a girl I always take as a paradigm for working with schizophrenics. She had been writing and majored in English. I got her when she was discharged from a hospital after an acute psychotic break. She came in here and looked uncared for and also moved in a catatonic way. She sat down, left the door open, and I asked her, "Would you close the door?" She didn't respond. So I got up and closed the door. She got up and opened the door. So I knew she did not want to be locked in here with me. She left herself an out. I told her she could stay and talk about whatever she felt like. She didn't say anything. She sat the whole session without saying a word, not moving her face at all, not really looking at me. At the end of the hour she got up and walked out. Didn't say goodbye. Didn't make another appointment. I didn't know if she would come next week. The next week she came, left the door open and sat down again and said nothing. I made myself available. I didn't read, or make a telephone call, or do anything on my desk. I looked at her and I stayed with her and said nothing. I just sat it out with her. She left, and I didn't know again whether she would come back. She came again and closed the door, and said nothing the whole session. At the very end of the session she looked at me and said, "What's my name?" I said, "I know what's your name. You're Irene; and what's my name?" and she smiled. The next week she started to talk. The talk at first was bizarre, and I didn't understand it. Then the next time she brought some poems that she had written. Then I realized that she was talking poetry, with a kind of elliptical procedure, and talking in the language of metaphors, and I could get in that way.

NK: So you were able to understand what was happening from your experience in poetry.

LP: Yes, without my knowing a lot of poetry and modern poetry in particular, I wouldn't have understood her at all, not for a long time. I would perhaps have given up, but I never give up actually. I don't push, but I am persistent. With schizophrenics particularly that pays off, because they really have withdrawn to that extent into a world of their own, because they don't feel understood. They are often very brilliant. This girl worked out very well. She started teaching in college and got married.

NK: So knowing the arts broadens one's capability to communicate and to understand more varied aspects of personalities. I'm wondering if any of your knowledge of music or literature went into formulating some of the Gestalt theory?

LP: Certainly the knowledge of literature gives you more insight into certain character structures, and of course psychology and existential philosophy have gotten much closer together. On the other hand, in the scientific community that is what is least accepted. They work with learning theory and conditioning, which is scientifically much more experimental.

NK: So the influence of the arts could be seen in the Gestalt emphasis on the intuitive understanding of the essences of things.

LP: On what I call the right-brain, left-hand activities, which in our left-brain culture have been left out nearly completely, being treated as somehow being eccentric. In Europe, eccentrics have a certain kind of respect. I remember when we grew up, one had an admiration for poets, composers, and artists —a particular species that was somehow on another higher plane.

NK: You feel that therapy is really an art.

LP: I wouldn't make such a division between therapy and art.

NK: Some people would talk about therapy as a technical skill.

LP: I think that's a great mistake. In Gestalt Therapy, I think any technique is applicable that is existential and experiential. We are not involved in just one technique. I would rather talk about style than techniques. Every therapist develops his own style, as an integrated way of expressing and communicating. You use technically what you have available in yourself, through your own experience. I have a lot available, because I have a very wide background and a deeper background than most people have here.

NK: So then, one's life experience and wideness of knowledge become very important to one's skills as a therapist.

LP: That's right. Whatever has been really integrated in your personality and has become your own support. By experience, I don't mean the collection of information. That remains introjects.

NK: Many people, when talking of their development as therapists, refer to means that I would consider very insular. They usually think of adding more experience with patients, or groups, or professional workshops. They stay confined within that framework. For instance, I don't think many people feel that extensive travel in other cultures is an experience that would enhance their therapeutic skills. Expanding one's knowledge of the world and bring it into one's work, perhaps even in a way that cannot be directly perceived, is not frequently emphasized. For me, the way artists do it is easier to see. Their visual and personal experiences, together with their inner sensations are always used as material to further their comprehension of the nature of the world and their place in it. Each new perception is added up, and then they are integrated in some way. From this the material can be brought out in a new way, with a new vision. I don't think many therapists approach their work that way.

LP: I must say that my style of doing therapy would be more like Paul Tillich or Martin Buber; they have had much more influence than any of the analysts or psychologists. Paul Tillich was my philosophy teacher in Frankfurt; so was Buber. What was important in Tillich as well as in Buber was the directness of their communication. They didn't lecture at you; they were directly talking to you, from a source in themselves; they had nothing to do with history or philosophy or any particular theory.

NK: So it was a deep, personal, and developed intuition that got communicated.

LP: Yes. That's what impressed me most, and of course historically they had very different backgrounds. Buber had a Hasidic, Jewish one, and Tillich, a Protestant, German one. Tillich had also been psychoanalyzed.

NK: In terms of personal experience—I wonder, for instance, if you went to hear a new piece of music, that you hadn't heard before, and it was a thrilling experience to hear the music, something that opened things up for you, would that influence change your work?

LP: It would affect me, and so it would also affect my therapeutic work. Even from the very beginning, musical experience was somehow opening up a whole world. I remember when I was five and started to play, that I discovered, or was taught, that I could sound more than one note on the piano at the same time, sound a chord, and that was absolutely—I still have the feeling of it—exhilarating. The experience of multiplicity, and perhaps through that, much less fear of multiplicity. For instance, if you only do folk singing and it is always one melody and the same, with no accompaniment, it's kind of simple, and if you build a whole world on that kind of simplistic idea, it's limited.

NK: That's a very interesting connection, because you're saying that it enabled you to experience complexity and in some way comprehend it. So I would think this enables you to be less anxious about it in yourself and in others and not try to simplify the other person, or their world. You would not push the other person to reduce some conflicts, dualities, or dichotomies, to make them less anxious. You could work with them to help them tolerate their anxiety about these complexities.

LP: I discovered my limitations on the piano. My hands are very small, and there are certain big pieces like Brahms, and Liszt, whom I didn't like anyhow, that I just can't play. Just as there are certain big constellations and events which I could not comprehend.

NK: That's true. In art you are very directly faced with your own limitations.

LP: Also with your own potential.

NK: I don't think you can ever experience it as purely in doing therapy, because of the factors the person whom you are working with brings in. There are always factors of the other person's motivation, capacity, or resistance and not only your own limits to contend with.

LP: The resistance is something that should not be taken as something negative; like in Chinese or Japanese body techniques, you take it as something to go with. Sensing limitations helps you explore the freedom you have within the limitations. If I had these enormous hands, I probably would have played a lot of Schuman and Brahms, and probably would have done much less Bach and Mozart.

NK: In doing therapeutic work, do you feel that there are certain kinds of personalities, or issues, that you cannot work well with, feel this kind of limitation there?

LP: Yes, I have felt it, but with increasing experience, I feel I can work with any kind of personality, if I let them be and go with what they are, not what I think they should be or become.

NK: So the limitations in playing music are much more clearly delineated.

LP: Well, perhaps the people that I could not work with would be the people who come to an agency. I have always worked with people who come either out of interest or people who could afford it. For a long time I took very low fees; still, they came mostly when they were students, people who had no money but who had some education. So I don't know if I could work with a really uneducated person.

NK: So you are saying that you and other therapists do not experience the full range of people, and so don't always experience the kind of limitations that they might have.

LP: That's why I think we should train many more minority and black people, who actually come out of the ghetto or still have more contact with it.

NK: Getting back to our original issues, do you think more artists should be trained as therapists?

LP: It's happening to some extent, that some dancers become movement therapists, and artists become art therapists. I don't know in the long run how much this will contribute. I find to a great extent that the good therapists are also artists, even if they are not well known as artists. They are also the people who read and are in contact with the arts, but they are not that many. Most of them, when they read, read professional literature, and they can hardly talk about anything else. I think these people are very limited as therapists.

NK: What are some of the limitations of those kinds of people as therapists that you can think of?

LP: As I said before, they would misunderstand anybody who talks in a way they are not used to.

NK: I think the worst danger is that they see one facet of human nature, and they feel that it is all of human nature. A narrow vision that is mistaken for a true vision. Other aspects that don't fit this narrow vision then begin to be considered as pathological. To get a deeper vision of human nature, most thinkers turn to the arts. Freud, for instance, had a great interest in primitive, as well as other, art.

LP: Yes, but Freud was actually an archaeologist. He collected antique terra cotta figures, and he was altogether, in his whole approach, an archaeologist who collected memories and interpreted them, because there is no direct access to memories, except in what is still there, right now, ways of behaving that have become a fixed gestalt.

NK: So as Freud is related to archaeology and history, Gestalt Theory could be seen as related to expressive art, that seeks the direct expression of feelings.

LP: The art that we were most affected by and grew up with was German Expressionism. There was also modern literature. There was a lot going on in drama. What influenced us was Brecht—*Mother Courage* and *The Three-Penny Opera*. We moved in this circle.

NK: Expressionism is again the new wave in art today, but I feel that currently it is not very good. The danger in expressive art, as well as in Gestalt Therapy, is that it can disintegrate into purely impulsive gestures that are not integrated with form or thought. It can become adolescent tantrums.

LP: I would say that is the right-brain activity without connecting to the left brain. It also has happened in Gestalt Therapy, and Fritz is guilty of that to a great extent. He disowned a lot of what he had. He was seduced by the West Coast so-called liberal humanism, which was simply laissez-faire and anything goes. He was perhaps relieved of a kind of intellectual rigor that he felt coming from Paul Goodman or from me. I think the West Coast is now recovering from this. A lot of those people had never read the second part of *Gestalt Therapy*, which I think is the most important. The other you can skip; that we can do now, and everybody does, in a much more sophisticated way. I think of people like Paul Goodman, who was an artist and an intellect. He was an erudite person. He talked sense. He was a man of letters of which there are hardly any here.

Chapter 14

Reflections on Unparenting

BARRY STEVENS

In Don't Push the River, *I referred to my "ex-son." Some people ask me what I mean by that. Others ask me how they can arrive at that with their children.*

Unparenting begins when the baby shows signs of wanting to feed himself and the parent lets him do it, when the baby shows signs of wanting to learn to walk and the parents lets him do it. When someone either pushes the child (giving him help that he doesn't need) or holds him back, this is not friendly. We don't let the child start feeding himself with a knife, or let him practice his wobbly walking at the edge of cliff. This is friendly. Friendly is going by observation and understanding. I must also observe and be friendly to myself. When I am tired and in need of rest, without which I will become cranky, I put the baby in the crib so that he is safe while I sleep.

The baby is constantly changing and I must change with him. How can I make a pattern, called rules, that will go beyond the present time? I can't. The pattern has been outgrown, often quite soon after I have made it. I'm changing too. Outer circumstances change.

Children are themselves great rule-makers, and use them in the same way that grownups often do—to get what I want, which is different from what I need. When the parent clearly differentiates between what he wants and what he needs, the child has a better chance of making this differentiation in himself. Yielding my want to another's needing works out well. Yielding my need to another's wanting is obviously a louse-up. As Fritz Perls said, "I can only give my surplus." When I give more than that, it's like spending money that I don't have. I'm not saying that a person shouldn't have what he wants, only that to recognize which is which clears up a lot of frustration and confusion. Getting what I want can prevent me from getting what I need, if what I want is to be taken care of and what I need is to get on my own feet.

What prevents me from living easily with changes is the rules, images, wishes, fears and so on that I have in my head. All of these illusions interfere with my letting be. Letting myself be. The problem is in my thinking. Without thought, I simply act and do in the moment, according to what is appropriate at the time. What I do is governed by observation as things happen, uncluttered by all the junk in my head. I don't have ideals, and try to change people to match them. In Chile, I remarked at lunch that it is lucky that the human foetus is carried inside, that if it were carried outside no one could resist giving it a pinch here or a push there to make it more like what we wanted it to be. A young Chilean who was very adoring of his two weeks old baby said "Oh, no!" The conversation moved on. A little later the young man said to me, sadly, "I *would* want to change the nose."

Some years after Abe Maslow wrote about self-actualizing people, he said that he must have left something out. What people did with what he'd written dismayed him. Fritz Perls clarified this by differentiating between self-concept actualization and self-actualization. Self-concept actualization begins with an image in my head. I don't know that it's an image. I think that it's me. I actualize the image, whatever it is. In this way, there's no difference between the hippie and the bank president, both of whom may also have self-actualizing moments. I have created another image, adding to the world of illusion. Self-actualizing has nothing to do with images. I free myself of images and what happens surprises me. I don't know what I will do until it happens.

When I become aware of images, thoughts (or pictures) controlling me, this is the first step in becoming free of them. When I let go of them, they do not influence me. I am not thinking about them. This is different from creating another image to replace the old one.

John is forty years old. On paper, he is my son. On paper, that goes on forever. I don't have to live with that paper identification. When I don't think of him as my son, I am free of all the personal junk in my head connected with "my son." Recently I wondered "If I thought of him as my son, how would I want him to be?" I let myself go into fantasy to discover that. I was shocked. The way that he is, which I like, is so different from the way that I wanted him to be when I thought of him as my son. He was a caricature. I even changed the color of his hair to fit the part. He was Desperate Desmond, my favorite comic strip character when I was quite small. Skinny, dark-haired, dashing, daring—and elegantly dressed. *Everyone* admired him, just as I did. What that did for me as his mother was that everyone got off my back about him. That felt good. I didn't like the way that I was when I fantasied myself as mother. I was complacent, vicariously enjoying what I had never been or done. When I don't think of myself as mother or of him as son, I like what happens. Small bits of time with him are satisfying. There is no demand—no need—for more.

The fantasy of "my son" was not at all what I had thought I'd want him to be. I had expected a conventional ideal, equally illusory but different. Does this fantasying about "my son" still go on in me? I don't know, and arguing about it seems to me not to accomplish anything. Whether it goes on or not, it is not influencing me. I am disconnected from it. I am, in this respect, awake—out of the world of illusion.

A young woman told me recently that the only man she is strongly attracted to at this time is a person with whom she can sit for long periods of time, sometimes saying something, sometimes saying nothing, with a deep feeling of peace and communion. She said that when she fantasies about him, "I'm entirely different! I don't like the way that I am then! I *like* the way that I am when I am with him."

When I was fourteen I stayed later at school one afternoon, and when I came home my mother was very cross with me. I had worried her. I had had a beautiful time that afternoon. Now, that was ruined. I felt bad.

When my sister's 17-year-old son was late coming home one night, his father took him into the study and gave him a dressing down. My sister and I sat in the living room, hearing this. My sister said, "I'm just so glad he's home!" I like this way better, but obviously the worrying was unfounded in both cases. It was self-torture that did nothing but torture the self-concept self. When something happens is the only time to worry about it, and then I am too busy doing what I can do. There is no time to worry-think. . . . Alisande was born of me fifty-one years ago. Just now, I tried fantasying her as my daughter. We'd both be smothered with demands! Children make these demands of parents, too, when they think of mother, father. Inventing impossibilities.

When I drop the labels, this is helpful to me in dropping images. When I don't think of myself as mother, parent, guardian or whatever, and don't think of the child as "my" somethingorother. I am more free. If I change the image from child to friend or pal, I'm still imaging. What happens between us when we have no images has no name. I used to think that unfortunate—how could I talk about it? Now I see that as soon as I put a name on anything a concept forms around it, and I'm back in the same old trap. Some things are not things, and when I don't put a name on them they stay that way.

When I think of myself as parent, already I have loused up, bringing in everything I think about being a parent. Impossible ideals. I cut myself in ribbons when I fall short of what I should be. How can I be what I am when I have an image of myself? Then I also have an image of you, and the two images go into a dance together or into a war, and both are illusion. I see this when I watch what goes on in my head.

Without the images, there is just you and me and what's going on now. Then, I do what I do and what I do is appropriate to the moment, uncluttered by the past or what I think I should have done or should do next time.

I don't always do this. I feel good when I do it, and I see where the only possible perfection lies. Giving up the struggle to make myself perfect or make someone else perfect—a scheme in my head that I try to actualize— and giving up blaming myself or others for lack of perfection. . . giving up praise, too. . . . I am much closer to where I want to be.

When I think "your child" I am in the same boat as when I think "my child." The whole human race is in the same boat. Instead of trying to get out of the boat, or to run the boat, or struggling to get to A-deck if we're in the hold, we might begin to observe the boat and what's going on in it. All of it is illusion, including the boat. What happens with illusions when I don't believe in them any more? Where do the fairies and goblins go?

(The) need (of the young child or infant) to love is so imperative that he is unconsciously willing to sacrifice his own nature in order to yield his will to that of his parents, to learn how to become the child whom they will accept with love. . . . He may lose all originality of thought and of imagination; he may become an unfeeling person, almost totally devitalized; he may suffer from chronic psychosomatic illness. This change of personality in many cases forms the initial step in the structuring of a neurosis, a consistent process with its own logic and laws.

Izette de Forest

. . . He is no longer young. Yet, she, the mother, is still playing the same role that she was when she was twenty, placing him above everything and everyone. And he, innocent and unwilling subject of the fantastic fascination he holds for her, wishes and waits for her death so that he may at last be free of being needed and loved by anyone, and therefore free at last to abandon himself completely to the abyss, an orphan of the world.

Marquerite Duras
commenting on a character in her
play, "Days in the Trees."

"Where have I come from, where did you pick me up?" the baby asked its mother.

She answered, half-crying, half-laughing, and clasping the baby to her breast: "You were hidden in my heart as its desire, my darling.

"You were in the dolls of my childhood's games; and when with clay I made the image of my god every morning, I made and unmade you then.

"You were enshrined with our household deity; in his worship I worshipped you.

"In all my hopes and my loves, in my life, in the life of my mother, you have lived.

"In the lap of the deathless Spirit who rules our home you have been nursed for ages."

Rabindranath Tagore

Chapter 15

Seven Decision Points

EDWARD W.L. SMITH

When Mark Stern first invited me to write something for this issue of *VOICES* devoted to Decisions, I felt nothing stir inside. The lack of inner stirrings to write about decisions is probably because of my feeling burned out with making big decisions. In the past year and a half my wife and I separated, I bought a condominium, she and I reunited, I sold the condominium, we bought a new house, we sold our old house, my partners and I bought land and a structure to be renovated into our new office space, I made a commitment to continue practicing with my partners, we added a new partner to our practice group, and I redefined three other major relationships. Each one of these events was a concatenation of DECISIONS—Decisions—decisions. And then Mark asked me again. And this time something stirred.

For some time I have been using a particular model in my training seminars which I have put off writing about. "Decisions" is central to the model. I have been using words such as responsibility, choice, awareness, and self-interruption. The word "decision" fits well, so I can share some aspects of this model in a way that will shed light on the process of decision.

Some background to the model: During my training in Gestalt therapy I felt frustrated by the lack of a systematic or coherent model. The Gestalt material was exciting and profound to me. What I needed in addition was a model which would give me a cognitive grasp of that material. I got along without such a model until I began offering workshops and ongoing training. Without the model I could facilitate exciting and profound experiences for participants, but an element was missing for their being able to use their experience fully when they returned to their own practices. The missing part was a cognitive model which could serve as a framework for all the rich Gestalt theory as well as a cognitive map to aid in negotiating the labyrinth of psychotherapy. Most of the elements of this model

98

are either explicit or easily extrapolated from the Gestalt literature. In addition to my organizing and extrapolating from Gestalt theory, I integrated some further insights from Bioenergetics theory and Psychomotor theory. I then flavored the model with my own stylistic touches.

The context of the model: When I think of any psychotherapy system or approach I think of several facets. First, there is an underlying philosophy or set of assumptions and values. Second, there is a theory of personality or ideas about how human beings normally function. Third, there is the theory of psychopathology or definition of what is problematic functioning and how such functioning comes about. Fourth, there is the theory of psychotherapy, or the views of what conditions lead to psychological growth and the cessation of problematic functioning. Fifth, there is a body of therapeutic techniques or the practical methods of actually making therapeutic interventions. All too often a therapy system is identified or even defined only by the fifth facet. The model I am presenting here focuses on the second and third facets, theory of normal personality functioning and theory of psychopathology.

Like any model, this model is a gross simplification. Its value lies in its describing and lending understanding to the human process which is the focus in psychotherapy. This model is concerned with the rhythms of contact and withdrawal, which characterize psychobiological existence.

A convenient starting point is the person's want. This "want" may be either a "need" or a "preference." By need, I mean those things which are necessary for survival, e.g., food, air, water, a certain range of temperature, sex, love, and so forth. A preference is what one chooses given that there are several options, any one of which meets the need. The goal, then, is the satisfaction of the want. Over a period of time the want arises again, and a life-long series of homeostatic cycles are set up.

This situation is complicated by the fact that several wants may be operating simultaneously so that a preferential ordering must be done. A person then responds to the emergent want which becomes figural out of the array of background wants. The person who has contributed most to my understanding of needs and their interrelationships is Abraham Maslow.

Let's look at the steps that take place between the arising of a want (need or preference) and the satisfaction of that want.

When a want arises there is a state of physiological arousal. This also can be termed "tension" or "excitement." The organism has become biochemically mobilized to a state of higher energy. This heightened energy state is differentiated and subjectively experienced as an "emotion," "affect," or "feeling." The emotion implies or calls for an "action" or movement of the energy into the musculoskeletal system. That action must become an "interaction" with someone or something if the final point of "satisfaction" is to be realized. The "contact episode" consists, then, of these several steps, and is followed by a natural organismic "withdrawal episode." The first half of the contact episode (want, excitement, emotion) is a function of "awareness," i.e., being aware that I want (need or prefer) something, being aware of my excitement (arousal, tension, energy), and being aware of the emotion (affect, feeling). This awareness serves as a focusing of my energy in the second half of the contact episode, the "expression" (action, interaction, satisfaction). Satisfying contact involves both awareness and expression.

The steps in the contact-withdrawal cycle are cumulative, each step depending on all previous steps for its success. If a given step is skipped, or not allowed in full form, the proceeding steps will be less well formed and the ultimate satisfaction is diminished or missed completely. There are also feedback loops such that later steps may enhance earlier steps. For example, taking action may enhance the felt emotion or if the action is not appropriate to the emotion the action may reveal to the person what the actual emotion would be if it were allowed into awareness. It's as if there were a reverberating wave which further enhances the previous steps as each new step is taken.

As long as these contact-withdrawal cycles emerge and recede smoothly, maintaining the organism and allowing for the meeting of the ultimate need—self-actualization—there is a state of psychobiological health. Two types of problems can occur, however. One type of problem is the absence in the environment of the person or thing needed for the satisfaction of the want. This type of problem is not a psychological one, *per se*, but is a problem of politics, economics, technology, ecology, or such. The second type of problem, equally serious in its potential is the psychological problem of stopping myself in my contact-withdrawal cycles short of satisfaction. A simple example: If I am in a desert with no water at all available, I cannot get my need for water satisfied and I will perish in time regardless of the level of my psychological functioning. If on the other hand, I have water but choose not to drink it because a voice inside speaking for my parents or sub-culture says I will burn in hell for drinking water not blessed by an appropriate priest, I will still perish. This is a psychological problem, obviously. I define *psychopathology as any pattern of habitual self-interruptions in the contact-withdrawal cycles.* These habitual self-interruptions tend to obscure the inner voice which speaks the wisdom of the organism and leads to cumulative self-alienation. And, the self-interruption is a decision.

There are several points of decision in a contact-withdrawal cycle. First is the decision to be aware of wants or not. The person who "decides" not to know her/his wants exists in a state of unawareness of organismic needs or the preferences which give one individual style. This is the patient who is blank when asked, "What do you want?" or "What would you like?"

At each of the junctures between steps in the contact-withdrawal cycle there is the decision to allow the organismic flow toward completion or the self-interruption which is a pseudo-withdrawal. The pseudo-withdrawal is a short-circuiting, where the ongoing flow has been diverted before satisfaction has been experienced.

The second decision point, then, is between "wanting" and awareness of "excitement." In self-interruption the potential excitement can be averted or the person can keep from awareness the existing excitement. (I will describe below the techniques for clouding awareness and for quelling excitement). This is the patient who just doesn't get excited or else doesn't experience the state of excitement which can be seen objectively by physiological indicators.

Between "excitement" and "emotion" is the third decision point. In this case the choice of lack of awareness involves a failure to differentiate the body arousal into a specific affective experience. This patient reports some version of "I just feel nervous," or "I'm just tense."

These first three decisions involve awareness. Will I allow myself to know what I need and what I prefer within the context of that need? Will I allow myself to become aroused, excited, and experience that? Will I allow myself to differentiate that tension into a specific affective experience? These are organismic decisions, decisions involving my whole psychobiological self.

The fourth decision point, or the movement from awareness into expression, is of particular interest because it involves putting energy into the musculoskeletal system. In "deciding" to take the step from "emotion" to "action" a whole new realm is entered, the realm of deliberate movement. The decision to self-interrupt at this juncture and remain in the realm of pre-motion is especially common in oversocialized patients. (The expressive therapies such as Gestalt, Bioenergetics, and Psychomotor focus on this transition to action in a manner which is totally absent in the purely talking therapies.)

Once the transition to the realm of expression is made, the next decision is whether or not to make the action an "interaction" with someone or something in the environment. Obviously, without this decision to interact there cannot be satisfaction. The patient who "decides" not to move to interaction either does her/his action retroflectively, i.e., with the energy directed back toward herself/himself, or takes action toward a displaced and therefore not fully satisfying target, or takes action with no target at all. This juncture is the fifth decision point.

The sixth decision point is whether or not to allow the interaction to be satisfying after all of the previous steps have been taken appropriately. The patient who self-interrupts at this point simply does not let the experience be complete.

Whether or not to "withdraw" following satisfying "contact" is the seventh decision point. Prior to "satisfaction" the target holds a positive valence, in the sense that contact with that target is pursued. At the point of satisfaction the valence becomes neutral. If contact is forced beyond that point, and the natural withdrawal is avoided, the contact becomes noxious rather than satisfying and the target comes to have a negative valence. The patient who "decides" not to withdraw is stuck in contacts which no longer satisfy.

These seven decisions are basic existential ones. The issue is, do I allow a natural flow in energy process, or do I override the wisdom of my organism and interrupt my flow out of bionegative introjected messages. The decision to self-interrupt at any one of these seven points means leaving a need or preference unmet, and thus the accumulation of "unfinished business."

Two obvious questions at this point are why does one decide to self-interrupt and how does one do so? Each of these questions invites a long intricate discussion. What I want to do here is offer only a brief answer to each.

First, the why of the decision to interrupt contact-withdrawal cycles. During early developmental years children are often told not to express a certain feeling in a particular way, or not to express that feeling at all, or sometimes not to feel certain feelings, or sometimes not even to have certain wants. These prohibitive messages may be either verbal or nonverbal. Because of the profound dependency of the young child, and her/his lack of personal experience against which to compare the parental messages, the messages are "swallowed-whole," introjected. During this phase of the socialization process, many of these introjected messages are bionegative, that is, they are socially arbitrary messages which do not support the aliveness of the person. The bionegative message is, then, a "toxic introject." There are two aspects to the toxic introject. There is the content of the message and there is the threat that if the message is disobeyed love will be withdrawn. An example is the statement to a little boy, "Big boys don't cry. Don't be a sissy." The content message is, "You should not cry," and the threat is, "If you cry I won't love you." Toxic introjects such as these are usually maintained, unexamined and unchallenged, throughout one's life. This results in conflicts between natural psychobiological needs pressing for aliveness and the toxic introjected message which calls for deadness. After the toxic message has been introjected, the threat of withdrawal of love for disobeying becomes a conditioned phobic belief in imminent catastrophe any time the toxic message is not honored. The toxic introject carries, then, a "should" (or "should not") and a "catastrophic expectation." The greater the number and severity of the toxic introjects, the more phobic is the person's life and the less aliveness is allowed. Given the presence of toxic introjects, and therefore the internal voice which says, "You should not. . ." and the expectation that if I disobey then a catastrophe will ensue, my "safety" lies in my limiting my aliveness. The self-interruption of a contact-withdrawal cycle is the very essence of limiting aliveness. Which kinds of contact-withdrawal cycles (based on which needs or preferences) I decide to interrupt, and at which of the seven decision points I choose to enact the interruption, is dictated by the details of the content of the toxic introject.

The "how" of self-interruption involves two methods which interact to enhance one another. Since satisfying contact involves both an energizing of the organism (excitement) and a focusing (through awareness) of that energy at the appropriate target, interfering with either energy level or organismic awareness will effectively interrupt the contact-withdrawal cycle. The basic method for blocking energy is to limit breathing. By tightening the diaphragm and intercostal muscles, particularly, and by moving the locus of breathing into the upper portion of the lungs, breathing is greatly restricted and provides less oxygen for the metabolic processes. The result is a restricting of available energy to the organism. Adjuncts to this restriction of energy include many factors which one can build into her/his lifestyle. Some examples are smoking, use of drugs, alcohol, poor nutrition, lack of exercise, lack of adequate sleep and rest, and lack of play.

The second focus in self-interruption of contact-withdrawal cycles is on the clouding of awareness. No matter how energized the organism, without clear awareness (what do I want, what am I feeling, what do I need to do, and with what or with whom do I need to do it?) the likelihood of satisfaction is nil. The method for clouding awareness is to employ ego-defenses. Several defenses are especially mentioned and focused on in Gestalt therapy theory: introjection, projection, retroflection, confluence, deflection, and desensitization. Without going into the details of each of these ego-defense mechanisms, I want to say here only that in each case there is a clouding of the awareness of what is wanted, or what is felt, or who it is that is wanting or feeling, or what is the appropriate action to be taken, or who/what is the appropriate target for that action.

In summary, I self-interrupt in a contact-withdrawal cycle whenever I come up against the voice of a toxic introject. That toxic introject declares what I "should" or "should not," and carries with it the threat of catastrophe if I don't obey. I then enact the self-interruption by de-energizing and by becoming confused (unaware). The exact point of interruption can be at any one of the seven decision points. And so, DECISIONS—Decisions—decisions. . . .

Chapter 16

The Yellow Brick Road is the Wizard, a Metaphor for Gestalt Theory

DEREK ECONOMY

The Wizard of Oz was hardly the all powerful mystical figure that legend had made of him. At the onset he is surrounded by a huge castle, clouds of smoke, strange frightening lights, and the thundering echo of his voice. All of this turns out to be media, in short—technique. A homesick little girl forgets being afraid long enough to call his bluff and he comes out naked and impotent. Abandoning his technique, the wizard, demythologized, owns who he is:

"Oh no, little girl, I'm not a very bad man," he replies to Dorothy's scolding, "I'm a very *good* man. I'm just a very bad wizard." And the four who traveled so far and faced untold dangers hang their heads. They had put all the power of a faith that brought them through the impossible onto the face of an impotent wizard.

Now something strange happens, something akin to the Zen experience of awakening and illumination of the spirit—satori. To their amazement the protagonists discover, with the help of the "wizard's" insight, that what they each had been seeking was theirs all along. (Somewhere between the fantasy of omnipotence and the fear of impotence is the fact of potency —the "very good man," abandoning the protection of his grandiose pretense, turns out to be not such a bad wizard after all.) The phobic lion knows he has courage after what he has been through. The tin man, rigid, non-feeling, compulsive, discovers that he has feelings. The schizophrenic scarecrow, whose body was once spread all over the forest floor, knows for the first time that he can think. And lastly, after the wizard flies away in the balloon, leaving her stranded, the abandoned little girl finds out that she has always had the power to be at home—the power was in the glass slippers.

"But why didn't you tell me?" she asks the good witch.

"Why you never would have believed me until now," the other replies.

As they followed the yellow brick road (an archetypal image of the Way or Tao) they joined together as a community of people, taking great risks together, trusting each other in the adventure of living, seeking the wizard to fill their empty places. And what they found was in the seeking. In the search, the struggle, and finally the despair of surrender (there is no wizard), we discover our true and whole selves, something that was—and is—ours all along.

Chapter 17

In Search of an Integrated Therapeutic Eclecticism*

AN INTERVIEW WITH JOSEPH ZINKER BY IRVING BAILIN

INTRODUCTION: *I chose to interview Joseph Zinker for this issue for a number of reasons. I experienced him in several weekend workshops over a period of three years in the early seventies. He has a unique style which, in my opinion, differs from most other Gestalt or body therapists I have observed. Not only does he come across sincere, involved, loving, and sensitive, but he attends to and integrates group process with individual work, so that the work becomes neither heavy nor boring. Joseph is extra-sensitive to the underlying dynamics of the person by observing the way s/he uses the body so that he seems to pick up the major themes and conflicts behind the avoid-dances. He "dances" with them, as it were, to heighten and focus the avoided feelings. He does this mainly by working metaphorically ·(I cannot remember his ever confronting, rejecting, or challenging anyone in the workshops which I observed). He works with*

---

* Note: The original interview from which this article was taken is available from the AAP Tape Library, 4850 Hickman Road, #14, Des Moines, IA 50322—Cassette #106, $11.00. Excellent audio. No typed script available.

106

the deftness and skill of a master surgeon, making the most difficult operation seem simple. He works with lightness, grace, and humor, always emphasizing the positive side of the polarities he extracts, and with such loving support that the breakthroughs I have seen people achieve (and achieved myself) have been deeply joyful in spite of pain. Not to be slighted in these breakthroughs is his remarkable ability to mobilize and maintain the interest and support of the group—he works constantly in the here and now with the body and the feelings. Joseph seems to be a loving grandparent to everyone he observes.

I.B.

Irving Bailin: Joseph, from your background and experiences of different therapists and modalities of therapy, why is it, do you think, that there is such heated dispute between body-oriented therapists and more verbal or mental therapies?

Joseph Zinker: I feel that people are attracted to different therapies in a sense out of their own pathology. For example, the obsessive-compulsive is attracted to a psychoanalytic approach which will make him or her even more obsessive-compulsive than before. The actor-outer who has blocked sensory life and the sharpness and clarity of personal awareness is going to want to cry and yell and smash pillows and will continue acting out. So, frequently, the therapies are not matched to the needs of the individual. Another ingredient that creates the split is that a therapist becomes converted to a therapy the way one would become converted to a religion and does not examine his or her needs as a total human being—or the needs of patients or friends. The psychoanalyst creates more obsessionals who are able to talk in greater and better detail about their phobias and stay phobic. The pillow-pounders and screamers are able to act on their impulses much more powerfully. But often they report a kind of homogenized peacefulness which lacks the detail of good, crisp awareness.

I.B.: This is almost an answer to the general question I planned to ask: Do the verbal therapies and the body therapies deal with the same problems, personality types, and/or growth issues; or are they dealing with different kinds of problems? Furthermore, do the patient or the method select each other, and are the outcomes therefore quite different for the different forms of therapy we are dealing with here? By verbal therapies, I mean to include psychoanalysis, client-centered, group therapies, cognitive, and rationally motivated therapies. Under body therapies I am including Rolfing, Bioenergetics, Gestalt, and all the Reichian forms.

J.Z.: There is no question in my mind that they address themselves to different issues and persons, but we have to be careful because there are different levels of sophistication. You and I are sophisticated enough to know that if after two years of psychoanalysis, we still have a stiff neck, we may need to integrate that with Gestalt and maybe Bioenergetic work. For the most part, the patient in the street hears about Irv or Joseph being a "good therapist" and comes in with only a vague idea about the method we use. In that case, the therapy most often is a method applied to every patient rather than fitting the method to the problem. I see this as the biggest problem our profession engenders: we tend to put a template on everybody—whether the person is a criminal, a neurotic, a psychopath, an arsonist who cannot love and touch another person's life, or whatever. We do the same routine that we have perfected on everybody we see.

I.B.: We have had a lot of heat around these problems with very little light.

J.Z.: My sense is that we need a theoretically elegant therapeutic eclecticism which would integrate a number of therapies in terms of the levels needed to reach a given person, taking into account both the development of the person and the way in which s/he actually functions from day to day. If we had such a theory, then we could have a whole diagnostic method by which to say, "Well, Irv has already reached a certain level of awareness, but his muscles are lazy; they are not as bright as his awareness." In fact, Wilhelm Reich pointed out that you have to do two kinds of analysis: the psychoanalysis in which you handle all the conflicts, and then the body therapy to get rid of the character armor that supported the neurosis in the first place.

I.B.: Kind of a total developmental overview?

J.Z.: Right. Even 30 years ago, Wilhelm Reich was already moving in that direction and then the whole thing disappeared when he died. I can give you one example of a very simple model in which this operates very beautifully with Gestalt, where you can take that model and plug in a different therapy depending on where the person is functioning at any given time in his or her life and where s/he is stuck at any given level of psychological functioning.

I.B.: You say you already have that model?

J.Z.: Sure, I wrote it up in my book, *Creative Process in Gestalt Therapy* (1977). For short, it is the Awareness-Excitement-Contact Continuum developed at the Gestalt Institute in Cleveland. Very briefly, it has to do with moving from sensation to awareness to mobilization of energy to action to contact to completion to withdrawal and once again into sensation. My theory is that you can take these various therapies and fit them into various functions within the cycle of the person.

I.B.: That sounds fascinating.

J.Z.: For example: Rolfing and Bioenergetics and Primal Therapy work at the level of mobilization of energy and action and contact. They do the least work in the area of awareness and withdrawal. To work on withdrawal you have to go to a Guru from India and learn meditation. That is one therapy you did not include. Why is it we are neglecting that? Is it because we are an action-oriented society? Here everything is action. You have to *do* something to make something happen! Now psychoanalysis neglects excitement, mobilization of energy systems, action systems, and focuses on different levels of awareness. You learn how you are aware, how to scoop up repressions and fully understand them. It does not guarantee in any way that you will change your action systems.

I.B.: It is like the experience I have as an unsophisticated musician. I play the guitar and sing. I play by ear. I have no musical training. Often I hear nuances very clearly in particular songs or voices, but I can't reproduce them. It's terribly frustrating.

J.Z.: That's a beautiful example. It's like you have an awareness and some sensation, but you have difficulty bridging your awareness and your sensation with some sort of skeletal-muscular activity.

I.B.: Yes, I'm missing the "means-whereby."

J.Z.: Exactly. And the very best psychoanalyst will not be able to help you however long and hard you work. Now the very simple model I'm proposing may not be able to answer all the requirements of a therapist, but if you use the cycle you will find, for example, if you are dealing with a criminal then you need to move into a cycle not from awareness to expression, but just the other way around: from expression to awareness. You don't need to teach criminals to breathe and scream. They can breathe and scream and kill ten people. You need to send them for psychoanalysis so they can understand how their behavior is fucking up their lives. If you have a plain ordinary psychotherapist who is an obsessional like you and me, what s/he needs is not more awareness but to be able to tell someone to fuck off and to really modify behavior in the direction of freedom of expression which the already clear awareness dictates.

I.B.: What you are saying reminds me of when I first conceived the idea for this issue of VOICES. I was with Bob and Mary Goulding at the Quebec American Academy of Psychotherapists Summer Workshop a couple of years ago and I shared a fantasy with them. My fantasy was that I was God—if you will remember, in fact, it was in your workshop that we had an ex-minister who was giving advice, rescuing everyone, and no one could make any contact with him, and I had the fantasy that *he* should play God and make a world of his own out of us and the universe-room we were occupying. Remember?

J.Z.: Sure.

I.B.: So in my fantasy in Quebec, *I* decided to play God and I came down on earth and scooped everybody out of analysts' chairs and couches and took them over and dumped them into this big circus where there were Rolfers and Bioenergetics and Yogas, Aikido's, Tai Chi's and all kinds of even crazier "meshugaas" going on. Then I scooped up everybody who was already there in that circus and dumped them into analysts' and client-centered offices, clapped my hands and proclaimed that I had solved all the problems of the world. The fantasy came from watching and listening to the defenses of therapists in the workshop.

J.Z.: That would be an act of charity and wisdom. The analysts need to breathe, move, dance; and the body folks need cognitive depth, clarity, and crispness. I had an interesting experience with a Rolfer. I swear to you, he didn't take five minutes to ask me anything about my medical history, my work, family life, nothing! He looked at my body and said I had the chest of a five year old, and went to work on me. He could make me groan, but I had the clear sense that he did not care about me as a person. He had only the respect for my body as a machine that needed correcting. But that is another issue having to do with the training of therapists!

I.B.: It does point up the issue that you started with though, that I would translate as, the patient tends to select the therapist who is congruent with his or her defense system so there is a mismatch in terms of the patient's needs.

J.Z.: Yes, there is no question about it. I have had a number of patients with histories of being schizoid, scattered, unable to focus, unable to ground themselves, who go into expression therapies. So you have the hysteric who needs to learn to focus going into Bioenergetics. It is crazy. I'm sure you can think of examples of really borderline people, very scattered in their awareness, doing work which just makes them more scattered.

I.B.: Joseph, I'm remembering a girl, very unfocused, in a workshop of yours six years ago. I remember the piece of work you did with her. You had her sit with her eyes closed and imagine that in her lap was a bowl of magic liquid. She was to dip her hands into the liquid in slow motion bring the liquid to her face and then very slowly wash her face with this magic potion that would awaken her.

J.Z.: That's beautiful, but I have no memory of that.

I.B.: I still remember it and the magic transformation that came over her afterwards.

J.Z.: I slowed her down. I am discovering a whole syndrome in people who are not grounded, the so-called hysteric, people who are not grounded in several basic ways. First of all, they speak very quickly like I'm doing right now because I'm so excited. Secondly, they hear voices in their heads which are competing—I don't mean psychotic hallucinations, I mean there is a lot of noise—static—in their heads. Thirdly, they don't experience the gravity in their bodies so they are always pulling up their shoulders, and their asses don't fully rest in whatever they're in. Before anyone can do any kind of work, awareness work, sensation work, movement work, they have to start with this base. A psychoanalyst or a client-centered therapist has to realize that before a patient can fully hear him or her, the patient has to be grounded in those three ways. Of course, before the therapist can hear the patient, s/he also must be grounded in those three ways. The moment the therapist gets stuck on content, listens only to the meanings, s/he is defeated.

I.B.: Because s/he has ignored process. Yes. Joseph, what are some more diagnostic indications for different forms of therapy? Who would you see as appropriate for specific methods like Rolfing and Bioenergetics and Gestalt or what-have-you? In our previous conversation, I mentioned to you that I found it difficult to work in a Gestalt framework with narcissistic personality disturbances. Because of their exhibitionism, that is all they seemed to get out of their work, or else they were so frightened and vulnerable about exhibiting themselves that they could not get into it.

J.Z.: It is difficult for me to translate classical psychiatric nomenclature into what we are doing phenomenologically. If, for example, you take someone who is high on a schizoid scale, what does that mean? It means that that person is not able to own his or her experience and understand its details. That means they need to bridge their sensation with their awareness. What kind of therapy does that problem require? It is a therapy that pays attention to your experience and not to my assumptions. That therapy could be psychoanalytic if it pays attention to sensation and not just words. It's certainly Gestalt. Rolfing? I don't see any Rolfers doing that at all. The Primal folks are dealing with much bigger pieces than that and my experience tells me such large pieces are indigestible; they cannot usually be integrated into the personality after the work is finished. The original Reichians might get into that. It depends on the sensitivity and personal development of the individual therapist. I don't know about the newer Reichians. To diagnose the schizophrenic or the schizoid condition phenomenologically means to say, "here is where we need to do the bridging." What we need is to teach persons to see and then connect the scene with their thinking and feeling. It is really not so simple. It is a complex diagnostic and methodological task.

I.B.: You're evoking some powerful imagery in me. You mentioned schizophrenics and I'm thinking also of borderline psychoses. Can you say more about the psychoses and dealing with them appropriately?

J.Z.: Once again, it has to do with the linking-up. I think what the psychotic does is jump from the sensation to misinterpreted awareness to action which may not relate to the original sensory experience.

I.B.: Like a little child?

J.Z.: Perhaps like a very frightened child. If I were psychotic, I would look into your eyes and then maybe "see" you examining my arms and then jump to the active mode of seeing you mutilate me. I might run before you got me.

I.B.: Are you saying in effect that the therapist has to supply the awareness rather than rely on the patient to produce it?

J.Z.: Well, certainly with psychotics I wouldn't start by getting into their fantasies of how they are going to be decapacitated or de-balled or whatever. That will only frighten them. They will have to do much smaller pieces of work on sensation. Gestalt has a tendency among many of us to be sweeping, broad, and bold. That level of excitement is frightening to psychotics. You have to keep them going back from sensation to awareness and again to sensation and awareness while paying attention to excitement. They must learn to identify the actual sensory roots of ideation. It boils down to how much excitement that person can tolerate before breaking and starting to flip out and "act out."

I.B.: Joseph, you have had a long experience in psychotherapy now—20 years. Let's go back. Do you see any change in prevailing pathologies between then and now?

J.Z.: Sure. I see more people now who are narcissistic, who do not have a sense of community.

I.B.: Do you agree with the criticism that Gestalt has encouraged this?

J.Z.: For the main part, I do. Especially the West Coast branch of Gestalt. I think that Fritz Perls was deeply misunderstood. You have to remember that he came out of a Victorian background in which he just naturally assumed some things about being a "mensch." We saw Fritz trying to break out of his own authoritarian mold. He was learning to ask for what he wanted out of a very rich apperceptive mass, of having done a great deal of service for others for 50 years. For *him* it was a very important transition in life. But when he encouraged young people to "wipe their own asses" and gave them

"I am I and you are you and if it happens between us it's nice, and if not it is too bad," he stimulated the "ME" revolution. So a whole generation of young people picked up these slogans and made caricatures of themselves with "I don't give a shit about what you think. This is what I want." For these children who never learned how to give, to keep wiping their own asses became a very lonely place. They were forlorn, hardened, and unattached. In marriage or living together, they didn't know how to give to and take care of the other person. They would insist on getting their own way. They would have to negotiate or argue about whether to go to a movie or not because they did not know how to compromise or to please the other out of love and graciousness and caring.

I.B.: It sounds like you're saying that in the last 20 years we have lost sight of what was really good and beautiful about the "Jewish Mother" and the capacity to take pleasure in giving and caring for another.

J.Z.: Yes, and we have also maligned religion. Even though religion deserved it for not updating its rituals to fit our spiritual needs and our existential pain, we ended up throwing out the baby with the bath water.

I.B.: Joseph, you have taken exception to the "I-focus" in Gestalt. Are you also critical of the contemporary trend to "Me-as-body" in psychotherapy, analogous to Jung's criticism of Freud's preoccupation with sex in psychoanalysis?

J.Z.: You know, I really believe in Freud's assumptions about libidinal energy, that the most profound inspirations grow out of sexual longings. I did very simple experiments with my painting. I found that when I didn't have intercourse for three weeks, I painted beautifully. The moment I had sexual relief my painting deteriorated. I did not have as much energy in it. We have to accept the fact that much of our creative energy grows out of the juices and chemistry inside us. But we cannot fixate at that level. For psychotherapy—and psychotherapists—to grow and develop, we need to grow at every level. We cannot simply learn how to be good listeners or how to be good body appreciators or how to move gracefully. We also have to learn the need for a sense of community, to be "plugged into" something outside ourselves. We need to learn the longing of the human spirit for transcendence. Carl Jung understood this, and he was no eunuch. He used to leave his wife alone, walk down several blocks to his mistress and screw his head off. He understood about having pleasure, but he was also a spiritual man.

I.B.: That's a dimension of Jung I never knew about. I did know about his spiritual side.

J.Z.: Obviously, if you have a rich life, you can appreciate that ascended dimension in humankind. To make our actions clear and strong requires the capacity to withdraw, to evaluate, to meditate, to think about how we have created the lives we have. If we can pursue those parts of ourselves and integrate them with the Rolfings and the Primal Screams and the group therapies and behavior modifications, then we can become whole persons teaching others to become whole persons. We need to keep integrating our meditative mysterious side with our bold actions.

I.B.: So what I'm hearing you say is that true spirituality as feeling and awareness has to emerge out of the awareness of the real needs and experience of our bodies. And this brings me to another problematic question out of my experience as a therapist. As I get more into body work, I find often as I am cueing in on the other's communication to me, I suddenly become aware of a twistedness in my stomach, for example, or a sharp pain in the back of my neck. I will ask the person what is going on in their body and they will tell me the exact thing that I am experiencing. I have found this also with a number of therapists I have talked to.

J.Z.: This is true for me too.

I.B.: So how do you deal with this, Joseph?

J.Z.: The same way that you deal with it. If I am in contact with a person, my body will mimic their stuckness over and over again. I will ask them to breathe, if I find myself short of breath, or take a deep breath for myself if they can't. That is the beauty of contact. It means that you are really in contact and aware of what is happening.

I.B.: Sometimes I go home overwhelmed by these sensations. I have to go out and run three miles or find something else to get myself out of these places. I'm curious to know how others deal with that problem in themselves.

J.Z.: There are different ways of doing it. One thing that I do is to move. I use movement in my work. If I begin to feel a pain in my neck, I won't look at the patient. I start working on my neck. Or maybe I get up and pace and ask my patient to pace with me in the office while talking. I try to put my tension to work and cash in on whatever I'm asking the patient to do. Just mimic the patient and join the patient in their new behavior. It's very enlivening.

I.B.: So you're saying that you are going to refuse to let the patient give you something that you don't want.

J.Z.: I don't want to take it home. I know very clearly the times I do, because I'm exhausted. I literally drag myself to my car. And this brings me to another dimension that is missing from this issue of verbal vs. body therapies: the dimension of systems. Let us say that you are seeing somebody who complains about not being sensitive to other people and you are able to tune in on their problem of seeing you as a person and how that is reflected in their body. Let's say that you have that integrated as a therapy. The problem still remains, how do they operate in this system with you and also how do they operate in the dyadic system with a significant other? I think this is the third piece we must tackle if we want to be holistic. No individual functions in a vacuum. Chances are this person has a contract with a significant other to remain insensitive. If you don't tap into that system and teach them—which analysts never do, by the way—how to break the system agreement for maintaining that insensitivity, you will not create lasting change.

I.B.: What you are saying, then, is that the character attitude of a person is in some way supported by a social-psychological system and that system has to be dealt with by them in some behavorial way in order to modify their character attitude.

J.Z.: Right. I will give you a very simple example, of projection. You come to me, and look at me and you say to me, "Joseph, you are stingy." Being a Gestalt therapist, I have you explore your own stinginess. Then I look at your body and I say, "Let's work on your body being more expansive." So far, so good. You achieve awareness of the linkage between thinking and feeling in your body. But you come back and you are still projecting. So then I say to you, "Bring your wife." Then what I discover is that your wife does not talk, does not tell you how she really feels and how angry she is. She creates an information vacuum into which you are forced to project. My feeling is that the social-system dimension is very important to add to the two that we are discussing. My prediction is that individual therapy will be used only in very special cases in the future. It will be the least-common form of therapy.

I.B.: Are you saying in effect that therapy of the social system and body therapy are going to be...

J.Z.: Hopefully, they will become integrated. My fantasy is, if you have a husband with a puffed-up chest, chances are that you'll find a wife with a collapsed chest. If you have a guy who projects and does not see, then you have a wife who does something with her vision or something with her body or with her movement so that *she* is not seeing.

I.B.: There is a Bioenergetic therapist here in Chicago, Bernie Liebowitz, who prefers working with couples because he finds this same dimension of a bioenergetic fitting in relationships.

J.Z.: He is already in the forefront of where I think we are going. Why pluck people out of the social system in which they actually function, do a beautiful piece of work, and then let it go down the drain when they go home?

I.B.: So, in effect, what you are saying is, whatever that body is that we are working with, that body is nevertheless supported in a medium and the medium must be looked at, not just the body manipulated.

J.Z.: Exactly. I couldn't say it better!

I.B.: Excellent, Joseph. I think that this has personally been a very productive interview, and is very valuable in terms of the questions that we are trying to confront in this issue of VOICES. Can you think of anything that we may have overlooked?

J.Z.: I think that the more we become aware of and work with the systems in which people actually function—coupling and family—the more we will reinforce the notion of the richness of community life and the less we will feel isolated as human beings. It is very clear to me that the "me" generation is on the way out. I'm very hopeful that the whole emphasis on "me" and "my needs" and "my growth" and isolation is going to die out because we cannot survive in a "me" world.

REFERENCE

Zinker, J.C. *Creative process in gestalt therapy.* New York: Brunner/Mazel, 1977.

Chapter 18

Toward a Bio-Existential Therapy Integrating Three Body Psychotherapies

JAMES E. DUBLIN

*A**ny adequate system of* psycho-*therapy is also a system of* somato-*therapy.* To illustrate why and how I have evolved to the point of making such an assertion, I shall begin with an extended personal note concerning my own work in various forms of therapy.

Long before I arrived at the study of psychotherapy, I had become an adherent of the line of philosophical thought broadly known as existential-ism. Imagine, then, my excitement at being fortunate enough to study with the renowned existential-phenomenological psychiatrist, Erwin Straus, and to have my first other-conducted personal therapy by Existential Analysis (I, too, had read Freud and done "self-psychoanalysis"). And imagine my dismay to find that I had experiential-existential-relationship therapy done on/to/with me and learned creditably to do it on/to/with others—only to not change personally in any remarkable way.

Still looking, I discovered and got in both ways into Gestalt therapy. Synoptically, I gave up my glasses (without which for eight years I had

115

been unable to see much), gained almost an inch in height (out of my formerly more humped back), lost about twenty-five pounds, divorced, remarried, and left the security of all institutions for full-time private practice.

I have no wish to self-disclose in order to secure sympathy for me personally or for the viewpoint I am presenting in this essay. Rather, to understand the next step in my quest, I must share two facts from my early life. The first is that I had a mild case of poliomyelitis in my right leg, inferentially at about age one, coincident with my learning to walk. This went undetected by my parents and left the leg completely functional but with a slightly reduced gastrocnemius muscle. The second fact is that when I was almost four my father was killed by a blow to the head by an unknown assailant, and my mother, pregnant with my younger sister, went away, to return only sporadically and briefly throughout the rest of her life. The germane connection to these two facts is that, although I had wept and raged and said goodbye to both parents in my Gestalt work, I felt very unfinished.

Then the simplest observation conceivable finally dawned on me. In all my Gestalt work, I had kept my clothes on. Thus, in a dual sense, *I scarcely had ever been touched.* To be touched, I had to discover Reichian and the various neo-Reichian therapies. The first time I spontaneously began screaming for/at my mother while having my right leg "worked" is not a therapy session I will soon forget. I dug Wilhelm Reich's books out of the dust and for the first time tried seriously to see at what point in his writings his paranoia shifted from heightened awareness to become dysfunctional. And in my own practice I began experimenting with touching patients more systematically.

But still, according to my still later work with a Bioenergeticist, the bottom half of my body was "not all there." For a long time, those were bone-dry words. I knew, finally, what they meant. While bodily and emotionally reaching out during a session with a female therapist, something trapped in my trapezius muscles broke out and ran searingly down my back. When "it" reached my gluteus maximus and semimembranosus muscles, they went into violent contractions of a convulsive proportion. In a standing bioenergetic stress position at the time, I was hurled to the floor screaming, where for the first time I caught a glimpse of my father's face. As soon as I could, I stood up, and after experiencing a terror unmatched in hundreds of hours of previous therapy, for some fifteen minutes, feelings I can only describe as "joy" poured from the upper half of my body into my lower half.

Ever since that day, my legs have felt perhaps twice as strong, and I have felt at least twice as giving and only half as angry. As a practicing therapist, the results were immediate and sweeping. I began deviating more and more from what had been my therapeutic stance, to transcend what I now see as the non-supportive, non-giving, relatively non-touching aspects of *Perlsian* Gestalt therapy, which I have elaborated in writing elsewhere.[1]

In the light of the additions of Wilhelm Reich[2] and his two best-known pupils, Alexander Lowen[3] and Fritz Perls,[4] to the base established by Freud, it is possible to say that an adequate system of psychotherapy has several requirements with respect to the body. It must holistically, orgasmically consider the whole person. Such consideration necessarily includes the person as experiential-existential body, or "body-subject." Either disregarded body or body-as-subject must be suspect as pathology. And any such pathology must be systematically referred to some conception of character type of existential mode of being-in-the-world. Further, the patient's awareness of mind-body unity or disunity must receive twofold consideration. His characteristic methods of avoiding such awareness must be systematically referred to some conception of defensive operations. And the extent of such awareness or lack thereof must be systematically related to his observed characterological rigidities.

By application of such criteria, it soon becomes apparent that many of what are today loosely called "body psychotherapies" are best described as adjuncts or techniques which can be applied in the service of, but do not of themselves constitute, systems of psychotherapy. For example, by criteria such as these, I do not consider Structural Integration, Postural Integration, the Alexander Technique, or Primal Therapy as practiced by Arthur Janov, to be *systems* of psychotherapy.

Even by the stringent criteria outlined above, I have found three systems of psychotherapy that "qualify": Gestalt Therapy, Bioenergetics Therapy and neo-Reichian Therapy. However I have found that any one of these three systems used alone has at least one very serious shortcoming. My integrative attempts have been an effort to minimize these shortcomings and to maximize the power inherent in each system. In this context, I first shall discuss Gestalt therapy.

The Gestalt therapist is attuned to posture, gestures, flushing and blushing, respiratory fluctuations, avoidant squirming and wiggling. And he is attuned to the voice as the music of the body, to intonation, inflection, automatic phrases, stammers and stutters. Thus he is attuned to manifestations of the body but not to *all* of the body; not to all or even most of the musculature, which, since the patient typically has clothes on, he cannot see. And if, typically, using the well-known "hot-*seat*," not attuned to such gross indices of the body as carriage, locomotion, deportment.

Secondly, Gestalt therapy is still dominated by nearly all aspects of the powerful personal influence of Perls. Thus it is essentially a non-touching therapy. The Perlsian definition of neurosis is in terms of gleaning environmental support rather than standing on one's own feet. Together with his oversimplified translation of the existential tenet of choosing responsibility as affording response-ability, this renders many Gestalt therapists positionally unwilling to take as much responsibility for the patient as is inherent in working directly on his body with the hands.

Finally, perhaps the greatest strength of Gestalt therapy is also perhaps its single greatest limitation. I refer to the Gestalt approach to the treatment of characterological rigidities, in combination with the Gestalt theory of change. The theory of change is paradoxical. This means that *primarily* awareness, as itself curative, replaces willful effort; with awareness development being directed toward perceptual-cognitive contactfulness with sensori-motoric-affective functioning in the phenomenological field. Only *secondarily* is there an emphasis on changing that functioning, via making novel contact with one's inanimate or interpersonal environment. In other words, the primary emphasis is on the patient developing more awareness of how he is, and only secondary emphasis is put on expanding the contact boundaries. Procedurally, this secondary emphasis is carried out via various contactful games and/or exercises, often in a group setting. I believe this aspect, the "creative Gestalt experiment," is broader ranging than the thrust of any other single therapy system. But it is often quite insufficient to enable the patient to make contact with his character--muscular armoring and/or his long-standing muscular constrictions and contractions which are "deeply repressed." Relying primarily on the principle of figure-out-of-ground by sensing, attending and concentrating, Gestalt therapy is a body therapy; but it is a from-the-head-down, mind-body therapy. In my experience it often needs help from neo-Reichian or Bioenergetic, from-the-body-up principles. To illustrate concretely:

John is a stocky, grossly overweight man with a huge head and a bull neck. He is a workaholic and some sort of alcoholic who compulsively gulps both drinks and food. He has been half-in, half-out of his marriage for many years. However all this is secondary to the presenting problem, feelings of panic whenever he sees or thinks about the big yellow m on the McDonald's sign near his new residence.

When he talks of, and in a Gestalt-type dialogue to and as, the sign, numerous tics and twinges around his eyes, nose and mouth are evident. When asked in Gestalt fashion to take ownership of these facial movements by conscious exaggeration of them, he is so out of contact with them that he cannot do so.

After a few weeks of therapy, in which I work essentially in a Gestalt fashion but also try, unsuccessfully, to loosen the musculature of his face and neck by Reichian-type massage/deep breathing procedures, he reports "strange sensations"; an "uncomfortable awareness" of his genital region when he thinks of or sees the sign, and "sometimes" when he contemplates sex with his wife. Again he is unaware that as he discusses this "new awareness," the facial movements are more active than usual. And again, when asked to take conscious control of and exaggerate the facial movements by saying "I feel..." he "draws a blank." And, again, in a Gestalt-type dialogue with and as the ɱ sign, he gets no affect, and nowhere.

I ask him to really take seriously bio-energetic exercises which I have shown him and which he previously has done at home only irregularly, falteringly and with "nothing happening." Diligently for two weeks he does the standard backwards and forwards stress-grounding positions of Lowen, tennis-racquet hitting of a bed, and retracted-pelvis, bent-knees falling-grounding exercises.

He then reports remembering having been given numerous soapy-water enemas as a boy of five, then having been chided for walking around in circles, unable to keep his hands off his buttocks. When he reenacts this experience in Gestalt fashion, he shows very strong affect and can take conscious control of the facial tics while expressing awareness of feelings of disgust, anger and excitement.

After retailoring them somewhat to focus more on loosening his pelvic and buttock muscles, I urge him to continue the exercises at home. He does so and after about two more weeks, fantasizes an aggressive sexual experience with his mother, unsurprisngly, from behind, with her standing bent over so that his view of her buttocks is as the ɱ sign. This fantasy is engulfing enough that he has sexual orgasm during it, with only minimal masturbatory help reported.

After this experience he abruptly stops overeating and overdrinking, reports that he no longer feels hungry all the time; that much tension is gone from his diaphragm-stomach-pelvic areas, that his penis in flaccid state is considerably longer and that he is having "good sex" with his wife almost daily. In a short time he loses thirty pounds and the facial tics virtually are eliminated, together with all fear of the sign.

With access to affect, dramatically improved, a Gestalt-Bioenergetic form of therapy proceeds much more rapidly and turns to his remaining existential choices, such as staying with his wife or divorcing.

In a similar sense, I find either neo-Reichian or Bioenergetics therapy to be severely limited when used alone. Before illustrating that, I should like to discuss what I see as the limitations of Reichian, neo-Reichian and Bioenergetics therapies. I shall begin with the basal system out of which the latter two arose, "vegetotherapy."

In his search for a concrete location in the body for "libido" and "repression," Reich posited seven transverse (i.e., "transverse" to the longitudinal axis of the body) rings of armor; beginning around the eyes and going down to, and lastly including, the pelvic-genital area. He held that the character-muscular armoring was always at these "rings" and was developed to prevent the flow of libidinal energy. The orthodox Reichian therefore still works, in order, down these "rings" until the musculature at each is loosened sufficiently. "Sufficiently" means that the patient, lying on his back with his knees up and his feet planted and breathing throughout the length of his body trunk, experiences an involuntary orgasm-like reflex. This reflex, a requisite for "orgiastic potency," is the ultimate criterion that a person is character-muscularly de-armored enough to experience, via the energetic discharge of sexual orgasm, freedom from anxiety and all manner of emotional inhibitions.

I largely agree with devastating theoretical and procedural criticisms which have been made of this foundational but now largely passé system of therapy.[5] I shall only say that Reich's conception of the etiology and form of the armoring and his manner of working on it are libidinal-categorical, orgasm-obsessed, and will not bear up under a phenomenological examination of the actual body rigidities. I am more interested in examining the neo-Reichian therapies.

Such neo-Reichians as Malcolm Brown, the originator of Direct-Body-Contact Therapy,[6] have "cleaned up" Reich's theory and practice by replacing libidinal conceptions with a two-part therapy process. The first part is de-armoring-touching-reparenting within the process of transference and counter-transference containment. This is followed by existential authenticity in late therapy; that is, person-expert/person vs- patient-therapist relationship. But they have typically remained concerned with notions of energy centers and have posited different notions of them. For example, Brown's "energy centers" follow and integrate the theoretical notions of D.H. Lawrence's "creative unconscious" and Jung's "collective unconscious" as well as retaining Freud's "repressed unconscious." Thus their systems, too, are theoretical-categorical. And they, too, have failed to perform a functional-structural-emotional analysis of the living, moving body, including its limbs in their relationship to the world and to the head and trunk of the body.

Alexander Lowen's Bioenergetics Therapy is the first body therapy which in my view even attempts systematically an analysis which is phenomenological, character-muscular and also functional-structural-developmental. It takes into account the usual results of the parenting process, as seen in bodily self-image, trust in relationships, and inhibition of aggressive and sexual attitudes. But more importantly, these factors are related to later modes of breathing, character-muscular armoring and to deportment; to man's upright posture, gait and weight-bearing burden. Lowen has avoided the moot question of the reality of any energy or energy centers. Thus he has examined man phenomenologically in his deportment and characterological essence from the ground up. As a consequence he has developed a therapy system which not only offers most of the better aspects of the other neo-Reichian therapies but also offers the profound concept of "grounding"—in the body; in physiological pleasure, in reality.

Brown has thoroughly criticized Bioenergetics as too directive, too interpretive and on theoretical grounds as confusing sheer vitality—as represented by the mobilization of the external muscular systems—with mobilization of creative energy used in higher, existential actualization. With this theoretical criticism I agree. But I wish to pass to what I consider to be a far more serious limitation. Neither the other neo-Reichians (e.g., Brown) nor Lowen have seen the full implications of Perls' transformation or functional re-definition of unconsciousness and self. Bioenergetics has not rid itself of a structural ego concept. It has not adapted a figure-ground conception in which self-function is not at all reified but is the "figure-ground process in boundary contacts in the organism-environment field,"[7] and in which therapy is therefore:

"...to train the ego, the various identifications and alienations, by experiments of deliberate awareness of one's various functions, until the sense of self is spontaneously revived that 'it is I who am thinking, perceiving, feeling, and doing this.'"[7]

Thus Bioenergetics therapy used alone does not integrate the owning, experiential choosing *Dasein* (being there) of Gestalt Therapy. To illustrate concretely:

Albert entered therapy over a year ago at a time of going through a separation and divorce, as a tall, schizoid, very intellectualized and affect-lame, passively angry man whose self-concept as a child was "a brain in a jar on a shelf." He did not work well in Gestalt-type dialogues or any psychodramatic-like procedures attempted. He would get to the edge of feelings, come out of the dialogue and direct analytical, intellectualized comments to me. So I tried Bioenergetic therapy and he found it much to his liking, being very concrete and offering dramatic results in terms of improved assertiveness.

Today, having terminated therapy prematurely before, he is back. And, after some three months of gaining access to affect through neo-Reichian, Bioenergetic and Gestalt therapy techniques, he has overcome primary sexual impotence, and has a lover.

But on this particular day he is extremely distraught that the woman with whom he is living will not fall in love with him—"commit herself," he puts it, as he avoids the word "love." He says that she has recently accused him of trying to control her, hold her down, "thwart her independence," and is preparing to move out to her own apartment. He reports paranoid ideation. When she types in the next room, he wonders what man she is writing a secret love letter to, etc.

I ask him to assume a position in front of a foam rubber mattress with his knees bent sufficiently to be on the balls of his feet but not up on his toes, his pelvis dropped all the way back, and to reach out with his arms and, breathing long and deeply, to stand there until he has to fall. After less than a minute in this position, a look of stark terror comes over his face and he emits a snarling roar and falls onto the mattress, beating it with his fists, sobbing, and screaming, "I hate them all (mother, former wife, current lover) and I won't fall in love."

When he sits up from this violent experience, I fully expect him to be able to discuss the profound implications of it in terms of his present functioning. But in talking with men about the experience, he denies what he has screamed and adamantly denies that he can understand any basis for projecting anything onto his lover.

Somewhat earlier in therapy he has left a Gestalt-oriented group in favor of intensive, bioenergetically-oriented individual sessions. I now suggest that he return to the group. He does so and we resume a Bioenergetics-Gestalt form of therapy, eventually with fairly dramatic results.

I attempt to integrate these three body therapies together with certain aspects of Transactional Analysis. My reason for integrating TA concepts is quite pragmatic. I have found that patients can understand what is going on better in terms of parent, adult and child ego states, strokes, pastimes, rackets, games and even scripts, than they can in terms of such concepts as introjects, organismic integration of dualities or polarities; and I have found that for those who have a need to talk about what is going on in therapy, such words as "implosion" and "explosion" are additionally terrifying. In practice, my TA work looks more like Jacki Schiff's radical reparenting therapy[8] in combination with Brown's Direct-Body-Contact Therapy.

My integrative attempt is part of my continuing effort to achieve a synthesis that I have decided to call "bio-existential." I have chosen that term on its etymological merits, as it derivatively translates something like, "life-giving-forth therapy." If realized, such a synthesis will be a step toward rendering truly redundant the still-necessary phrase, "psychotherapy *and* the body." It will be a therapy which retains the best aspects of Gestalt, Bioenergetics and neo-Reichian therapies, but not one which stands strictly on its own two feet, as Perls protectively and narcissistically proclaimed to be the case with Gestalt therapy. Rather, it will be a therapy which is open to a truly phenomenological, atheoretical reception of any procedure useful in the cause of bringing forth thwarted, blocked life while at the same time translating all forms of "it" into responsible choosing. If by any chance I have seen a little farther down the road, it is, as Sir Isaac Newton put it, because I have stood on the shoulders of giants.

REFERENCES

[1] Dublin, J.E. Gestalt therapy, existential-Gestalt therapy, and/versus Perls-ism. In *The growing edge of Gestalt therapy*, E.W.L. Smith, Ed. New York: Bruner/Mazel, 1976.

² See, e.g., Reich, W. *Character analysis*, 3rd ed., trans by T.P. Wolfe, M.D. New York: Noonday Press, 1961. And, by the same author and translator, *The function of the orgasm*. New York: Noonday Press, 1961.

³ The span and development of Alexander Lowen's writing and theorizing can be examined by study of his first book, *Physical dynamics of character structure*. New York: Grune & Stratton, 1958. And his latest, least technical statement, *Bioenergetics*. New York: Coward, McCann & Geoghegan, In., 1975.

⁴ The development of Frederick Perls' system of therapy can be traced from its theoretical conception in his first book, *Ego, hunger and aggression*. London: Allen Unwin Ltd., 1947, to its methodological explication in his most clinical book, *Gestalt therapy verbatim*, J. Stevens, Ed. Lafayette, CA: Real People's Press, 1969.

⁵ Brown, M. The new body psychotherapies. *Psychotherapy: Theory, Research and Practice, 10*, 1973, 98–116.

⁶ Brown, M. The healing touch. Unpublished book-length manuscript, Xerox, 3125 Claremont Ave., Berkeley, CA.

⁷ Perls, F., Hefferline, R., & Goodman, P. *Gestalt therapy*. New York: Julian Press, 1951, pp. 230–235 intermittently.

⁸ Schiff, J. *All my children*. New York: M. Evans & Co., 1970.

Chapter 19

Gestalt Therapy Discussed: An Interview with James E. Simkin

ROBERT L. HARMAN

Jim Simkin died in 1984. He had been a long-time member of the American Academy of Psychotherapists. An internationally known Gestalt therapist, he was regarded by many as a master therapist. In this interview, Jim deftly integrates his discussion of the theory, practice, and development of Gestalt therapy. This interview was recorded in 1975 and was recently "refound."

Bob: Today I'd like to talk some theory with you. I am particularly interested in contact. I've been reading Perls, Hefferline, and Goodman (1951) and one of their definitions which I'll paraphrase is, "Paying attention to, being aware of, directing my behavior toward what is novel and what is possible to be assimilated from the environment and the rejection of that which is not assimilable."

Jim: That's what it is, what it is perceptually, paying attention to that which grabs you, that is novel, which is interesting, and so on. There is more to the definition than that. You have to know where it occurs. It occurs at the contact boundary. Where there is a sense of "me and not me." Another thing that is important to know about contact is that it is always sensory, so there is some sensory awareness. The awareness is not cognitive nor is it affective.

B: Where does the "motor" part come in?

J: I should say sensory-motor.

B: That would be seeing, hearing, touching, smelling, tasting, and moving.

J: Right.

B: How does awareness fit in?

J: Awareness is the modality of knowing that contact is taking place. Awareness is not contact. Awareness is the way in which you know, so that it is more than contact. Awareness isn't thinking or feeling, it is more *than* either. Awareness is focusing and focusing is part of contact.

B: There are times when I feel totally involved in a task, such as doing therapy, baking bread, listening to music, something like that. I feel so involved that I have no other awareness, everything else is out, in the background. I don't have an awareness of my involvement. Would you call that contact?

J: That's when you are confluent with what you are doing to the extent that you have lost your contact function; you don't have you observing you, you have become part of the activity, confluent with it. You are "one" with the activity, you have lost your contact boundary. So, contact has been lost, you are as one with your activity. It's like some good sex where you and your partner are as one. So that point at which good contact is lost is when you are no longer able to pull back and observe, you are no longer able to do the contact-with-drawal number. In confluence, awareness is lost as you and object/activity become one. When you and your basketball teammates function so smoothly together that you are no longer aware of your moves, your team is confluent. In that kind of automatic relationship you become part of a team. When you are confluent, you are out of contact with; you are into an automatic, habitual, broader thing. So someone out there doesn't see you but sees the union—a couple making love, or a team.

B: So part of the risk in contact is getting lost, losing one's self in a confluent relationship.

J: Yeah, there are certain kinds of activities where confluence supports the activity better than contact. There are other activities where contact supports the activity better than confluence. Therapy, for example: Most of the time what facilitates therapy is contact. There are times when you get so intimately into what you are doing with the person you are doing it with, that you lose perspective and become confluent. That's not necessarily bad, it may be if that lasts a long period of time or if neither of you is watching the store so to speak. There are times when neither of you watching the store may be OK; if that continues for a long period of time it becomes antitherapeutic. There is no growth possible in a confluent relationship.

B: Is contact possible with anything except another person, like oneself for example?

J: Yes, when I go into myself and am aware, or when to you I may seem withdrawn, I'm not withdrawn. I am withdrawn from the interpersonal and I'm in contact with the intrapsychic. So I distinguish two kinds of contact. One is interpersonal, or if it is not with another person it is interenvironmental. Another kind is intrapsychic, and I'm very much aware when I'm with being in touch with me, I don't lose awareness. Sometimes I/we go into a groove/ grave and only become aware retrospectively. Then, there is no contact, there is withdrawal.

B: Is what you are talking about now the same thing Fritz Perls was talking about when he talks of the three levels of awareness, the intermediary or the DMZ he sometimes called it, along with the other levels?

J: I'm not very clear on the underlying theory of that. I find for me what I just said to be enough, to be economic as opposed to the zone business. We may be saying the same thing in different ways.

B: I'd like to switch to a different topic now. Some observers/critics of Gestalt therapy in groups say that we really don't do group therapy, that we do individual therapy in the presence of others. At times that may be accurate; what I've noticed about your style is that if someone has something to say, they say it. Mostly, you appear to stay out. Are there some guidelines, some rules you set for yourself about staying out?

J: You're talking about group interaction?

B: Yes, and your attitudes about interaction, how you work with it, facilitate it, discourage it, or whatever.

J: Ordinarily what I do when somebody has something to take up with someone else in group is to withdraw and stay available. I'm involved, but not participating. Occasionally, I'll facilitate, when I think there is some kind of obvious unfinished stuff and one or the other is avoiding. I may interfere when I think somebody is playing therapist, or doing a number on someone else; what is going on may be either irritating to me or I believe it to be countertherapeutic to some therapeutic outcome. If what is going on out there appears genuine and active, then I can become background and let that be foreground. I don't have to be on stage all the time and my coming on stage is in terms of what I think is missing, or perhaps somebody is dumping (projecting) their stuff onto someone. The way Cindy Sheldon works, for example, in facilitating group interaction is quite different; she is more interested in that than I am. Erv Polster is more into using the group. My style is more setting the stage for one-to-one interaction within the group, so when there is one-to-one interaction within the group it is like a natural outcome of my style; others may be different.

B: You mentioned if someone was "playing therapist" you often intervene in some way. What do you mean by that?

J: Someone in group may offer ideas, suggestions, or as you remember last week while you were working, one person came and sat in the empty chair. You felt that was an interference and waved him away. If a person is taking care of himself or discourages someone from "playing therapist" I don't interfere. If I see him play therapist, or lay some kind of a trip, or using this to avoid his own work, then I would interfere.

B: Sometimes in group, after a person has worked, others come in with feedback, or attempt in some way to "make" the person feel good, or something that seems to distract/deflect from the working patient's experience. How do you handle this?

J: What I usually do is I'll allow this for a bit, then I'll come in and say something like, "What are you doing?" or "What do you want?" I'm asking that person to attend to his or her own process. I might say, "I've been paying attention to what you are doing and to me it feels like chickensoup. I'm getting uneasy with your saying 'there, there, everything will be all right.'" Some comment about where I am. When I ask people to pay attention to their own process, if they do I'm hooking them into the next encounter or piece of work. How I do this may depend on if I have made comments like this before, or if I have worked with this group before. The person then has some grounds for understanding, to be able to pick up what is foreground for them in their process. If I've done this several times then I may say where I am and put a hook in for that person to pay attention to what they are doing and to come on stage with what their process, what their want is.

B: What I have observed about some of the visiting Gestalt therapists here is that some seem interested in the individuals in the group, not the group *per se.* While others may actively attempt to facilitate group process.

J: I think that the Polsters divide their time into three segments, that is, their time when they are training. About one-third of the training time is devoted to dealing with group dynamics where they would be heavily invested in group process. Another third of the time would be devoted to didactic material, lectures, bringing in speakers on topics such as how existentialism ties in with Gestalt therapy. The other third is spent in triads where one person is therapist, one person is patient, and one person is supervisor. Erv and Miriam would visit each triad, sometimes they would intervene, or be available in some way. Their orientation seems to be more group process than mine. They do a lot of things which may involve all the group.

B: I'd like to discuss another topic. I'm thinking of the unsophisticated patient, the one who knows nothing about psychotherapy, let alone Gestalt therapy. For example, a college student from a rural area. Do you do anything to "orient" a new patient like this, to orient them to your style, to how to be a patient, in other words?

J: What I like to do if I am working with someone who doesn't know the rules is what I used to do when I worked with groups. I would spend 20 or 30 minutes at the start of each group doing some orienting. Let's say you have an intake process at your Center, and new people would be assigned individually or to a group for an orientation group session. I would tell them what they are getting into, there are certain rules and games in Gestalt therapy and you may want to demonstrate some of these experientially with a volunteer during the orientation session. If there is a need for more exposure to the rationale, rules, and so on, you could hand out a copy of Levitsky's paper, or write one for your purposes. You may consider developing a film segment of someone's work as well. So the new patients get a real feel for what it will be like. At the beginning of the film I made at Bradley University, I said a little about the contract. During the orientation period I would make the contract clear: what you are available to do, and so forth. I also say something to brand new people about why I reject the "why-because" game. I may do this humorously and get my message across. So I think orientation is useful. It may be economic to do this in group.

When I work with somebody who is new to Gestalt therapy in an individual setting, I do the orientation in an individual way. I don't use film clips, articles, and so on. I use the "here and now" situation. I give a rationale for what I've just done so the new patient isn't left hanging, and as things go on this lets the new person know that you know what you are doing, and you are willing at least in the beginning to let the person know your rationale.

B: Also, with an individual, as concerns and issues emerge from the individual during the orientation, you could deal with them in the immediacy of the session, and experiential learning can take place.

J: Right. Also, I may need to say something like, "Right now I think you are asking me a lot of questions as a way of avoiding." Share with the person rather than withhold. So then the person is aware that you share, and make very clear that any time the patient comes for therapy you assume the person wants his or her privacy invaded. So my question may be an invasion of the patient's privacy, that is asking the patient to pay attention to, to be aware of his or her process. I also tell the patient, "You are entitled to the same privileges I am, if you want to know where I am, ask me." I will tell the patient that if you don't want your privacy invaded you can tell me and I'll respect that. I make this clear to all new people and at the beginning of every workshop.

B: I am remembering the workshop last week where there were seven or eight of us in group every night. It seemed to me that two or three of us did much of the work in group.

J: Right, group can be a place to hide. If someone is getting into some heavy stuff during the individual sessions then they may be resting or withholding or avoiding in group. If someone has been having an easy time in the individual hour they may be working real hard in group. When someone is real frightened and this is part of their character structure, I don't push them in group.

B: When someone comes to group and doesn't do anything do you say something to them? When this happens in my group I may inquire, for example, "Are you getting what you want?" I don't make them do anything.

J: I don't believe that you don't make them do anything. I think you delude yourself when you say that. When you ask them that in a group you are "making them do something"; when you ask that in private then you are curious and you're not putting pressure on them. When you ask that in group you could be pressuring or doing an emotional blackmail number. It's not why are you coming, it's why aren't you participating. So I make a rule never to see somebody only in group, I want to see them individually. It doesn't have be weekly, it could be once a month or 6 weeks. I want a time where we talk to each other without the pressure of me and the group. When I was in private practice, patients would say to me, "I want an individual hour with you but you are always so booked up." So I would leave the hour before group open and announce to the group that I have an hour open next week and who wants it. Then they could schedule it if they wanted it. If more than one person was interested, they could split the time or work it out in some way. If no one wanted it then I would have a little break.

B: How do you feel about inquiring of group participants, "Where are you now?" instead of "Why aren't you participating?"

J: That I do, something like that is OK with me. Some comment indicating I'm interested and that I'm aware you haven't said much. I may do this when making systematic rounds so the person doesn't feel singled out. I like at least once in a group to hear where a person is, or a reporting of their awareness, something like that.

B: Sometimes when I make rounds I develop a curiosity about what a person says or does so I will say something like, "I'm curious/interested in what you are saying/doing, that is something we could work on." How do you feel about something like that?

J: Fine, I would add, "I know we don't have a contract to work and I'm curious, are you willing to say more?" That gives them a real option, instead of just a hook. How you do it makes a difference as to whether you are hooking, seducing, pressuring, or allowing the person to have options. I don't fundamentally object to hooking or seducing somebody when that is done with awareness on the part of the therapist. As a general rule I am against "hooking" without making it clear that's what I am doing.

B: Some Gestalt therapists start new groups by involving the group in some kind of exercise, that is, if no one wants to work. Then after the exercise the therapist may inquire of the participants about their experience, their awareness during the exercise. This helps the patients become accustomed to talking in front of others, to express their awareness, and sometimes they discover something to work on.

J: I think that is fine with a new group. You would want to be sure to let them know that if they have something they want to do that you are available. If no one has anything they want, I will usually come up with something I want rather than just sit there. I do that more with a new group. I don't do this with a group that has people in it who have worked with me before and/or with a training group.

B: This is the third time I have asked you this in the past 2 years so I must be blocking or forgetting, so I want your answer on tape! During my first month of training, in group, you would invite a feedback after a piece of work. I don't think I have ever seen you do this in a therapy group. What is your rationale for this?

J: The function of the feedback is to tie the work in with some theory or concept, to show trainees how something may fit. I also will want, especially therapists, to get more into the habit of sharing where they are: a lot of therapists hide behind questions or make critical statements instead of sharing or disclosing what they are experiencing. The feedback has two functions: one is to help group members/therapists see how the experiential work fits into the theory part; the second is to encourage therapists to share where they are, what their experience is. I don't ask therapists to make clinical impressions, in fact, I discourage that.

So, with a therapy group I'm different. One problem is that the person could do a TA number, "now I understand," and that becomes an introject. If patients experience something and disclose it voluntarily, that is OK. But I don't give the theoretical construct in a therapy group. In therapy groups, I share where I am, I seldom talk about theory. My theory supports me and I don't want to use it to hide behind in a therapy group. I'm wary of Gestalt therapists who are exclusively operating from hunches, or if it feels right, or "don't know why I did that, I just did." I am wary of Gestalt therapists who deal exclusively with a cookbook approach. Some combination of understanding theory and going with what is happening can work, some shuttling back and forth. Patients don't need to understand theory and they too can use it to avoid, to cop out.

B: Sometimes in spite of how you may want it, for example, someone may come in with the "clinical expertise" in a therapy group. How would you handle this?

J: I may discourage it, I may come down hard on that person. If a person is persistent, I may ask that person to try it on for himself or herself. Is this a projection? Very often it is, and they are eager to put it "out there." I may say "what you are offering is possible and would you try it on?"

B: Other than Fritz Perls, who do you consider to be some of the major contributors to Gestalt therapy?

J: I consider it a must for any Gestalt therapist to be familiar with some of the work of Laura Perls. Her article, "Notes on the Psychology of Give and Take," is must reading. She gets into some of the relationship between Gestalt therapy and community of Gestalt therapy and sociological implications. Another of her articles, "One Gestalt Therapist's Approach" (Perls, 1970) is a response to certain specific questions and is an excellent contribution. There are a couple of other articles she has written recently, I can't remember their titles, I think they are excellent.

You are familiar with the work of Erv and Miriam Polster (1973) and I think you have worked with them. I think their book, *Gestalt Therapy Integrated*, is must reading. Gerry Greenwald's concepts of behavior that can be nourishing or toxic are around here someplace in manuscript form and I think is interesting reading. If you haven't seen it, I suggest you read Bob Resnick's article, "Chickensoup is Poison." Bob has also developed a style of working in which he may, for example, if he is working with someone who is into suffering, ask the person to teach him how to suffer. So the sufferer must get into what he is doing to himself.

B: You have been using the term "must read." Are there other articles or books that you consider must reading?

J: Yes, there is some more reading that I consider the "well-rounded" Gestalt therapist would be familiar with. There is this psychiatrist in the Los Angeles area who wrote on the Gestalt therapy theory of change. His name is Arnold Beisser (1970) and his article, "The Paradoxical Theory of Change," is a must. If you understand that article you understand how to conceptualize existential theory and put it into a Gestalt framework. An article by Van Dusen touches on this concept. Some of Erv Polster's articles that have appeared over time are important contributions. Paul Goodman, who did the theorizing for the second half of *Gestalt Therapy*, made important contributions in that book and in some of his essays. Abe Levitsky (1976) is emerging as someone who theorizes about Gestalt therapy. He has several important articles out now. John Enright (1972) writes about the application of Gestalt therapy in various settings. Some of his papers are a little techniquey but solid. I would consider Walter

Kempler (1970) as making important contributions to family therapy. The book edited by Fagan and Shepherd (1970) is a worthy contribution.

B: Let's go into another topic. The other night when I was working in group, when it became clear to me that I was torturing myself, I could literally feel myself changing. I felt lighter, less burdened. The awareness of how I was doing something seemed enough for me to change.

J: What you are on to is two kinds of learning. One kind of learning might be called trial and error, the "Aha" experience, or even insight; there are other names for this as well. The other type of learning is an incremental kind of learning where the reinforcement gradually builds up to where something becomes clear and it is not really one-trial learning, it builds, so in this type of learning you may be consciously aware of an "Aha" but it has been building, reinforcing all along. We may also be talking about going from the general to the specific in learning.

The theory in Gestalt therapy is that if you are aware, meaning fully conscious, fully open to what is ongoing, that's all you need to do. You don't have to topdog yourself, bully yourself, program yourself, and so on. One-trial learning works if you are all there. So you can get an "Aha" and the impactfulness is such that you will no longer be anti-organismic, you'll no longer be with partial awareness. Perls claimed that you don't need anything except awareness, that awareness is enough for change. Maybe, with certain personality types like the addictive personality, awareness doesn't seem to be enough. The awareness isn't full enough, and it may be that something more is necessary for change. It may be that for some to change, along with awareness, you would have to program something, do something deliberate, build some support; awareness alone isn't enough. For me, most of my changes that are important have occurred without any programming at all.

B: What do you mean by programming?

J: Deciding, willing something to happen or to change, promising, consciously determining to be some way. Some of my changes may have incorporated some willfulness. Some systems of therapy, TA for example, would say you can't change without willfulness, that you have to program, to decide to start a new life script. The Gestalt theory would differ, on the contrary, awareness alone *can* be enough. I'm mostly with the Gestalt approach where awareness is enough and at times see programming as a necessary addendum.

If you get the "Aha" and clearly see what you're doing, and you don't do anything else and you stop doing what you were doing, then you have the evidence that awareness is all you need. My theory, my conviction, my belief that I teach to therapists is based on how I have changed. The more I experience that awareness is enough, the more I promulgate that point of view.

B: Some of the therapy I did with Erv Polster when he was here as a visiting therapist was very intense, very dramatic. One time I did a 2-hour piece of work around some issues with my father. I hardly remember the work, yet I have been much more comfortable and less burdened around my father ever since.

J: Mostly, if you don't understand, don't remember, and can't replicate something that has happened, that's a good sign. Sometimes when I have a good cognitive map, I'm not all there. My intellect, my computer is there but there is not a complete gestalt. When all of me is present and things click and fall into place, a gestalt is completed and I let go. When I let go, I finish, and I may not remember.

B: Sometimes it seems like in therapy we start with something; 30 minutes later we are into something else; in between time something fantastic has happened and it is hard to make a connection. There is evidence from the patient and the rest of the group that something great has happened.

J: That is what I would call the creative act or the artistry of therapy. From my point of view you cannot be a competent therapist without being an artist. If you are only an artist and don't understand the science of what you are doing, don't know some of the "rules" of your science or art, then you are handicapped in that you can never teach that to anyone else. You may be a fine therapist, and a lousy trainer/teacher. It may be that one knows all the theory and science about painting and can't produce a painting. That person might be able to teach painting and there is something missing, he can't paint. The best combination is to know enough science so that your artistry is supported and you can do therapy with some rationale, some base.

For one to be trainer it is necessary to be more than a good therapist/artist. One needs the support of theory, training is more than encouraging people to do their thing.

B: By support do you mean a thorough knowledge, a grounding in Gestalt therapy theory?

J: Yes, and more than just Gestalt therapy. For example, if you are a therapist who comes out of a background of behavior modification, or if your background is Adlerian, or whatever, as a trainer I need to have some awareness of these so that I can tie them into Gestalt therapy. So I know how they compare to Gestalt therapy theory, how they overlap, and where they part company. When I talk to you and you know nothing about Gestalt therapy but you do know psychoanalysis, knowing how to put some of what you know into Gestalt therapy terminology will help me talk to you. So I can, because I have the necessary support, communicate with you in their theoretical language. You know Perls just didn't come to Gestalt therapy out of his head. He had a background of psychoanalysis, he worked with Reich when Reich was formulating some of his "body armor" theory, he was familiar with Otto Rank, and so on. One could be a tremendous therapist, but if you aren't familiar with the above, the theory, you can't be a good teacher/trainer. If you read *The Autobiography of Alice B. Toklas*, by Gertrude Stein, you can get some idea of that circle, of how they influenced each other. If you know that Fritz had some ambition to be an actor and at one time worked with Rinehart, that will help you understand how some of his style developed.

Some therapists may have real good self-support, be real solid, be good therapists with a good reputation. I don't think they should teach or train with that alone. They need the environmental support, the theory, and background I am talking about.

REFERENCES

Beisser, A. The paradoxical theory of change. In *Gestalt therapy now* (pp. 77–80), J. Fagan and I. Shepherd, Eds. New York: Harper Colophon, 1970.

Enright, J. Thou art that: Projection and play in gestalt therapy. *Psychotherapy: Theory, Research and Practice, 9,* 1972, 153–156.

Fagan, J., & Shepherd, I. (Eds.). *Gestalt therapy now.* New York: Harper Colophon, 1970.

Kempler, W. Experiential psychotherapy with families. In *Gestalt therapy now* (pp. 150–161), J. Fagan & I. Shepherd, Eds. New York: Harper Colophon, 1970.

Levitsky, A. Combining hypnosis with gestalt therapy. In *The growing edge of gestalt therapy* (pp. 111–124), E. Smith, Ed. New York: Brunner/Mazel, 1976.

Perls, F., Hefferline, R., & Goodman, P. *Gestalt therapy: Excitement and growth in the human personality.* New York: Julian Press, 1951.

Perls, L. One gestalt therapist's approach. In *Gestalt therapy now* (pp. 125–130), J. Fagan & I. Shepherd, Eds. New York: Harper Colophon, 1970.

Polster, E., & Polster, M. *Gestalt therapy integrated.* New York: Brunner/Mazel, 1970.

Van Dusen, W. Existential analytic therapy. In *Recognitions in gestalt therapy* (pp. 29–41), P. Pursglove, Ed. New York: Harper Colophon, 1968.

Comment

by Edward W.L. Smith

Bob Harman has given us a gift in his sharing of his recently discovered interview with Jim Simkin. Jim was not a polished writer nor an eloquent speaker, as the syntax and grammar of this interview attest. He was, however, a master therapist and a master trainer, as shown to all of us who knew him in those overlapping capacities. The recording of the words of this Gestalt therapy pioneer is of immense value.

Perhaps the most important point which Jim made in this interview is that, "One-trial learning works if you are all there." This may very well be the key which unlocks the mystery of the Gestalt approach. Read, again, "One-trial learning works *if you are all there.*" This conditional clause is the *raison d'etre* of most of the principles and techniques of Gestalt practice. Gestalt focuses on the moment-to-moment process of awareness.

Techniques come into being for the illumination of my spontaneous awareness as it unfolds, and the clarification of how I avoid that spontaneous unfoldment of awareness. In my avoidance, I am *not all there*, so I don't learn very well. The well-timed, process-focused Gestalt intervention invites me to "invade my own privacy," as Jim would say, and come to experience what I am doing. When I experience what I am doing, how I am undermining my organismic process, then I can choose to do otherwise. But, as Jim has pointed out, this is not a "willful" choice. (Does anyone of experience still believe in New Year's resolutions?) No, it is an organismic choice which follows naturally from full awareness. If you have experienced this, then you know it is true.

To paraphase Jim, the Gestalt approach sets the stage for one-trial learning by powerfully inviting one to be all here. . . now.

Comment

by Joseph Zinker, Ph.D.

A critical reader, especially one who appears to know something about the subject matter, may have a tendency to examine minute details, get cranky, and even nit-pick. I remember a reviewer who did a critical evaluation of my book, *Creative Process in Gestalt Therapy*, chapter by chapter, section by section; he even had an opinion of the little bit of poetry that I (self-indulgently) inserted into the book. It was the only review that didn't appreciate my effort to show how exciting and vibrant the therapy process can be. He didn't see, hear the whole. Now, Bob Harman's interview tempts me to split hairs. Could he have raised deeper questions? Could he have been less gentle and more confrontive? Perhaps philosophical? It was clear to me that Bob had a deep respect for and curiosity about Jim Simkin's work. That's good enough for me.

Now, what stands out for me about Jim's ideas? The theme that emerges has to do with respect. Respect is taught to group members: Don't interfere with each other's work; don't "lay some kind of trip" on one another. Jim makes similar requirements of himself as a therapist: He makes sure not to "hook" an unwilling participant into a "piece of work." The atmosphere in Jim's consulting room is one of respect and choicefulness. The person *contracts* to work or to experiment. A therapy that emphasizes respect for boundaries and choicefulness is one that emphasizes learning through expansion of awareness, including, of course, the awareness of one's own resistance to learning or to contact. What does Jim do with newcomers to his groups? He does not push his stuff on them, he orients them to his way of working. He is also interested in not invading the person's privacy and puts out the following notion: "Any time the patient comes for therapy, you assume he or she wants his or her privacy invaded." (Jim refers to his interpretations or questions as "invasions of privacy," rather than to abusive physical behavior or true seductiveness.)

Again and again we hear Jim protecting the client/student: "I know we don't have a contract to work and I'm curious, are you willing to say more?" Jim's work has a kind of formal quality and I wonder how much room he created for playfulness or humor. Perhaps Bob would be able to answer that question since my contact as an observer of Jim's work took place many years ago—and my own observations may have been too formal or too earnest to allow for the perception of humor.

As I read the interview I realized that I missed seeing Jim Simkin's work and teaching when he was at his best. I suspect that may of us will miss him in the years to come. Thank you, Bob Harman, for this opportunity to "visit" with Jim.

Figure 2. "Introjection" (Ed.)

Figure 3. "Confluence" (Ed.)

Figure 4. "Projection" (Ed.)

Figure 5. "Toxic Introject" (Ed.)

Part II
Gestalt Practice

Psychoanalytically, the compassionate man refuses to accept his own maiming.

Paul Goodman

"MOTHER SEEMS TO FEEL, WE'VE REACHED THIS STALEMATE BECAUSE YOU DON'T KNOW WHAT YOU'RE DOING!"

Figure 6. "Remaining Infantile" (Ed.)

Chapter 20

A Workshop
with Laura Perls*

Laura Perls: The perception of reality is the awareness of what is, and what is depends on whatever you bring to a situation in yourself and whatever happens to be available in the situation. It depends on interest and availability. Right now I am aware of the shifting of attention; and now I am aware of a lot of faces of whom I know one or two before and all the others are somewhat strange and you all look more or less expectant. What do you expect?

Bill: I'm feeling very happy to be with you again Laura, very happy. I feel tears coming to my eyes. It's been a long time, ten years maybe, since before Fritz was gone.

Laura: So you are aware more of your memory than of what is right here?

Bill: Memory in the here and now, side by side. The learning I had from you and Fritz comes back to me, fine memories. I'm happy to be here again, very happy. Side by side.

Laura: So you look very sad.

Bill: I don't feel sad. My tears are tears of joy.

Laura: (*To group*): Don't leave it all to me.

Ann: You have so much energy.

Laura: How do you know?

Ann: Because I see it.

Laura: What do you see?

---

* Excerpts from a workshop given at the annual Institute and Conference of the American Academy of Psychotherapists in New York City on October 11, 1980. All names have been changed to insure confidentiality.

Ann: Energy emanating from you. You have a sparkle in your eyes, a good muscle tone.

Laura: I also don't feel very much at ease right now. I am, as I said, faced with a lot of new people and that is always the situation on the boundary, where I and the other meet. The boundary concept is really crucial in Gestalt Therapy. That is where awareness takes place. That is where the excitement and the interest is and that is also where the unease and the embarrassment may be, the insecurity, the uncertainty, and if one can't tolerate that uncertainty it turns into anxiety. If you try to cover it up then either you have to withdraw, because you feel too anxious, or you try to brazen it out with grim determination and then you make an insensitive contact. Contact is on the boundary, and in order to make contact with a really new, different other you have to have enough support for it, and for me that is another crucial concept. One always talks about contact—making contact and being in contact and having good contact or erratic contact or no contact—but contact can be only as good as the support that is available. And by support I don't mean just my presence as a group leader or as a therapist, my availability, but what the patient or the client or the trainee brings to the situation. Support is everything that one has assimilated and integrated. What has not been really integrated, really become you, becomes a block, becomes a fixed gestalt, which is in the way of the ongoing gestalt formation, and that is really the aim of any good therapy: the ongoing gestalt formation where whatever is of greatest interest to the organism, to the person, to a relationship, to a group, even to a nation, comes into the foreground and becomes gestalt, something that stands out from all the rest. In the foreground one can cope with it and work on it, with it, through it, so that it can be in one way or another disposed of, finished, so that the foreground then becomes free again for the next relevant gestalt. And what we have to do in Gestalt Therapy and any good therapy is really to focus on the fixed gestalt and the behavior and the principles and ideas, and it's mostly all the things which we take for granted. It's what in psychoanalysis is called resistance, and it's not enough to explain the resistance, to interpret it, or to see it as a transference phenomenon; but it is something that has become automatic, it has become second nature, and all so-called resistances are originally acquired as assistance for something in some situation, in an early situation usually. And if it is useful at that time it tends to become automatic, you rely on it, and what is automatic you are not aware of anymore: "That's how I am; that's how I have always been; I can't do anything about it." And what we do in Gestalt Therapy is to de-automatize the fixed behavior, the fixed muscular attitudes, the fixed ideas, principles, and ideals. . . .

You know, if you really make contact, you don't say, "I am making contact with you." That is a technical term and when I talk about it I can talk about making contact; but I look at you, I'm talking to you, you are looking at me, you are thinking of something else. . . . And now? You have in your whole attitude and posture something challenging. Just exaggerate it.

Ann: I'm sure I'm trying to grow taller.

Laura: What do you say now to me?

Ann: If you challenge me, I'll feel challenged. I don't feel challenged.

Laura: OK. What are you enjoying right now?

Ann: I'm enjoying your trying to find something to reach me and I really appreciate that. I'm not quite sure—part of me starts to want to respond.

Laura: Part of you. On the one hand. And on the other?

Ann: I'm not sure what I want to do.

Laura: Can you make a dialogue between these two parts?

Ann: I did have an anticipation of being quiet. You're not letting me be quiet! It was like my own rehearsal, and so I feel on the one hand a bit trapped.

Laura: You came with a kind of a fixed gestalt. . . .

Ann: To level. To let myself level, but I essentially wanted to be quiet, like, experience more internally, I'm really being pestered to be outward. I can be excited about wanting to be more in touch with you and our relating. I feel kind of open and pleasant really. I'm past now. . . because I wanted to be quiet and you haven't let me. I could have told you to go to hell.

Laura *(To group)*:   If anyone makes any observations which are pertinent to what's going on, please come out with it.

Eve: I don't know what's going on but I don't like it. I don't know what my expectation was—some kind of experiential group—but I'm sitting here getting angry about what you're doing but I'm not sure why. I don't know how long I can sit here. I'm thinking, am I going to get bored or angry or what?

Laura: You say you are bored or angry or nearly so and you say it in a very quiet voice. Just do that intentionally.

Eve: You mean exaggerate my posture?

Laura: Is this the only movement you can make in that position?

Eve: I can't even make any movement in this position. . . .

    I'm trying to walk differently from the way I think I usually walk, by keeping my chest up and not worrying about my posture that much but I've wanted to learn how to walk better.

Laura: Actually what one does in walking is that one transports one's whole bulk from one place to another and the center of gravity is in the pelvis and that must go forward and the legs are really only catchers. If you start with stiff legs then you walk more or less like this and everything is back, you see, you really stiffen your legs, it throws the pelvis back and then you have to hold yourself up from here, from the chest and shoulders. The support must come from the upper carriage and that gives you enough space to breathe and it also supports your guts. When this is too far back then you literally spill your guts unless you stiffen your muscles. If the pelvis is under then the guts are supported, you *have* guts and the upper part of the body remains free for orientation and manipulation.

Eve: I always have the sense of being pulled down on this side, like a gravitation, though I try to fight against it.

Laura: Just come a little bit further in. Ya, this is rather higher. Lie down on the floor, on your back. Put your knees up a bit, your stomach and relax, and your head loose, and inhale against my hand. You see, you pull all the air up there. Actually, in the prone position, stomach breathing gets more into action if you don't prevent it. You automatically and habitually pull everything up here. . . . Inhale against my hand and make that hole in the back bigger and exhale as if you were exhaling right here through the middle of the spine, not pushing but just letting the air flow out and let the spine glide against the floor. And see what happens with the pelvis when the spine straightens out more. You can practice this also against the wall or against the floor, and one's doesn't have to be that straight all the time as when one is against the floor but what I am after really is the mobility of the spine so that you can mobilize any kind of support that is necessary for whatever you are doing at the time. Just roll up with the head first. . . stretch your legs and roll down again from here, lean everything forward and roll against the floor, and now the other way, put your legs over your head. You can do it, you see, you have the mobility here. Now go down slowly, one vertebra after another. Actually all the vertebrae can be moved separately except the last three or four that are linked at the tail end. You have the mobility still so you can do it comparatively easy but of course in order to acquire a different habit one must first feel what one is actually doing and then you can experiment with doing something else. I was lucky I started that choral dancing when I was eight and then later did a lot of other choral dance and eurythmic work in the other German systems and once you have acquired that kind of support the mobility really holds good all your life. I'm 75 and it's still there, I don't think I could do a lot of the work I am doing without it. So it's a very basic support: the breathing, the alignment, and the freedom of head and shoulders. Now . . . are you aware that your left shoulder is much higher than the right?

Eve: Yes.

Laura: Do you feel the tension?

Eve: No, I feel the pull of gravity on the other side, this side.

Laura: Just come up again. (*To a group member*): Put that away, it doesn't help taking notes. (*Laughter*) You are pushing and pulling, you see. . . . Let's try it. Ya, the other leg, the same way, ya. Very controlling. Do that intentionally. Do you feel that you pull your leg?

Eve: Not a lot.

Laura: And most of the time you left your eyes on me and I felt as long as you do that you are looking in some way for I don't know what—approval?—for approval that you are doing it right?

Eve: Probably.

Laura: And to that extent you are not really in and with the movement but more on how it looks or how you look to me. Actually I don't criticize in that way that something is right or wrong or you should do it better. I take it the way it comes, the way you do it, and that's how it is at the moment and we start with that.

I would like to say a little more about support and contact. Contact is not something that one is in or out of but something one makes, one does; and one also does whatever is in the way of making contact; and the awareness of that is what we are supporting in Gestalt Therapy, the awareness *how* you intefere with the free flow of awareness. . . .

Gus: . . . I would very much appreciate your making a contract with somebody to do some work so everyone could watch.

Laura: Well, what about you?

Gus: Fine.

Laura: What do you want to work on?

Gus: In general I've been aware of my dreams and transformation that's taking place in me. I'm giving away clothes. I'm buying different kinds of clothes. I'm saying all kinds of things to me in my behavior. It's new. And I'm aware I'm looking away from you and grabbing some of the things that have happened in the last day or two that I haven't put together yet. I haven't really chewed on them enough and I'm mystified as to what I'm saying to me.

Laura: Are you aware that after every sentence you either smile or bite your lips? Do that intentionally. Exaggerate it. How do you feel when you do it?

Gus: Like I'm clamping down. And to me, that's part of the issue. Much of me—I'm going back into the past again but it's very familiar to what's happening with me now—in relationship to a significant other friend of mine. We're swapping roles; it's new to me. It's just within the last day and I'm getting used to a new assertiveness I've not had. I like it, but it's strange and a little scary. I'm strange, I'm a little scary. I'm aware that as I own it, my jaws are a little looser. So I'm able to bring in air easier and give myself some energy.

Laura: You ought to let it out and then talk with nothing. Just inhale and let your voice out on "AH" so that it hits me.

Gus: AHHHH.

Laura: Much more.

Gus: AAHHHHH. I'm aware that I stop. . . .

Laura: You push it out from here. Really fill yourself, let it come in and then let it out. And whatever you want to say right now, feel it however you can, like a recitative in an opera.

Gus: I think I could be Boris.

Laura: Sing that.

Gus: Boris—how's that?

Laura: Sing that.

Gus: BORIS. . . .

Laura: See when it's all out, you start talking. The voice carries on the exhalation. That's why singing is such a good exercise for people who don't let out their voice, don't use it. Then you get into this kind of indefinite thing, generalizing, making up in quantity what you don't get across in quality. Quality comes through letting the energy go through.

Gus: I'm aware of breathing deeper and my asshole is unwinding. I'm aware of sweating a little right now, perspiring.

Laura: You let it out everywhere else except the voice.

Gus: That brings a flood of past associations, because I've been accused of being too forceful.

Laura: Be too forceful right now, or what you think is too forceful. Get up and throw your weight around.

Gus: Laura, I wish you'd do something for us. We've been sitting here like bumps on a log.

Laura: Speak for yourself.

Gus: I've been sitting here like a bump on a log. I've been aware of Hal falling asleep and I've been aware of my own falling asleep and I agree with what's been said: We've been talking too much and not doing enough and I feel much better now that I'm talking and doing something. Now that I'm doing it it doesn't sound all that forceful.

Laura: And again you smile at the end of every sentence.

Gus: Yeah, "Don't hit me, I'm smiling you know." It's almost. . . I expect to be punished for being forceful. Yes, that goes way back.

Laura: Well, just look around. Who would punish you here? Tell us. . . .

I am reminded of an experience I had several years ago when I was at Martin Buber's 80th birthday party, and Erich Fromm was giving an address and in the course of the address he said something: "Power is what makes machines or animals out of people" and I felt he was really not giving himself credit as a therapist and I wanted to say something at the end and then Buber got up first of course and thanked him for the address and said, "But in one respect I don't agree with you. Power is not only this or this. . . ."

I pay so much attention to support functions because if the boundary experience is disturbed by insufficient support, the boundary, the discrimination between what is me and what is the other becomes blurred and malfunctions and that opens the door to projection and introjection so these are not really the primary things to cope with—you can talk about it until you are blue in the face—but you really have to strengthen the support functions.

Laura: So who wants to work?

Liz: I'll work. Which shocked me cause I came here thinking "I'm not going to work." I don't want to deal with it. I was thinking that already. I don't know how to say it in a Gestalt way.

Laura: There's a Gestalt way?

Liz: This weekend I've been holding on to anger with my husband about something that I've made into a tremendous thing. It's not that it's nothing, which is what's unusual in our relationship, but I've really been very angry and trying to be angrier than I am, trying to not talk with him at all, and to act very angry and be very hostile—and I think act angrier than I am, making a mountain out of a molehill—not a molehill but it's not a huge thing and I am aware of wanting to make a mountain out of it.

Laura: Why do you have to do that for?

Liz: That's what I don't know. It's not usually my style, so that it's not at all clear to me why I want to do that. I could tell you what it is.
Laura: Do you feel he doesn't react otherwise?
Liz: No, I can't say that. He's usually a pretty sensitive guy.
Laura: Can you make a dialogue right now with him? Talk with him about this.
Liz: "Look, I'm really sick and tired of when we get angry, that I kind of start the overtures of, 'Let's talk about it, let's understand what's going on.' Sure, if I start then you'll talk to me and you'll reply but why should I always have to start that kind of a dialogue. Why can't for once I get angry and you should come to me and say, 'Let's talk about what's going on.' Well, you will, but I haven't talked to you since—what, Friday? Thursday night? This is Sunday? How long are you gonna wait? I know eventually you will; I'm not gonna move out. You'll eventually come out. Why should I have to go through all this? And the longer you don't talk to me, the angrier I get, you know that."
Laura: What is he saying?
Liz: What is he saying? He's saying, "I've been acting friendly. If you could talk to me, I would talk to you. I tried to discuss everyday life with you; you won't talk to me so why should I make myself vulnerable? Why should I make myself vulnerable to you when you're so angry? Nothing's such a big thing that you have to be so angry about it. I mean, if you're angry then you talk to me. I don't want to make myself vulnerable. And besides, I think I'm right. I think I'm right and I don't want to say I'm wrong when I think I'm right." That what he'd say.
Laura: With whom did you have to do that when you were a child? Shut up and not say anything?
Liz: Who did *I* have to do that with? My mother always told me I never shut up. My mother always thinks she's right. Either you don't mention it or you agree with her or you have a big fight or you walk out and you say "All right, Mom, it's all right." I mean to this day she always thinks she's right.
Laura: And you change your tone of voice? That's something that I noticed immediately that you speak frequently, "That's right,ok."
Liz: Kind of like angry and attracted at the same time.
Laura: Like showing your teeth.
Liz: People tell me I'm a lot like my mother. (*Laughter*)
Laura: This is what always happens. Children imitate with awareness what they admire and want to be like; and they identify unawares with what they can't stomach in any other way. And that way they avoid the outside conflict and they set up an inner one.
Liz: I'm feeling that I'm feeling very pulled in. I guess I'm feeling that I really would like to punch my husband now and I know it has nothing to do with him.
Laura: I wish you would make a dialogue with your mother and really tell her.
Liz: Tell my mother? I was about to say "what"? "You know, Mom, I'm really sick and tired of your always having to be right. I'm also sick and tired of every time I tell you that, or try to talk to you or try to share what I feel

about what goes on between us, that you kind of either get hurt, or you get this "Oh my God, Liz, I always have to walk on eggshells with you. Can't I just tell you what I feel? If I tell you what I feel or what I think, then you get all upset. What is this? You're a grown woman. I should be able to talk to you, you know. If I don't agree with you then you get all upset." That's my mother. And I would say back, the same thing to her, right? "That's not it, mother. If I don't agree with *you*, you get all upset. You know, your idea of being understanding and empathetic is to go through all the motions of being understanding and empathetic, but it's not really understanding. It's really kind of coping with, putting up with, loving, but it's not really understanding. It's not really trying to understand what I'm feeling. I feel you always come out of a defensive position, even though you don't seem defensive."

Laura: I see you are both reproaching each other and in that way trying somehow to restore the original confluence to be in one camp or in the other. You want her to be more like you and she wants you to be more like her and to agree and none really acknowledges the other one as the other one. Could you say right now how you are different from your mother.

Liz: "I guess I'm different in that I have a life in which I'm willing to take more risks than you are, and maybe I'm not different underneath in being more rebellious but I think I've given myself permission to do what I want to do. I think that you really chose to lead a life of conformity and that we're very different in this way, and I know it bothers you that my life doesn't conform to what you would consider to be the perfect life, and it bothers me that it bothers you that I live my life the way I do and that my sisters and my brother live their lives the way they do. It bothers me most of all that you're so hurt about it, and that you feel like such a failure. Where did you go wrong? All your friends' children married well-to-do men or women who are Jewish and live in the suburbs and have three kids. I'd just like to live with your disapproval. It's harder to live with your feeling so really hurt and disappointed in yourself. I guess I keep wanting somehow either to make it up to you, though I'm not willing to do that at my own expense, or at least to get so angry at you—Can't you see that things are alright? You're making yourself miserable for nothing."

Laura: You see, that's really her responsibility. And you're making yourself miserable over that—that's *your* responsibility.

Liz: The point is, it's like I know that I'm making myself miserable over this thing with my husband.

Laura: There is the same thing, that you don't fully acknowledge the difference, and let him be. I think that he lets you be much more than you let him be.

Liz: That's true, that's definitely true. I'm spoiled, I'm so used to his letting me be that it's precisely about something that he wasn't letting me be about that I said, "He's not letting me be. How can he do that to me!"

Laura: You want him to be mother?

Liz: Oh yes, I want him to be the good mother, sure. Most of the time he does pretty good. Maybe that's the other side of it. I'm very aware of the part— I have a two-year-old and I'm pregnant and part of really what I've been feeling is, "How can he treat me that way when I'm pregnant?" Now I'm aware that I need special consideration, not that there's anything specially wrong, but I need special consideraton and he shouldn't put more demands on me.

    I want to say something about the content of our fight because it may be relevant too, which is that I have a friend who is bisexual but most of whose affairs are with women, and I arranged to have dinner with her and I mentioned it Thursday night when I came home—"By the way, I'm having dinner with this friend." And he got this real attitude—"How come you have to see her every so often?" (That's like about four times a year.) "How come you have to see her, why do you have this compulsion?" He didn't say that but that was the indication, and then he got into all this thing about why she would want to see me but I know that's not true. If I were having supper with a straight friend he would say "Oh" or whatever; he wouldn't mind—he's not like that but he and I knew that he was threatened. I have other gay friends and stuff and I knew he was threatened by the idea that maybe I'm gay. And uh—

Laura: What does it mean to you?

Liz: Well, that's what I'm asking myself too, because why should that upset me so much? Because it's very much in contrast, you know, I mean I feel like first of all if I were gay, I'd be gay, it wouldn't be like the end of the world and if I were bisexual, I'd be bisexual, that's all on an intellectual level and I don't feel like. . . .

Laura: How do you feel?

Liz: You're asking me how. I'm avoiding it. I think I feel very mixed. I guess just as there's a part of me that's glad I'm white (that's a terrible thing to say, right?) I guess there's a part of me that's glad I'm straight. And. . . 'Cause I know what I kept saying to myself is "Shit! Now come on, I'm raising this child and I'm pregnant. I'm going to have another child and all that the idiot could come out with is: She doesn't know that I'm straight." If your own husband doesn't know that you're straight who's gonna know you're straight? Like I mean, but it wasn't really on a real level. I wasn't really taking it as an insult about my sexuality, but I was wondering why should this upset me so much. That's why I thought I should bring it up.

Laura: Any comments?

Eve: I don't think that its coming up at this time and also coming up with your feelings about your mother is unrelated to your being pregnant and being connected for a time to a child.

Liz: I was feeling very strongly but it had a strong feeling connection to me of, "How can he say that to me when I'm pregnant?"

Laura: Make a few generalizations about gay people.

Liz: Well I guess I'll just say what comes to mind even though I'm not proud of them. I'm feeling like this really goes against all my beliefs. OK. Gay women don't like men. I don't believe it but I'll say it anyway. Somehow the strongest thing that came to my mind is that gay women are choosing to live their lives without men.

Laura: Are you aware that you are saying all that without any energy?

Liz: Maybe I was saying that without energy, but I was feeling something kind of deep when I said that because something kind of came together for me that what being pregnant means to me is that it means to be tremendously dependent on my husband. I mean he does about 40-60 of child raising. I work, and he's home when I work, and I'm home when he works, and we don't see each other very much and it's not just having another child, it's also him too, and now it's going to be more of giving of ourselves and taking away of ourselves and my being much more dependent on him and especially the first year, I mean, really, I don't know how people raise children by themselves, I really don't know. And I guess I was feeling at this time that "I'm making myself so vulnerable to you, how could you say that to me?" Really, cause there's no way that I would have chosen to have a child on my own without his support at any time. Certainly having one and knowing what I'm letting myself in for, I choose to do another one.

Laura: What are you letting yourself in for?

Liz: Not sleeping at night, not ever being able to go to the bathroom by yourself, never having any time to do anything when you have any energy, not having time to read, not having time to be a person except for being a person with your children.

Laura: It would be so much easier to be gay.

Liz: Yes, it would be a whole lot easier.

Eve: You might not even be pregnant.

Liz: Well, we planned this child. Maybe that's why I want to be angry with him; maybe there's a part of me that says I don't have to deal with this if I'm not talking to him. He'll go to bed, I'll stay up and read and go through my mail, I can't do too much, but in some ways it's like having stolen some time for myself, if I'm not talking to him. At least the time I would spend with him right now I could have to myself.

Laura: Did you want this second child or is it an accident?

Liz: No, we planned this child. And I'm very excited about it too. There's that side of it too, but you know we have a two-year-old. It's the memory of what the early part of it is like, it's not very far away. And two is twice the work of one.

   I'm feeling a hundred percent better. I'm feeling I can go home and talk to him. Of course he doesn't know where I am today. I said, I'm not going to call him and tell him where I'm going. He probably went home and thought "I'll have some peace and quiet for a change."

Sam: Have the two of you talked about it a lot about having one more child?

Liz: Why did you ask that?

Sam: I asked it because I wondered if that's one of the reasons about him not talking to you now. I kept hearing the word "support"—support—support.

Liz: I guess what you're picking up is that probably what we both feel is that we're operating at maximum now, between really trying to be there for our daughter and really trying to be there for each other and also working and leading our lives, that it doesn't feel that there's a whole lot left over and if you're going to have another child and give a whole lot more, then you have to wonder how much we're going to have left over for each other. I think we're both feeling that, so that maybe we're both feeling in need of love.

Laura: You talk about energy and possibly not having enough and at the same time the way you hold yourself is really a way of depriving yourself. You talk about having to do things at the same time—you know, when I sit like that I feel more like withdrawing, not doing anything. (*Apparently Laura does a bit of work on how Liz is sitting.*)

Ann: I want to take back what I said about there not being anything to work on. I would like to explore what happened to me—I told you that I was touched and you looked back at me and I let you touch something inside me. I think I know what it's about but I'm not sure. I'm living in a new town and I'm 50 miles away from my friends and I'm working in a hospital primarily with people who are terminally ill and it is very touching to work them but they do not let me touch them very much. Physically, they will let me hold their hand but they have a lot of distance. And I feel like I come away with a gap most of the time. And I guess I don't know what to do about that. I don't know how to reach more, or if I can't do that, it should just say well. . . .

Laura: For whom do you have to do that, or want to do that for?

Ann: I'm not sure. That feels confusing because I don't have my support, my support people are not with me any more, so I have all new people and I want somebody to touch me and I want to touch them and the flow's not there in this new place, and I feel very unsure about what to do.

Laura: Do you make other contacts, apart from the hospital?

Ann: I've been there two months and. . .

Laura: The people in the hospital, they are dying and they don't care so much, they can't give you very much except perhaps a certain example of how one faces it.

Ann: They don't want much from me. I think that's the other part of it.

Laura: You want to be needed.

Ann: I think so. I hadn't thought of that before but now that occurs to me. I don't think they need very much.

Laura: Who needs you most right now?

Ann: I don't have somebody that needs me. I don't have somebody outside me that needs me right now.

Laura: It's a difficult thing you know. It's something you want but it's not something you absolutely need. A child needs it, growing kids need it, one needs it at certain moments of one's life.

Ann: I think when everything changes for me the way it's done recently I once again feel like I need it because I didn't have much of that as a child, so I feel needy about it again. But it's good to be reminded that I don't need it like I once did.

Laura: You were also told, you don't need it, you have everything? Something like that.

Ann: Not in so many words, but, yes.

Laura: Start a whole row of sentences with "I want."

Ann: What I was first aware of was that I wanted contact with you, I want to look at you, I wanted you to look at me, I want to talk to you, I want you to hear me out, to hear you.

Laura: Do you need your glasses all the time?

Ann: Pretty much, I can't see.

Laura: Take them off.

Ann: Take them off? OK. I know you're there but I can't see your face.

Laura: What do you have to do now in order to see me again.

Ann: Oh, come closer. OK. Now I can see you.

Laura: Leave your glasses off whenever you don't absolutely need them. You see, you grab with your eyes, that lengthens the eye muscles and you get more and more short-sighted. Close your eyes. Relax, try to get the feeling that your eyes are falling back into your head. How are you breathing?

Ann: A little bit shallow.

Laura: When you open your eyes open them softly and let come in whatever comes in. Don't grab for it. Whatever you see. Close them again. Feel any tension anywhere?

Ann: A little here and a little here.

Laura: If you would exaggerate that, emphasize the tension around your eyes and your cheeks, your mouth, yah! How does that feel?

Ann: It feels like crying of some kind. A little crying. . . .

Laura: What didn't you let yourself cry about?

Ann: What don't I let myself cry about? Now? When I was little or when I was grown up? When I was little? How unhappy I was, then. That's what I didn't cry about when I was little, and I did not grieve when I lost people.

Laura: Well, Freud said that already, that one has to do the mourning labor, and that goes with crying. And one cries about loss, or not getting or not having what one wants or what one needs. That's why infants cry such a lot because they can't do anything else about it, whatever they need. Grownups cry when they lose somebody or something or a relationship. Who do you think of?

Ann: I think of two or three of my friends whom I left that I miss a whole lot.

Laura: Talk to one of your friends right now. Tell them how you feel.

Ann: "I miss you. . . so much (tears). Sometimes I don't have anybody to talk to about things that matter. . . . I don't have a shoulder to cry on—yet. I don't have anybody who puts their arm around me—yet. . ." (long tearful silence) I think it feels like if I cry I'll quit missing them and I really don't want to quit missing them, 'cause I don't want to give them up completely. (Much fuller crying.)

When I cry, I cry out of my skin, it's not just out of my eyes.

Laura: How do you feel now? Listen to your voice.

Ann: Better, not so tired.

Laura: (*To group*): Any questions, any comments? Who wants to work with a dream?

Mara: It's a recurring dream about being in a room.

Laura: Say it in the present, "I am..."

Mara: I am in a room, and there's all my papers and magazines and they're suffocating me, but I'm afraid that without them I'll die or there won't be any tomorrow and I don't know how to stop being suffocated or how to get out from under or what to do about the papers and the books and there seem to be more and more books and papers.

Laura: Identify with the papers.

Mara: Well, I'm the papers that you may need to teach this course again. I'm the papers that you may need to write a book. I'm the papers that you may need to give to patients to read. And you really can't get rid of me."

Laura: What are you saying?

Mara: That I'm stuck, that part of me wants to get out from under, and yet part of me is really scared.

Laura: Make a dialogue between these two parts.

Mara: "I would like to be free. I would like to start over anew, fresh. I would like to have a clean room and a clean office."

(As papers): "You can't do without me. You'll never know if you'll need me again. Or you will always need to have something to do in the future, so that you'll know you'll survive. You need to have me there with you."

(As self): "I really don't need these papers. I'm scared, but I'd like to free myself so I can be more creative, free from thése papers and from these past experiences."

Laura: You find you are suffocating under that....

Mara: Yes, under the pile.

Laura: So what do you need more?

Mara: Free space—air—

Laura: Are you breathing right now?

Mara: Not well (takes deep breath). I don't give myself the space.

Laura: Ya, you're half suffocating yourself all the time.

Mara: Part of me feels protected by the papers and the other part of me feels suffocated.

Laura: What do they protect, your papers?

Mara: They really—I have my little animals that I take with me each time that I go to the hospital and then I survive. And it's like, if there's papers around they're like an indication that I'll be back tomorrow. I haven't settled on staying alive; I know I'm going to, but I haven't settled on it. The papers are an indication that I exist and I will exist....

Laura: If you could change the dream, how would you change it?

Mara: The dream is also reality. How would I change it? Boxes of material and to have to read everything, for which I certainly don't have time and never will, that somehow if I'm existing or surviving or working without them, then somehow, though I get anxious even thinking about even just checking the box I can possibly do it. I don't know. It's really scary.

Laura: And now you are looking at it, really for the first time. All these papers protect you against people.

Mara: Against people?

Laura: Papers you can read, you can occupy your time. You can surround yourself with it, build walls of paper.

Mara: But I don't really do that. They're like having sleeping pills in the medicine cabinet without ever taking them.

Laura: Ah! You just have it in case....

Mara: In case—yeah.

Laura: Security at any price, if you took sick.

Mara: I don't know. I know I made a move and I got a good medical report, so I wiped that connection out. And I certainly don't sit with the papers. I basically am with people most of the time. One of my decisions is that writing is a lonely occupation and I don't do that.

Laura: You are a room full of papers. Identify with that.

Mara: I am a room full of papers? God! I'm ugly and messy and most people are not too crazy about walking into that room. And it upsets my husband a great deal. And it also upsets me but I feel trapped.

Laura: You *are* it.

Mara: I am the room with the papers?

Laura: What are you doing right now?

Mara: Well, I'm trying to get rid of the notion that there's a mysterious something inside me which will grow and kill me one day. I know that that's not really true cause I've had good medical observations and I've also learned the Simonton technique BUT what scares me is that I won't do the technique well enough to survive, I won't do it right—and I even did it with them in that way. I made my drawings and then got scared about them and crossed them out—that I won't have the right imagery to work well and that's probably what's stopping me from getting rid of these papers.

Laura: You try to live up to the image you have of yourself, to be right and doing things just so.

Mara: No, I just want to stay alive.

Laura: Forever?

Mara: No, for a certain length of time, and I gave the responsibility to medicine and people are telling me I really have to take it on myself and I have to be—you know, this holistic medicine and stuff—I have to be responsible for myself. And that's very scary. I know I can do both. I also know that if the imagery doesn't work, there's always a doctor.

Laura: Ya, and one doesn't stay alive by working at staying alive.

Mara: I know that.

Laura: You stay alive through making alive contact.

Mara: I certainly have plenty of support and loving people, but mostly I've been in the hospital a lot too and the papers, somehow this fake security blanket...

Laura: What's going on right now?

Mara: I keep wondering what's going to give me the peace of mind to clean up. To do it freely and feel OK about it.

Laura: What do you feel right now?

Mara: I still am feeling a little bit scared.

Laura: You're breathing rather shallowly again.

Mara: I keep seeing that room and wondering when I'm going to approach it and what am I going to do with it when I do.

Laura: You are continually ruminating and worrying about what you are *going* to do and what's *going* to happen and in that way possibly missing out on what's available at the present time.

Mara: Except that this time I was much better; I was less anxious about seeing the surgeon.

Laura: Most people think always only of their front, that they have to present a good front, that they must be right. But it's the back really that gives you support and makes it possible to get the breathing support. Backbone and guts—that's really what's called courage. This is why I'm so keen on this coordination and alignment, because you certainly feel different when you are straight in your back and have room to breathe and you can hold yourself together. Don't think of those things as just being up here (*Laura points to head here*) that you have a body, but *be* a body. The English language says very well. "When you *are* a body, you are *some*body."

Mara: I gave my body to the doctors and I'm just reclaiming it. I'm just taking it back now. . .

Laura: Any questions?

Dan: I have one. I became aware that with a number of people who were working, there were hand gestures, things that they did with their hands, that were in the background and seemed to me to be part of the gestalt of what was going on. And I'm sure you were aware of them too. And I'd love to know—for you—why do you choose what you choose in terms of what you bring from the background into the foreground? I work so much more with the body in terms of—"look at what you're doing now, don't change it, and what might it be saying?" etc. and I was contemplating as you were doing it whether you were dealing with what was being said rather than what the background was bringing up. I'd like to know where you were at with that.

Laura: I deal with what I feel is the easiest to deal with. I had the impression here, and particularly with her before, that dealing simply with the way she was holding herself or the movements she made or didn't make, that it didn't register really.

Dan: That's a good concept—what they're ready for next.

Laura: So I thought that working with the dream and the dream content was more useful at this point, and I came to the body at the end.

Eve (*To Dan*): I had a thought, partly so much it's for me and I want to say it to you too, just the little bit that I did plus the other things that are going on, the irony that I'm feeling and that I saw with you is the irony that the things we think support us and sustain us and make us feel safe are the things that destroy us. And I see you taking those notes and her trying to get you all day to stop and you're filling up more pages and I was thinking about what I've done with my back that I thought was supporting my life and supporting me and it's really what, over time, destroyed it.

Dan: I want to say that I commend you on coming forward as you did, especially that you seemed critical earlier, and for you to come forward and openly explore something like that, I commend you for it.

Laura (*To another group member*): What's going on with you?

Len: I'm just really appreciating you, really enjoying it.

Laura: That was difficult to see, most of the time. You sit there nearly all the time—and I can't help noticing it because I'm directly opposite you—with a kind of grim expression on your face, or no expression.

Len: I was really enjoying it, just enjoying it, taking it in, and marveling at it. I walk away with a sense of being with somebody who really knows just what to do. It's kind of like an awe thing.

Laura: I am so aware of the tension in your face which is occasionally relieved by laughing when something funny happens, somebody says something. Do *you* need the glasses all the time?

Len: Unfortunately.

Laura: Get a little closer and take them off. Let me see your face. What do you see now?

Len: Still a little blurry, but it's better.

Laura: That can get better only if you relax. I recommend that you close your eyes and let them fall back. Close them softly; see, you let them twitch now; keep breathing; let your mouth loose; it's so covered up with your beard I can hardly see it, but there's a lot of tension. When you open your eyes, open them softly and just let come in what comes in. Don't grab.

Len: Sol's red shirt—and your smile.

Laura: You can see quite well.

Len: It's really quite interesting, 'cause things really are clearer. It's weird. (*Laughter*)

Laura: Leave them off as much as possible when you don't actually need them. Of course, it's a kind of wall. When you wear them, it's a kind of a wall; it makes for distance.

Len: I have to admit, I couldn't see his face hardly at all before and it's clearer now.

Laura: Well, when your eyes are more relaxed you see better.

Len: I've just really been enjoying you.

Laura: For most people who don't have much experience in Gestalt, or have their kind of experience in what I call "West Coast Gestalt" they don't appreciate the minimal work, and I find that it is more easily assimilated and therefore keeps better.

Len: Just from watching you work with other people, I got some insights into myself, in terms of some things that I need to let go of, and I think there's still tension there because they still have to be dealt with but I think I know what I have to do and I guess that feels better.

Laura: And you talk in a should language: "I know what I have to do."

Len: I want to do it, I really do. It's just not going to be very pleasant.

Laura: You look very different now.

Len: It's getting clearer. (*Laughter*)

Hal: Want to work on a crazy child dream that I have?

Laura: Yes.

Hal: It's good to work with you again, Laura. I had a dream a night or two ago, not remembering as much of it now as I did. I'm walking in the street and I'm seeing the largest fattest thickest tallest weeds I've ever seen in my life. The street is filled with them and they are all purple. People are running away and I'm walking in the direction in which they are running away from. I am coming right around the corner of a building. There's a part of a body and I can only see the lowest portion, like a leg, and I begin to look up and it's a purple monster. I haven't had a monster dream since I was a very little boy and I'm 56 years old and it was the tallest biggest fattest ugliest monster I've ever seen and it was solid purple. I become very very frightened. That's all I remember.

Laura: Be the monster.

Hal: You want me to get up and be the monster? You mean act the monster? "YAHHHHH! I can kill. I have the power to kill. I am a purple monster and I will eat you up. AGHHHHH!!!"

Laura: How do you feel as the monster?

Hal: Scared, very scared. I feel it in here, I'm feeling it right now, in my stomach. It's my anger. I'm very very frightened of it. It's very powerful.

Laura: Who are you angry with?

Hal: Beginning when? In the here and now I want to bury my hands.

Laura: Otherwise you might do what?

Hal: Choke, beat, kill. Angry with my wife, angry with my kids. Very angry. I'm thinking right now of the weeds growing in my back yard.

Laura: Be the weeds.

Hal: "We're ugly. Ugly weeds. Fuck up your gorgeous garden. You spent so much money and so much time and so much effort making your beautiful garden and we fuck it up, because nobody wants to pull us out. Look how ugly your garden looks now. Your beautiful Shangri-la is ugly, full of ugly weeds." The house that I bought two years ago that I put up for sale, and I really had weeds growing there, because nobody takes care of it.

Laura: What do you do?

Hal: Suffer a lot. I'm not going to go pull the fuckin' weeds. Selling the house. I don't have the time to take care of weeds; I don't want to anymore. The house didn't do for me what I wanted it to do. I'm thinking of how upset many of the people are who come to me for help, come with a head full of weeds and we pull out the weeds and you've got bare earth and it feels like it's empty but you have to wait for the flowers to grow and that takes time.

Laura: To whom are you saying it?

Hal: Because I left my wife, early part of the summer.

Laura: That's why you can't get angry with her?

Hal: Oh, I can get angry with her. It's my kids I can't get angry with.

Laura: Right now, make a dialogue with your kids. Take your hands out of your pockets.

Hal:	"I'm so goddammed confused with you all. On the one hand you tell me you're not passing judgment; but what you're doing makes so much noise I can't hear what you say. I see what you do constantly. You do make judgments. I'm pissed off at you." I think I'm pissed off.
Laura:	Try to feel how you are saying that, how you are holding yourself.
Hal:	I'm holding myself down. I'm keeping my fingers spread apart. . . .
Laura:	Is anybody listening to you?
Hal:	And whining. Who's gonna listen to somebody who whines?
Laura:	Pick yourself up.
Hal:	Wow! I'm remembering when I used to get angry my mother would call me bulldog. "Bulldog, what are you angry about?" "Fucking angry with you kids 'cause you're stupid, because you make a choice to choose to believe one side of the story because I keep my mouth shut, kept my mouth shut for many years." Big joke in our family, everybody sees the Hal who's angry in the backyard but nobody sees the Hal who got shitted on in the kitchen and then was told, "What are you angry about? Keep your mouth shut, you sound like a bulldog." I'm feeling like a miserable wretch.
Laura:	Can you argue with your mother? Argue back. You're the bulldog.
Hal:	"YAGHHHHH!! Fuck off! I feel so fuckin' angry. I really could be a people-eater, I'm so so fuckin' angry at you all. You counter it with stuff I can't fight back with and you say things to me like, 'You're angry a lot. And if we all don't believe you, what part do you play?' Fuck you kids! I paid a fortune for your therapy and you give me back that kind of shit."
Laura:	What do you expect? (*Laughter*)
Hal:	God, I'm angry! Feel so powerless to do anything about it.
Laura:	What did you expect from therapy for your children? That they should be nice and quiet?
Hal:	I think that I would have expected for them at least to come to me and say, "Dad, what's your side of the story? Dad, what happened through all these years?"
Laura:	You want them to be like you, understanding and quiet and interested; and again you want the confluence.
Hal:	They're not like me; they have to be what they are.
Laura:	You know, there's something I learned from my first analyst when I was 23 or 24 years old. Aggressive people you have to meet with their own weapons. If they are nasty to you, or noisy. . . .
Hal:	Usually I can do that with most people, but I don't do it with my kids.
Laura:	What are you afraid of?
Hal:	Scared they'll leave me. I'll lose my grandchildren.
Laura:	As though if they need you they won't leave you.
Hal:	I know that's true. I know. I had the dream before this weekend and I did some of this work in a workshop that I went to Friday and Saturday before we came here and I know I have to face up to them. I know. I took off the bracelet my wife gave me for my fiftieth birthday, threw it on the floor, ended up putting it in my pocket. I know I have to face them with my anger; even if it doesn't go anywhere I'll feel better.

Laura: If you don't express it at the time something occurs that makes you angry, you accumulate a lot of resentment, a lot of unfinished business, and you poison yourself.

Hal: That's true. I recognize I'm the purple people-eater; that part of me I can see. I don't know what part of me are the weeds, purple weeds.

Laura: Be a weed. How do you feel?

Hal: Stuck! Stuck in the ground, can't move. OK. I get it. I thank you.

Laura: OK. I think our time is pretty much up.

Chapter 21

The One-Hundred Dollar Check

THOMAS L. MEYER, ACSW

C*athy had been a member of our group* for several months. This particular meeting had been dragging along, with more than the usual amount of bullshitting. After about forty-five minutes I was feeling rather useless, announced that fact, and inquired whether anyone had any "work" they'd like to do. Cathy replied in the affirmative (I noted she chose to wait until asked). She mentioned she had a "thing" about checks; a phobia of writing checks. So much so that she had been to a hypnotist, where she had not been "helped." She described her "thing" as a "monkey on my back."

Bob (co-therapist) asked her to try a couple of encounters, e.g., between pen and check, ten-foot pole (between pen and check), etc. Cathy chose to get "stuck" each time. Bob dryly announced his fantasy that the hypnotist ended up hypnotized. I was feeling frustrated and annoyed; Cathy and I played "Push," which ended in a wrestling match. We both felt better afterwards.

After a short silence Cathy offered—quite offhandedly—the fact that everytime she cashed a check at the base PX she would have to include with the endorsement, "USN/Deceased." I gave her a pen and check and asked her to endorse it. She signed her name only. Bob asked her to continue; she hesitatingly added her husband's serial number and "USN/Deceased," and sat staring vacantly at what she had written.

Tom: Where are you right this minute?
Cathy: I'm sitting at the diningroom table with George (voice choking).

160

Tom: What is happening?
Cathy: He's making out the budget, writing checks...I'm sitting and crying.
Tom: What aren't you saying?
Cathy: I'm not telling him...(breaks into tears)...I'm not telling him. "You're not going to be writing anymore checks." (silence—she continues weeping)
Tom: (pause) I don't know what to say to you at this point, Cathy, or where to go from here.
Bob: What else aren't you telling him?
Cathy: That I'm scared, frightened; that I know he's going to die.

It had become clear that Cathy had not yet "buried" her husband. We discovered that he had been a pilot, that his plane had been lost at sea, and that his body had not been recovered. There had been a memorial service but no funeral. We decided to hold one:

Tom: Where will you bury him?
Cathy: Arlington.
Tom: Please go there now. (pause) When you get there tell me what you see.
Cathy: (after a short silence) An empty hole in the ground.
Tom: Nothing else?
Cathy: A Navy jet is flying over, waving its wings "goodbye." That's all.
Bob: I'd like you to be that jet that's flying over. Tell me what you see.
Cathy: A cemetery, freshly-dug grave...(voice fades)
Bob: He's still not in it. (Cathy shakes her head) Then try putting yourself in that hole.
Cathy: (lies back) I'm in the hole. I see a plane flying over, wagging its wings. I wave back (waves with her fingers only, her hands crossed on her stomach). It's comfortable.
Bob: So you choose to pre-empt his place in the grave, and at the same time you give some physical indication you're still alive.
Cathy: (nods head, cries)
Tom: (after pause) Do you know what happened? How he died?
Cathy: I have a good idea (her voice goes flat).
Tom: Then I'd like you to take a trip; to be a passenger on that flight.
Cathy: (startled and seemingly bewildered) To be on that plane!?
Tom: Yes.
Cathy: (pauses) Okay. (looks thoughtfully and speaks slowly) It's an A3B, kinda small (voice fades).
Tom: Where are you?
Cathy: In the plane.
Tom: Have you taken off yet?
Cathy: Yes. From the carrier.
Tom: You're flying now. (she nods) You're inside. Look around and tell me what you see.
Cathy: I see the crew performing its tasks. I'm sitting behind the co-pilot.
Tom: They have no names.

Cathy: I see Mr. N., Mr. S., George, and a young kid—I'll call him Tom—who's just along for the ride.

Tom: Okay. Fine. Please continue.

Cathy: (frowning) We're on fire all of a sudden. And the radio's out.

Tom: How do you know you're on fire?

Cathy: The buddy plane flies very close... they write the message on a chalk board. (pause)

Tom: And now?

Cathy: They're going through emergency procedures.

Tom: They?

Cathy: (voice trembling) Mr. N., Mr. S. George is strapping Tom into a parachute and explaining about bailing out over water.

Tom: Go on.

Cathy: They're yelling. "Let's get the hell out of here." (pause) They're leaving the plane. One... two...

Tom: Who is leaving?

Cathy: Nr. N., Mr. S., Tom... (voice fades)

Tom: George?

Cathy: (crying, shakes her head and bites her lip)

Tom: He chose to stay. (Cathy nods, crying bitterly)

Bob: (after short silence) Go back to the plane. This time I'd like you to tell George what to do.

Cathy: (snorts) Tell him what to do? You have to be joking. I never could tell him what to do.

Tom: I find it difficult to believe that you're going to simply sit in that plane, mute, and think to yourself, "I can't tell him what to do," and do nothing.

Cathy: (voice soft, shaking) Think about us, George.

Tom: I'm sure he can't hear you, what with all the noise and screaming and shouting.

Cathy: (loudly) What about us!? (bursts into tears)

Tom: (pause) What does he do?

Cathy: He doesn't pay any attention. (sobbing)

Bob: (after pause) So it's time for you to get out of there. Get yourself a parachute.

Cathy: (looking around) There aren't any. There weren't enough.

Bob: Ah! Yeah. There weren't enough parachutes. What happened to George's?

Cathy: (crying) He gave his to Tom.

Tom: So he not only chose to stay with the plane, he also chose to die.

Cathy: (nodding, crying) Yeah. And he was the only one with kids.

Bob: It's time for you to leave now. Conjure up a chute. (pause) What are you doing?

Cathy: I'm strapping it on... sliding down (to escape hatch)... I'm out now. Dangling... (long pause)

Bob: Well?

Cathy: I'm still dangling.

Bob: Yeah, I know. Let us know when you hit the water.

Cathy: I'm in the water... struggling... can't swim.

Bob: Come on, come on. You have a life vest with those chutes. You don't have to swim. You can float.

Cathy: Can't find the tube.
Tom: It looks like you still may not get out of this alive.
Cathy: There! I've got it...floating now.
Bob: What do you see there?
Cathy: Water. (looks around) I see the plane burning...falling...exploding. (voice shaking)
Tom: And George?
Cathy: (sobs) He explodes with the plane.
Tom: Again.
Cathy: (louder, crying) He explodes with the plane.
Tom: He may have survived the explosion.
Cathy: (shakes head) No, I don't think so.
Tom: You don't *think* so.
Cathy: I *know* so!
Bob: (pause) So what do you say to George now?
Cathy: (softly) Goodbye.
Bob: Louder!
Cathy: (sobs) Goodbye!
Bob: LOUDER!
Cathy: GOODBYE! (covers face, sobbing...long silence)
Bob: Okay, Cathy. Come back here now and tell me what you see.
Cathy: (looks around) People.
Tom: Who?
Cathy: (facing each person) I see you, Tom. I see you, Bob. I see you, Cathy. I see you, Pearl. (eyes fill) I see me.
Tom: What do we all have in common?
Cathy: (looking puzzled) We're here?
Tom: More basic than that.
Cathy: We all have problems?
Tom: Still more basic.
Cathy: We're alive.
Tom: Right. We're alive. You're alive. What's the difference between you and George?
Cathy: (hesitating) I'm alive and he's dead. (tears)
Tom: Again.
Cathy: I'm alive and he's dead (burst into tears, sobbing).

I was feeling very warm and tender, and Cathy and I held each other for quite a while. Bob was treating himself to some coffee, and when we left the room, he noted Cathy leaving, puffed-faced, red-eyed, smiling wanly. She stopped briefly and made some body moves to suggest her slight embarrassment at being seen in "public" in such a state.

Bob complimented her on her "work." She seemed pleased to have his "approval." He then suggested she demonstrate for him what she had learned; he suggested she write a check. Cathy promptly brought out her check book and, unhesitatingly, wrote me a check in the amount of one hundred dollars, noting at the top of the check, "for services..."

Chapter 22

The Power of the Gestalt Dialog in Dreamwork: Integration of a "Multiple Personality"

JAMES E. DUBLIN

I have very little, yet, to say about psychosis. We are working always with op-posites, polarities. But I see the polarities in, for instance,...schizophrenia...

F. Perls, *Gestalt Therapy Verbatim*

Steven,[1] an athletic-looking, handsome college junior, took an attractive young woman to a fraternity dance. When she left with another young man, described by Steven as a "jock," he fled to his apartment and gulped a handful of Valium and half a quart of vodka. When first hospitalized, he was affectively and associatively psychotic. When the structure of the hospital and some phenothiazines had leveled his affect and tightened his associations somewhat, I picked him out for an attempt at intensive psycho-

---

[1] For purposes soon to become clear, the patient's real first name is used, with his express, written permission.

therapy. Over a two month period, he remained overdefended, essentially non-participative, and hostile to the idea of therapy. Under pressure from his parents, he left the hospital, to resume college work. Reluctantly, he joined a weekly out-patient group. At the third meeting of the group following his release from the hospital, he failed to show and his friend, Tom, also in the group, reported that he had seen Steven wandering about the campus in what sounded to me like a fugue state. Two days later, before he could commence his comtemplated "soar," he was removed by police from the roof of a tall building, and re-hospitalized. In a grandiose paranoid state this time, he was delusional in an interesting way (having for a "companion" an old high school chum, "Cathy") but, mysteriously, was motivated for and optimistic about therapy.

In individual sessions, he was surly and resistant to experiencing his feelings. But in the intensive (daily) group, he was suddenly very self-disclosing. He now revealed that some material he had presented during the previous hospitalization was fictional. For example, he had returned from a furlough wearing an eye patch and claiming to have been "stoned" by "Rednecks" who did not like his mod dress and had "taunted" him, called him "gay," etc. He now revealed that he had purposely struck himself in the eye with a smooth stone, secured the eye patch and made up the story, for purposes of "sympathy seeking." I began to see just how creative his symptomatology could be, and, for a time, violated one of my hard-learned principles of therapy by missing his form in favor of attending to his tricky, manipulative content. Thus, his fellow patients in the daily group first pointed out what I certainly should have noticed, that Steven seemed to have two distinct styles of dressing, not from day to day, but serially, for a week to ten days duration. Thus phenomenologically grounded, and beginning to notice other consistent but serial patterns of differences, I concluded that unfolding before me were two distinct personalities. These two personalities were not entirely dissociated each from the other in Steven's awareness. Therefore, I have put the term "multiple personality," in quotes. I shall simply say that in the kind of language Bleuler used in describing schizophrenia, he was "splitting-off," but rather than in the usual fragmented and unpredictable way, he was manifesting two composite, consistent part-selves.

As one part-self, Steven was humble, shy, incompetent, and thoroughly externalizing. In a flat "hill twang," he elaborated the "it" that was responsible for all his difficulties—the small, mining-town environment from which he hailed. His parents, siblings, teachers, townspeople, merchants—everyone, said Steven—were unappreciative of his sensitivity, intellect, poetic receptiveness and perceptiveness, devotion to liberal causes, etc. Steven himself identified this part-self as "Steven-the-Martyr," but did not find it ego alien and continued to justify it at every occasion. During his week-to-ten-day enactments of this role, he consistently wore dungarees, levis, overalls, work shirts, railroad caps, etc.—working man's attire—and was fairly unkempt. Behaviorally, he was dull, sluggish, lethargic, passive, and indifferent.

The second part-self to become evident posed a striking contrast. Extremely urbane, clever, witty, verbose, and energetic, this Steven was regarded by young women his own age as "very cool." Following the same temporal pattern, for a week to ten days he looked as if he had just stepped from a leading boutique. Not only was he "mod," but a rakish flair and a tasteful flamboyance typified his dress. And he acted the part to the hilt, often getting off amusing puns or quips, and at a kind of literary repartee he was a master. In contrast to the "hill twang" of "Steven-the-Martyr," this Steven spoke with very good diction and articulation. Steven identified his part-self as "Fritz-the-Clown."

Steven found "Fritz-the-Clown" much to his liking, and relished the attention showered upon him by other members of the group. When questioned about his origin or the derivation of the title, he was wittily guarded. When his friend, Tom, knowing that Steven had recently read *Gestalt Therapy Verbatim*, proposed the theory that this part-self was Steven's attempt to mock Fritz Perls (and me), Steven got into the challenge. At the next meeting of the group, he wore a purple smock with yellow flowers pinned to it, a false beard, and imitated his notion of Perls. Interestingly, the loosening up that seemed to come with the emergence of this part-self resulted in Steven loosening up in individual sessions, so that he would now enter into dialogs between the two parts.

After considerable dialog had occurred between these two part-selves without much discernible change in either, the therapeutic process suddenly became very tumultuous, and a very problematic third part-self emerged. Steven carefully concealed this one from the group, and asked me not to discuss or implicate it there. When I refused, he asked to quit the group. Trying to build trust, I agreed. Steven identified this one as "Stephen-with-a-p," but offered no descriptive such as martyr or clown, and carefully guarded every hint as to its derivation. "Stephen-with-a-p" could best be described as a grandiose paranoid schizophrenic seething with rage and pervasively projecting and displacing these feelings. As this part-self, Steven believed that he could shoot "Steven-the-Martyr" and "Fritz-the-Clown" through the head without harm to "Stephen-with-a-p," and laid a plan to prove it to me. Although he never quite refused to work in a Gestalt dialog fashion in individual sessions, he acted out in the hospital between sessions, particularly with members of the group, from which he now was extremely alienated. When he threatened to kill me and several members of the group, he had to be confined for a short time. His dress and speech were those of any 21-year-old, college-culture youth.

After some two months of intensive therapy (5 sessions per week), about half of which included "Stephen-with-a-p" in dialogs with either or both of the other self-splits, as suddenly as it had appeared, this part-self disappeared. Resuming his pattern of alternating at about weekly intervals between "Steven-the-Martyr" and "Fritz-the-Clown" phases, Steven asked to and was permitted to rejoin the group. About a month later, "Fritz-the-Clown" disappeared, and again under much pressure from his parents to resume school work, Steven was discharged to continuing out-patient therapy. And after about a month of weekly group meetings, he reported, in group, a dream too long for verbatim reproduction, but presented synoptically and in vivid detail below:

Lying on his bed, he begins seeing dots, and is aware of great tension in his spine and teeth and a ringing in his ears. A batwing with great, sharp teeth flies partially into the room, and is flopping against the door, but, waving the batwing back with the sweep of a hand, "Stephen-with-a-p" enters, walks over to Steven, taunts and tells him he is evil briefly, then takes on a smiling countenance, shrinks to six inches in height, climbs up on Steven's right shoulder, and informs Steven that he (Stephen) has come to tell him "who he is."

There follows a scene in which Steven is quite young (3–4), is fallen on by his drunken father at a boisterous party, and screams. The homuncular Stephen tells him that the origin of "Steven-the-Martyr" lies in his hatred toward his father and his commiserative identification with his seductive mother.

Immediately, Steven sees himself at about age ten, trying to electrocute one of his brothers by encouraging him to hold a copper wire and bar he has rigged to an open wall socket, setting the carpet on fire in spots, and being screamed at by his mother.

Suddenly the picture switches, and, still at about age ten, Steven rams a screwdriver up the left nostril of his other brother.

The homunculus explains the origin of "Stephen-with-a-p" in terms of fantastic sibling rivalry, and asserts that for the next several years (10 to about 15) Steven is good, quiet, attentive at school while at home he is a thief, liar, and murderously manipulative. Until, says the homunculus, at age sixteen. Steven seriously injured his knee in a football accident.

Abruptly, the next scene of the dream finds Steven, fat and on crutches, going down a hallway in his high school, being jeered by fellow students about his fat stomach and "deformed, hunchback" look.

The homuncular Stephen explains the origin of "Fritz-the-Clown" as a jester who in this way minimizes ridicule by beating others to the punch, ridiculing himself, then, finding this way of being interpersonally rewarding, cultivates and perfects it.

As suddenly as he appeared on Steven's shoulder, the six-inch narrator disappears, and Steven wakes, "trembling, perspiring, and very strung out."

In a therapy session lasting over four hours, Steven took the part of each symbol in this dream and dialogued in a first-person, present-tense manner with all the other symbols and himself. After much sobbing, raging, beating, kicking, cursing, etc., his last experiential dialog is with the homunculus who had perched on his shoulder. With genuine affect, he thanked him for his interpretive services and said a tearful goodbye to him. Following some cognitive consolidation, Steven reported that he felt energetic, light, free, and like he was "newly born."

Shortly after this dreamwork, I left the area of Steven's residence and university, and he opted not to transfer to another therapist. That was in 1972. I have received regular reports, a couple from him and several from persons who know him in the community. Apparently, he was thoroughly integrated, for ever since the work on the dream he has functioned as a creative, industrious graduate student with an interesting interpersonal life.

To be part of such a powerful piece of work in relatively short-term therapy was a peak experience as a therapist. However, that is the least of my reasons for sharing this case. It illustrates the relative unproductivity of the traditional nosological entities and argues for the depth therapist functioning phenomenologically, with the actually appearing events, rather than theoretically-categorically. It argues for the case made by Laing (1965) that psychotic symptomatology, including the schizophrenic "lifestyle," is frequently avoidance of rather than the result of "craziness," and that to be integrated, a divided self may first need to be more fully and explicitly divided. It illustrates what I have asserted elsewhere (Dublin, 1973), that with such a Laingian model of psychopathology, Gestalt therapy can be effective with selected psychotic persons, whereas they are usually considered too fragile and in need of too much support for this kind of intensive work while in or recently recovered from a psychotic state (e.g., Shepherd, 1970). It argues against the usual criteria for diagnosing multiple personalities in terms of dissociative, hysterical phenomena, and argues for the Gestalt theoretical position (Perls, 1969) of alienated or split-off self as a nosological entity or condition more fundamental than established syndromes such as "schizophrenia." And finally, it is a testimonial to the power of the Gestalt dialog in dreamwork, a fact not that evident from the published pertinent work, which for the most part has been done with persons much less seriously disturbed. This may be another way of saying that the Gestalt dreamwork method is a powerful instrument for operationalizing more concretely the notions of the creative unconscious as espoused by Jung, John Perry, John Lilly, and others.

REFERENCES

Dublin, J.E. Gestalting psychotic persons. *Psychotherapy: Theory, Research, and Practice, 10,* 1973, 149–152.

Laing, R.D. *The divided self.* London: Penguin Books, 1965.
Perls, F.S. *Gestalt therapy verbatim,* John Stevens, Ed. Lafayette, CA: Real People Press, 1969.
Shepherd, I.L. Limitations and cautions in the Gestalt approach. In *Gestalt Therapy Now,* J. Fagan and I.L. Shepherd, Eds. New York: Science and Behavior Books, 1970, pp. 234–238.

Chapter 23

A Gestalt Awareness Process for Working with Problem Drinkers Who Do Not Want to Stop Drinking

PAUL E. PAIGE

In the last decade, I have had the good fortune to work with over 3000 people who were seriously involved with alcohol abuse. Within this spectrum were included simple excessive drinkers, problem drinkers (alpha alcoholics), people who manifested physical dependency and were out of control in their drinking (gamma alcoholics), people who had consistently maintained a controlled drunken condition (delta alcoholics), the episodic drinkers who go on binges (epsilon alcoholics), as well as the neurologically damaged and Korsakoff syndrome patients. This experience has been in a variety of settings: private outpatient clinics, private hospitals, county hospitals, state hospitals, skid row, recovery homes, legal justice system, and in private practice. In working with alcohol and other drug abusers in a variety of settings, my experience has been more successful than not; and as a result I continue to pursue this area of investigation and intervention. At this point I want to share a clinical perspective that has evolved in working with alcohol abusers who say they do not want to stop drinking.

An enduring question that is always present with every good clinician is how do we effect successful treatment of those people who did not respond to whatever approach we used at that time? After hundreds of therapeutic "post mortems" with people who were unsuccessfully treated by a variety of therapies, several insights emerge. Summary remarks usually include statements to the effect that: (1) the patient does not want to stop drinking; (2) the patient has a way to go before he hits bottom and is ready to change; (3) the patient is not serious and does not have enough motivation. These judgments may in fact be true, and/or they may be explanations for clinical and therapeutic failure on the part of the professional therapist or counselor. I believe the latter is more true in most cases that are unsuccessfully treated.

Recently, in reviewing about 1,000 case histories of people who had deteriorated enough to be hospitalized in a state hospital, the most outstanding feature noted was that all of the people had received treatment at least twice before the last hospitalization. All had been hospitalized at least once before and had tried to utilize at least two community rehabilitation resources; physicians, Alcoholics Anonymous, outpatient clinics or medical hospitals. These patients consistently reported having attempted actively to utilize at least three of these resources at different points in their drinking career, and consistently reported little or no success.

These patients reported that they were "motivated" in at least two of their "sincere" attempts at obtaining help early in their drinking career before they had lost everything; *but* they had not been able to stop drinking, or they could not maintain their sobriety long enough. A surprising finding, in reviewing this case history material, was that all of the patients within the year prior to admission to the hospital had had significant periods of sobriety and had not been drinking continuously. Also, nearly all reported extended periods of sobriety (nearly six months) within the last five years. All of them had been able to stop drinking and did. This was surprising, since most of these people reported that they were not able to stop drinking, and they had in fact stopped. Yet they started again.

This distinction is important; that there was not *continuous* drinking. Evidently, the period of abstinence was not satisfying and complete enough for them. There was something vital and important missing in their lives, and in the ways they were attempting to straighten themselves out. Sobriety in and of itself was not enough.

FACTORS IN UNCONTROLLED DRINKING

Individuals who are experiencing difficulty through problem drinking and who refuse to stop, regardless of environmental and personal pressures, suffer from a lack of ego strength. Ego strength is defined here as the ability to identify with one's emotional and body state, the ability to control impulses and the ability to direct functioning into appropriate reality tasks. High ego strength has been related to successful treatment in psychotherapy and used as a prognostic factor in determining outcome of treatment. A simple formulation is possible: ego strength is necessary for self-control.

Usually behind the problem drinker's reluctance to stop drinking are: 1. Inadequate resources to deal with internal distress and disorganization; 2. lack of alternates to drinking as a coping mechanism; 3. inability to feel what is going on in their bodies as a result of the anesthetic effects of alcohol and propreoceptive anesthetic (they are cut off and have lost the "feel of themselves"); 4. positive benefits are still being achieved through the use of alcohol; 5. maintaining the illusion that they are a "happy drunk" most of the time; 6. basic fear that they will not be able to stop even if they try as hard as possible.

The last item, basic fear that they will not be able to stop even if they put everything into it, is the central issue of concern. When a change agent (physician, minister, court, therapeutic counselor), is able to get a "commitment" or promise from the patient to "try" to stop all drinking immediately, both the therapist and the patient are forced into an impasse; and the patient does not have the ego strength or the resources to face or go through such an impasse. The patient retreats, feeling less than he did before; more inadequate and more convinced that he is not able to control himself or sustain positive action on his own behalf. An all-or-nothing imperative sets him up for another failure that further damages his ego and depletes what motivation the patient may have. At this point he may lose confidence in his ability to mount an effort on his own behalf, and he may lose confidence in the professional with whom he is working.

I have seen physicians, therapists and counselors set up an all-or-nothing ultimatum; when the patient "fails" to meet the therapist's expectations, he is admonished for his lack of sincerity or seriousness. The patient will usually fade into the distance and disappear, or he will come back again to get beaten over the head with his inability to control himself, *which is his basis for seeking professional advice.* The key is that the person does not know *how.* Physicians and other professionals tell the person *what* to do and do not work with how to accomplish this. This is the arena of Gestalt Therapy, the *what* and *how* in the *here* and *now.* Working centrally with the what and how is necessary and sufficient to effect stabilization.

A major axiom that repeatedly emerges is: If the patient is not in treatment, you cannot treat him. The converse is true also: As long as he is involved in treatment, then treatment is possible.

De facto with the person being in treatment, he wants something and is willing to invest his time, money and whatever little else is available at that moment. This "whatever little else" that is available may not be enough to accomplish anastrophic results like cessation of all drinking immediately. However, whatever is there is enough for a humanistic counselor to start working with. As a matter of fact, what is at that moment, with that person, is all there ever is to work with. It does not really matter how little or meager the resources the person is presenting; he is there, concerned, wanting and in my opinion workable. The basic approach is to start where the client is, not where we would like him to be. Take him seriously. Begin a systematic approach to engage him in treatment; sustain and maintain his motivation; build his ego strength, his knowledge bases, and begin to increase his alternatives to the use of alcohol. As long as the person is coming in, and is there, he is workable. A professional need not throw the patient away because he does not meet specific expectations. To do so makes the therapist no different from lay people who have done the same.

DIFFERENT TYPES OF PROBLEM DRINKERS

In general practice we usually see three types of problem drinkers: 1. The person who has a serious problem with alcohol, where substance abuse is seriously interfering with one of the major life processes, and the person does not recognize or accept that alcohol is the problem; 2. the person who acknowledges that alcohol is a problem and freely admits that he *has* to stop, wants to stop, and thinks he is not able; 3. the person who intellectually admits that alcohol creates problems of health, employment, relationships, or with the laws and says he does not want to stop drinking.

I work in several ways with the different types of problem drinkers, depending on who they are, the resources available, the best possible way to effect intervention, based on their reality and the way they present themselves to be worked with. The possible modes of intervention and goals are: 1. Working directly with the person, directly on his/her drinking; goal is no drinking or other drug abuse (legal or illegal); 2. working directly with the person, and indirectly on his/her drinking; goal is no drinking or drug abuse; 3. working directly with the person, and directly on his/her drinking; goal is limited and controlled drinking; 4. working directly with the person, and indirectly on his/her drinking; goal is limited and controlled drinking; 5. working indirectly with the person who is a problem drinker (working with a wife, child, relative or close friend) and directly on drinking; goal is self-adjustment, being a real resource and helping the problem drinker; 6. working with a spouse, child, relative or friend and indirectly working on the drinking; goal is self-adjustment of the person that I'm working with, exploring what is possible in the affected relationship, and controlled or no drinking.

The third type of problem drinker usually seen in general practice is always the most difficult and frustrating type of person with whom to work and is the subject of this paper. Frequently we see the waste of human resources and potential of people who have a serious problem, who do not want to stop drinking, freely admit that they like drinking and still get a lot from it. The situation is usually complex, where there are one or several coercive agents who are pressuring the person to cease drinking altogether: 1. Mandate from physician that the person will not live long; 2. ultimatum by spouse that he or she will leave or kick out the problem drinker; 3. ultimatum by boss that employment will be curtailed; 4. ultimatum by legal authorities for suspension of license or jail.

It is important to understand the background of this person in order to treat him. The patient has been manipulated and coerced into treatment to change behavior that he really does not want to change. The person has had subtle and obvious pressures applied, has been threatened by the most important people in his life, and yet his drinking behavior has not changed, and may have in many cases worsened.

The person has presented wishful thinking and promises like, "I'm going to stop drinking," and yet he persists in his drinking behavior. The person in effect is being sent to a counselor or doctor to be further manipulated, or changed by a professional change agent. *In my experience as a counselor and psychotherapist, I have not been able to get anyone to do what he or she did not want to do.* I have learned this lesson over and over again. Ultimately, people do exactly what they are willing to do. If the professional accepts the mandate made to the person that he stop drinking completely, then he becomes a part of the alcoholic game of "bet you can't stop me." If the therapist is a skillful manipulator, and if the patient's cost of drinking is high, there may be brief periods of sobriety and abstinence, but there will always be brief and protracted drinking bouts. The counselor will always wind up defeated, feeling frustrated and used.

Siding with a person's resistances and changing personality resistance into personality assistance has been implicit throughout the evolution of Gestalt Therapy. Arnold Beisser[1] has conceptualized this as the theory of paradoxical change: "Briefly stated, it is this, that change occurs when one becomes what he is, not when he tries to become what he is not. Change does not take place through a coercive attempt by the individual, or by another person to change him, but it does take place if one takes the time and effort to be what he is—to be fully invested in his current position. By rejecting the role of change agent, we make meaningful and orderly change possible."

This feeling of being frustrated and used is common to most people in the helping professions and the basis of their refusal to work with these types of patients. It is my opinion that professionals who have these experiences have set themselves up for this by siding with the coercive agents and then become an extension of the person's conflict, as he asks the patient to do the impossible (patient's view), completely stop drinking. This is what Fritz Perls[2] has called a top-dog/under-dog struggle, with the change agent winding up as the under-dog.

What I suggest is that the counselor side with the person's resistance and work within that framework on the side of the patient; and help him learn to use himself instead of abuse himself and alcohol. When a professional sides with the resistance and is willing to work with what is, he will discover that personality resistance will change into assistance and that the patient will trust him and be willing to explore new ways of seeing and being in the world. A danger exists that the professional may become another coercive agent crystallizing the person's resistance and his stubbornness by demanding that *the person stop drinking immediately.*

Mark and Linda Sobell[3] have pointed out that in some cases, during acute drinking, insistence upon abstinence as the *only* possible treatment goal may be unrealistic or harmful. The person may try his best to abstain from all drinking and find that he is unable to tolerate the *immediate* consequences of not being intoxicated and not having this coping mechanism available to him. What results is another failure and collapse of inspiration and motivation to do something about himself and his problem. In spite of the consequences, the person continues to ingest large amounts of alcohol and continues to perpetuate or worsen his condition. The Sobells point out that the issue here is not the morality of the consequences, rather, the reality of the person involved in the consequences.

The third type of alcohol abusing patient really knows that he is hurting himself; however, at this point in his life he is not able to face that hurt and pain by himself. His reality is that he does not have any better alternative that he knows and trusts will work for him. He is faced with an impasse: stop using and abusing and do what? Additionally, these people do not have the basic trust and faith in themselves or the professional they are working with to go through the impasse. The patient's impasse soon becomes the practitioner's dilemma: the patient has to stop drinking or he is not going to get better, and I cannot help him.

AN AWARENESS PROCESS

An alternate to the dilemma—abstinence or rejection—is what I call a *controlled drinking schedule*. I develop a contract with the patient to bring his drinking under control and begin dealing with the consequences in a realistic step-by-step fashion. By controlled drinking I mean: a specified amount, at a specified time, under specified conditions; with an explicit contract agreed upon and freely entered into by both parties, the counselor and the patient.

In most cases, the person is not fully aware of how much he is currently drinking. He may know that he is drinking too much and is not fully cognizant of what that really means.

The *First Step* is for the counselor to go over the last week and establish a good estimate of the quality, quantity, circumstances and financial cost of the drinking behavior. This will establish a base line to work from and give the counselor an idea of the depth of the problem.

The *Second Step* is to have the person keep an accurate record at the end of each evening of the day's drinking, quality, quantity, circumstances, with whom and the cost. This method will bring into awareness exactly what he is doing to himself. The record will give the counselor some idea of how motivated the patient is, and how well he can follow directions.

The *Third Step* consists of a study of the structure and function of the drinking behavior. Pay attention to details and find out what the different parts of drinking means to the person, before he can deal with the whole. Find out what parts the person likes, what parts he gets something from; what parts he does not like and from which he gets negative benefits.

The *Fourth Step* involves a complete and detailed record kept of every use of alcohol, detailing the "solutions" that alcohol is providing for the problems being coped with, exploring and specifying alternates that are mutually acceptable.

The *Fifth Step* is the developing and detailing of the therapeutic work necessary to develop functional and creative alternates to some of the real problems the person is facing, such as handling anger, anxiety and awkwardness, etc.

The *Sixth Step:* The person is fully aware of the extent of the use and abuse of alcohol and specific areas are targeted to "work through" therapeutically. Concomitantly, there is a cessation of the use of alcohol as a means of coping when the function of the use is no longer needed. The person no longer needs to rely on alcohol as a means, but can use his own resources and be free to choose what he wants to do, use or abuse himself.

When a person becomes aware of the structure and function of his drinking, it begins to change immediately. From the focus on drinking we begin to expand awareness with the person, of himself and the world. The problem drinker begins to learn-discover possibilities for his own growth and development and to generate his own creative adjustment instead of using alcohol or other drugs to cope with the world and himself.

SUMMARY

A clinical attitude on the part of the professional is described which, when adopted, can make the therapeutic work possible. This clinical perspective is not unique to Gestalt Therapy or a humanistic framework; however it does afford the most congruence from the perspective. The process outlined could be taken in conjunction with many different therapies— with different results.

In general practice we see three types of alcohol abusers: (1) the alcohol abuser who does not accept that alcohol is a problem; (2) the alcohol abuser who freely admits that alcohol is a problem and that he has to stop; and (3) the alcohol abuser who intellectually admits that alcohol creates problems of health, employment, etc., and refuses to stop drinking. A clinical approach to working with this resistance is recommended. The professional does not side with the coercive agents; rather, he engages the person in treatment and sides with his resistance, in order to get the person stabilized. Thus the real problems with which the person is having difficulty can be successfully treated. Alcohol, as such, is not the problem, rather it has functioned as a "solution" to a variety of problems these people have faced.

REFERENCES

Beisser, A.R. The paradoxical theory of change. In Gestalt therapy now, J. Fagen and I.L. Shepherd, Eds. Palo Alto: Science and Behavior Books, 1970.

Perls, F. The Gestalt approach & eye witness to therapy. Palo Alto: Science and Behavior Books, 1973.

Sobell, M. and Sobell, L. Individualized behavior therapy for alcoholics. Research Monograph, California Department of Mental Hygiene, 1972.

Chapter 24

MSIBTTBUD
and
MFIBTBUD

STEPHAN A. TOBIN

My Sickness is Bigger Than The Both of Us, Doc (MSIBTTBUD) *usually has some condition that a physician has diagnosed as an illness.* The ones I have seen either have had a psychosomatic disorder or were schizophrenic. MSIBTTBUD pays lip service to wanting to change and tells the therapist how much he suffers with his affliction and how fervently he wishes to get rid of it. That's not the least bit true. His illness is his major source of contact with others, his best (and often only) friend, his means of controlling others, his major topic of conversation, and frequently his meal ticket.

One MSIBTTBUD was a man who called me in desperation from some public building. He told me he was in therapy already, but that he wasn't getting anything out of therapy and needed to be seen right away. I consented to see him on the following day. When he came in he announced that he was a paranoid schizophrenic and had a 100% service connected disability from the Army. This meant that he received a modest sum from the government to live on every month, and that he didn't have to do any work to support himself. He was both pathetic and amusing because he was so transparent in the way he used his psychosis to deal with the world.

I have found MSIBTTBUD persons impossible to treat. The longest a MSIBTTBUD has even stayed in therapy with me has been four sessions, and he was a hypochondriac who was pressured by his family doctor to

178

get treatment. The median is one session. MSIBTTBUD doesn't ever want to get rid of his "ailments" and has probably come for psychotherapy only because someone pushed him into doing so.

Similar but somewhat more amendable to treatment is My Failure is Bigger Than Both of Us, Doc. MFIBTBUD is bright and obviously has ability, but he has made a mess of his life when he shows up at the therapist's office. His background is generally that others gave him double-bind messages when he was a child. "You're worthless unless you succeed," is one message. "You don't have the ability to succeed at anything" is the other. Faced with this kind of dilemma, about the only way MFIBTBUD can succeed is by proving that no one can force him to be successful, including his own Topdog. MFIBTBUD sucks people into trying to help him achieve intellectually or financially, and then frustrates them. The result is a covert feeling of triumph over his "helpers." Unfortunately, however, MFIBTBUD can't even let himself enjoy that feeling of power because he usually is not aware of his game and feels too guilty himself about not getting anywhere in life.

As in all other games with difficult patients who play *Helpless* or a variation thereof, I make no attempt to get MFIBTBUD to stop playing his game or to succeed. Instead, I try to get him to become aware of his game and one way to do that is to ask him to play it on purpose.

MFIBTBUD was a man in his early thirties who had a perpetual look of gloom on his face. His only interactions with the other workshop members were comments by him about what a failure he was in everything he did: In his work, in his romantic life, and in his relationships with other people. Finally, on the morning of the last day of the workshop he said he wanted to work with me. Here is a recreation of my work with the man, whom I shall call Jim.

Steve: What would you like to work on?

Jim: I wanted to work on my relationship with women. I was recently engaged, but the girl broke off the engagement at the last minute. I really feel lousy. I never seem to get along with girls. They go out with me one or two times, then they don't want to see me anymore.

Steve: How do you feel about that?

Jim: I feel lousy! I feel lonely all the time and depressed and—and just plain lousy! You would too if you were in my boat.

Steve: Yeah, you do have a certain aura around you of a loser. There's several nice looking single girls in this workshop but I'll bet that none is interested in you.

Jim: I wouldn't be surprised. I probably wouldn't want to go out with me if I was a girl.

Steve: I have an idea. I'd like you to play a girl and tell Jim—put him in that empty chair there—and tell him what you think of him.

J.G. (Jim as girl): Well, you're not bad looking; you're a little skinny, but you're not ugly. I don't know, you always look so crabby and depressed. I don't think I'd be interested in you.

J.S. (Jim as self): I don't blame you, I don't have anything to be happy about. I'm even probably going to lose my job soon. I don't think they're very pleased with me at work—I don't blame them, because I don't do very much there. I don't have any hobbies, I don't read. I don't do anything!

Steve: You know, Jim. I'd like you to go around and tell everyone about what a failure you are.

Jim: Okay, but I'll probably fuck that up too (group laughs). (Goes to first group member, Leslie.) Leslie, I am really a failure. Nothing I do comes out right. I don't get along with girls, I get fired from jobs, I can't do anything right.

Leslie: That's too bad, I really feel sorry for you, Jim.

Jim: (Moves to next member, Jane.) Jane, I'm a terrible failure. I—

Steve: (interrupting): Start boasting about what a failure you are. Tell them how great you are at failing.

Jim: Okay; Jane, I'm the greatest failure in the whole world. I do less with more potential than anyone else alive. (Jim's voice starts to sound more alive and more excited.)

Jane: Look, why don't you just try harder? You're a pretty nice guy, but you sound so dead and gloomy that I wouldn't go out with you. If you were more cheerful and didn't put yourself down, I might.

Jim: Oh, that wouldn't do any good. It would be just an act. Anyway, my breath would probably smell, or you'd have just gotten engaged or something. No, it's just no use. (Moves on to next member.) Ray, I'm the biggest failure in the whole world. I just can't succeed at anything!

Ray: I'd like to suggest something you could do to be a success, but I feel kind of helpless with you, man. Everytime anyone makes a suggestion, you shoot it down.

Jim: Well, I just know it wouldn't do any good.

Steve: I'd like to change the task. As you continue, Jim I'd like you to tell everyone that they can't make you become a success. That you refuse to succeed no matter how hard anyone tries to help you become a success.

Jim: Okay. Stan, not only am I a hopeless failure, but you couldn't succeed with me if you tried. I am the biggest failure in the world and I defy you to try to make a success out of me (Jim's voice is suddenly very strong and very much alive and he is smiling for the first time during the workshop. His posture is erect instead of hunched and he is now looking at people instead of giving them side-glances, as he had done before.)

Steve: That's great, continue.

Jim: Mary, you could lend me a million dollars, buy me the best clothes, and fix me up with the ugliest girls, and I'd still blow it! I defy you to make a success out of me.

Mary: *I* feel defeated (laughs). No, Jim, I think you have a lot of potential and are a pretty nice guy. I think you just put yourself down; if you didn't do that so much, you'd be okay.

Jim: Oh no! Don't say those awful things! I'm the greatest failure in the world, and *you* can't make me into a success. Nobody can, I'm too good at failing.

Mary: I give up, you win.

As Jim made his way around the group, he became more and more aware of how much excitment and energy was wrapped up in this game he played with himself and with the world. I didn't have much contact with him after that, only a few individual sessions and a workshop a year or so later. My impression of him was, that he had ceased to play his game with such intensity and, although he wasn't exactly setting the world on fire, was at least letting himself be successful in some ways.

Chapter 25

Comparative Therapies for an Itch

ROY O. RESNIKOFF

While in my residency training, like most trainees, I imagined that I had every malady that I read or heard about. When I thought about the chronic itching sensation I had near my left-forehead hairline—a symptom whose first appearance I could clearly recall during a math class in high school—I couldn't help but wonder: Had I been so maternally deprived that I was regressing to auto-erotic or autistic stimulation as described by Mahler? (1968) Was I so narcissistic that I needed external stimulation to remind myself where my boundaries were (Kohut, 1971)? Was I engaged in a masturbatory equivalent, especially since my skin irritation sometimes went along with hair twirling and could be soothing? Was I really masochistic and self-mutilating, expressing my aggression in an autistic way (since at times I would scratch this itch)? Was the itching sensation really a compulsion indicating an obsessive neurosis (Shapiro, 1965)? Was I identifying with my critical father, who perhaps was jealous of my special relationship (as the youngest of three sons) with my mother? Was I having a teenage identity crisis? Maybe I just hated math? Interestingly, as I was ruminating about all these possibilities the spot felt more irritable and I scratched it more. To my dismay, I gradually found myself with a chronic localized hairline sore a little less than the size of a dime. My wife called it a "pick."

Because I was a psychiatrist in postgraduate training I sought out several different therapies, ostensibly for the training involved, but leaving myself open to opportunities to gain personal insights along the way. Although I was not seeking help specifically for my "picking" habit, it was a clear-cut psychosomatic symptom and lent itself to easy presentation in different therapeutic settings. I would like here to describe four different therapies, using varying orientations, all dealing with the same symptom, and in the process to demonstrate some of the therapeutic approaches available to people with problems. The four approaches to be described are (1) Gestalt therapy, (2) Psychoanalysis, (3) The redecision approach (Transactional Analysis and Gestalt), and (4) The Strategic hypnotic approach. I did not consider biochemical or strictly conditioning approaches such as biofeedback. Although I have had other contacts with varied therapists and varied settings, this discussion will be limited to four specific approaches for purposes of clarity.

First, a little background on my symptom. I have bitten and picked my nails as far back as I can remember and carved up a school desk on a regular basis in the first grade. My actual hairline itching, and the scratching of it, began as I became worried about my math performance in high school. Worries about college or medical school exams would exacerbate irritation of the small area of skin involved as would my trying to concentrate on various reading materials. Sexual tension release could temporarily reduce my awareness of the symptom. So could a glass of beer.

GESTALT THERAPY (Polster, 1973)

My contact with Gestalt therapy has included a three-year postgraduate training and supervisory program; the instructors were a married couple well known in their field. Personal work was included as part of the training program, partly for demonstration purposes. Usually I joined a group of eight trainees in the leaders' living room. At times I asked to be the focus of the group's attention and at other times my reactions to others led to my being the focus.

The major goal of their therapy was to promote awareness of current perceptions, first within the individual, and, later, in the individual's contact with others. Group members could also try out new behaviors with each other or dramatize a conflict.

In my case, the therapist promoted awareness by instructing me: "Instead of trying to decrease the itch, close your eyes and give special concentration to this sensation." Interestingly, paying more attention, without touching, lessened the irritability of my skin problem; the therapist then suggested that I could allow my skin itching to join other sensations in my body rather than remaining an isolated symptom. At one point the therapist, typically sharing his own reactions to patient work, sat with me intensely imagining and experiencing what it felt like to be itchy. He shared with the rest of the group the excitement of the sensation. For further personal contact, on one occasion, I was asked to either pick or soothe physically (since the symptom seemed to encompass both polarities) the therapist's hand, instead of myself, depending on my sensations. My self-contained ("retroflexive") activity changed into an interpersonal touching communication. In addition, when I felt the urge to "pick" I was asked to convey this message in words rather than pick on myself. (For example, saying "I don't understand" to another person rather than picking on myself.) Also, being asked to show the "picked" area to the group revealed my embarrassment about the symptom and provided another contact medium leading to new understanding about my fears of criticism and rejection. A further experiment with the group included my verbally "picking" on various people's faults. This was quite easy to do in my mind but less easy to do face to face. The issue of picking on myself became quite obvious at that point.

The Gestalt trainers that I experienced were experts at finding the positive element to any problem. At times this took the form of finding how a particular activity or symptom was developmentally, if not currently, useful. My picking was positively compared to being highly discriminatory. To further reveal the psychological polarities of "picking," I recall having an experimental dialogue between my discriminating, preoccupied, picky side (characteristics I associated with my father) and the nondiscriminating, self-interest side (more similar to my mother) of my personality. My picking and being discriminatory was seen as a problem only when taken to an extreme.

The Gestalt approach emphasized discovery of potential messages included in the sensation of itching as well as enacting these discoveries right at that precise moment during therapy. Understanding the early roots of my symptom flowed naturally from this discovery process. The therapy emphasized the potential symbolic messages that the sensation of itching conveyed both to me (for example, my need to be soothed or criticized) and toward others (for example, wanting to confront or pick at them).

THE PSYCHOANALYTIC APPROACH (Greenson, 1967)

I have completed five years of four-session-per-week traditional psychoanalytic therapy. Again, the therapist was well recognized in his field but was less well known nationally compared to the Gestalt therapist above. Again, as in the other approaches, the itching symptom was only a small focus of the total experience.

The setting was an office with a separate entrance and exit. After entering, I lay on a couch looking at the ceiling. (After a number of months I was able to pick out six different patterns in the ceiling's soundproofing.)

In psychoanalytic work, my free-floating thoughts to various aspects of the itching sensation were crucial, as well as how I imagined my therapist to be reacting to a person who would have such a symptom. In some detail, we explored how I even "pick" on myself for having a pick. Instead of simply condemning myself for what I had labeled "preoedipal" or "oedipal" behavior, I was encouraged to accept all the various aspects of my character as being me—not something to be diagnosed, otherwise pigeonholed, or discarded.

As with my symptom, my therapist was attributed with picky as well as soothing maternal qualities. At other times he seemed to be perfect (like I imagined my father to be), very powerful (like I imagined my mother to be), or incompetent (also attributed to my mother). My picking was associated to all three qualities, either related to my frustration about not being all knowing and omnipotent, or related to the anxiety about feeling helpless. Compared to the Gestalt approach, there was less instruction on how to develop fantasies and less formal experiments to facilitate the process of understanding the roots of my symptom. The basic format, however, encouraged discussion of my thoughts and feelings toward the therapist. Before beginning analysis I envisioned spending endless tedious hours intellectualizing about my past. Instead, focusing on my frustrations and admirations regarding the therapist, as well as letting my mind wander, led to a fascinating "present" experience.

Although mostly focused on the process of my "transference" (reactions and projections regarding the therapist based on my past) and changing my self-concept, I was amused when the psychoanalyst humorously did acknowledge that it would help if I "just stopped picking."

The frequent and long-term nature of the therapy gave importance to everyday matters, and gave time to internalize a positive analyzing mental set as opposed to a picky, destructive mental set. I still imagine conversations with my psychoanalyst when I am feeling pick-o-rific.

REDECISION THERAPY (TA-Gestalt)—(Goulding, 1978)

This approach emphasized analyzing the early developmental decisions a child makes—decisions that still operate actively in adult life, often without one's awareness. Redecision work thus involves attempting to activate the feelings that were involved in making that original decision, and then using adult awareness in redeciding what is—or was—needed to solve an old problem that is still causing conflict. I got to know redecision work in a 50-hour contact with a well-known couple who have a national reputation in transactional analysis and redecision therapy. Twenty therapists-in-training met for one week at a retreat. The conference room was set up with the leaders in front and the participants seated in a horsehoe-shaped arrangement.

After hearing the description of my symptom and understanding the comforting as well as the aggressive aspects of my skin problem, the therapists suggested a preverbal experiment. I had mentioned to the therapists at one point that my mother had always insisted that she had to get dentures because all her calcium had gone into milk to breastfeed me and my brothers. To experience the guilt and anger of feeling that I had somehow hurt my mother by breastfeeding, the therapist told me to fantasize and then enact (physically and with sounds) biting her breast. This, to my surprise, was a very emotional experience for me. Afterwards, the therapists had me choose a nurturing woman in the group to comfort me. The redecision that took place was, that if my mother felt bad about "sacrificing" her milk, I could redecide not to feel guilty about it. That was her problem, not mine.

In videotape work with the same therapists, I saw that the left side of my face (on which the itching was localized) was more immobile than the right side. The right side would reveal grimaces, smiles, and frowns, while the left side was relatively still. This fact seemed to provide personal evidence for split-brain phenomena; that is, my left-sided symptom seemed to be an attempt to stimulate that side to include more emotionally and personal contactfulness. (Later in Gestalt work I practiced exercising the left side of my face to include the expression and fantasies revealed by the right side. Later in psychoanalytic work I also began to accept the right side of my face (and its revelations) which I had previously seen as the problem side.)

STRATEGIC, HYPNOTIC THERAPY (Haley, 1967)

For this therapeutic approach I visited a nationally known hypnotist for two days. I was attracted to this therapist because of my mutual interest in family therapy. I was also interested in strategies of problem-solving therapy especially for use in the early phases of therapy. The therapist was perhaps doing a lot more than I was aware of, but here are some of the things I think happened: First, while in a hypnotic state, I was able to recreate, at the therapist's suggestion, beautiful, enjoyable experiences from my childhood, such as lounging around Cedar Brook Pond feeding the ducks. While I was under hypnosis, I was told to focus on a bouquet of lavender flowers in front of me; the therapist simply said that in the future when I was feeling like picking, I could, instead, think of lavender flowers. The underlying process, I think, was to condition my previous positive childhood memories at the pond (symbolized by lavender flowers), together with my current negative symptom—the picking. The therapist stated over and over again that the power to solve problems comes from the client's own psyche and experience; the hypnotist simply helps develop the process of using this power. My power in this instance was the ability to appreciate a beautiful pond and recall this beauty.

This particular therapist is also known for his story-telling ability which he apparently uses to give indirect suggestions to avoid patient reluctance toward change. The therapist seemed to feel that a part of my self-picking was a frustrated wish for fame. He described his own experience of trying to enjoy activities for themselves, rather than always anticipating what might result from them in the future. The suggestion to me was obvious. He also used his well-known food stories about how two people with different gastronomic preferences could each enjoy a meal in their own way. The client (in this case, me) was left to find what might apply. I could easily apply the idea of being less harsh on myself as well as enjoying what "food" (job, sex, money) is available (without hateful envy).

Reviewing these four experiences, what struck me was that they were all different but all useful. All the therapists were unique individuals who had qualities that at times superceded their theoretical schools of therapy. All appeared quite mature personally and professionally and had a developmental sense of how problems and symptoms developed; I clearly respected and admired the therapists involved. The strategic hypnosis approach was the least overt, but, as I recall my psychoanalysis, the latter was the hardest to characterize in a few paragraphs. Psychoanalysis used the content from the other three experiences but there were less clear-cut behavioral enactments to recall.

My main purpose in this piece is twofold. The first purpose is to explore the psychology of a specific symptom. The main point I have illustrated is that this symptom has multiple dynamic and developmental origins and can be used as the starting point for many directions of self-awareness. All the concerns listed at the outset during my training were partially, but not condemningly true.

The second main goal is to offer some comparison between varied therapy approaches—both old and new, directive and indirect. The redecision work and the strategic therapy both emphasized rapid change. The Gestalt approach and psychoanalysis both offered small changes, repetitively reworked over a period of time. With these latter two approaches, contact with the therapist and discussion of that contact was especially important. The personal power of the therapist was important with the redecision and strategic work but the therapist-patient interaction was less of a discussed issue in the content of the therapy. For readers using this article as a guide to therapy, again, I was impressed by the fact that therapists with different schools of thought and different personalities could all be useful; in all cases, however, I had a good "gut feeling" about the therapists.

As I write this piece, the self-questioning, picky part of me rekindles my impulse to "pick." My concerns are: Will the reader understand that this paper only represents one small fraction and example of the therapies involved? Will the reader be overly picky and critical of my character style? Have I paid sufficient attention to the intent and process of my discussion with lesser emphasis on the potential recognition? Will I regret exposing weaknesses in myself?

The fact that I have submitted this paper without excessive rumination or picking further reinforces my conviction that the therapy experiences described above were helpful. Although I still pick at times, my picking feels more creative, friendly, and interesting.

REFERENCES

Goulding, B., & Goulding, M. *The power is in the patient.* San Francisco: TA Press, 1978.

Greenson, R. *The technique and practice of psychoanalysis.* New York: International Universities Press, 1967.

Haley, J. *Advanced techniques of hypnosis and therapy.* Selected papers of Milton H. Erickson, M.D. New York: Grune & Stratton, 1967.

Kohut, H. *Analysis of the self.* New York: International Universities Press, 1971.

Mahler, M. *On human symbiosis and the vicissitudes of individuation. Volume I. Infantile psychosis.* New York: International Universities Press, 1968.

Polster, E., & Polster, M. *Gestalt therapy integrated.* New York: Vintage Books, 1973.

Shapiro, D. *Neurotic styles.* New York: Basic Books; 1965.

Chapter 26

Humor
and Gestalt Therapy

ROBERT L. HARMAN

Several years ago, I was leading a group which somehow managed to atrophy right before my eyes. Not only was there a lull in activities, a veritable lethargy had set in. This lull stimulated me to tell a story.

"Well," I addressed the group, "there was this old couple from the Ozarks." (The sudden shock of a story coming on perked up a few heads.) "Grandpa had died about a year earlier and Grandma lay on her deathbed. As was the tradition in those parts, the whole family, children, grandchildren and great-grandchildren, were gathered around her. The room was crowded, Grandma began to reminisce: 'You know Pa and I got together in 1913 and moved to the farm. We intended to get married when the preacher made his circuit, but the first World War came along and the preacher got drafted.' She looked around the room and continued, 'There wasn't no hurry cause we wasn't going noplace. So, soon we had Billy, and then Suzy and Jack. Then the war ended and we hunted around for another preacher. Took us a while, but we finally found one. So we made arrangements to get married, but darn if the depression didn't come along and we didn't have no money to pay a preacher. By that time, along come Sarah, Clyde, Bobby Joe, and Wilma. Anyway, just when we was thinking again about marrying, World War II begun and all the boys had to go. By the time the war ended, some of you had children of your own, and me and Pa didn't think it would look right if we got married then. You know, we didn't want to cause you no embarrassment. Well, what I'm trying to tell you is that Pa and I never got married.' A great hush fell over the room; everyone was stunned. Grandma looked about weakly, then mustered her last strength and said, 'Well, one of you bastards say something!'"

The joke proved to be an elixir. We've always known the curative effect of a good laugh. Humor, they say, is the "best medicine"; we've heard it purported to cure what ails an individual, but what of its effect on groups? It seemed that the combination of the laughter and the metaphorical nature of this particular joke got us through the impasse and moving again. In fact, at subsequent group meetings, during slow times, all I had to do was threaten, that is I would *mention*, that I "knew this joke" and before I would get the words out someone in group would announce his or her intention to "work." I found myself having to contend with such impertinences as "Someone hurry up and do something before Bob tells his joke." The story became part of this group's history, something to be passed on. Occasionally, even still, I get a request to tell it. Yet, somehow, it has *never* had the impact it had the first time, when it seemed to fit so perfectly.

The first telling of this joke was spontaneous; it developed out of the natural phenomenology of the group. At other times, I planned its telling in order to "get the group moving"; and most other times it flopped. There are a couple of lessons, here, that fit with Gestalt theory, as with other modalities. First of all: do not "try" to be funny. Humor can only be curative when it is natural. Secondly, remember "timing." At times humor may not fit and may deflect instead of facilitate.

I savor the memory of a week-long Gestalt workshop, led by Jim Simkin in which humor was central. Most of us were struggling with those awful, yet familiar, dilemmas: boredom, marriage, divorce, unfinished business with dead or dying parents, and so forth. Yet I cannot remember ever having laughed so deeply or so much for a long time as I did that week in Big Sur. Jim's was a natural sense of humor and timing blended with his skill as a therapist. As I remember it, there were some funny people there and the group's humor, in that situation, seemed to assist in defusing the intensity of what most of us were experiencing and to render our problems tolerable. In this case, and in many others, humor was the lubricant that kept us rolling.

More specifically, though, humor can arouse or excite. This arousal function is necessary for what Gestalt therapy has termed "contact," without which not much happens and therapy becomes a stale, sterile "talking about" problems. Such contact with others or with alienated parts of oneself is necessary for change and is, in fact, one of the curative factors in Gestalt therapy. Humor, then, serves very well as an arousal vehicle for contactful episodes.

A good sense of the comic also enlivens! It charges people up. Naturally, this is true for therapists as well as for their patients. The humorless are usually dull; they lack any aura. My hunch about people who appear to have no humor is that they have lost touch with their polarities. In therapy, with such individuals I may propose some type of polarity experiment. I may "out-serious" them until they begin to laugh at me or at themselves. If they are trying desperately to make sense, I may make deliberate nonsense. The point here? For every pronounced trait in one's personality, the polar opposite has probably been squelched. As a Gestaltist, I am interested in developing an awareness of that polarity. Humor, as an enlivener, literally adds more energy for living.

We need to know on the other hand, that humor can also serve as a deflector, acting as a shield. Every attempt for serious contact can bounce off or be deflected. In this manner, some people make themselves unavailable for contact. This sense, in them, is actually pseudo-humor which serves to insulate them from the rest of the world. Instead of being funny, they soon become stale—predictable.

There is something distasteful to me about the phrase "using humor in Gestalt therapy." It smacks of technique, and I have a bias against a technique-bound approach to psychotherapy. Such a usage might imply that humor is, in some sense, the essence of Gestalt therapy. It is not, just as the "empty chair" never was. Humor is a natural expression that should not be inhibited in the name of "working with serious problems." Therapy can be serious without being somber. Usually, I feel free to laugh when something impresses me as funny or to say something "funny" if that is what is foreground for me.

At such times, even a joke may be useful—especially when the joke serves as a metaphor for what's happening in the group, as in the one about the "couple from the Ozarks." An apropos joke reflects the phenomenology of the group, or of the patient's problem, and the patient may accept the "punchline," that is, receive the message of the joke, with much less resistance than if it were presented in a confrontational style.

In Gestalt therapy, a certain "lightness of heart" can serve several purposes: as an arousal source that excites and enlivens; as a way of being contactful; as a way of working through an impasse; and as a way of defusing from an intensely threatening situation. On the negative side, humor for the patient can be a deflection away from contact; while for the therapist it can become a gimmick or technique that can or "should" be used.

Chapter 27

Expanding on the "Here and Now" and the "Void": The Mystery of Life

MARVIN LIFSCHITZ

What has impressed me about Laura Perls is her openness to new directions in Gestalt Therapy. Laura Perls (1976) has expressed a belief in, "Gestalt Therapy in itself as a continually ongoing innovation and expansion in whatever direction is possible and with whatever means are available between therapist and patient in the actual therapeutic situation" (p. 222). Laura has always struck me as more flexible and open to the Gestalt process itself than her late husband Fritz Perls. It is to this openness I respond in sharing my further evolution as a therapist and human being.

These last several years I have been integrating Gestalt Therapy with contemporary psychoanalysis. For the purpose of this paper, I am going to focus on Gestalt's emphasis on the "void" and the "here and now," along with Wilfred Bion's concept of "O," or the "emotional truth" of a session. I will also discuss some elements of Henry Elkin's (1972) developmental theory and address the link between these concepts in terms of how they affect the therapy process, and how they affect human experience and development.

Joel Latner (1973), commenting on some of the principles of Gestalt Therapy, reflects on the healthy aspects of emptiness and the void. He states,

To be empty is to be open to all the possibilities. This ensures that whatever gestalt develops will be able to draw on all the pertinent aspects of the field. Once we begin to judge, we can no longer allow the gestalt to emerge freely. Our thoughts and opinions about what we experience interfere with the experience itself, narrowing the possibilities. Latner goes on to discuss the concept of creative indifference, the organism at its zero point, open to what will come. (pp. 28, 29)

As a Gestalt therapist, I have attempted to integrate these theories into clinical practice. I have developed more than a respect for these concepts. My positive belief in the richness of emptiness and the void has given me greater courage in helping my patients and myself to let go of some controls and harmful defensive patterns.

Along with my respect and awe, I've had a special reverence for the "here and now." I used to do workshops called "Trusting the Here and Now," and the awarenesses and emotional truths that emerged from people's psyches made me treasure the "here and now." Even though in my own life I had and have difficulty staying in that plane, I knew in my heart from the experience of these workshops that something powerful and holy was operating. It wasn't until I came upon the teachings of Wilfred Bion that I was able to link up my respect for emptiness, the fertile void, and the "here and now" with his concept of "O," thus gaining a firmer foundation for a deeper understanding of these principles.

Michael Eigen (1981) a contemporary analyst and scholar of Bion, writes in his illuminating paper:

Bion uses the sign "O" to denote ultimate reality. For the psychoanalyst the O (ultimate reality) of psychoanalytic experience is what might be expressed as the emotional truth of a session. Strictly speaking, as psychoanalysts we live in the *faith* [my underline] that emotional truth is possible, even necessary as a principle of wholesome psychic growth. In itself the emotional truth at stake may be unknown and unknowable, but nothing can be more important than learning to attend to it. This is a paradox: an unknowable is to be the focus of our attention. Our faith in something important happening when we reach out toward the unknowable sustains the attention that clears a working space for truth. (p. 423)

In working with my patients, the reverence and awe I've had in staying with not knowing as patients explore their inner space, being in the "here and now" (to let whatever happens to emerge), has been my way of being involved in reclaiming faith.

I was letting myself be open to faith; I was letting myself be open to a healing process that was an antidote to the omniscient therapist and being in the world in a "know it all" and controlling manner. In Bion's terms, the analytic attitude is freedom from memory and desire. In Bion, faith is linked with openness to "O"; it is an area in which once again I was open to the mystery of life.

I began thinking about my birth and patients' births. There is a faith inherent in the baby's not knowing what he/she is getting involved with in the world. With all my neuroses, I somehow managed to survive and maintain some openness to what some analysts call the rape and bombardment of stimuli from the outside and inside. I managed to experience my helplessness, and my rage, and by blanking out and losing my mind to avoid the pain of mother not being there for me. I have been frustrated by my instinctual demands and urges, even with good-enough mothering. What is also mind staggering is that the first object for myself, and my patients, is not really mother. Elkin's (1972) brilliant developmental theory, reflects on this experience. He makes a strong case that the first object is really the primordial other. The primordial self and primordial other each is subject and object to itself. In Western society, primordial other has been called God, that is, that which you can't touch or see and that something unknown is "what is."

It would seem to me that being open to "O," in the "here and now," and experiencing faith in the unknown has been with us from birth on. Before the baby actually experiences his/her embodiment, and before discriminating his/her self from the mother, a primordial consciousness has evolved. As Elkin so masterfully describes, there is a death and rebirth of self-awareness; the primordial drama of a baby crying, and its terror and helplessness, and its losing consciousness and coming out of it again. The primordial other has indeed resurrected me. . . . Every human being who has survived has had some experience of love and caring, and of some resurrection. . . . This is all occurring before mother, as we know her in the material world, is experienced. To reexperience this area of our life and to assimilate it in some fashion in the therapy process, would be to undercut major obsessions with mother and father problems.

The more I work with patients, and in my own analysis, I feel the basic foundational experience in human nature is to reclaim this openness to the void, the unknown, and to faith in process and evolution. How faith has been smashed and lost, and how it can be regained and recaptured, is at the heart of human experience and of the therapeutic process. To be linked to this spirituality that is greater than we are, and yet does not diminish us, is something holy and wholling to the human soul.

As I write this article, I am deeply moved regarding the fragility, beauty, heartache, terror, and openness to the mystery of life and the creative fullness-functioning of the void.

REFERENCES

Bion, W.R. *Seven servants*. New York: Jason Aronson, 1977.

Eigen, M. The area of faith in Winnicott, Lacan and Bion. *International Journal of Psychoanalysis*, 62, 1977, 413–433.

Elkin, H. On selfhood and the development of ego structures in infancy. *Psychoanalytic Review*, 59, 1972, 389–416.

Latner, J. *The Gestalt Therapy book*. New York: Julian Press, 1973.

Perls, L. Comments on the new directions. In *The growing edge of Gestalt Therapy*, E. Smith, Ed. New York: Brunner Mazel, 1976.

Chapter 28

Intimacy in Psychotherapy*

IRMA LEE SHEPHERD

I do not believe I have to make a case for the importance of intimacy or closeness in human experience, since history fully attests to the drive for human consciousness and awareness to be shared and communicated. The quality, nature, styles, procedures, and problems of relationships have been described in diaries, journals, novels, poetry, drama, and, of late, in scientific investigations and case studies. Certainly, many of the problems which bring people to seek psychotherapy are those which have to do with failure to achieve closeness with others, fear of intimacy, lack of skill in making contact, or knowing how to support or maintain satisfying relationships.

A person does not develop if validation of his perceptions and experience by caring persons is absent. One's knowledge of self remains unfocused and uncomfortable, one's view of others and the world distorted, and one's skills for living diminished when one is denied intimate contact in infancy and childhood.

Many of the theorists of psychotherapy emphasize the importance of intimacy. Freud spoke of the goals of human development and of psychoanalysis as being able *to work* and *to love*. Eric Berne specified the goals of Transactional Analysis as autonomy, intimacy, and spontaneity. Perls described one of the goals of Gestalt therapy as "I and Thou—Here and Now," another as differentiation and integration of the person, and skill

---

* Based on a presentation for a symposium on Intimacy in Psychotherapy, American Psychological Association, San Francisco, California, August 1977.

in contacting others in healthy confluence. My own goals for myself and in my work as a therapist parallel these: intimacy with oneself and the skill to be intimate with others. I am certainly speaking of loving here and have no quarrel with the guideline to abundant living in Jesus' dictum "Love thy Neighbor as Thyself." It makes sense to me that the basic nature of reality is energy which has as its major characteristics *consciousness* and *unity*, and that we contact this reality most fully in our moments of open, unguarded loving. (Berne suggested that one was very fortunate if one experienced ten minutes of genuine intimacy in a lifetime.)

Intimacy comes from the Latin word meaning *within*. To me, intimacy means to be open and unguarded in the deeper aspects of my person. The process of being intimate involves knowing or seeking to know. I believe all human beings yearn to know and to be known and that these processes are interactive, and mutually facilitative of deeper levels of personal knowledge. In intimacy what is revealed and shared is that which is deeply personal, basic, most important, experienced almost as the core of being or soul, that which may often have had to be defended from others and even hidden from oneself. To risk closeness with another is to risk remembering old pain from violations of trust and openness in early development, and evoke the early non-verbal conditionings that don't respond easily to cognitive formula. This may account, in part, for the commonly observed symptoms and crises in adolescents and young adults as they pursue and establish intimate relationships. That which is anticipated as being satisfying instead evokes anxiety and depression and may lead to the felt need for psychotherapy.

Thus, the psychotherapy experience may become a potential laboratory where the person may learn how s/he blocks himself or herself from being intimate, and begin to develop skills for being close. The therapist becomes the teaching partner in this endeavor.

What are some of the therapist behaviors that we might describe as evoking intimacy or facilitating the patient's increased knowledge of self and his or her responses to another? I might interject here that the limits placed around the therapy situation—the boundaries of time, place, confidentiality, and protection—provide the necessary sanctuary for what is a delicate process. The limits provide protection from intrusion and distraction, and allow for concentration and focusing. Also, the therapist's own self-knowledge and skill in centering and clarity about his or her own limits are essential.

Some of the behaviors that may invite a closer sharing of one's self include eye contact, talking or listening, and touching and holding. Paying attention to another by steady contact with eyes is one of our earliest ways of relating ourselves to others and the world, and perhaps the most basic way we have of letting someone know we are listening and communicating presence. The looking and seeing must not be too intrusive or too intense. The other side of this is the willingness to be seen and regarded, undefended. Sometimes, patients have to be taught to risk seeing and being seen, to learn to trust their eyes again, thus reducing the power of images in the head which get easily substituted for reality. Eyes have been called the "mirrors of the soul." Indeed, they are very sensitive indicators of our feelings and our fears, and as such, often say much more than words.

However, words are important too, to clarify experience and disclose the self with increasingly refined shades of meaning. Through selective shared disclosings, we deepen our sense of self and feel less alone in the universe. Much can be taught in therapy about risking with words and moving towards strength through tenderness for onself and another as words and feelings are united in integrated expression.

Touching and holding, when not forced, driven, or contrived, but following the therapist's genuine response to the patient, may also be powerful in the process of restoring whole personness. In my experience, holding and comforting often precipitates grieving and then facilitates the ending process of grief. Physical contact may sometimes be the only vehicle for releasing bound energy that was once feeling which was powerfully held back and frozen. Learning to reach out, reach for, touch, and find another person there who is not avoiding or controlling or exploiting or punishing is important in restoring confidence in very natural ways of contacting and engaging. I also include here spontaneous expressions, such as hugs of joy and affection, and pride and congratulations which may have been absent and sorely yearned for in the patient's past. Affection invites affection, attention invites attention. These experiences and skills become part of the patient's new way of being, and can be generalized into relationships in the world. This is, of course, the aim.

The major caution here is that the therapist be clear about his or her own needs and motives. If the therapist is afraid of intimacy, avoids it, or is deprived of close relationships in his or her own life, then difficulties will surely follow. If the therapist is afraid to accept loving and feels unworthy, then he or she may well recapitulate the patient's experience of trying to love parents who felt unworthy or afraid and who pushed him or her away. When the therapist becomes aware of anxiety, confusion, or obsessions about parents in this process, he or she can seek supervision, consultation, or therapy to help clarify personal and therapeutic options.

Patients may well test the limits in intimate contact, particularly in touching and holding, attempting to get the therapist to help them avoid deeper issues by asking for nurturing or comforting when these are not relevant. In these instances, the therapist needs to be clear, able to differentiate between manipulation and genuine affect, and to maintain the commitment to one's own authenticity.

Of the ways by which intimacy with oneself or others can be avoided, one of the most common is going through any of the behaviors of intimacy without contact, and here is one more about which I want to be very clear. Talking, looking, and touching can be sexually oriented and provocative, and in a culture that often frantically and compulsively presses toward easy sexual release, these behaviors may have no other goal. Individuals may very successfully avoid relationships through quick and early and excessive sex. The anxiety of possible closeness or avoidance of pain in therapy may be experienced as sexual tension by patient or therapist. I believe that it is the therapist's responsibility to deal with this issue openly as with any therapeutic issue and not to act it out with the patient. The therapist may very well need to support the patient's permission to be sexual in the world, but cannot be the agent of experience without therapy disappearing. Such behavior closely parallels incest, and is just as confusing to the patient if not more so. This, in my opinion, represents a breach of contract, unless possibly for those therapists who make their intentions clear in their initial contracts.

Intimacy in or out of therapy cannot be expected, forced, or contrived. All one can bring is openness, unguardedness, and a willingness to wait for those connections with the deeper self and the depth of another person to bless us with this happening.

Chapter 29

When Is It Wise for the Therapist to Give Information About His or Her Own Life and Ideals to the Patient?

EDWARD W.L. SMITH

When I agree to be a psychotherapist to someone, I agree implicitly that the primary focus of our work will be on that person's growth. Therefore, I want my sharing of my ideals and information about my life to be in the service of the patient.

Much of the artistry in therapy is in the timing. So, I want to share when the patient is poised to hear.

I want to share when my sharing lets my patient witness my being open and honest and see that I survive and mostly prosper from such risk. This is my living an example of intimate contact.

When I can inspire or give permission to my patient to be more alive by my stories of living with reasonable risks I want to share those stories with as much detail as necessary.

Sometimes my story can serve as a guide if my patient is now on a path which I have traversed. I may share my struggles and resolution of such a path.

Caveat: Sharing is not wise when it comes from the therapist's own narcissistic needs, or needs for personal therapy.

Chapter 30

Interpretation Is. . .

An intellectual shortcut. It promotes introjection rather than assimilation and integration, and thus is a waste of time. A phenomenological-existential method facilitates immediate experience, works through details of resistances and blocks (the fixed gestalten), and thus facilitates more thorough assimilation and ongoing gestalt formation.

LAURA PERLS

The attempt by one person to translate the unique experience of another person into significance extending beyond the raw event.

MIRIAM POLSTER

Chapter 31

Gibberish

STEPHEN A. TOBIN

One technique I have found very effective in my Gestalt therapy work is to have clients communicate in gibberish instead of words. I have found that many persons actually obfuscate communication when they use words by rehearsing and censoring so much of what they say that they lose all emotion that could have been in their voices.

Getting such people to communicate in gibberish can have the effect of: (1) making them aware how much they *don't* communicate with words; (2) getting them in touch with feelings that are usually excluded when they talk to others; (3) getting them in touch with others in a more meaningful way than they are used to. Frequently clients refuse to communicate in gibberish because of embarrassment; those that do, however, are sometimes very surprised at what comes out.

For example, about two years ago I ran a weekend workshop in which was a young man who was a severe stutterer. He had had much psychotherapy and speech therapy but, while his stuttering had decreased, he still stuttered rather badly. His voice also had a harsh, grating quality to it and, while listening to him talk to another workshop participant, I began to feel tortured by the sound of his voice and his stuttering. On a hunch I suggested he play a sadistic torturer with everyone in the group. He readily and eagerly got into the role, and began to tell people what brutal things he would like to do to them. Amazingly, he stopped stuttering! I then asked him to start talking to people in gibberish and the change again was amazing; the harshness became pronounced so that he began to sound and look very different. Instead of his usual strained, dead, passive, dull, well-meaning demeanor, he sounded and looked graceful, alive, aggressive, frightening, and very angry. His stuttering and strained voice turned out to have been an indirect way of both expressing anger and of avoiding awareness that he really was angry.

Since he didn't seem particularly frightened at discovering all this rage inside himself and his speech was much approved during the rest of the workshop, I think the results may be lasting.

Chapter 32

Don't Be Satisfied Until—

ERVING POLSTER

What leads to success in psychotherapy?

If a patient were to ask me, "How can I be a successful patient in psychotherapy," I might well tell him that if he really means the question, this would be half the job. The rest would open itself to us as we proceeded in the therapy.

That sounds half-wise and half-buck-passing, so I went on trying to think of the answer, not for my patient, but for Voices, where I am not faced with a particular person's asking. So here are four of my guiding principles:

1. Teach me (your therapist) all you can about yourself, and don't be satisfied until I have learned what you are trying to teach me.
2. Never take unfruitful sessions for granted.
3. Know where you left off last meeting, and if it is not finished, go on from there.
4. Continue "therapy" on your own, away from the therapy office, either by doing specific homework which we may set up, or whatever else you see that you can do to make a point of growing.

Chapter 33

To Shed Respectability

SOL S. ROSENBERG

Into the mouth of Jack Tanner (Man and Superman), G.B. Shaw put the words, "The more things a man is ashamed of the more respectable he is." Tanner continues: "For if I were ashamed of my real self, I should cut as stupid a figure as any of the rest of you. Cultivate, a little impudence, Ramsden; and you will become quite a remarkable man."—In my experience the patient who derives the deepest benefits from psychotherapy is the one who experiences the growing courage to shed his respectability. For optimum results the patient must respond to the therapist's adroit resistance analysis and/or permit a relationship so full of trust that he can risk exposing all that he has been, wishes to be, and is.

Chapter 34

Intervision

GROVER E. CRISWELL

CLINICAL SITUATION

Recently there was an incident in one of my therapy groups which brought up for me the issue of therapist responsibility and patient responsibility. The issue is the appropriate limit of responsibility which the therapist takes for patients during therapy sessions.

The incident occurred in an ongoing Gestalt group of eight patients which I lead by myself. The group meets once a week for two hours. The usual format is to begin with a brief "check-in" during which each person, including myself, says how he or she is feeling and any interesting or important happenings of the past week which he or she wants to share. The patients also indicate whether or not they would like to "work" that evening. Following the check-in people take their turn working, negotiating the order as we go. I work in the style sometimes referred to as "one-on-one in a group context," for the most part. Sometimes other participants are invited into the work by the patient who is "on" or by me for feedback, sharing of their relevant experience, or for role playing. And sometimes we move into group discussions or group "processing" if that is what emerges as most important.

In this particular evening all members were present. One of the men, M, had missed a previous session during which there had been a discussion about keeping check-ins brief so as to allow more working time. Several members had noted that for some weeks the check-in time had been getting longer and longer and they agreed that they would prefer to keep more time available for individual work. In his check-in, M said that he didn't want working time that evening, and would like to share something important that had happened. M had been unemployed for many months and talked about the job he had just begun a few days before. As he talked he expressed his feelings about being employed after a long hiatus (he had resigned his last job as a social worker). He got into his feelings about being unemployed during those months while his wife supported him financially and how he had doubts and fears now about being able to keep the new job. Several people responded to M with supportive comments.

Prior to M's check-in, W, a woman in the group, had checked in saying that she had taken some big risks that week and was feeling very vulnerable. She asked if she could sit by me. At the end of M's check-in, W, still sitting by me, picked up on something M had said. W told M that he had said he wanted a "couple minutes" and then talked considerably longer and that he frequently presented himself that way—indicating that he wanted very little and then taking more. M responded that he hadn't taken much time for the past several weeks and had a right to the time. We assured him that the amount of time was not the issue. The issue was the way he didn't ask in a straight manner and thereby probably didn't get the full support from others that he wanted.

What ensued was several back-and-forth comments between M and W culminating in M's shouting angrily at W. So, in brief, what happened is this: W said she was vulnerable and sought support by sitting beside me. M said he wanted a "couple minutes" and talked longer, opening up his vulnerability. W confronted M on his style of asking. M obviously felt bad, being confronted while open and vulnerable, and responded with anger to W. W was the target for anger while vulnerable. The result was two hurt people. Two people, open in tender places, interacted in a way that they both felt hurt and angry.

I will discuss below what I did and my rationale for it. What I would like is to hear what other people would do in the situation presented. I want to know others' thoughts on how much intervention they would do in this situation, how much responsibility they would take to protect the two patients involved.

*   *   *

I recognized that both W and M were exposed in tender places and that rough treatment would be hurtful to either one. So, any intervention on my part needed to be gentle. As I saw it both W and M were in error. First, M was not being entirely straightforward when he said he wanted a "couple minutes" and talked longer. Second, W's confrontation was ill-timed. Even though it was a valid confrontation, it was not congruent with M's open position, having just expressed fear and doubt. From his position of hurt following the confrontation, he became angry and directed that at W who was still vulnerable.

I intervened with W by suggesting that she stop her confrontation. I said that given that she was feeling vulnerable, my guess was that she would not get what she wanted for herself by continuing. She stopped. With M, I clarified that the issue was not his right to the time, but his manner of asking. He kept not hearing that and escalating his anger, so I let him rave until he felt finished.

A helpful theoretical point which I learned from the Polsters is that in growth from the blocked level of emotional expression through the inhibited level there is an exhibitionistic level before the level of spontaneity is reached. During the exhibitionistic level the patient is trying out new behavior and is, of course, somewhat clumsy and ill timed. In addition, the patient is precarious in their newness of expression so criticism or punishment at that time can strongly reinforce movement back to an inhibited or even a blocked position. I see the therapist as having responsibility to provide enough safety during that exhibitionistic phase.

Both M and W were in this exhibitionistic phase, risking the expression of their fear and doubts. This is still new for both of them. Interestingly, W's confrontation was also new behavior. What I wanted was to maximize the safety for both M and W in their exhibitionistic expression, and that felt like a tightrope act.

My intention is to bring this incident up in a session soon, at a time when neither of them is feeling particularly tender and express what I have written here.

EDWARD W.L. SMITH

RESPONSES

Edward, your intervention fits the context of the one-on-one Gestalt group model. Within this framework, you, M, and W are the central characters in the therapeutic encounter. The awareness and exerted energy are, in a sense, continued in this sub-system of the group. Your response to the situation is sensible, although I am puzzled by language like, "As I saw it, both W and M were in *error*" (underlining mine). In my view, each person's experience is "correct" or "right," in the sense that it has intrinsic phenomenological validity: for me, W was right, M was right, and you were right. Your intervention came from your heart, from wanting to spare both individuals more pain.

My hope is that a lesson was learned by M regarding his lack of communicated clarity and by W, who put a contract, a principle, before her compassion.

When we look at your situation through the model of Gestalt Group Process (see Elaine Kepner's chapter in *Beyond the Hot Seat*), you did not use the full resources of the group. What was happening in the total group during the shouting match? You speak of "patient responsibility" vs. "therapist responsibility." Within the context of this model, the *group* is your patient also. The whole system is the patient and also carries some responsibility. Had you been able to express your concern regarding the generated pain and asked for their feelings, you may have discovered that, at that moment, the group's energy had risen and that others may have mobilized to support either M, or W, or both. In joining you, the group may have taken a more active role as a change agent. They may have asked you to let the action go on a bit longer, encouraging W and M to experiment with new behavior.

I find that, often, a group can provide support to both hurt parties and, at the same time, teach them something. The therapist is no longer the lonely long-distance runner, carrying the whole load. In this way, the pent-up energy of the group would have been creatively utilized, resulting in group contact, resolution, and relief.

I have often found that the group as a caring community may have more wisdom than is available to me in a given situation.

JOSEPH C. ZINKER

To begin with, I find the context presented by Smith with a missing part. Smith's "check-in" with the group—how *he* was feeling, etc.—is missing.

If I am leading a group and believe that two members of a group are hurting each other, I think it is my responsibility to share my belief: "To me, it looks like each of you is hurting each other," *and* then add how this affects me. "I don't like what you are doing to each other,"or "I can still remember the pain I felt when my parents hurt each other," or whatever truly reflects how I am affected by W and M's exchange.

Meaningful contact in the context of Gestalt Therapy is a two-way street. The Gestalt therapist is a model and his/her behavior will often set the tone in a group, especially where the work is on a one-on-one basis within the group setting. I prefer to work, as much as possible, on a horizontal level rather than on a vertical level with the group participants.

Working in the I-Thou (horizontal) context means sharing my thoughts and feelings. This does not mean abrogating judgment. Presumably, well-trained and emotionally mature Gestalt therapists will not be "acting out" with their patients—nor will they be making pronouncements, interpretations, or judgments *about* what is going on in a vertical manner, leaving themselves out of the interactive process.

The cutting edge in Gestalt Therapy takes place at the contact boundary. In order for the "you" to discover where s/he ends and the "I" begins, it is necessary that the "I" be transparent, sharing, and fully present (i.e. contactful).

JAMES S. SIMKIN

This very nice example of therapist responsibility from Edward does highlight an issue that Gestalt therapists often disagree about. My view is that I want the group setting to provide a place where people can expect safety and support, thus allowing them to risk opening deep wounds. Just as a surgical room must be kept scrupulously clean, so must a vulnerable patient be provided protection, and I am willing to do this, preferably in a way that allows both attacker and attacked to deal with issues that underlie the conflict.

In response to this incident, I would have stepped in after the comments got underway, saying that W was taking another risk in confronting M, possibly because she didn't like anybody (including herself) being timid and fearful these days. Then I'd have said to M that I'd like his getting angry at someone who sounded like she were criticizing his way of doing business. But maybe there was some extra anger because his topdog had been yelling at him overtime lately and he didn't want anyone else chiming in. To be sure, it feels better to fuss at someone else rather than oneself. Then I'd suggest that each of them sit back and decide if they wanted to do some topdog-underdog confrontation with themselves after the rest of the group had checked in. After that, maybe they'd be ready to get back to dealing with each other.

At least in retrospect, having had plenty of time to reflect, that's how I'd have liked to have done it. Had I been sitting on the firing line with Edward, I'd have been satisfied to have done as good a job of separation and protection as he did.

JOEN FAGAN

Recently I was on the client side of this issue in a Gestalt Therapy group. I felt left, unprotected, vulnerable, dropped! I had expressed a feeling strongly and strong feelings had been expressed to me in return. There we both were, retreating and stuck in a Mexican "stand off." We didn't know what to do. What were the others in the group feeling and thinking? In fact, where were they? Faces stared off into space, some with blank expressions, other in terror and pain. And more important, where was the group leader? Why wasn't he interacting with us—helping us to sort out the pieces; helping us to confront ourselves and our projections;

eliciting group involvement? He was not there for us! Does it really matter why? A group norm was being set: This was not a safe place. A protective boundary was not being established and without it there would be no group unity and only limited taking of risk.

KATHRYN P. VAN DER HEIDEN

The incident reported by Dr. Smith is an interesting one for me and raises several issues including the one of responsibility. First of all, the group activity seemed routinized with the "check-in" and then members working. It wasn't clear to me what the therapist does during check-in time, what responsibility does he feel for "working" with material that surfaces at that time? This part of the group sounded dull to me and I wasn't surprised to read that members were asking that check-in time be cut short in order to give more time for working. In the incident, I would have commented to M that he said he didn't want to work and was bringing up several issues, would he be interested in working on them?

The therapist in this incident seemed paternal and to look upon responsibility as protection. My experience with patients who say they are feeling vulnerable is that it has been helpful to explore how they experience that feeling. Frequently, the actual feeling is one of excitement, while in their heads they are predicting dire consequences. At least I want to explore what feeling vulnerable means for each person who experiences it.

I believe it is my responsibility to assist patients in becoming aware that they have and are making choices. Also, I have found that the vulnerable patient is not necessarily fragile and I do not have to be gentle with them. The woman in this incident, W, started out by saying she was feeling vulnerable and asked to sit by the therapist; before long she is confronting M. Wow! She doesn't sound vulnerable to me. I would have explored this more, probably asking her to move away from me to experiment with her own support system. With M I would ask him what he was hearing specifically that made him angry. I would ask him to speak directly to W in a contactful way, not to rave.

Fritz Perls used to equate responsible with response-able or ability to respond. Both M and W seem able to respond. Had I been the therapist in the incident I would want to be able to respond in a way that would engage M and W in a contactful encounter leading to closure.

ROBERT L. HARMAN

END COMMENT

I want to elaborate further on a couple of points. One of the important "gate-keeping" functions of the group leader is to keep the members of the group current on the operating procedures of the group. Evidently the group in this incident had changed what had been a behavioral contract, taking a lot of time to check in, and had decided in M's absence to focus this ritual toward more brevity. Was he thus "set up" for the confrontation that came by not knowing the new contract? A protective function of leadership would be to let M know that new agreements were in effect.

My other concern picks up at a point prior to the intervention. It has to do with the clinical judgment that "protection" was needed. When are clients really vulnerable and when are they presenting themselves that way as a form of manipulation? We are not given enough of the action to know for sure, but was protection really needed in this situation? I agree with Bob Harman that neither M or W sound *that* vulnerable to me. Turning the Gestalt spotlight on ourselves, I am aware that sometimes what I construe (clients are not the only ones who project!) as a "need for protection" is the shadow side of my need to be in control, to not "let things get out of hand." When am I projecting my own need to curb the intensity of the interaction and protect *myself* from my own anxiety and when is there a real need for protection? The issue is often not that clear. I need to check my own processes in those moments and the group, as suggested by Joseph Zinker, may be a good resource with that. If I jump in to give too much protection, if I assume too much responsibility in that direction, then I may communicate to clients that they are incapable of dealing with bumps and bangs, the false accusations, the unfair dealings of the world with them. If I cut off the action too quickly, I may teach that anger is always the destructive experience which most of us were taught, that they are too fragile to stand toe to toe and irrationally yell it out, that a way cannot be found *through* the storm to that quiet place of resolution. If I protect too much, then the illusion is supported that a "good Daddy" is needed to make things right and I inadvertently support core dependency needs.

How do I determine the moment to "stay out of it," even when the interaction feels painful for them and me, and when do I "jump in," making the decision that the immediate hurt outweighs the potential good? I check inside me, with the energy and responses of the group, with what I know about the protagonists, recognize I will make mistakes, and go with my felt response.

G.E.C.

Chapter 35

A Voice from the Past: Gestalt Dreamwork with Jim Simkin

ROBERT L. HARMAN

Jim Simkin died in 1984. He was a long-time member of the American Academy of Psychotherapists. An internationally known Gestalt therapist, he was regarded by many as a master therapist. He was unerringly accurate in zeroing in on a person's characterological traits and themes. For many years he had confined his practice to training therapists in Gestalt therapy. Many therapists who encountered Jim during weeks or months of training at his home in Big Sur found that their lives were irrevocably changed as a result. I find that I am still changing. That is what this story is all about.

THE DREAM

What caused me on this morning in February, 1987, to notice the cassette tape on my bedroom shelf? I must have glanced at it hundreds of times during the past 2 years without any conscious thoughts. This morning I decided to take it with me to my office so that I could store it with other tapes I save. Was it fate, a coincidence, or, as my Ericksonian friend says,

"Jim continues to work with you through your unconscious." At any rate, I brought the tape labeled by me as, "Simkin, definition of contact, work on my dream, 1/16/75," to my office. Presently I am editing a book on Gestalt-therapy theory, so I decided to listen to the first part of the tape. But I'm getting ahead of myself, I need to take the reader back to January, 1975.

At that time I was in my second month of Gestalt therapy training with Jim Simkin. I had contracted for an apprenticeship kind of month, opting to skip Jim's traditional month-long training workshop with seven trainees. My daily routine consisted of a therapy session, a tutorial/teaching session and an occasional group session, all led by Jim. During my free time I chatted with Jim, visited with the rest of the Simkin family, played a spirited game of hearts, soaked in the hot tub, read, or hiked the Big Sur trails. It was truly a wonderful month for me.

Jim felt good the entire month. He was verbal, sharing, and warm to me. We spent time informally talking about his days in training, and he shared with me what he called his "historical file" which included postcards from Fritz Perls and brochures announcing training workshops by the New York Institute dating back to the '50s. It was during this month that Jim and I developed a closeness that lasted until his death in 1986 (my Ericksonian friend says we are still close).

I left Lexington, Kentucky, early that month suffering from prostatitis and an unpleasant relationship with my wife. She had not wanted me to go for that month; we had fought about it and were strained and tense with each other. For example, when I called home from Big Sur she refused to talk to me, telling my son to tell me that she had nothing to say to me (10 years later we were divorced and I have remarried). I was also struggling some over my relationship with my father, who was chronically ill and had become addicted to prescription drugs. I had been working on these issues and others during my individual sessions and in group whenever we had one. This is background information for what was going on with me that month.

The morning of January 16, 1975, I tape-recorded my session with Jim. The first part of the session we discussed the Gestalt concept of contact; the second part of the session I worked on my dream with Jim. It is this tape that I decided to bring to my office, slightly over 12 years after the taping. I had a cancellation the very day I brought it to my office. During the time I would have been seeing a patient I decided to listen to the theory part of the tape, thinking it might relate some way to the book I am editing. That portion of the tape was interesting; when it ended I heard my voice on the tape ask Jim to work on a dream with me. For fun, I thought, I decided now to go ahead and listen to that part of the tape as well. It is this dreamwork that I present here.

Bob: I would like to work on a dream that I had last night.

Jim: You were saying something about having an upset stomach or something like that.

B: Yesterday morning I had a stomachache until lunchtime. This morning I felt OK, I didn't eat as much for breakfast. I had some anxiety yesterday; I wasn't in touch with where it was coming from.

J: The dream was last night, as far as you know were there any dreams the night before?

B: O yes, gobs of dreams the night before. I didn't have the upset stomach when I got up, it was after I ate breakfast.

J: OK.

B: In this dream I am going to the post office. Only the post office has moved and to get my mail, as everyone has to do, I have to listen to a postal clerk give a commercial on some kind of powdered laundry or dishwashing detergent. I have to stand in line and they have big blue bags, plastic bags of this detergent, and I'm thinking as I stand in line, "This is weird, these people doing a commercial." When I get to the counter I'm waited on by a short, stocky lady with glasses who gives me my mail. I say to her, "I really resent having to put up with this commercial to get my mail." She gives no response and I say louder, "God damn it, I really resent having to do this and hear this commercial to get my mail." She says nothing and as I turn to go out, I hear someone in line say to someone else, "Can you imagine that guy in a social group?" I turn back *very* angry. I'm not sure what I say, I may swear at her, than I say, "I'm in social groups all the time, it is just that I am angry at having to do this." Then I ask the people in line for their names and addresses, they wonder what I want them for and I say, "I just might file suit against this woman." One guy says he doesn't want to get involved, nevertheless, he writes down his name and gives it to me. That portion of the dream ends and I take my mail and leave.

Outside I remember that I have left a big, flat package on the counter. When I go back in, the counter has grown high or I have shrunk, I'm not sure which, I have to reach up to get my package and I'm worried about it or some other packages falling on me. Nothing happens and I go out thinking everyone is looking at me and I don't give a shit. I go out and there is a footbridge of some kind to cross to get out of the Post Office. It is a weird footbridge in that it looks OK and then there is another deck to walk on that is built about 3 feet above where one would normally walk. So you have to walk to that and take a step, a very high step, to get up. I awaken at that point. So that's it.

J: There is one message which repeats in your dream and that is the high step or the high counter, where you have to reach up and there is some danger. Where you have to take a high step there is some potential danger.

B: Right.

J: And that is twice. Start by being the blue bag of detergent.

B: I'm a blue bag of detergent. I can be used for laundry or dishes. I'm a blue plastic bag and my insides are a white powder and I'm at the Post Office. People have to be told about me, about my cleansing power in order to get their mail. If they don't listen, they don't get their letters, their goodies—I'm associating now with cocaine which I read about last night before I went to sleep. That's what I look like. I'm not cocaine, I'm a cleanser. I could clean up dirty mail. I don't have a name, this is weird, the postal people are giving testimonials about me and I don't have a name or a label. Bob out there doesn't know for sure what I'm for.

J: So the essential quality of you is that you cleanse and you're not labeled.

B: Yes.

J: Now can you get in touch with any part of you which cleanses, cleans up messes, and you don't have an adequate name or label for you?

B: The mess I'm thinking of is cleaning up with my wife and me.

J: My hunch is that it has more to do with your father. The last thing you do is to associate your cleaning up with is to have read something about cocaine. It is more apt to be related to being hooked on drugs or something than with your wife. I would imagine it is more in that direction and that is what you may be cleaning up.

B: I'm having an "Aha!" When my father was ill this fall and had surgery he became very angry that I didn't come home, he wrote me a disowning type of letter. I spent some time cleaning up that mess, explaining to my father that my brother hadn't informed me of the surgery until almost a week later.

J: How did you clean up the mess?

B: I wrote him and told him that I didn't know about his surgery until after it happened. I just told him what had gone on. He wrote back that he understood.

J: Now be the stocky lady at the counter in your dream.

B: I'm a postal clerk, people have to come to me to get their mail and this guy behind me talks to them about this detergent. We don't do very much talking, we give out the mail and people tolerate us, except for Bob who makes a commotion. I have difficulty imagining him related to other people the way he is here; he is angry, not making sense, now he is talking about a lawsuit. I have some size this way (sideways), I'm not very tall, if people just stay in line and not make much of a hassle I'll give what they want.

J: That's another message that repeats itself, in one part of your dream you get smaller one way and in another part you are also smaller and wider. Can you identify with being smaller than you are, shorter than you are, thicker than you are?

B: I'm not really in touch with anything. . . . Yeah, some of my products, some of my writing—you have told me this and an editor has told me this—some of it may lack depth. Perhaps there is some knowledge part of me that is like that. Are you hunching on to something else?

J: Well, the hunch that I have has to do with the other meaning of small, which is being petty. You talk about a lawsuit; I was imagining that there is a part of you that is litigious, petty, maybe stubborn.

B: Stubborn, no doubt about that! I'm not recalling pettiness, stubborn to the point of many times sticking with something I could well let go of.

J: Be the package that is left and you retrieve with some effort.

B: I'm a flat package, brown wrap, sort of like a record package, though I'm thicker. I could contain a book though I'm much wider than most books, I could contain reprints. I'm heavy. From the high counter, if Bob didn't get a firm grip on me I could conk him on the head. I wouldn't damage him severely, but I am heavy. Jim, I'm getting in touch again with this squashed, flat feeling. I'm flattened out, I'm squashed.

J: What do you do to squash yourself, to flatten yourself? What stands out for you as a way of keeping yourself down or keeping yourself squashed?

B: Self-torture perhaps.

J: Also, you are apologetic. If your wife blows or something, you listen and you are apologetic. If you father blows, you explain or you are apologetic. I have rarely seen you take a stand where you are angry even though you don't have a right to. You are seldom arbitrary. You take a lot of unnecessary crap perhaps, like listening to a commercial you have no interest in. Part of you resents being the way you are and blows, part says this guy couldn't get along very well in social groups. You're not fully accepting of your right to be angry without some good rationale.

B: That seems a key sentence for me, I need a good rationale.

J: The one thing you avoid like anything is being arbitrary or irrational.

B: Arbitrary yes, irrational I don't know. Anger I avoid if I don't have a reason.

J: Or if you can't come up with a reason.

B: I'm saying to myself: Is this bad? Is this something I want to stop? This is how I am. I'm not sure I want to change.

J: Yeah, you're having a dream where this is the only place your anger can come out. It doesn't usually come out or isn't allowed out when you are awake, when you are in charge, and you allow yourself to be angry only after you get your goodies. You go through all this shit, you listen, and so forth, then you get angry. Then this part of you says this guy doesn't belong in a social situation. Then there is gossip and you get even angrier, become litigious. Sounds like there is a conflict there. That you're not completely satisfied even though you may say rationally, it's OK not to be angry. At some level you don't fully accept it or believe it.

B: I'm recalling some incidents of being angry and not saying much directly, pretending as if they were no big deal. I probably appeared grumpy and didn't say much. We've touched on this before and in some way I want to deny.

J: You keep convincing yourself that this is no big deal, nothing to get annoyed about. I'm obviously annoyed and I ought not to be, it will blow over. This denial of "I'm an angry guy," either results in eventually ulcers or migraines, or a heart attack. The retroflection becomes implosive and you wind up with some kind of somatic problem. Or, you become potentially dangerous, so when you blow, you blow sky high. Some of your anger gets out a teensy bit and people see you as looking angry or irritated. What you experience in some of this, in dreams you can experience your irritation or anger. You become aware of your hanging on, your stubbornness; and you are also aware of consciously that you are irritated, annoyed and "it's no big deal." Or some sloughing off, I don't know if there is enough of a safety valve there that you can get rid of without injuring yourself or others. So that the affect that does build gets retroflected, stored, and then an explosion. You don't need a safety valve with your kids; you do need a safety valve with your father, your wife, and your boss. The part of you that is the underling, that waits on you, that controls; the part of you that wants some goodies is very irritated with the clerk part that controls you.

B: This all fits and what I don't experience are the symptoms that I think would come from retroflection. I don't have many complaints.

J: Well, you have a little touch here and there, such as a stomachache, prostatitis, nothing tremendous. Maybe just reminders that you are doing a number on yourself. Not so blatant or damaging as an ulcer and it does give you an appearance of an angry person. The prostatitis may be a way of getting back at somebody. If you look angry, you're sending a message; if you have some irritation, can't or won't function or perform, there is a message there. It is not a very heavy message. What I believe is this lack of breadth, not being willing/able to go into depth in something, is also characteristic. Whether that is good or bad is another issue, it goes with a projection/denial way of being in the world. It goes with a little bit of the Pollyanna stuff. It may or may not be suitable. I don't believe you question too much, nor would you have too much in the way of dreams which are conflictual if this wasn't a problem for you. There may be more depth to you than you are allowing and so you may be getting a message in your dream. There is certainly more depth to you than squatness, part of you that has you by the balls controls you; on the surface you stand in line, part of you is not that malleable or that allowing. I would begin to see other ways of resolving the conflict other than being flexible and pleasant and then blaming at the end. You can get your mail without going through this number. One of the things you pride yourself on is that you are different, you don't go through some numbers to get promoted. If they want to promote you, fine. Then again you may have a conflict about how different are you: Are you really different or is your difference a projection/denial number or a facade? It may be basically that you really don't care. Organismically, that is how you are, as opposed to role playing.

B: Yeah, what I want to do is find out! Does this fit for me, is this me or what? Am I role playing or not? I'm not sure I know how to find that out. I don't know how to experiment with this.

J: When you tell somebody "I'm not interested in what you have to tell me," as you did to this person in group the other night, he was persistent about telling you something and you dismissed him. Then you didn't feel guilty or have afterthoughts, then that is how you are. That is congruent with how you are. If you "dismiss" and then you worry about it later and wonder "did I hurt that guy" or if you have difficulty falling asleep, then you have been role playing "as if" you are dismissing. You may get some evidence that you aren't that disinterested. When you say to your wife, "no matter what you say I'm going to Big Sur," and then you are concerned/worried about how she is feeling, then you are role-playing being disinterested. The essence is can you let go and go on to whatever is next. When you find that you are letting go and you're not having dreams about it, worrying, developing symptoms, and so forth, then you probably have really dismissed. You have organismically finished. One thing you could do to experiment is to be deliberately arbitrary, to tempt the Gods and see what happens. Do you then get symptoms, have dreams, and so on.

B: Some things I have worked on here the past couple of weeks I have let go of, others I haven't.

J: Right, when you work on something and you let go, feel finished, then that is congruent for you. If you don't let go then it isn't congruent.

B: OK, I would like to stop here.

While listening to this tape I noticed how strong, clear, and lively Jim's voice sounded. It was almost as if he was in my office now, having this session today instead of 12 years ago. Other things that stood out for me technically were Jim's interpreting parts of my dream, which he clearly did at times, drawing on his knowledge of previous work that I had done. Toward the end of the session he was giving me "homework" or suggestions on how to experiment with some of my discoveries. Neither interpreting nor giving suggestions are strongly associated with Gestalt therapy. Yet they seemed a natural part of the session and to emerge from the session. My biggest surprise while listening to the tape was to discover that I am still struggling with some of these same issues *now!*

These themes came out for me during the session: (a) I rarely get angry without a good reason, (b) I avoid being arbitrary or irrational, (c) I allow myself to get angry after I get "goodies," and (d) I keep convincing myself that important things are "no big deal." It was the last point that hit home. Shit, I thought, I'm doing that now with my wife! After mulling this one over I reached that metaphoric point of ejaculatory inevitability, I could no longer contain myself so I called JoAnn (my wife).

I expressed to her that I wasn't feeling patient, that there is an issue in our relationship that I was passing off as no big deal, that I'll wait patiently until it changes. That was not true, it is a big deal and I want to discuss it tonight.

The final point of this story is that I did express my concern over this issue to my wife. I did this not to "make" her change in any way but for me to feel fully expressed, to be congruent as Jim called it. By allowing myself to make a big deal over something, I feel more vibrant in my marriage. Jim's voice from the past, as accurate today as it was 12 years ago, has made it possible for me to enrich my marriage.

"Awopbopaloobop, alopbamboom!
Tutti frutti, oh ruddi,
Tutti frutti, oh ruddi,
Tutti frutti, oh ruddi,
Tutti frutti, oh ruddi,
Tutti frutti, oh ruddi,
Awopbopaloobop, alopbamboom"
—*Little Richard, 1955*

"Lose your mind and come
    to your senses."
—*Fritz Perls, 1969*

Rick Gilbert

Oh, I wasn't
thinking of
jumping!

Figure 7. "Manipulation" (Ed.)

Part III
Gestalt Training

Martin Grotjahn

THE NARCISSISTIC FROG:
"But I do not want to be a prince!"

Figure 8.   "Beware of the helpers. . ." (Ed.)

Chapter 36

Notes on the Training of Gestalt Therapists

ERVING AND MIRIAM POLSTER

WHO COMES AND WHY

Gestalt therapy is rarely taught in depth in universities. This is due only partly to the system's traditional myopic infatuation with the proven. Gestalt therapists have not, until recently, been very articulate in describing what they actually do. They insisted that the doing was explanatory enough in itself. This did not make them attractive academic risks. Nor have they characteristically sought (or comfortably occupied) such structurally constricting positions as universities offer. All too frequently, alas, they have also been gratuitously obnoxious to people who don't swing into linguistic synchrony with them. So, most of the training and education of gestalt people takes place in extra-academic training centers where trainees come out of their own inner surge rather than educational fiat.

Through the charisma and extraordinary artistry of Fritz Perls in demonstrating his concepts transparently and quickly, and through his aphoristic slicing through verbal red tape, he almost single-handedly dramatized the simplicity and beauty of powerful present experience. This view resonated well with the existential momentum of our times and present experience; later, in the hands of other talented gestalt therapists, thus metamorphosed from a contemplative philosophical premise into visibly profound actuality.

Not surprisingly, therefore, gestalt therapy promises profound personal experiences both for the therapist and client. Furthermore, it leans into applications which transcend the traditional fact of psychotherapy. People come

225

to us for training from a broad human spectrum which radiates beyond the accustomed therapeutic triad of psychiatrist, psychologist and social worker. Professionals interested in affective education, in the humanization and productivity of organizations and in the accentuation of feelings of community life, as well as those newly welcomed into the confrontation with personal malaise—ministers, counselors, psychiatric nurses, etc., have discovered that interpersonal contact is a vital force in their work and are looking to gestalt therapy as one way of learning more about it. Even those who have never viewed themselves as more than only peripherally involved in human correctiveness; physicians, architects, lawyers, theatre directors, etc., are looking for ways to apply what we have to teach about human contact and expression in their own work.

Nevertheless, the greatest interest in training still arises from the healers who, at many levels of training and experience, want to move into a new stage of intensity and fascination where they depend less on professional assurances formulae, and rituals of competence and more on their own assessment of what is missing from the substance of their work. They seek, it seems to us, to work specifically with a certain teacher of a certain method to be *personally* taught and inspired. They welcome the impact that one human being can have on another, be he teacher or fellow trainee. Arriving together in postgraduate training programs, these people usually find new professional liveliness and discover, as a bonus to their search for the personal mentor, a mutuality among their colleagues which enlivens and adds spirit, unique applications and meanings to concepts which might otherwise seem very dry.

THE RHYTHM BETWEEN CONCEPT AND PRACTICE

Gestalt therapy, being action-oriented, has been vulnerable to an anti-intellectual bias. This is not hard to understand in view of our distrust of the proof-ridden, infertile influences which contaminate many educational experiences. Nevertheless, the gestalt counterforce has frequently been overreactive to these poisons with an insistence that no explanation was better than too much explanation. So, though the personal force of Fritz and others among us in workshops, movies, books and demonstrations has turned people on to gestalt therapy in vast numbers, there have been too few opportunities for solid grounding in the fundamentals of gestalt therapy. We believe that this is a lacuna which gestalt education must fill in order to express its full scope as a verbalistic system in which action and meaning reverberate in perpetually continuing interplay. We want concept to emerge organically from action, each development uniquely forming from a specific engagement between people, either in therapy or in a training program where gestalt therapy is being taught.

In our programs, therefore, formerly at the Gestalt Institute of Cleveland and now at the Gestalt Training Center—San Diego, we have explicitly accentuated the relationship between concept and practice. Lectures are not a dirty word for us, but they are short, pithy and frequently spiced with humor. Laughter doesn't obscure a point; often it makes it even clearer and lubricates what might otherwise be a lugubrious passage. This is also as true of therapy itself as it is of teaching.

We augment all our lectures with demonstrations of how the concept advances the therapy. For example, if we are discussing conditions at the contact boundary, we work with one of the trainees in front of the whole group and show where his personal contact boundary is and how this limits or enhances his possibilities for making contact. We also will create experiments which lead him to expand these boundaries. Suppose, for example, a person is compulsively modest and makes a boring story out of what was otherwise a lively adventure. He might be asked to notice himself on the verge of blushing as he tells of the experience. Then, through feeling the blush, he may discover his warm radiance instead of his expected painful embarrassment; he becomes more likely to move into pleasure-ridden contacts than he was before. Or in working with a warm and welcoming woman, we discover that she characteristically stops herself after taking only the initial step in an overture to someone else, and frequently winds up feeling disregarded. She practices making not just the first remark but also adding a second and lo! the follow-up gets her the response that she has been missing so far.

In our demonstrations, we may stop the action (when stopping is suitable, as it frequently is) to comment on the process and the underlying methodological considerations and to discuss alternative therapeutic possibilities. We also may teach how the experienced therapist is free to slough off the concept after assimilating it into his system of spontaneous reflexes. Or a student pair may work in front of the group, guided by one of the training faculty who offers suggestions about therapeutic choices from which he or she may move into doing what is stylistically right for him or her.

After the demonstration, the group divides into practice units of three people, one of whom will serve as therapist, one as patient and one as observer. Each person gets a turn at each position, the therapist practicing the demonstrated technique as far as the patient's actual need permits. The faculty rotate among the triads, supervising students. The therapist-trainee gets a chance to practice his craft, the patient-trainee works through issues of genuine personal concern, and the observer-trainee exercises his perceptiveness and sensitivity in giving instructional feedback. They all share their observations of how the therapist's actions enhanced the therapeutic process or interrupted it. Colleagueal teaching among the trainees is prodigious and the close relationship with faculty makes teaching an intimate and personally relevant experience.

PERSONAL GROWTH

Plenty of personal growth occurs as a result of our demonstrations and practicums, but we nevertheless also set aside another large part of our day for an actual therapy group where personal growth and the opportunity to be witness and participant within a gestalt group process are our primary purposes. We believe there is no reliable substitute for the therapist-trainee discovering patienthood firsthand and working through the many specific barriers which bind us all. Thus, the impassiveness of one of our group members, the arrogance of another, the brooding physical strength of still another all intrude upon or distort their interaction with others and are crucial to their professional as well as their personal development. When one of them can discover, as he experiences his impassiveness, for example, that it grows in volume and intensity until at last he explodes into the realization that he can't bear to be hurt again by his love for other people, he can then explore his chances to experience this love safely and, if the experience ends happily, he increases his own sensibility to his patients as well as other people in his life. To multiply descriptions of this phenomenon in group therapy would be to belabor what is already well known, namely that therapy expands the boundaries of people's customary behaviors and feelings. The therapist must include within his scope as a human being a very wide range of such behaviors and feelings if he or she is to transcend the position of mechanistic technician. Studying about Africa, or any other unfamiliar territory, is not the same as visiting there to say nothing of living there for a time.

In some training programs in gestalt therapy, the main force of training *is* personal therapy. We do not go this route but we do agree that it is a crucial part of a global training.

PEER LEARNING

The opportunity for trainees to learn from each other pervades any good training environment. It is often overlooked that one learns not only from teachers, but from one's fellows, particularly when they communicate that chunk of their own experience which no one else could duplicate. When we were in training we had some of the great teachers of our era, including Fritz Perls, Paul Goodman, Paul Weisz, Isadore From and Laura Perls. Nevertheless, our own personal experiences, though mightily shaped by these teachers, were also affected by our peers whose characteristics demanded not only our coping with them but also encompassing their natures. Our relationships were forged out of and included interactions with people of vivacity, magnificent bodily movement, paranoia, rollicking humor, business acumen, grandiosity, mendacity, all of which were far better represented in the shadings of our colleagues than by even the great teachers to whom we were privy.

One of us, Erv, still remembers how he learned from a fellow trainee to move his pelvis while dancing, or his first close relationship with a homosexual man or his being confronted for the first time with his innocence in office and money matters or his introduction to unfamiliar literature. Such mutual therapy continuing day to day was lush compared with the occasional contacts with our leaders.

So also among our trainees; they stimulate each other, instruct each other, inspire each other, challenge each other, recognize each other, support each other. This happens naturally just living together. It also happens in the practice triads where our trainees, who are often brilliantly sensitive, mutually affect each others' work with direct commentary. We also encourage this colleagueal effect in the demonstrations when we stop the action at various points, asking such questions as, "What would you do now?" "What are you perceiving?" "What theme do you identify?" "What experiment might you set up at this point?" These and comparable questions always elicit a whole range of responses, most of which are right on target, all of which show a different slant, an individual perspective which is the unique interaction between each trainee and the so-called patient.

FUNCTIONS OF THE TEACHER

Ideally, the training and education of a psychotherapist forms where there is maximum opportunity for personal expressiveness and interaction and where there is time to allow a repertoire of personal style and relationship to ripen and enhance what is being learned. In a sense, what we try to teach, (ignoring obvious exceptions for the moment), is that everybody is right. Not in the usual sense of "right" but only in the sense of whether, given what the therapist-trainee has said or done, he or she can find the consequent way, the harmonious next step, following through, moving from one moment to the next in a natural drama where personal expression culminates in completion and meaning. If one person wants her patient to speak to his father in the "empty chair," another says to exaggerate speaking as you are, with tightened jaw, and another says try growling like a lion, they may each be "right" just as long as they follow the natural line of expression which develops as the instructions or interactions continue. All roads lead to where the patient needs to go, if you follow him faithfully. We try to teach the sensitivity for following each road in its own valid direction.

The same is true for the validity of the teacher. His own style communicates in ways that go beyond the teaching of specific techniques. If the teacher is a clown and can combine humor with pathos, the student may discover that humor and pathos are mutually lubricating aspects of the same world. If the teacher is a provocateur, the student may experience the power of an invitation into novelty—part challenge, part support—where by beginning to growl, snarl, claw at each other and circle each other warily like a pair of felines, therapist and trainee may move from a sense of inalienable distance into a union between previously disparate beings. If the teacher is transparent and able clearly to articulate what he experiences either in himself or in the trainee, the student is moved to let her own reverberations guide her in her work. She becomes less concerned with maintaining distance and prior habits than with adding her own voice, whatever it may be, to the therapy. The functions of the teacher are limitless; he or she may cajole, inform, tease, confront, entertain, guide, berate, consult, advise, hearten, challenge, shape. . .

The teacher also must have inspirational powers and skill which, through his craftsmanship, show the student the magnificence of the craft itself. The student, aroused by knowing that such profound experiences are possible, becomes motivated to risk, to invent, to be absorbed into a process where he practices not only routinely but with his own sense of interpersonal journey. The teacher simply shows the student what is possible. The student, beginning from here, takes this sense of what is possible and combines it, reworks it into a sense of what is possible *for him or for her.*

EXTENSIVE OR INTENSIVE TRAINING

In the anarchical orientation which has infused the gestalt training process (not hard to understand when you remember that one of our mentors was Paul Goodman), the extent and style of training has ranged from sudden weekend revelations followed by more or less sporadic weekend infusions thereafter, to three or more years of structured training and on up to ten or more years of professional and personal devotions. These choices are dictated by more than caprice; often they represent the most practical way of getting as much training as possible given considerations of time, money, geography and available leadership.

The more we came to recognize the shortcomings in such catch-as-catch-can training, the more we moved into actual training designs. Currently there are two major forms into which such training programs have evolved. For people living in the local community where there is a resident training center, an extensive program of training has been devised. Here, trainees attend frequent sessions, usually weekly, for an extended period of time, possibly two or three years. In contrast to this, for out-of-towners, there is the intensive training program of briefer duration, lasting one or two months, occasionally longer. Each of these training structures has advantages and disadvantages.

In the extensive training program, time itself is a growth factor. What has been learned, both in the didactic and experiential sessions, can be assimilated slowly in the intervals between meetings. There is also richer opportunity to try out what has been learned in one's actual work setting and an opportunity for consultation about the results of these try-outs. Often the program of the training center itself may offer opportunities for co-leadership with senior staff in weekend workshops of on-going groups, where supervision is a part of the experience. In addition, the fact that all the trainees live in the same general community maximizes the chance of building a supportive network of colleagues who can serve both as resources and consultants. Still further, individual therapy with a member of the training faculty becomes viable as a training adjunct.

There are also some disadvantages in the extensive approach to training. One is that an evening meeting after a hard day at one's "real" work (which is the customary scheduling) can be over-ridden by residues of practical day-to-day concerns. In some ways it is like taking a night-school course; one may indeed learn a lot, but it is a far cry from the total immersion of full-time enrollment. The buildup of momentum has to recur at every session, making up for the weekly recess. Also, a not unimportant factor is the dependency on the limited number of local training faculty whose skills and styles may or may not be commensurate with the needs of a specific trainee. One way of ameliorating this limitation is to invite visiting trainers to supplement the local staff by giving workshops during the training year. Finally, a well-established training center may train individuals who want to become senior staff and themselves train others, but there may be only limited opportunity to admit new faculty, and they are then left to their own devices in a location where there is already a solid training program in gestalt therapy.

The intensive program, on the other hand, is a full-time engagement even if only for a limited period. Being away from one's working world assures minimal distraction and a high level of fascination with both the training program and one's colleagues. It is the only game in town, and it infects trainees with a zest to learn all they can while they're there. There is also a heightened sense of diversity and novelty among one's colleagues, often accentuated by the fact that they have come from scattered places; Africa, Utah, Australia, Germany, Vermont, New York, the Netherlands, California; with all the cultural reverberations this sets off. A new community is built. The momentum of its creation is like all birth and excites and vibrates through the whole training period. This can, however, turn into one of the sadnesses of the intensive program when, at the close of the program, this community disintegrates, like a nomadic tribe, and each person is faced with applying what he or she has learned in what may be an unreceptive or unsupportive home base, deprived of the nourishment which fellow students might provide. It is frequently important to include the issue of re-entry into one's local community as a part of the training experience.

Also, the pace of the intensive program may be so rich as to make assimilation not only exciting but also painful. Dividing the intensive program into two or more units, separated by an interval of time, say six months or a year, can be helpful in fostering a sense of continuity and an opportunity for renewal and the ripening of understanding and familiarity. In addition, the development of homework, something to be focused on between sessions, can tie together the person's experience between what he has learned in the training program and his experience in his own work and community. For example Jean may decide to focus on the surface of the interaction between herself and patient without her previous attempts to analyze or diagnose what is happening, Ted may try to use his own awareness more in his therapeutic action, or George may follow up a new use of the metaphor, right on for his style, but not yet fully assimilated. With the faculty, a trainee can identify ways of practicing these new modes and figure out how to communicate this experimentation to a faculty mentor in the interval between training units. When he or she returns for the follow-up period, it will be at a new level of skillful functioning.

CONCLUSION

Though we believe in a structured and orderly progression in teaching basic principles of gestalt therapy, we are not in love with schedule and frequently take soundings to see where our trainees are and what their current needs may be. We often start the session by asking what unfinished business there is, if any, from the previous day's work. We can easily set aside the schedule and deal first with what is figural at that moment. When that is completed, we are ready to pick up what has been put aside.

Basic to this freedom to respond to the present moment is a respect for the starting point from which each individual participates in the program and a wish to attend carefully to his movement through the program, not taking it for granted like an eight-day clock, which once properly wound up and set going is supposed to keep ticking along without a hitch.

It is also deeply important to us to honor the unique individual style of each trainee. We have often heard how much variety people find in the different gestalt therapists they have observed. This is not accident. Our belief is that gestalt therapy offers a range of techniques and therapeutic possibilities from which a practitioner can compose a repertoire of methodological approaches that harmonize with his talents and his values. We try to stretch the range of what is therapeutically possible from him without trying to fit him into a mechanistic model where he can presumably work as easily with the hot seat, say, as he can with dreams. No one can do everything equally well. The object of our training is to accept what a person knows he can do well and show him how to do it better and to discover what he can do well that he may not yet know about and help him to do that, too.

What we are saying is that the training and education of a gestalt therapist must be compatible with what we believe to be the best elements in gestalt therapy itself. It has to be humane and responsive in and of the present moment rather than being distracted by futuristic concerns. It has to call forth the most sensitive and responsive contact between the human who is doing the teaching and the human who is doing the learning. When things are going very well indeed in a training program, sometimes it is hard to know which one is which.

Chapter 37

Bringing in the Wives

KALEN AND JESSICA HAMMANN

Τhe notion that a person must live continually two separate lives, in worlds often connected only by his own passage between them, ought to be a shocking one to anyone whose picture of ideal human functioning includes the idea that it be integrated or "all of a piece." Yet the assumption that one's "work" or "professional life" must be separate from one's "personal life" so permeates our society that most of us accept it without question. "A man's home is his castle," from which he sallies forth to do battle with whatever dragons he has chosen, and to which he then returns—a castle inhabited by others who know little or nothing of his battles except from the stories he tells. Strangely, the coming of "Women's Lib" hasn't changed this much. The usual picture of the "egalitarian marriage" has *two* people sallying forth instead of one, but the "personal life" both return to share generally has little to do with the workaday activities of either. If a person finds his work an unpleasant, painful chore, this separation can at least help him forget the unpleasantness during his hours of re-creation. If, however, his work is a center of meaning in his life and an arena for his growth, the separation brings fragmentation and the kind of pain evident in the letter which gave rise to this issue of *Voices.* *

We'd like to tell you about an attempt we've been making to counter some of this separation between the personal and the professional in our lives. It seems to us that while it has many roots, the separation is perhaps

---

* Anonymous. Alienation of Affection: A Wife's View of the American Academy of Psychotherapists, *Voices*, Vol. 6, No. 3, Winter 1970.

234

most strongly fostered by the kinds of training most jobs require. When someone is trained to be a dentist, it never occurs to anybody that his training amounts to more than a set of specialized skills. As a result, it never occurs to anyone that the aspiring dentist's spouse would benefit—unless she, too, wished to become a dentist or perhaps her husband's dental technician—from going through some of the training with him. As a result, once he's had the training the dentist finds he can't really talk with his spouse in any meaningful way about what he does at work: without the training she truly "wouldn't understand." And though many believe that being an effective psychotherapist requires a person to draw on all that he is, and that growth as a therapist therefore must involve growth as a total human being, training to be a therapist is still organized almost everywhere on the "specialized skills: only aspiring professionals need apply" model. The result is generally that therapists' personal lives are as separate from their professional lives as everyone else's; when they try to share the desolation of their uncertainties and the exhileration of their triumphs, they too find that their spouses often really don't know what they're talking about.

Since at that point we didn't know any better, when a group of us got together and arranged with a faculty from the Gestalt Institute of Cleveland for a program to train gestalt therapists in the Boston area, we set up the program the same old way. Although thirteen of the sixteen people selected for the program were married, there was only one couple in the group (us). And even though we both *were* "professionally" interested in Gestalt therapy, the Cleveland faculty were dubious enough about the wisdom of having us in the group *together* that we had a special extra interview to discuss it with them. After a little initial shuffling around, then, the group consisted of three single people, one married couple, and eleven married people without their spouses.

Despite the selection team's attempts at balance, the group also consisted of thirteen men and only three women (a single woman, Jessica and another married woman.) (Indeed, part of that "initial shuffling" included the addition of one woman to an original group of thirteen men and two women!) Perhaps in part for that reason, many of the group's first meetings were stormy ones, in which recurrent battles among the men played a dominant part. Whether because they missed the moderating nurturant influence of women in general, because they preferred a more even sex balance for other reasons, or simply because our being there provided an example that led them to think of the possibility, a number of different people began saying things like, "You know, I really envy the two of you being able to go through this training together." "I wish I could share this experience with my wife the way you're sharing it with each other."

To understand what happened next, you need to know something about the way our training program is organized. About once a month, and for extended periods in the summer, we meet for an intensive workshop with training faculty from Cleveland (or, occasionally, elsewhere). Between those workshops, we meet Thursday evenings to handle whatever business we need to do and to consolidate what we've learned in the workshops. Pretty soon we were discussing the idea of having any spouses who wished to come to the Thursday night sessions, not just to "socialize," as had happened once already, but to participate with us as we "worked" with what we'd learned. In favor of the idea were those who argued that what we were doing would, in itself, be beneficial to anybody and they'd like to share it with their wives;[*] that they were changing in ways their wives found difficult to understand or to deal with and they'd like their wives to be a closer part of that change process; that studies show there's less hostility and tension in groups of men and women subjected to crowded conditions than in groups of all men; that what was already a good experience for them would be much enriched for them if their wives could be there with them; that they found it increasingly hard to separate who they were as therapists from who they were as husbands, and hence the distinction built into our group seemed artificial; that they felt sympathetic to their wives' unhappiness at being excluded from something so important to their husbands; that having the wives more actively involved would help our group move in the direction of a mutually supportive community; and probably more we don't remember. Those against adding spouses argued that the group was already so big that some of us participated very little; that at this point in their marriage they were just achieving a somewhat precarious autonomy and ability to more be separate from their spouses which the proposed change might undermine; that when marital difficulties loomed large it was important to have a supportive group as a haven which did *not* include their spouse; that increasing the size of the group would mean watering down training, or at least less chance to "practice," for those of us in the original group; and probably more. Intriguingly enough, we don't remember anyone arguing that the training was so specialized that it would be irrelevant to the spouses.

We finally decided to try it, at first on a temporary basis and then, encouraged by how well it seemed to be working, as a regular part of the structure of our program. We found that by dividing up into two or more groups, with different composition each time, we could solve most of the problems associated with increasing the size of our groups, as well as give

---

[*] The only married woman in the group (besides Jessica) was opposed to the idea of having spouses present at our working sessions.

people the option of working with their spouses or sharing the general experience but working in separate groups. Not all the spouses came, nor did everyone attending come every week, so we were able to discover that even intermittent attendance by the spouses wasn't disruptive to our training. And most of the benefits we'd hoped for were occurring.

Most of the benefits, but not all. From the beginning the workshops with Cleveland faculty in general had been much more intense and growth-filled experiences than the Thursday night "consolidation sessions." For many, excluding the wives from those workshops meant that the most exciting sharing they'd hoped for was not taking place. Accordingly, we began talking about the possibility of including the wives in the workshops too. Special meetings were held to discuss the idea; telephone calls were made (to Cleveland); eloquent letters were written. We decided to try it, at a ten-day workshop scheduled for the end of August (1971). We figured that with the exra time and with the two senior staff members from Cleveland who were already planning to be there (instead of the one staff member and one trainee who'd worked with us on the weekend workshops) we'd have the best chance of dealing successfully with whatever problems the change created.

The problems we'd feared simply failed to appear; the workshop was a huge success. For many, it was the most exciting, fruitful combination of personal and professional growth they'd every experienced. The workshop design suggested by the Cleveland faculty deserves some of the credit, for it provided a fine blend of varied activities, groupings, and formats. We began each day with a meeting of the whole group for a lecture-and-demonstration on some aspect of gestalt therapy by the Cleveland faculty. We then met in groups of three (whose makeup varied every day) for "practicum," attempting to use what we'd just learned as we alternated between the roles of "therapist," "patient," ("therapee??"), and observer. In the afternoon we met in two groups (whose membership stayed the same throughout the workshop), each meeting with a faculty member from Cleveland (and one joined in addition by a recent graduate of Cleveland's training program) for therapy sessions with no preset agenda. Some of the seven wives who joined us seemed quite comfortable—and were quite active—from the beginning. Others seemed to find the leaders' and members' attempts to "make space for them" to come in if they wished, helpful. Many felt awkward at first playing the role of therapist in the practicum sessions (and some found it easier to do so if they could use the observer as a "consultant"), but by the end all were doing so with considerable aplomb and often with great effectiveness. As the workshop closed, many of us expressed the deep satisfaction we felt, on many levels, with the experiences we'd shared.

It seems to us that our experience suggests a number of potentially useful conclusions, at both a specific and a general level:

1. It seems clear (contrary to the assumption usually made, at least implicitly) that a training program can be joined "in midstream" by a large number of new people—even people with past issues and outside relationships with the original group members—without disaster.

2. We now know, if we didn't before, that many people do feel excluded from their spouses' training programs and would like to participate in that training. Perhaps most crucial, we now know that many spouses can participate in such training programs in ways that not only do not disrupt or dilute the training but rather actually enhance it.

3. We've learned that couples can be in such a training program without couple issues taking center stage very often: individuals can still work as individuals even with their spouses present and sharing in what's going on. And professional development can remain the major focus of that work. At the same time, we've found that the continuity and involvement of a group like this can provide great support and a rich opportunity for work on couple issues when these arise.

4. Not all spouses do want to participate in such a training program —or want to participate in the same ways. (For example, in the afternoon groups in our 10-day workshop some people were in the same group with their spouses and some were in different groups. Both seemed to benefit.) And it's not necessary that all do participate in the same ways for the addition of spouses to such a program to "work."

5. In making a change like the one we've made, it's apparently helpful and may be necessary for success to talk about the issues involved, to plan a workable design for working with the new, larger group and to do some specific "gatekeeping" (spacemaking) for the new members.

At a more general level, our experience suggests that at least for therapists the currently widespread pattern of separation between professional and personal life, with its attendant tensions, may not be necessary or even desirable. While none of the wives has begun doing therapy herself, a kind of sharing of husbands' professional life and professional development is occurring which was impossible for many before. And the fact of this sharing opens up the possibility that if they wish to spouses can become powerfully helpful resources in each others' professional work.

"*If they wish to . . .*" Our experience seems to substantiate the notion that no one model is best for everyone. For while many members of our group pushed for and welcomed the addition of their wives to the group, others continued to feel that for them it was most satisfying and growthful to have husband and wife keep their professional lives separate. Our experience, then, does not imply a new prescription which all individuals— or all groups—"ought to" follow, but rather demonstrates the viability of an exciting new option, available to whoever finds it attractive.

Chapter 38

Teaching Therapy Through the Lives of the Masters: A Personal Statement

IRMA LEE SHEPHERD

I *doubt that psychotherapy can be taught,* even as being an artist or a teacher cannot be taught. There is, of course, learning involved, but this comes primarily from the process of apprenticeship. The single most important factor is the impact of the master and his personal skill in unlocking and releasing powers of personhood related to the creative process undertaken. While it is possible to teach the student specific techniques or responses without the power and authenticity of the person, these are transparently learned techniques artificially applied. It is a false belief that if I know how to "do therapy," then I am a therapist.

The long process of apprenticeship is primarily a relationship and a cumulative relationship that goes back through the master himself having been a student of another master and so on, transcending generations. (Accounts of Zen masters imply a pride in the genealogy of masters.) Part of the skill of being a therapist is bringing to bear in the specific moment, in a way that transcends time, the accumulated wisdom of experiences mediated from all those disciples where the central search has been for meaning, wholeness, relatedness, truth.

The beginning student therapist has access to his own person and his potential powers as a therapist in only a limited way and, also, only limited access to the person of his own teacher and supervisor. Initially, he does not have enough of a sense of his own personal impact in the process of therapy, or of the personal resources that can be brought to bear.

In training the beginning therapist, one way to assist him in gaining access to more personhood in a short span of time, offering the possibility of genuine assimilation of personal skills and confidence, is to have him become a "master therapist" through the study of biographical material. This assignment, given as part of the first therapy course, asks the student to discern from his reading the major events and happenings in the life of the master therapist that led to his choosing to become a therapist, and the particular developments in his approach that have resulted from his own person, values, and struggles.

The student makes a first person 30–50 minute presentation, with the other students interspersing questions and comments to the "distinguished visitor." After the first few presentations, heated exchanges occur, as Sullivan challenges Freud, or Ellis disagrees with Perls over issues of dynamics, procedures, ethics, etc. Occasionally, the guest may choose to demonstrate his skill, as the time Reich chose a hapless student and marked off in chalk various body zones, or when Perls chose to talk directly to his mother rather than gossip about her as he recalled his family.

Students report a high level of learning about masters with a minimal effort at memorization; which is to say, they report learning with pleasure. Those listening to presentations report acquiring a clearer understanding of the historical antecedents of schools of therapy. Most important, students evidence a clearer sense of themselves as therapists which allows them to begin work with patients with some confidence, recognizing that they are beginners; but then, the masters, too, were once beginners.

What I believe the master therapist or teacher does is to help the student release within himself his own powers of listening, perceiving, and being, in his own style and out of his own person as he touches the life of another. I believe the self-aware purposeful use of presence to be the single most powerful force in positive intervention in the life process of another. And I believe this to be true in any creative field, but most especially, in the work of psychotherapy.

Chapter 39

Undelivered Commencement Address

JAMES E. DUBLIN

Here at the Midwestern Psychotherapy Institute we have not been very formal, perhaps to a fault. I did not say anything to you when you finished the year-long Gestalt-training track. We had some fantastic psychotherapists in here, as guest faculty, and they, and I, taught you what could be taught in such a short time, and you were examined, and given a certificate. With those certificates, and the fare, you can get on the bus that runs to the airport. There, you can get on planes darting here and there, and really get trained. But you've got a start, and having said nothing formal, and realizing that I should have, here it is.

Take the path against the water running backwards. Stroke strongly against the current. Follow your will against the natural dragdown. At first, say nothing. Be silent and look into the darkness. Feel its uncertainty. Do not have intent or definition. Go with where it feels right, into the darkness. Before the explosion is the imploding, but before that, is the turning loose of all support to stand alone.

After the first long night, at first light, there is no assistance either. Stand quite still with your natural curiosity, and do not let those who will try take it away from you. Do not conform to the long white coat, or the short green one. If you do your job, they will not really fire you, though you may think they are going to. Walk alone at 3 a.m. beside the river or the railroad tracks and write a song. If it seems appropriate and you are not just showing off, sing it to the next one you see, patient, client or consumer. If s/he complains that you're not doing therapy, make him or her help you search for the hidden microphone until s/he laughs at himself or herself, even if the session runs over, or goes for half a day and someone else has to wait.

After the darkness comes the mist. Do not hurl yourself into the mist of phenothiazines, crippling labels, or the flow of money with your calendar filled and a waiting list. Look closely at the shapes in the mist. They are dark and shadowy, so sniff the air if you have to. It really is okay to have feelings and to model them. And beware of the yellow creature hiding deep in the mist in a three-piece suit, or otherwise uniformed for the day. Look at his sweatshirt, front and back. If the back says scientist-practitioner model, biological-nutritional model, weekend-breakthrough model, etcetera, have no truck with him. Know that being-with is not the same as reciprocal inhibition or systematic desensitization, and that neither of these, as long as the label lasts, is being there.

At the third juncture, go quickly to the baptismal, agnostic as you may be. Even if you are building a system and the journals are printing it, and even if it has a name which is different from any of the others, keep tuned to looking for the exception. Keep still. Keep some ethics going, but don't wash your own dishes every night. By now, you can always hire a part-time maid. Learn to paint, or draw, or dance if you can't, or carve useless things out of hard wood and set them about the window sills of your office, and when other professionals ask what you are doing, don't shrug your shoulders (that can be taken for indifference), but laugh. Get on the edge and be ready. When you find a match, strike it, for God's sake. Make a little noise, even if you get your fingers burned. Bring her into fourth or fifth and slam that hammer down. On the bad curves, watch the center line where the white light will come, eventually.

Now you're out of the mist. Now it's day and night. Be there. Don't be too tough, like Fritz Perls was, and Jim Simkin is, and like I used to be. Let them call you at home. Give it over to them. The warm woollies don't really run out. Don't even count them. After all, if worst comes to worst, you will know some of the best therapists in the country who won't even charge you a regular fee. The story of humpty dumpty is overplayed and undersimplified. At midlife, see the needs of others.

When the creative energy starts to come, be not afraid, but read all of Wilhelm Reich again, carefully this time. Take off your blanket and stand naked, contained in your skin. Seek to lose all you have to your name. Let them know you as Bill, Dick, Jane, and Sue. Do not seek power or dominion. Be very careful while checking on the one to also sneak a glimpse at the other. You never can tell, no matter how many like him you've seen. Maybe she is the one who can only get it together by being just a housewife. Do not offer yourself as sacrifice. Remember always that the rules that have to do with transference are made by people who cannot touch others except with the lights out and after they are married with mom's and dad's approval and a hired limousine to take them honeymooning at the local Hilton. But watch that swelling head. If now you want to write a book, go read Dr. Seuss. Be a root. The smoke will lift.

Now every commencement speech must have a reference to being a good team member. After all, we have to keep this country going until the cowboys, or Indians, Russians or Israelis—somebody—blows it up. The really great coaches never stop drilling in the fundamentals. Know when to run and when to punt. Go home. Go back where you started. Grow sideways too. If your midriff starts to bulge, take up jogging, or tennis again, or T'ai Chi. Anything to keep your body together with your mind and spirit (while we still talk that way). In this sideways growth, give more. More! Do not, I say again, do not sacrifice yourself, but if you haven't done it on the way up the ladder, get a job in a Community Mental Health Center. Maybe in the mountains somewhere, or any inner city will do. Perhaps you've gotten spoiled. See those who rape their daughters, shoot their women, sell their body for cash with which to support their habit, or their mother, the bag woman.

After the darkness, the mist, and the smoke, you will come to the place of the turning around. It may be dust in a deep hole. Ride the wind out, spurring it as you do. True, that requires choice, and passage after passage. Land on a cloud and rest awhile, or keep on flying. Soon you will see that rocks and stuff are alive too. Be consoled that you cannot create a better world. It is not absolutely true that every time the only way out is through, but as a presumably trained existentialist, personally I wish they had never hung those signs on the walls of the head shops in the sixties.

On a crisp autumn morning, skip to work, and at noon, play hopscotch. Remember, the children know. Listen to them. If a ragamuffin gives you a wild flower, take it into the case conference in the early afternoon. And do not explain it to anyone. Pick a four-leaf clover, or an Indian guide named McIntosh and wearing a kilt. If you work for others, let them know that they buy only your time. Do what you damned well please on weekends. Try not to let them dress you up like clowns. If you have to be a clown, dress yourself. Wear a silly hat. Jump suits are becoming passé, even on the West Coast.

Well, this is it. I resent you for not having the grace to insist that I deliver this speech, for surely you all must have known that I had written it fairly carefully, even if only in my head. I appreciate your paying your hard-earned thousand dollars each for a fee. We put all of it we could into equipment, video-tape, etc., so that the Institute can keep going, maybe, even if I go from here. I regret that we didn't have a really big bash at the end, with a spitted lamb and a prize for the best original poem, song, or vaudeville routine. I know you understand, now, that I was sick and getting sicker, and eventually came down with diabetes, had to quit boozing, and had a really bad time for a time. So, good-bye. Hit the road and if you have to, hit the streets. And don't look back. The lawyers may be gaining on you, for alimony, *zum beispiel*. Pay them no heed. If there is really no other way to sleep at night with integrity, go to prison. There are more Johnny Cashes and more Merle Haggards there, needing help to get out to play and sing. Wherever you go, make music, while you're young and after you're not. Play a kazoo at a cocktail party in Beverly Hills.

Since a very tall tree is one way out of a very deep hole, learn to climb. Become a monkey if you have to. Climb to the sun. There's water there for the thirst, and rest, and peace. But not until you journey into the sky where the homeless wind lives.

And, oh yeah. One last thing. Set the alarm, get up, and go to work, like all the rest of us do.

"DAMMIT YOUNG MAN, I HAVE BEEN IN THERAPY A WHOLE YEAR! WHEN AM I GOING TO BE MORE LOVABLE?"

Figure 9.   "The patient expects from the therapist what he/she won't do for himself/herself." (Ed.)

Part IV

Views and Reflections by Gestalt Therapists

I am in exile. Like everybody else, I live in a world that is given to me—I am thankful for it. It is not made by me—and that too is very well. But it is *not* my native home; therefore I make poems.

Paul Goodman

"I'M GETTING 6 ☆☼‼6 TIRED OF BEING SO ☼‼★☆6 SWEET ALL THE ♨‼☼☉! TIME ‼"

Severin

Figure 10. "Self-Image" (Ed.)

Chapter 40

The Village Idiot

NEIL LAMPER

"Blessed are those who know the secret that there is no secret."

—*Lamper, from a play written in the former time.*

And then I bought the cycle. I did that; at least I did that. I did not do it by regulation but by my way, on impulse. Some say this cycle was part of the craziness but ask me; I say it is the functioning of the wisdom of my organism. Those who call me crazy simply do not see that at the age of forty-four, a man can ask for a sabbatical and then ride a motorcycle 13,000 miles, living first in a commune and then in the desert along the way. But this is what I did and I will tell you about some of it.

The training of the therapist is a risky business; it must be understood. The Tao speaks plainly on this point: beware of The Way, there is only your way. Too often a scholar is someone who does not own himself and so he studies to own another. From his earned eminence he imposes the pattern of his idol on others and condescends to their shortcomings. And often a therapist will plod a safe path in his own preparation and then seek to open others to infinite variety. Along my way I needed courage and strength and a fleeting kind of faith that slipped in and out of my grasp. This faith is like a tantalizing woman and she still plays with me while I write this. I follow my way and sacrifice the blessing of The Brotherhood but the excitement of my search lifts me aloft and I soar in realms of freedom with a feel more solid than air. Now I know the myth and adventure of the Holy Grail, or the Menorah, or Sacred Wood, whatever, and the myth is myth but the faith is real. And your way is your way; the only requirement is faith.

In the beginning my way was books and schools and I took them in stride and did well. Even then the foolishness, or sense, stopped me a step short of official certificates issued by states and academies. Perhaps only a lobotomy can change my pattern of response whenever One Way is declared sacred. The only blessing I've had for twelve years is my Ph.D. and it hasn't helped my hives. Neither have the shots of the allergist. So in the Spring of 1970 I went crazy.

At the time I didn't know it. At the time I simply did a number of normal things. Fritz had talked with me at Esalen and asked me to come live with him in his commune in Canada. I returned to Michigan and applied for a sabbatical; that's normal, isn't it? And isn't it normal to provide income for my family of six left back in Kalamazoo while I follow the wisp? These things must be understood.

And I did my daily chores well, "like falling off a log," is the phrase. I wound my internal clockwork tighter and tighter but in the Spring couldn't feel it yet. I ignored symptoms. I avoided contact with my colleagues, preferring the company of women. By the time my sabbatical began my family lacked a father and husband anyway and a crazy man is no substitute. I accepted new clients and made my diagnoses during the first fifteen seconds of the initial interview and then proceeded to pound those poor people into the shape of my arrogant phantasy. Even that isn't much different from what many others do but it is still the manufacture of madness. The people in my groups became angry with each other and held whispering campaigns over the telephone between sessions. Husbands moved out and spent nights drinking and then went and blackened the eyes of their wives. Madness is contagious and spreads like cancer. I know it's true that way when I say it.

Look here: I'm not giving you ten pages of elephantshit. I'm sharing with you what I did and even telling you how I did it. I'm not talking about a weekend trip to Scarborough Fair.

Now I know any other way would have been insufficient. My way is my way. I'm scared to death of motorcycles and would never even ride backseat on one. My son is going around the world on a BMW cycle and he can have it. He wiped out in South America and almost died mired in the mud of Africa but made it to India for six months of study in Banares. He can have it. I must have had cycles registered in my broken brain and when I went into the local shop to inquire about the durability of a BMW, I suddenly bought a Honda 350 and a jacket and a helmet and visor and windscreen and gloves and boots all in one fell swoop.

Chuck sold it all to me at a good price. He had a date and was in a hurry. He set me astraddle the machine in the parking lot and when I succeeded with one pass, corner to corner, he pointed me homeward. I made it by amazing grace and fell in the driveway and burned my leg. Early the next morning I pounded on the door of the cycle shop and asked Chuck how much he would give me for a used cycle. I was astonished to discover that my machine had depreciated two hundred dollars over night. What's a madman to expect?

My sabbatical began in one week. I used the time well. I abandoned my individual patients. Why not? I was crazier than they. I terminated my groups, spoke to my banker and arranged all family business by alphabet in the desk drawer in the livingroom. I sent an agonizing letter to John Warkentin and even though I caught him at the time of his own grief he replied with compassion. My friends and medical colleagues regaled me with predictions and calculations of just where my carcass would be scraped off the pavement. I was so afraid of a broken back, or neck, I shook the cycle all over the road while I put 500 miles into it so I could have that first checkup before I left. Then I strapped on my gear and pretended I didn't see the bewildered tears of my family. How can young children see that a father is crazy when tears of love blind them? Tell me about that one.

I wobbled down the driveway and began the 3,000 miles to Lake Cowichan, Vancouver Island. Of course Fritz was dead but that's his business. Dead is dead is dead. I already felt warm towards Janet Lederman and her little book about anger, and Gentle Jerry Rothstein was always kind in his letters. So what could I lose? My mistake was that I expected the wind on my face to cure me but how could it cure me when I still didn't know I was crazy? Now I can look back and see that first I must own the craziness and not project it out onto the whole world, and admit what is and see it and hear it well down into the deep places.

I will not lie; it was terrible. Each day I prayed for transcendence and only tumbled deeper into pain. I couldn't take my eyes from the road for a second and so I saw no majestic scenery. I almost crashed broadside into another cycle on my first 300 miles and only a scream of fear at the last instant saved me. I miscalculated curves, too much and too little, and cursed my clumsiness. I didn't dare drive very fast but June days are long days in Canada and I covered 450 miles each day. One day I was angry at myself for not meeting my quota on the previous day and I made 624 miles. I began these days at 8:00 a.m. and bought whiskey along the way and stopped to drink and sleep at 10:00 p.m. I had no confidence yet on the cycle and three things that scared me were cities, stops on the city hills and crossing steel bridges. I held to the cycle so tightly that I gave myself the deadhand. My hands became claws curled into mere hooks and after a few of these long days of driving I could not button, zip, or even lift my hand to my face.

I will not lie and suck sympathy so I must tell of some of the good times. I will tell of how I began to come out of it although I did not know it at the time. What clarity is possibly in insanity? I was high in my head all day and my thoughts raced 'round in circles, so I was not in my body and the fine muscular adjustments I needed to cycle well were lost to me.

Some force of wind and weather played on me and the endless expanse of distance always before me began to stretch me out. Now and then I could shut off my head, and body and brain came together and I would caress a curve with just the right amount of finesse. There is a split second when going into a curve where your head must be free to process all the subtle data coming from your body. When you do it well there is an integration of all of it and you feel the power and thrill of how well you do it. A moment later I would flash back into my head and in phantasy plot out an article on the correct use of the mind. I cornered all teachers in my head-trip and lectured them that they stressed memory as the work of the mind when it is obvious that the mind is to process data from the senses. Being myself oblivious to the obvious I would then overshoot the next curve and wobble back onto the road.

A therapist often hangs with his own kind and even an evening at the opera is apt to end with conversation about passive aggressives. A man need not go crazy to escape this but as I hurtled along the highway I began meeting people devoid of psychologese. My cycle required adjustments along the way and at 500 mile intervals I stopped at the red and white Honda sign and talked with the cycle freaks. My bike was new and the model unseen as yet in Canada and the magnitude of my trip raised excitement and some envy. Old timers sauntered up and admitted racing cycles when only the Indian and Harley were available. They told me the only time they ever got hurt was when they drank and drove, and they said not to worry about my tenseness, that when I relaxed too much I'd be dead, that the tension would leave around 5,000 miles. And midway across the continent I left the cycle for a major tuneup and while walking in the little town I became aware of a new way of walking, of a lightness to my step and I felt young and strong and alive and the craziness did not seem so bad.

Now I can look back and see how the wisdom of my organism caused me to be in a way that was curative, though unknown and unintentional at the time. Small incidents with no spectacular meaning registered with me and I began to re-weave my consciousness into the larger fabric around me. All along the way, hours of the ride rolled me through the north woods and vast expanses where I felt the full weight of silence. I did not know at that time that sound is sometimes curative and a way out of the impasse, a way to halt a chronic implosion. I was not concerned with knowing and when I knew something in every cell in my body, when feeling flowed, I burst out into song. At one time songs dormant for forty years spilled out of me complete with tears. I didn't understand any of it but I did not obstruct it. Now I look back and recognize a whole course in therapy balanced finely there on a hurtling cycle. The peculiar virtue of a crazy man is that as he had nothing left to cling to he can let it all go and let it be and get out of his own way. I didn't understand a thing in my head but being of sound body there was no obstacle to my cure and each song ended in good, belly-breaking laughter. Even a crazy man enjoys the bounce of his belly.

Insanity is a mucked-up medley of the head with little awareness of the simple goodness of existence. The way of the wind and the playful pressure of the weather was lost to me except in the extreme. Cold night-time rain forced me to consider my soaked skin and even though I felt like I rode in squished piss at least I felt. I was sure my crippled hands would never heal and for this I stumbled, humble to lay me down to sleep each night. I had another lesson in humility high on the plains of Saskatchewan. At the end of the long day, the 624-mile day, just at dusk while standing in the saddle to ease my sore ass, the world's largest jack rabbit bounded across the road in front of me. Even my madness didn't erase the knowledge that a split-second difference would have destroyed me. Is it so crazy to get killed by a bunny? Think on these things.

Truly, I still controlled my destiny for the most part and that very control killed almost all spontaneous response in me. Nature and chance now and again mounted a counter-campaign and what seemed a curse became blessed cure. By faith we are made whole and by chance we are taken off the hook. By chance I ran out of gas at the top of the Continental Divide. I swerved and swore and read the roadside sign: Hill—Next 20 Miles. Mountains stood sheer to my right; far down on my left the bubble and tumble of a canyon stream. There was no traffic and with my cycle silent I floated like a feather in a vacuum. I heard the sigh of space in the trees and sometimes the stream. A hawk hung over my shadow for a time and then dipped in salute and veered off. So far in life I have been unable to fill my barns with the earthly goods that rust doth corrupt; that freefall down the canyon is one of the treasures I've laid up for myself in heaven. What else is a poor man to do?

I also had a moment when wind and weather and Perls and McLuhan and Lamper and God all came together. Don't ask me what order; is there status in heaven? For a full afternoon I skirted a summer storm: deep gunmetal gray on my right, primary blue on my left. A strong, head-on wind sometimes struck me almost to a stop. Each time the road curved I had to learn a new lean and suddenly, clean-cleft, as by a knife, the wind was at my back and threw me at fierce speed along the road. I screamed with joy and knew that God is a God of curves. Man's thought—shapes of Aristotle and Gutenburg—may be linear but life is nuclear, circular, curves, a spiral. And now my mind, for a moment playful, strayed from curves to women. Such sweet dalliance; such a stew of storm and sensual ecstasy.

Is the earth flat? Is there an edge? I circled Vancouver and stood at Horseshoe Bay with the land behind me. I looked out over the water at the islands of the Inland Passage. I felt the momentum of my long ride subside and as yet I had no excitement to arrive at the Institute. Apprehension involving new people is my pattern and to them I give the power to accept me. A British Columbia ferry hove to and a group of islanders exchanged places with me, my cycle and a couple hundred cars and other people. During the two-hour crossing I drooped at the fantail and watched the gulls eat the boat's garbage. I considered going up on to Alaska but I'm too stingy to lose a down payment on a workshop. Which choice is crazy? Enlighten me.

I had a vision of the Gestalt Institute as a group of tents pegged beneath the branches of giant trees. I drove with some caution south from the boat dock at Nanaimo. I had no idea which small, twisted road would take me to the Promised Land. I do not like to ride after dark but when I found my road it was under construction so it was a black forest in which I stopped for gas and directions. The Chinese grinned and said, "You mean those kooks along the road to Youbou?" I didn't bite and he said, "About a mile and a half out of Lake Cowichan, on the road to Youbou. Turn right at the pub." A group of Sikhs with turbans padded across the main street of Cowichan and my mind reeled to the former time poised at the edge of the land of the Hittites, Jebusites and Amorites. Here we were, the Chinese, the Indian, Canadian, the Jew and the goy. Surely his eye is on the sparrow, so do I worry about them? The day is sufficient.

It is only now that I look into the mirror and say I am whole. And when I hear the pretentiousness in that—the invitation to a mindfuck—I don't even lay it on me that heavy. I rub my buddhabelly and let my face fall slack into a vacant grin. I know what I know; only the village idiot knows as much and the world over we have a secret sign, we of the Secret Society of Village Idiots. You're damn right we're exclusive; it takes work to get here. One of our members put it this way: sell all you have and give to the poor; then come live with me. Sheer idiocy. Later on the same nut said to let go of your mommy and daddy, your spouse and kids and stand strong. Jesus Christ! Pure Gestalt.

I want to be careful to tell the truth about Cowichan, the Gestalt Community. It's nothing special; there are no scrolls there. It's like a girl I had with a funny nose. I loved her. Is that something to explain? You may look at her nose and laugh but I'm an idiot and will kiss and fondle her nose and drool dew dust on her lips. I will show you how this works. Recently I wrote a Song of Love about Cowichan and mailed it off. Many responded with the exhortation to let go of Cowichan, that it is my crutch. Bullshit. I love Cowichan, is it something to explain? I was born there. "To suffer one's death and to be reborn is not easy." I stand alone and have immense power. So what is this Eleventh Commandment: Thou shalt not love? "My beloved is like a gazelle. . ."

I arrived at The Sign of the Gestalt Institute at 10:00 p.m. Dark, silent. A waif walked by with a plate of chicken and I asked for Jerry. She giggled and disappeared. I saw a light in a building and made for it and knocked on the door. A voice said to come in so I pushed the door open. A naked man and woman looked at me from their chairs. Some scene: two naked idiots and a crazy man in boots, gloves, a helmet and a mask. None of us smiled. We fluttered as nonchalant as lords and ladies of King Louie's court. They said Jerry must be somewhere.

I gave it up and found an empty cabin. All night I tossed and turned. "On the one hand... but on the other hand." Are there no graves in Egypt? Early the next morning I uncovered Jerry behind a newspaper. I pinned him to the wall with words. I slaughtered him with questions. I shifted and swerved and feinted with my logic and then pranced in for the kill with my *non sequitur*. Sheer brilliance. I bowed to a round of applause and took a curtain call. Jerry sat unperturbed by my stellar performance and said, "You're crazy." Crestfallen, I maintained my brittle smile and watched him peel a banana. When you're up against the wall and it's to the death there's nothing as disemboweling as a banana. Something about the shape. Milk and honey I can take but a banana is something else.

Jerry ate the banana and smelled the skin. Then he said it was all right by him for me to be crazy but he didn't like to have me drive him crazy. He said maybe I could leave him alone and go outside and begin to experience the grass and sun and trees and water. This took some time. Time I had. And it took some juggling and balancing from the other people there. This I got, a true kind of love. Nobody did anything for me and nobody laid anything on me.

At Lake Cowichan the genius comes in regular garb; the healers wear pants and they work a shovel, and hammer. I told you long ago I did well with books all my life. Each time I studied the droppings of a great mind the man was so far ahead of me, way up in cosmic dust, I could only sit and sulk and somehow escape my own failure. The only guy that ever made any sense to me said it with simple words. Early in the recorded Hebrew myth he told a loser named Job to get off his ass and do something, and later on in the same myth he told everybody to care for everybody. Jesus Christ, you can't get it much simpler than that. I can't possibly give you all the details about life at Cowichan. I only want to say that it's there and that it's no Mayo Clinic. And that it's all process and it's subtle and simple and that I cured myself there and I was born there, with a little help from my friends. I also know that since leaving the location—in body, not spirit—I've had no luck telling about it. Most of the fat Pharisees with whom I rap rear back on their pipes and beards and condescend to me and my simple commune, Cowichan. Here are some of the most frequent traps laid:

"But are those people happy there?"
"Isn't it a copout to go and live there?"

> "What would happen if we all did that?"
> "Who does the dishes?"
> "You mean they operate without a resident psychiatrist?"
> "How did you feel about the drugs and free sex?"
> "It can't work; it's your imagination."

Good Christ, I know how you felt only you didn't blow your cool. You still forgave their ignorance and I wanted to smash them somehow. Telling me honey doesn't exist when I'm dipped in it. But then if I blow my cool they are right on all counts. If I blow my cool then it's true I am not happy and it's a copout to find it only on location and the cure is only in my imagination. So I grin and shuffle a little bit and I tote that barge and lift that bale and tear ass down to Paw Paw on my cycle for a cup of coffee. Sheer idiocy. Render unto Caesar what is Caesar's; I know what I know. Getting uptight is my own crap and I take responsibility for it. When I go slack I have fun with it and then sometimes my accusers relax and sigh and listen and I can hear the hurt in them. This is in the great tradition of the Court Jester, the Village Idiot. You can hear it clearly in *King Lear*. On my 3,000-mile cycle trip from Cowichan back to Kalamazoo in December, I re-read The *Rubaiyat* and discovered that Omar Khayyam said the same myth all over again and didn't get hanged because he said it funny.

Right now I'm losing the simplicity, I'm preaching. Maybe the preacher is the biggest idiot of all. Back to the simple things. I'll tell you simply about my craziness and cure at the Cowichan Community.

I lay on the grass. I saw the sky; I felt the soil. Early each morning I jumped nude into the cold water of Lake Cowichan. Later, in November, I fell out of the canoe into the icewater of the river Cowichan. Hydro-therapy, water cure. I began to shut up my infernal internal dialogue. I slept nights. That's simple.

Jerry said, "Just hang around and define your work space." That's the heaviest any instruction ever got and that was laid on gently. Had I not done any work my whole role in the community would be different and it's my problem, no one else's. We don't have any directors, nor leaders. We're all in it together. A community is a community is a community. I did an experiment with simple, tiny words and got the feel of that. One day I worked hard all day with the thought in me that I worked for *them*. I was full of resentment and I went to lift my bale and sprung my back and suffered the pangs of hell for 30 days. Then one day I worked hard all day with the thought in me that I worked for *me*. I began to give orders and pin rules to the bulletin board and I saw the long road to dictatorship stretch before me. At night I was tired. And I worked hard all day with the thought that I worked for *us*. Aha! Peak experience; a mini-satori. I laughed and danced and sang and took a coffeebreak soaking in a hot bath and felt so much love and joy and power, I felt the cosmic orgone flowing through me. What? Reich? Of course, he was crazy, too. We idiots keep our own counsel; it's a simple thing.

I pulled on my boots; I donned my gloves and doffed my hat. I walked around. I had Selig in mind. The community needed a Selig. Call me Neil, my name is not Selig. I began where I began. I began at the beginning. I cleared the grounds. I built a fence. I cut the grass and sawed the wood. I roofed the shed and added a room and moved the garbage and made a new compost pit and organized the lumber and shelved the tools and salvaged the logs and moved the boats and cleaned the roof gutters and nailed the door and replaced the window and piled the junk. Much later Janet Lederman made a haiku of it. "You came here and began with a fence and then cleared the grounds and then cleaned out the stream." I did that; it's a simple thing.

Janet returned to Cowichan after I had been there a week. I read her book a year before and fell in love with her. I still don't know her; I still love her. Janet is tough. Janet hurts. Janet is a mother; Janet is a little girl cuddled on a lap. Janet never gets sucked in, she is invaluable. She asks for nothing and gives nothing unless you can see under all the crap and see that she gives everything. She doesn't even know the one time I observed her unobserved and saw the tears hanging in her eyes. Ach. Let it be. Do tears clarify the Dead Sea? It must be understood.

The simple things cure. Psychiatric evaluations and differential diagnoses are elephantshit. My colleagues respond with, "If we didn't have the etiology we couldn't treat." We have it and we treat and our clients still go nuts. Nuts is nuts is nuts. If you gotta go nuts you gotta go nuts. Anyway, there are nuts and nuts. The real nut is the Chairman of the Board.

Nature cures. When a meeting at Cowichan turned rancid I ran across the road and crashed through the trees and briarpatch. Me and Brer Rabbit. I smothered my face in moss and running pell mell down to the stream I sank ankle deep in swamp swill. When it rained I sat and soaked and studied the delicate ecology of a fallen tree. Holy Cow, Great Pumpkin, an' all them other expletives. That's how I felt; that's how I feel now, writing of it. I could pass that tree a thousand times and not see a thing but now I could see the busy fungus doing its work and as I sat the whole tree came alive and we smiled at each other and had a strong communication. A certain caption of a poster is true: Stand still and look until you see.

At the beginning, full into my craziness, I had to be clobbered now and then to own that craziness and not lay it on others. The waif of my first night at the community turned into the Lovely Diann by daylight. She's organic. It must be understood. She makes salads out of steamed nettles, and huge broths out of huge clams. And when I chattered incessantly she said, my god you talk a lot. And when I kept it up she said shuddup, and when I rattled on into high gear she left. With her I discovered the organic cure of silence. Once a week for the rest of the seven months I spent a 24-hour period in silence. Most of the times the others didn't even know I was on a silent trip. So my reward is in heaven where moth and rust do not *etc., etc.*

Silence cures. I do it now in Kalamazoo. My kids laugh and try to provoke me to talk. If they get too close they get spit. When I'm silent I hear people, I hear the entire universe, I hear whatever space I'm in. Most of all I hear me. It's a feeling: these things are all in the body. We can feel them if we listen. I can hear myself at center; I hear myself when I get off; I hear confusion, tightness, anxiety and craziness. I can experience these now when I talk, now, when I write—if I listen. I feel much different when I'm together, balanced at center, from when I begin to stray off into one of the concentric circles around the bullseye of the target. If I listen. I'm learning to listen when I'm off and just sit. It's organic.

Work cures. Work that makes use of the head only and not the body is a curse. The works of Bach and Beethoven and Mahler have body, so does the work of Steinbeck, Milton and Einstein. The Congressional Record does not have body, neither does the committee report, nor the minutes of the meeting. It's a problem. If you're stuck with paper work in a paper world you find your body on the side. Good, better, best and Selig says that when what you do for work expresses the whole of who you are, you got it together.

We needed a fence so I cut logs for posts and dug post holes. And when I got traumatic phone calls from home, and then when my son dropped out of sight for eight weeks in the Middle East, and the law was on my ass, and my colleagues were furious at me, I put down the shovel and dug the post holes with my fingernails. I have met the village idiot and he is me. My eyes could see only the four square inches of the post hole and my ears could hear only my heart, my breathing, and my scratching. The whole world could have exploded and I would know only the hole. One time Janet watched and I didn't know it and later she said, "Who needs therapy when they can do that?" A four-inch posthole is not the Promised Land and soil is not milk and honey but being an idiot I'll take what I can get. I know what I know.

There is more, much more but I am after no Moby Dick and my name is not Ishmael. In the beginning was uncalculated craziness and at the end of my cure is peaceful identification with idiocy. A mind that found itself. If you journey to Cowichan your path will be different. It's a deal. Our community is different every day. We don't package anything; we're a process, a flow, a river by a river. The cure for a beat brain is elusive. Janet works hard and with brilliance but she brooks no bullshit and whenever I came to her with a bag of it she went to sleep. She always knew what was going on and if she didn't she acted like she knew. Can an idiot tell the difference? Once she said that sometimes the ones who resist the longest have the best center when they finally plunge headlong into it. I got the message and could relax and move a little in my space. Then once after a phone call there wasn't any me left and I sat *uumph* in the grass, that sound like when a man gets the wind knocked out of him, and I stared at a piece of dirt and I was a piece of dirt. Janet came and squatted nearby and waited and when I finally looked up she said, "Can you let it be?" I felt the soft support instead of frustration. A beautiful thing Fritz said during his last year here, that Gestalt is not rules, it's wholeness. Janet hovers around and has eyes and ears and knows and goes with it and there is healing in her wings. It is strange, so strange now, while I write it. I am somewhat back into it and my arms drip wet with sweat and my pen seems not to touch the paper. The bottom is fearsome and my breath heaves and bounds at the contemplation of it.

I know about craziness. Craziness is uptight is projection is judgment. A crazy man, Nuremberg, the world. A crazy man can't stand his innards and he looks around and he lays it on and he blames and he judges and he kills. From nothing to nothing. Read it in The Rabaiyat.

Jerry is quiet, Jerry is gentle. Jerry isn't about to allow anyone to crash in his space. In silence I found my way to Jerry and in that quiet space is beauty and a genuine soul. Jerry is free of judgment and such soulfood is rare. John lives in the woods and makes musical instruments out of silex coffee jars. When I'm with John I always feel good. It's not to be explained. When I complain to Vaughn that I can't saw straight across a board he doesn't get sucked into my Bad Neil game. He pauses and then tells me that anyone who works with wood must love the wood, that a tree is a long time growing, that there is a quick death and the least we can do is slow down and love the wood a little. Deke tacks a sign to the board that there will be a sound session at seven. We gather in the lodge, we listen, we breathe, we make sound. Somehow I feel a little more together. Ray plunks his guitar and lets kids make words to his chords. Later he helps adults re-discover the world of the young by taking roles in that world. No lectures on adolescence, just young feelings with movement and play. Sara weaves and is herself a delicate fabric of great beauty. There are others, we are a sweet smorgasbord. It's enough to know about it. Somehow healing hovers, whether in me, there, or in the air. It is not to be explained; it is to be experienced. It is what Fritz wanted it to be: a therapeutic community. It is there; it's enough.

Three steps forward and two back, said Fritz. It's true. I learned the difference between the feel of steps back and on the bottom. I left the community for a time and went to San Francisco. To my insanity I added despair; the time in the community should have knit me all together, I reasoned, back in my head again. I didn't know then that it's not the time that counts but the timing. I hated what time I spent in the city and as often as possible went north to Bolinas and Bodega Bay. I sat and watched Pacific waves and listened and heard how at the end of the ebb is perfect silence while the energy gathers to fling forward once more. I sweat through five workshops and sulked between them. Finally Elaine yelled, "Will you quit cringing?" Help comes in many forms; must it always be acceptance and love? Sometimes a yell is more than a yell.

Whenever I consulted my head I could find no reason not to return to Michigan and my people. The head of an idiot is not too good. Somewhere in my organism there was a sense of incompleteness. I didn't know this but I felt it. I knew the completion was not one of myself as a finished product but of this segment of my journey. Even now, writing this, I also read from Robinson Jeffers, the poet, and scan descriptions of the Big Sur written by poetic naturalists. I feel the same pull: center off-center; back-forward. At that time I knew I would interrupt something if I stopped what I was doing to return. And yet there was no fun to the idiot, no pleasure, no looseness. Instead of silly flop the idiot was stiff tight. Some idiot: a wrong word and he'd kill. A true idiot is warm and does not murder. Only long afterwards does a man see that such a period of disintegration produces the next step forward. Can a man see the mystery when he's in it?

What is chance, that we are mindful of it? By chance I browsed in a Berkeley bookstore. By chance I picked up a photo-essay of Death Valley. By chance the idea of going there, to live with nothing, on the floor of the world became a fixation. By chance this idea filled me day and night so full I had room for nothing else. I closed accounts around the Bay. I spent a week of gut belly sensual fun with my wife in the pine needles around Idaho Springs, Colorado. The desert lurked, sulked in my blood and, returning to where I'd tied my cycle, I packed, all in a furious flurry, and headed deeper into the unknown.

Mountains are mysterious and brood on their haunches; the sea moves always and heaves and has immense power. I feel full of fun and frolic in a forest and I talk with trees. At the time of this journey I wanted to divest myself of everything. I wanted no gear and I wanted silence and bare survival. I talked with people who wanted to equip me but I took only a little money for gas and I took my sleeping bag and a waterbag. I took no tent, no tools, or food. When I got to Death Valley I felt what I was after and it was life, not death. In all of time primal wandering has been done in the desert. The space and apparent emptiness of the desert has encouraged man to see life at the most elementary level. Milk and honey, trees and hills all divert man's attention but in the desert he is only where he is. In the desert silence shimmers and fades into haze in all directions. Vast distance and close scrutiny are in constant exchange. In my bones I felt home, no mystery, just belief that man came from here. For the first time I knew my condition: IS. I was content and wanted to stay. Both idiocy and sanity were irrelevant. Can anything be measured against endless space?

And so I did that; at least I did that. I did not do it by regulation but by my way, on impulse. I listened, I went to the desert and listened. I heard eons of time, I heard centuries. I heard the beginnings of man. I heard timelessness. I heard how time is a lie, there is no time, there is only change of form. And space, always space. Space, space, vast, infinite space. Limitless space. And I heard silence, total silence, limitless silence, overpowering, powerful, awesome silence. The silence of big; the silence of the immense power and dignity and integrity of the universe. I saw this in the faces of the Indians I met and I saw it etched on the rock-face. I heard the omnipotence and omnipresence of creation; and I heard the earth and its fullness. And I heard the Babel of man and his squeaking and my caterwauling. And I was stopped, stoned. Stoned in the desert. And I heard me.

At night I cycled, or walked and twice crawled to some kind of a flat space where I spread my bag and, clothes, curled into it and hid my head. By day a huge knife hung on my belt but at night it was tô my hand. Once a snake and once a rat sniffed me but they were insignificant in the way of the desert and the possum's play of the dead served me well. An idiot is already at an end, and a wise man knows everything is a beginning.

Early each morning I was up and on into some canyon, some young wash of 130 million years of age. Tall, brash stalk, I strode seven-league down severe cuts, hand-hewn of layered silt and slain mountain levels. Centuries of silent space sculpted small rocks and fractured mountains and wrote the history of the world into both. I climbed ridge tops and, looking like a fly pasted against the sky, gazed across the floor of the world, saw another ridge rise to wall the far side of the valley, saw the dry river of salt crystal wind the valley floor, saw specks of mine ruins hang in the hot haze. Sheer awe filled me each day. Mornings I walked canyons, probed prehistoric caves and crawled abandoned mine shafts. Afternoons I studied contour maps and plotted my course to evening camp ground. Early morning and late evening the entire valley is a gigantic artist's palette and the colors of the silent ages slide down the ridges, across the valley floor and seem to sink into the salt silt at Badwater, the lowest spot. I watered at Stovepipe Well, Scottie's Castle and Mesquite Campground with the hidden spring.

I trailed the bighorn sheep with no success, they have retreated high into the hills to escape man. The valley is the home of the descendants of the Twenty Mule Team borax mules and I had better luck tracking them, even to being attacked by the world's largest jackass. An idiot is no match for a jackass and when I could I hid behind a bristlecone pine. At five in the morning, to escape the heat, I slid to the bottom of the Ubehebe crater, I broke my bike and abandoned it and spent a day scaling Telescope Peak. I met professional climbers, well equipped, but in my search for my own primal pulse I went with no food or water, no shirt and with broken boots. What I found was blisters and burnt skin, the lot of an idiot. One day, seeking to suck up the ultimate atmosphere, I rode the bike in my undershorts and, at high speed below sea level. I ripped one ear drum to shreds. Now the idiot both hears and babbles less, a blessing to us both.

Looking back I know this experience in the desert was not the same as that of a man sailing the world in a small raft. All things considered, however, my way of life for a brief time in the desert was new to me. At night, curled and cold into my bag, with no one near my small fire of pine cones crackling against the desert shadow sounds, I thought of my huge suburban house, of my garage full of machines, of my university tenure, my clients and my family and felt like an idiot away from all that duty. And smiled. And never felt better. I knew the feel of letting go; as far as I knew I might remain there forever. I'll tell you a little of how this is.

Each tiny thing was an ultimate. An old timer came down out of the hills and left with me a half loaf of bread and coffee grounds for ten cups. I had a four-inch square piece of saran wrap which was as important as my retirement policy. I took out the contents of my tube patching kit to use the container for coffee. The lid of the canister had holes in it so I screwed the saran wrap into it. The bread suffered from the heat so I hung it in the stream of evaporation from the waterbag which I carried on my cycle. Such training is excellent for the eyes and ears of the therapist. In no course, clinic, or institute did I ever find such valuable exercise for my eyes to see and my ears to hear. And in the desert I came to my true and honest beginnings, my stance in time as man only. In the desert I stood stripped of all roles, facades, possessions and responsibilities. And by paradox I felt the strength and power of my role as a man, and I was rich and able to respond with integrity. This kind of fecund aloneness is not a neurotic escape from people. To have another person nearby would take me one step away from myself and at this time, having never felt it, I needed the feel of my own pulse.

I did not find the truth in the desert; it must be understood. The desert is a space and I went to it. I opened my eyes and I saw; with ears to hear I heard. You have your truth and I have mine. If you read this and rush out to buy a cycle and retrace my trip you are a fool and miss the whole point. A fool is not an idiot and there is only one idiot to a village. This entire story is a metaphor.

I left the desert, of course, as the play ends. Only the fool says in his heart there is no God. All the rest was anti-climatic but still necessary, I spent a night under the stars over Chew's Ridge, at the fire tower camp of

Fred and Linda, old-time guardians of the Los Padres forest. During my month at Big Sur I helped Selig put a roof over his head and with Barbara, Russ and Dewey covered the Esalen gardens with a blanket of steaming compost. At times I was tempted to join the theraping of the therapists around me but I held fast to my idiocy and remained true to myself. It must be understood. I needed time to seal my eyes and ears open. It was not a thing of my head but of some wisdom of my organism. I felt each call to return to Michigan ill-timed, out of focus, an interruption but I could not explain it. I could only gurgle like an idiot. I felt the wheel of time circling in me and the arc was not complete. So again I shut my mouth and stood with Selig and we mourned what is left of the Big Sur.

Then I went back to Cowichan for a month. Then I organized the grounds and cleaned the stream. Then I spent a day overcome by something I never experienced before and can't explain; with my eyes I saw the constant undulation of birth movement and travail beating in the universe. Then I woke up one morning and it was time and I slipped away.

Chapter 41

Babel Maneuvers— Notes for a Study of Confusion*

WILLIAM R. TAYLOR

One learns in life to keep silent and draw one's own confusions.

Cornelia Otis Skinner

Confusion: the state of feeling/thinking muddled, mixed up, uncertain, paralyzed, unable to decide or act. Most of us seem to tolerate only a few seconds of contact with our own brand of primal chaos before we mask, bury, displace, evaporate, project, or otherwise rid ourselves of this unmentionable condition. And so there spreads over the conference room or through my mind/body an opaque polyfilm of elided contradictions. Because of our collective silence on the topic I have come to view confusion as the single most important commodity smuggled into the cortical gray market today. The potentially lethal psychodrama of confusion at Three Mile Island has strengthened my conviction.

In this article I want to recount and reflect upon some of the causes and symptoms of confusion in myself, in others, and in the human-service professions generally. Most of my current ideas have taken shape in the last four years, but I can see important areas of confusion in my own life going

---

* Author's warning: Acute attacks of confusion have occurred in some readers of this article. Although the source of these inflections has not been identified, I notice a tendency to place blame upon the author.

back to the mid-1960's. At the time, however, I did not recognize the role that confusion played in my struggles. My lack of insight reflected what I have come to view as a key defensive process: As professionals we often do not see our own confusion; moreover, the methods we use to mask our confusion usually worsen either our own or someone else's.

SOME EARLY PROFESSIONAL REFLECTIONS OF CONFUSION

Two struggles stand out in my early professional years (1965–1970), neither of which I would have seen as arising from confusion at the time. In 1969 I left analytic training after three years of training analysis and a year of course work at a "liberal" Freudian institute. In addition to the neurotic roots of this decision, I also see that I had not found a way to integrate two treatment approaches that I considered equally valid: psychoanalysis and family therapy. The proponents of each method tended in that era to deny either the validity or the existence of the other, which left any open-minded clinician with the confusion of trying to integrate without a role model with which to identify. I now believe that the tunnel vision of any school of therapy represents a survival tactic necessary to protect the faculty from confronting their own confusion. This masked confusion usually gets externalized onto the trainees, if they keep any degree of openmindedness intact. At the time, however, I dealt with my still-unlabeled confusion by breaking off contact with formal schools of therapy and their adherents. This withdrawal may have enabled me to become sensitive to the general topic of confusion. It also permitted me to carry out a slow integration of the psychoanalytic and family therapy approaches. At the same time, my withdrawal reflected a long-standing conflict involving distance and closeness. I think this happens often: The individual stands at the intersection where confusion-generating forces (in this case the tunnel vision of faculty in competing schools of therapy) interact with his/her personal conflicts. I have not found any theoretical framework that can adequately describe these interactions among confusions and personal conflicts. Although the concepts of cognitive dissonance bear upon the topic, the proponents do not appear to have extended dissonance theory sufficiently for my purposes.

To resume the story, by the mid-1970's, as I headed into my forties, I had sought out additional training experiences in Gestalt therapy, social literacy, and various shared-leadership support groups; I had also begun personal therapy with a bioenergetic therapist, working on some of the resistances I had come to recognize through the training experiences. The sum total of these exposures led me to begin seeing my own and others' confusions more clearly. This represented an initial step in a process of integration that I expect will take the rest of my life.

At the same time that I had begun this prolonged withdrawal/integration period with regard to psychoanalytic and family systems approaches, I had also opened a second front in my then-undeclared guerilla war on confusions. In 1969 I entered a crisis of confidence with regard to my expert role as a child psychiatrist. Often I found myself in the position of making overt or covert predictions about a particular child's future development, such as when called upon to recommend a treatment program. Behind most recommendations lies an implication that without the treatment, trouble (mental disorder) will occur at some point. My discomfort arose from the assumption on the part of others that I knew something about child development that permitted me to make predictions beyond such commonsense notions that past behavior tends to predict future behavior. I searched the literature and finally wrote an article pointing out the lack of a theory of child development adequate to the task of prediction in child psychiatry. I can appreciate more clearly now my confusion over the general silence on this topic: Did the experts really not know that they did not know? How could I deal with the major limitations in the field in a way that did not alienate the patient and family? How could I teach medical students developmental theory when these fallacious misapplications abounded? I resolved the dilemma at the time by deciding that I could work as a therapist to alleviate pain without making predictions about the future.

Aside from my personal struggles in these two areas, the small, newly formed group with which I then worked had its own confusions. None of us recognized the extent of our individual and group perplexities. I only knew that I did not fit that particular academic setting and so left to enter private practice. Few groups or settings can deal with confusion except indirectly, through conflict, territorial disputes, or other struggles.

My double withdrawal—from formal schools of therapy training and their adherents, and from academic psychiatry—probably set the stage for my first actual naming of confusion. I had not yet begun to see my own confusion in 1973, but I became alert to the impact upon parents, for example, of the great confusion *among* professionals (including myself) who deal with learning-disabled children. I began to see when I caused confusion and when I alleviated it in patients and families. I did some workshops with parents of learning-disabled children around the topic of confusion itself. Their enthusiastic response (being parents, they had fewer defenses against confusion than professionals) led me to start noticing the rare allusions to confusion in "the literature." I also began cataloging the sources of confusion and discussing the topic with colleagues and friends.

By 1976, I had begun to "own" my personal and professional confusions, at least for brief periods. I would then bury the whole issue for months at a time. Each resurfacing usually brought a new dimension: I began to see some of the intersecting sources of my confusion from my family of origin, on the one hand, and in my culture and historical epoch on the other. I became increasingly convinced that the topic of confusion warranted real study and I began more seriously to search reference works and textbooks for any mention of the state. In 1975 I had begun writing the seemingly endless sequence of drafts that led to this paper; with each new attempt at writing I realized how much background I lacked in philosophy and history when approaching such a topic. Around the same time I suddenly realized that artists and a few creative scientists in the last century in the West not only faced their own confusion but also demonstrated the generative power of confusion once befriended. (Eastern philosophy seemed to have made a more comfortable place for confusion and ambiguity centuries ago.) I came to view the present state of the world as inevitably evoking confusion, though most of us lack the support and training which might enable us to turn it into an asset.

A BRIEF CATALOGUE
OF SOME SOURCES OF CONFUSIONS

Out of these efforts I would like to offer the following abbreviated discussion of some of the sources of confusion that have struck me (in both senses of that word). Because some of these sources interact with one another, I envision someday a great diagram, with boxes and arrows depicting the complex mutual influences among them. For now, I have promised myself to remain content with written descriptions.

a) *Information overload.*
Each year there appear in print over *one hundred thousand* articles bearing some relevance to the behavioral sciences. The number of new books tops twenty five hundred. I come into contact with perhaps one tenth of one percent of the avalanche. When I first made these calculations I felt an intense need to cower in panic, covering my head with my arms, warding off the overwhelming mass. To ignore this flood breeds ignorance; to embrace it, confusion. To try to keep up with new material necessitates slighting the old and vice versa.

b) *Information lack.*
Despite this deluge of articles and books there exist significant gaps in our knowledge. A few random examples: careful studies of lithium carbonate in adolescents (lithium is used in adult psychiatry for manic-depressive and

other cyclic depressive disorders.); follow-up studies of residential treatment; laboratories and personnel for the computer processing of EEG's; a theory of child development adequate for making predictions; comparison of different approaches to teaching learning-disabled children.

Although these lacks could produce primarily ignorance, I believe confusion results from a denial of our ignorance, and the hiding of ignorance under jargon.

c) *Contradictions.*
Conflicting opinions, findings, or approaches can generate confusion. I have already described my confusion in trying to integrate contradictory approaches to therapy. The information overload contains countless examples of contradictory findings, sometimes offered in apparent ignorance of others' results.

Beyond these contradictions stand such profound upheavals in culture as the change in our views of men and women. These changes produce conflicts between old and new ideas about sex role, for example, with attendant confusion.

d) *Others' defenses against their own confusion.*
Several common coping techniques used, I believe, to mask confusion may increase the net muddle in the listener or reader. Examples: The speaker buries his/her confusion under jargon; conferees argue some minor or unknowable point, bypassing the underlying confusion; tunnel vision, discussed above, avoids confusion by denying the alternatives to a given approach; pseudoscience, as illustrated by undocumented assertions about blood sugar or oxygen level (variables that *could* be measured but weren't in these instances) leave an informed reader or listener with confusion as to the place of critical thinking in the world view of the author or speaker, while simultaneously masking the latter's confusion about complex physiological processes.

These four factors operate in other professions and fields than human services. A research-laboratory director in a chemical company told me how he learned to capitalize on management's confusion by not totally changing his lab's goals and activities each time a new directive came down. By keeping a small effort going on the supposedly abandoned projects he could salvage some useful data and more easily start up again when the inevitable change at some future point brought a project back into favor. Usually there existed enough confusion among his bosses to permit him to bank certain fires rather than extinguish them. Similarly, an insurance executive responsible for billions of dollars in investments cited confusion as a central reality of his life in the company. Thus, the river of confusion sweeps into its flood people from all walks of life. In the next section I will discuss several other sources of confusion in a broader context than the human services.

e) *Secrecy and deception.*

The Nixon era heightened my consciousness of the long history of secrecy, image building, and deception by leaders in government and business. Ernest Becker (1975), in *Escape from Evil*, says "the talent to mystify others is the queen of tyranny" (p. 13). Thus, a part of my confusions over the past decade and a half reflects active efforts by my leaders to create exactly that state of affairs. I now believe that secrecy and deception serve another purpose: the masking of the leaders' underlying confusions through the creation of out-groups and enemies. If I as a leader can become preoccupied enough with external threats I can bury my own confusions behind the stone wall of counterespionage.

This technique of maintaining power through the sowing of confusion goes back at least to the tower of Babel, where the Lord curbed the over-reaching ambitions of humans (the attempt to build a tower to heaven) by causing them to begin speaking different languages. In the resulting confusion, the tangle of tongues licked the pile of stones and the use of mystification continued unchallenged, perhaps until Marx. Our need for mystification leads us to collude with our leaders' confusion maneuvers, unless our critical thinking awakens us.

f) *Paradox.*

Another powerful source of general confusion stems from the paradoxical nature of many situations in which common sense or our first belief leads to error. Watzlawick, Weakland, and Fisch (1974) in *Change* depict the paradoxical and painful reality that most problems get perpetuated through misguided attempts at solution. For example, the more a mother tries to check up on her daughter (and solve the problem of "keeping her out of trouble") the more the daughter may withhold, leading her mother to think she has something to hide, etc. These authors cite the need to try to catapult the stuck individual or family out of the box of conventional thinking, into a realization that they have trapped themselves in a paradox.

In philosophy, Kierkegaard and many others have portrayed existence as an array of contradictions and paradoxical predicaments, a theme also developed by Becker. He argues that we have to shrink our vision in order to survive (i.e. to defend against overload-confusion) but that this shrinkage paradoxically deprives us of the broad understanding we will need to counteract the effects of that shrinkage. Bateson (1972), steadfastly resisting shrinkage of perspective, has spread his attention over the broadest possible range, seeking common patterns in embryology, cybernetics, and psychosis. Bateson explores the regions where thought bends back upon itself—one definition of paradox. A random collection of paradoxical (and often confusing) situations might yield such observations as:

- The more I learn, the more I see the limitations of my knowledge and range of my ignorance;
- the harder one applies a wrong solution, the worse the problem becomes;

- the more important a political event, the less the likelihood of our receiving a true account;
- the more important the information I have about a patient or the family the less freely I can talk with others about the situation;
- the more limited or distorted the point of view, the more arrogant and malignantly persuasive its adherents;
- the more power the person has, the farther out of touch s/he gets from the people.

g) Unrecognized ignorance.
Some of these paradoxical situations highlight the "fact" that we lack an adequate framework and langauge within which to discuss the complicated arrays of forces within a family, a social network, a government, or an ecological system. But in contrast to the kinds of recognized gaps in knowledge mentioned in section (b), this lack of unifying framework goes too often unnoticed. *We do not often enough remember that we do not know.* Furthermore, the attempts at dealing with our core thought processes by such theorists as Bateson, G. Spencer Brown, and Francisco Varela require sustained effort on the part of the reader and contain no ready formulae that a therapist or an urban planner or a governor can adopt.

INTERACTIONS AMONG SOURCES OF CONFUSIONS

Although I have decided not to include a systems diagram of these various forces in full armor assembled, I do need to make clear the central message of this paper: *These "external" sources of confusion interact—among themselves and with my "internal" (neurotic) sources—to yield a situation that, if unrecognized, will worsen over time.* More importantly, even if recognized, the array of forces fits into no current theoretical framework that can guide us toward its ultimate detoxification. Thus, we live with a risk of getting caught in a spiral wherein the sources of confusion, our defenses against it, and our lack of a coping framework all accelerate in a dance of collective cognitive death. Following Walter Wink's (1973) schema, the dialectical movement seems to circle from *fusion* (not seeing the confusion, merging oneself with a confusion-masking world view) through distancing and critical perception to *confusion;* from confusion we move to a grappling with the problem using confusion-coping tools (see below); from grappling we proceed to——where? I don't know the outcome of the grappling process, having so recently emerged from fusion and distancing.

TOOLS FOR COPING WITH CONFUSIONS

Although no single frame of reference appears able to handle the dynamics of confusion, a number of writers have broken the silence on the topic. The

Polsters, Perls, and Stevens come to mind. Watzlawick (1976) in *How Real is Real* portrays the effect of confusion in catalyzing the victim's creative problem solving (Ch. 2 & 4). Watzlawick also depicts, as few others have done, the delusional quality of an erroneous solution to a confusion situation. Such wrong beliefs get defended tenaciously and may have a powerful and contagious impact upon others who share the confusion.

In addition to the Gestalt techniques for reducing confusion, other approaches have emerged from the fields of psychosynthesis, organizational development, and future planning. For example, some of the various priority setting or values clarification exercises can serve to reduce confusion in an individual or a group. The cross-impact matrix, used in future forecasting, organizes a variety of trends and factors in such a way as to highlight the impact each variable has upon the others.

Cognitive-dissonance theory offers a potentially useful set of concepts for dealing with some confusion situations. However, I find many important instances of confusion where the fundamental assumptions of dissonance theory seem to need modification. In addition I have not seen any writer apply the concepts in a way that deals directly with dilemmas familiar to me. And finally, in exactly that area of greatest interest to me as a clinician, namely, individual differences in tolerance for ambiguity and in personal styles of resolving cognitive dissonances, "the concept becomes confused" (p. 229) according to Wicklund and Brehm (1976). Thus, ironically, dissonance theorists become confused about their field in precisely those areas where their concepts might be useful in dealing with individuals. As with other schemas, their attempt to understand confusion breeds metaconfusion.

CONFUSION AT THE DOMESTIC SUMMIT

Elizabeth Drew's (1979) account of the Carter Administration's "domestic summit" at Camp David provides material for a case study of the dynamics of confusion. At one of the meetings, in which President Carter and his advisers discussed the best diagnosis for the country's malaise (surely a topic worthy of at least a bit of confusion), the group split into opposing camps. (Polarization and conflict, in addition to the other functions they serve in a group, can serve to ward off confusion by allowing participants to build a case for their own side of a question, derogating the potentially confusing opposing view.) At the next meeting, criticism of the Cabinet appears to have served to deflect confusion through scapegoating. In the days that followed, bitter arguments continued and the confusion broke through in a complex series of meetings described as "chaotic" by an aide. The process ended with no agreement on what the new look in Presidential image should be, though the lack of agreement went unrecognized at the time. Finally, the confusion was externalized onto the body politic by the unbelievable sequence in which the President's energy speech was followed within forty eight hours by the "firing" of the Cabinet members. Drew states that the White House staff were "utterly unprepared" for the storm that followed. Drew describes literally world-wide bewilderment and a feeling that things had gone out of control. Thus, the original confusion underwent denial and externalization far beyond the confines of the original group. I find the subsequent amplification that apparently can occur when confusion gets masked in high places of particular interest.

CONCLUSION

I have written and discarded several closing passages. One contained a sermon about the value of group consciousness raising in dealing with confusion. I decided that I haven't had enough experience with that approach to hold it out as a solution. I had considered closing with a series of maxims about confusion. I did a draft of a confusion questionnaire for readers to return. Still another ending compared the symptoms of confusion to the vapor tracks of particles (individuals) moving through a cloud chamber; the chamber's magnetic field corresponded to the forces of confusion within a family or organization. The resulting trajectory reflects both the individual particles' energies and other characteristics and the magnetic force applied by the experimenter. But I couldn't decide who corresponds to the experimenter. The Experimenter?

Finally, I begin to see my confusion about how to end. Hello, confusion. I thought I had laid you to rest with this paper.

Confusion: Don't fool yourself! You've only drawn a rough sketch of me, and a rather unflattering one, at that. I can help as well as harm, you know.

W.T.: Just when I think I've gotten you under control...

Conf.: You missed your own point! You can't get me under control singlehandedly. You need to work on me, with me, harness me in some kind of group situation.

W.T.: I've tried. But I don't know what kind of group, where to find it, what perspective, what framework. I feel confused...

Conf.: So muddle. Wait. Experiment. Hunt. Hope.

REFERENCES

Bateson, G. *Steps to an ecology of mind.* New York: Ballatine Books, 1972.
Becker. E. *Escape from evil.* New York: The Free Press, 1975.
Brown, G.S. *Laws of form.* New York: Bantam Books, 1973.

Drew, E. Phase: In search of a definition. *The New Yorker.* August 27, 1979, pp. 45–73.

Perls, F.S. *In and out the garbage pail.* New York: Bantam Books, 1972.

Polster, E., & Polster, M. *Gestalt therapy integrated.* New York: Brunner/Mazel, 1973.

Stevens, B. *Don't push the river.* Moab, Utah: Real People Press, 1970.

Taylor, W. Developmental theory: Unsolved problem for child psychiatry. *American Journal of Orthopsychiatry, 41,* 1971, 557–565.

Varela, F.A. Calculus for self-reference. *International Journal of General Systems, 2,* 1975, 5–24.

Watzlawick, P., Weakland, J., & Fisch, R. *Change.* New York: Norton, 1974.

Watzlawick, P. *How real is real?* New York: Random House, 1976.

Wicklund, R.A., & Brehm, J.W. *Perspectives on cognitive dissonance.* Hillsdale, NJ: Erlbaum Associates, 1976.

Wink, W. *The Bible in human transformation.* Philadelphia: Fortress Press, 1973.

Chapter 42

A Personal Experience with Institutional Reinforcement of Retroflection

JOHN H. GAGNON

Retroflection is the act of turning back toward the self an energy that otherwise might be directed toward the environment (Perls, Goodman, & Hefferline, 1951, pp. 146 ff.); and as defined by Laura Perls in person in 1981. Chronic masturbation is an example of turning sexual energy back upon the self while depression and guilt can be the retroflections of anger and resentment respectively. It is these latter two retroflections that I want to discuss.

Over the past nine years during which I have been a psychotherapist I have witnessed numerous examples of reinforcement for retroflection brought about by institutions established for the mental and physical well-being of patients. Before I became a Gestalt therapist, I was never quite clear about the healthy need for angry and resentful expression but I often felt uncomfortable with the way in which these feelings were handled in institutional settings.

At one mental hospital where I trained, I saw several patients express anger in loud yelling or in punching a piece of furniture. These patients were restrained with camisoles, put in isolation rooms, or tied to their beds. One patient who kicked a standing ash tray over was wrestled down by several aides and put in a strip isolation room in a less "progressive" ward. I remember thinking, "God, if I were in this place I would have lots of reasons to be angry and would want to express this. What are patients supposed to do?" Obviously what they were supposed to do and in fact did do was to suppress any expression of angry feelings. Depression was rampant and so were all kinds of psychotic symptoms. I can't help but wonder how these patients might have been helped by not only allowing them to express anger but, in fact, even encouraging them to use punching bags, cushions, Batacca bats, or whatever to get rid of angry feelings in safe and acceptable ways. Years later when I directed a program for schizophrenic patients I and my staff found that the Gestalt practice of allowing and facilitating anger and resentment was responsible for reducing depressive and psychotic symptoms in the patients we treated. Again I found that the administrative structure of the institution for which I worked did not support such therapeutic interventions and considered patient behavior regressive "acting out." The more I learned about the benefits of helping patients to undo the chronic retroflection of angry and resentful feelings the more I facilitated patients in the expression of these feelings. Over the years I often heard from patients that other treatment settings had discouraged such expression.

As much as I had experienced the institutional practice of the repression of feelings I was not prepared for what I would experience in the summer of 1981. In June of that year I was in a very traumatic moped accident in which a tractor-trailer truck ran over my legs. I found myself in several hospitals which were eager to repair the physical damage that was done to me but were so uncomfortable with the expression of anger and resentment which were part of my grief process, that they reinforced my own retroflection tendencies in these areas. The result was that I became quite depressed and only found relief when I was discharged back home where I could work on releasing these pent-up feelings.

The first hospital I was sent to had to deal with the acute emergency of my accident. My left leg had been totally crushed and had to be amputated 7 inches below the knee. I had nearly lost all of my blood supply and was given 13 units of blood to bring me out of physical shock. My right leg was also crushed, the ankle was broken, the foot turned around 180 degrees and the lower leg denuded of skin and fascia. I spent the first three weeks in a morphine delirium and was shortly thereafter placed on other pain medications and Haldol and Elavil to thwart any depressive symptoms that might develop. I was drugged and foggy most of the time. It wasn't until I was leaving the first hospital and sent to another place for skin grafts that I really experienced intense feelings. I found that there was a general acceptance of sadness and crying by nurses but not by my doctors. The doctors would often point out to me that I still had two arms, was not a spinal-cord injury, and was lucky to be alive. I kept thinking, "I'm not crying for what I've got! I'm crying for what I've lost!" I never let anyone at any hospital discourage me from crying. With anger I was less self-supportive; however, I was not externally supported at all.

The real intense rage hit me after I was in the second hospital about one week. I was so overcome with the intensity of the anger that I became frightened of it. I knew that I needed to do something physical to express it but I was on my back, in traction. I tried using fantasy at first. I imagined myself destroying the truck that had hit me, using a sledge hammer. I even fantasized breaking the driver's legs. This still didn't help with the intensity of the fury. I wanted to hit, to punch, to scream, but there was no useful way to do this. I tried hitting my pillow but found it too soft to get any feeling of release from hitting it. I also tried twisting the pillow and got little release from doing that. I began telling my doctors and nurses that I was feeling lots of anger. Both groups said that this was part of the grief process and would say nothing further. I sensed their reluctance to see me release this anger. At no time did anyone, the medical staff or the psychologists sent to me, ever try to help me express the intense anger that I felt. I didn't want to yell or carry on in my room alone for fear of reprisal (being moved off the floor I was on, for example).

Nurses were especially uneasy around my anger and if I even spoke to them using an angry sound in my voice they seemed to leave my room sooner.

I also had an experience that served to frighten me further and to increase my overall level of rage and frustration. One night at approximately two a.m. a nurse came into my room to change an I.V. bag. Instead of shutting off the roller valve at the end of the tubing she left it open. I woke up to see the liquid level dropping in the I.V. tube. Then I saw the meniscus enter my arm. Moments later in my groggy, sleepy state I felt the air bubbles ripple through my heart. I immediately became alert, realized that air was running into the tubing and into my vein, and I grabbed the I.V. tubing and pinched it closed.

I told the nurse quite angrily that she had left the valve open. She was from Jamaica and didn't speak English well. I felt frustrated. I called for a nursing supervisor and the next day for the doctor in charge. I told both of them what had happened. They both dismissed the incident as something that could easily happen and told me it took a lot of air in the vein to kill someone. I felt unheard and deflected. My anger built up.

Finally, one nursing supervisor to whom I spoke told me that she would help to get my anger out without reprisal from the hospital. I asked her if she was uncomfortable with intense anger. She said she was not.

Before she came to my room I got hold of a shot-filled weight bag for exercising my arms. I found that I could put the bag on the bed in a position where I could hit at it with my fist. All day long I experimented with taking short, not too loud, wacks at the weight bag and this felt right.

At ten p.m. the supervisor came on duty. She came to my room and said she would help me express my anger. At first I realized that I couldn't shout or make lots of noise because I'd wake other patients so I tried telling her *about* my anger while I punched easily at the shot-filled bag. She became very uneasy with my punching, admitted that she was uncomfortable, got up and left.

The next week I felt worse. I became totally retroflected. My anger was all focused on myself. I felt tortured and miserable. This condition got worse over the next couple of days. I began to lose sleep and became horribly depressed. I could find no object to focus anger at. The nurses were always sweet and gentle; visitors were always concerned and kind.

One day in desperation I sat up and tried pounding on my pillow. The noise brought in a nurse. I had to explain to her what I was doing. My sense was that if I made too much noise I would be restrained or moved to the psychiatric ward. Also, I had to become intellectual in order to explain myself to the nurse who had come in. This succeeded in pulling me out of touch with my feelings. The depression and fear increased. So did my Haldol and Elavil doses.

After one month at the second hospital I was returned to the first hospital for rehabilitation therapy. The psychologist who came to see me said that while it was normal to go through sadness and anger as part of traumatic loss, I ought to look at the bright side of things. I received platitudes aplenty from the whole medical staff about how lucky I should feel and again I experienced very little real support for the strong emotional pain I was in.

One nurse who had worked in a psychotherapeutic treatment setting before was willing to stay with me when I cried. I found this companionship very helpful. However, everyone seemed uncomfortable with anger and I again had the sense that if I expressed it I would be placed on the psychiatric ward. One patient on my floor began to call out in anguish and was moved off the floor. This confirmed my fear of being seen as crazy if I acted out and so I retroflected more.

I have been out of the hospital three months now. I am still working on all of the feelings of my loss and of having to live mostly in a wheel chair or to walk short distances with great effort and pain, using an artificial leg. I still get depressed from time to time but I have gotten back into therapy with someone who is not afraid of feelings and who can facilitate the expression of everything including anger.

I can't help but think that my emotional recovery would have been much easier if someone on staff had been trained in Gestalt therapy or Radix and had helped me to release the tremendous rage I held inside.

I feel disappointed with the discomfort with feelings I saw in the medical staff. I often felt abandoned by doctors and nurses when I was in touch with deep feelings and this only served to pull away support for me and my emotional needs. In spite of the years of training I had in Gestalt therapy myself, I found that the lack of support for feelings, especially anger, had a particularly negative effect on me. It encouraged my own retroflection tendencies and increased my depression.

While I know that not all institutions reinforce retroflection I believe now that what many other facilities need to do is to train members of their staff in handling and facilitating feelings. I think that all such institutions should be equipped to help patients express, with physical acting out if necessary, the tremendous pent-up energies they have, and after my own experiences in the hospital I am especially aware of how important it is to help traumatic-injury victims deal with the anger they feel for their loss.

I hope that this paper can stimulate some changes in those institutional policies which reinforce retroflection in the individuals who come to these facilities for emotional as well as physical help.

REFERENCES

Perls, F., Hefferline, R., & Goodman, P. *Gestalt therapy.* New York: Dell, 1951.

Comment

Edward W.L. Smith

I was both touched and aroused as I read this piece by Gagnon. His statement is poignantly personal and delivers a protest badly needed. I felt touched as I remembered several incidents in my life in which I was strongly encouraged to retroflect my anger, my sadness, or my sexualized love. My experiences are, however, pale when contrasted to the one Gagnon describes. The protest aroused me, for it is about a situation which I have witnessed often in institutional settings.

The practice which Gagnon protests, the encouragement of retroflection of strong and oft-labeled "negative emotions,"is very common in institutions and is extremely destructive. Furthermore, my guess is that some of the VOICES readers support this destructive practice, out of ignorance of the nature of the healing process.

Several years ago George Taylor and I were co-leading a Gestalt workshop at Marco Island, Florida, for the Division of Psychotherapy of the American Psychological Association. I ran into a man who had been my supervisor in diagnostics and psychotherapy during five months of my internship in the late 1960s. Having not seen each other in some time we exchanged amenities and then he remarked that he had seen on the program that I was offering a workshop on Gestalt therapy. I said yes, and he followed up with a story about Gestalt therapists he had observed. He told of having attended a workshop once in which a woman became upset in her work and began crying. Two or three therapists, each identifying himself as Gestalt in orientation, took turns working with her. But, he said, "They must not have been very good, because one tried to work with her and she just kept crying. And each of the others took a turn and they just made her cry all the more!" He was pressed for time and I didn't push him to explain. I was upset, though, to think of how many interns may have received that attitudinal message.

The problem in encouraging retroflection by prohibiting expression of feelings is that this interferes with a natural process. If the natural process of expression is blocked, then that energy will be perverted and do its unnatural damage to the self or others. Reich wrote of this perversion of the natural urges and saw it as so common as to refer to the blocking of the natural urges as the "emotional plague." "Plagued" individuals, he believed, were so threatened by healthy emotional expression in others that they actively sought to suppress such. My experience has suggested to me that "institutions of healing" tend to be heavily staffed by individuals who meet Reich's criteria for the emotional plague, and emotionally free staff members are less in evidence, except for those times when they are reprimanded for allowing patients to "act out."

Final comment: Jim Bugental called attention to one of the ethics of humanistic psychology as being the valuing of non-hedonic emotions. I see this as of basic importance and as having far-reaching implications in the practice of the facilitation of healing and growth.

Chapter 43

Time to Work. . .
Time to Play

BUD FEDER

1977 and I am forty-seven and tired of day-in, day-out, week-in, week-out working as a clinical psychologist—this despite a varied work schedule including clinic administration (part-time), therapist (part-time), supervisor (part-time), consultant to schools (part-time), etc. The sum of the parts is wholly too much.

What to do? Can't stop earning as much as I'm accustomed to, can I? Kid expects, wife expects, I expect. . .stuff. Tough! From now on:

1. Two or three hours off the middle of each day for: tennis, jogging, sunning, reading, sexing, cooking, sleeping, i.e., taking care of me.
2. One week off every month for traveling, staying home, catching up on—chores mental or intellectual, such as a recent book with Ruth Ronall, *Gestalt Group Approaches*.
3. And still three weeks off every summer for that special vacation.

Friends, it's working—and I'm playing. Clients don't always like it—so we deal with that, often creatively. Sure I make less; so I spend less. Does your '79 Datsun really make you happier than my '67 Volvo? Does your meal at the Four Seasons (fifty bucks per head) pleasure you more than mine at the New Delhi (four bucks per head)?

All of my grandparents lived well into their eighties. Me too, I hope.

Chapter 44

Dead Tired and Bone Weary

GROVER E. CRISWELL

Somewhere out of my Oklahoma past the slang title for this article jumped to mind as an apt metaphor for exhaustion. I've become convinced, however, that being "dead tired" is not the same as being "bone weary." Or to say it another way, being tired is different from being fatigued. The causes and experience of each are similar, but in fact are quite different. Depending upon which state we are in, the necessary response to get us into another space will vary. Another preliminary conclusion is that tiredness can be useful in our functioning as psychotherapists while fatigue interferes with it.

The quickest way to point up some of the differences between tiredness and fatigue will be to relate two recent clinical experiences. The first has to do with a 35-year-old female client I had been seeing (she has now terminated) for about six months. Her wealthy husband had left her three years ago and she felt frustrated around trying to get a life going for herself. She dependently clung to the hope that another wealthy man would appear to take care of her and she would be able to continue her life as it had been before. She resisted any suggestion that would move her life in another direction, brushed aside any owning of the fearfulness her rigidity seemed to indicate, and would produce elaborate defenses for why things had to be exactly as they were. In spite of the fact that I would be energized in the sessions before and following her, I found it extremely hard to stay awake when with her. I was bored and only with difficulty could I keep my energy going. I would try to engage her, look out the window, walk around the room, would try again to find an opening, talk about what she was wanting from therapy, suggest termination, but no matter what, the situation continued to feel deadly. In looking back, I think I did not take seriously enough my tiredness and how hard it was to get around it. My afterthought is that she should have been working with a woman where the male-female passive/aggressive dynamics might not have been so paramount.

The other clinical situation involved a weekend intensive group and the dynamics of fatigue. I had been working almost non-stop for two weeks, having allowed myself to book two weekend groups in a row. I'd been up late the night before and the group started early. My most physical symptom, besides low energy, was a familiar pain behind my right eye that persisted throughout the day. I had little appetite and was aware of resenting the group and my inner tapes about responsibility. I was very susceptible to the negative inner voices that questioned my professional ability, whether they would like me or not, and whether I had anything to offer. Ugh. I don't like being in that space. I find it—not surprising— hard to get with people, my intuitive juices don't flow, and I have to rely much more than I like on past experience. To use a flying analogy, my senses are in a fog and I have to trust the instruments for guidance. The weekend turned out alright, thanks to a co-leader and an enthusiastic group, but my functioning was impaired, mostly in my own inner experience of how I usually work.

Tiredness, therefore, seems to be an acute condition with a fair amount of correlation to the energy expended. If I exercise for half an hour, I'm tired. The sensations are pleasant ones of release, and shortly I am ready for other activity. I put in my work day and when I come home, I'm tired. Generally some relaxing activity in the evening and a good night's sleep leaves me feeling refreshed. There are variables. Toward the end of the week, my tiredness increases. I find new clients take more energy. Doing administration saps more than when I am engaged in psychotherapy. If I am dealing with personal or interpersonal conflicts, I am more drained. When I am not paying enough attention to what I need in exercise, nutrition, sleep, and fun, I tire more quickly.

When my tiredness is on this level, I find it extremely useful as a dynamic in psychotherapy, not to mention in the conduct of my personal life. When I'm working with a client and begin to be aware of tiredness, the first thing I check out is what I am doing with myself physically. How am I breathing? Have I fallen into the breathing patterns of the client? How am I sitting? Where are my areas of tension? Does the tiredness have a focus? Behind my eyes? In my shoulders? My stomach? My hands? I listen for the messages and for the fantasies of what that part of me wants to do if I were to do an action. Sometimes I discover that I have been sitting too long or in an out-of-balance position, but most of the time I'm sitting *on* something.

The second thing I'm curious about when I experience tiredness is what feeling am I blocking? Tiredness becomes a way of pushing down a feeling that wants to emerge. Suppression takes energy. My tiredness can be a symptom of when I am beginning to shut down and I allow myself to open up to that feeling. In one session with a client where tiredness tugged at my sleeve, I found a resentment I had pushed aside about his call at the last minute to cancel our previous session. In another, I looked under the feelings of tiredness and got in touch with some sexual feelings I wasn't acknowledging to myself. With another the feelings were ones of danger and the client volunteered that she was feeling self-destructive and not telling me. This is where tiredness feels akin to boredom. Tiredness is the result of paying attention to what we find uninteresting, and/or not attending to what is more compelling.

A third focus when I begin to feel tired is to look at my mental functioning. I often notice that my head feels tired when I am thinking too much. This results not from the activity of thinking but *how* I am thinking. When I am thinking holistically, images, thoughts, associations, metaphors, and stories flow. My thinking is grounded in me. There is little wear or tear. When I am tired, I am generally *working* at thinking and the process gets sluggish. The internal economy of my energy is out of balance and I am figuratively standing on my head. I have seduced me or been seduced into abstraction, generalizations, logic, or other such irrelevant meanderings that sabotage therapy. The antidote is obvious, getting myself connected again in the here-and-now, and the result generates new vitality.

In psychotherapy, tiredness is not only a persona, but an interpersonal event. Everything that goes on during the therapy session (not to mention a lot of what happens outside the session) is of significance in the therapy. So it is with tiredness. I key off of my own processes, including being tired, to let me know what is going on in the session, and I also encourage the client to do so. I have them attend to their feelings of weariness, lack of energy, or tiredness, especially when these feelings seem to make a sudden or unexpected appearance. During a recent session a client was talking along in a fairly calm way about his week when he started yawning and indicated how tired he was feeling. He'd really not wanted to come because his week had been so hard. So I had him be the part that didn't want to come. As he gave that part energy and a voice, what he exploded into were a lot of negative feelings he was having about me! A therapist friend of mine believes that any time tiredness is present in a session it is a transferential issue where either the client (or the therapist!) is needing to express some feeling directly to the other. That certainly was the case in this situation and tiredness was the key.

In any case, where tiredness is present we go searching for a meaning. If you look upon tiredness as an energetic withdrawal, it may signal an avoidance of material with which the client doesn't want to deal or is conflicted about. It may be issues related to the structures of therapy (time, money, etc.) or feelings they are having about you as the therapist. Sometimes the feelings of tiredness need most of all the response of rest. Once a harried industrialist came into a Gestalt marathon. In response to the opening instructions to "get in touch" and "go with the flow," he lay down and slept for half of the time. There are moments when this is the most appropriate response!

When we proceed now to the matter of fatigue, we are looking at a quite different phenomenon. With tiredness, as I have indicated, there is an ebb and flow that is grounded in the present. As a dynamic, it can often be useful in the conduct of the therapy. Even when it isn't, we can generally get around it to be with the client. With fatigue, we begin to shut down and our energy is drained. It interferes with our functioning as a psychotherapist. Fatigue begins as tiredness, but somewhere along the way we have crossed a line, often without even knowing it, entering into a state of exhaustion. On a muscular level, this is quite easy to demonstrate. Just start bending your arm back and forth at the elbow until you are tired. Now keep doing it beyond the point of tiredness. Your first sensations will be painful ones and then it will begin to feel like the energy drains out of the arm. You are exhausting the arm. Technically, you are producing metabolites (carbon dioxide, acid phosphate, and lactic acid) faster than they can be eliminated. Fatigue is our body's way of telling us to stop. It is possible to run over these insistent messages and to keep bending your arm. Just distract yourself and focus on something else. The movement becomes automatic because you have detached. Eventually, of course, the arm will stop and begin to spasm. What we have isolated here in an arm is what happens on a more total organismic level with fatigue. At this point, I want to mention the other way in which the fatigue substances accumulate in the body because it is pertinent to our discussion of the fatigue of the therapist. Toxicity can develop in the body from too little exercise or the absence of other activities that speed up the elimination of the toxic material. The toxicity settles into the muscles.

Now I want to make a generalization from what has been said: Fatigue is a direct consequence of not taking care of ourselves and is a self-destructive pattern. It becomes a chronic state that develops a cumulative power. We can detach and keep going for awhile before the body rebels. I generally find that what happens for me is that feelings of irritability develop and my mood becomes somewhat depressed. In fact, fatigue and depression seem to be "kissing cousins." My energy level then goes down and my body registers its discomfort. I feel a tightness in my muscles, my breathing gets more restricted, and I feel tension in the back of my neck. Occasionally, to make a pun of a biblical phrase, my right eye offends me! All of this, of course, has an effect on my mental functioning, but the mind has marvelous powers to keep going by the magic of detachment. When I am distracting myself, I can go well beyond my limits before my mind is compelled to pay attention.

Fatigue comes from not taking care of ourselves, from going beyond our limits. The line between being tired and being fatigued is a personal one determined by a number of variables: age, health, amount of physical exercise, nutrition, stamina and how well we pace ourselves. The clarity of our psychological processing is no small part. Emotional toxicity also accumulates into fatigue. The beginning therapist will often tire more quickly than a more experienced one and will often have more tendency to push the limits. Whatever the reasons, when we are in a fatigue state, we are in an emergency situation, both personally and interpersonally. We are vulnerable. Getting into another space means we have to take our situation seriously. During the weekend I mentioned, I took care to conserve my energy, factored my fatigue into my responses, lay down and went through relaxation exercises at the breaks, and opted out of a party for that night to sleep twelve hours. Oh yes, I also cancelled everything but play on weekends for the next two months. Sometimes getting ourselves out of the fatigue state and back in balance means giving attention to relatively simple needs. Rest. Relaxation. Vacation. Exercise. Less work and more play. Finishing unfinished business that is weighing us down. Getting our system clear. However, when we are often in a state of fatigue, we need to remember its cumulative momentum and the damaging results. Fatigue regularly and dutifully collects its toll. Major revision in our style of living is then required if we are to continue as effective therapists who also model the health we would facilitate.

My belief is that fatigue only interferes in the practice of psychotherapy and serves no useful purpose. It is a destructive source of static. Tiredness, kept within limits, can be a rich ground out of which important meanings emerge.

Chapter 45

Anxiety—the Perverse Traveling Companion

EDWARD W.L. SMITH

For most of us, anxiety is a traveling companion on our journeys into intimacy. As we move toward intimacy, the mutual exploration of our personal, private ground, we keep anxiety closely with us. We may abandon anxiety for awhile, moving forward, only to turn a corner and meet it head on.

The promise which anxiety makes is that it will warn us of, and thereby protect us from, dangers. And these dangers are presented with a certainty which makes ignoring them seem absolutely foolhardy. Anxiety demands at least a delay in the trip, a detour into "safer" (so anxiety promises) and more superficial public territory. These detours can become the itinerary of a lifetime.

So, anxiety is the tocsin and the detour guide. It scares us with the warning of imminent danger and then offers a path to safer ground. Only one catch. Anxiety lies.

Anxiety is the perverse half-sib of fear. Fear is an indispensable traveling companion on all long journeys. Without it we wouldn't survive more than a few trips. Fear is well educated. It uses its eyes, its ears, and all of its sensory equipment. It also remembers. This means that it has only to carry an alley cat home by the tail one time to learn an important lesson about alley cats. (Appreciations to Mark Twain for his insights about empiricism and caution.)

So fear is a protector from real dangers. It warns us of the presence of something which indeed will harm. Of course, this is within the limits of fear's education. Sometimes fear is misinformed and therefore gives warnings about things believed harmful but actually not so. But fear is honest.

To the best of its knowledge, what it says is dangerous, is. And fear is open to revising what it knows, based on new sensory information and carefully evaluated second-hand reports. Fear keeps a close watch on reality.

Not so, anxiety. Anxiety acts like fear, but with a major difference. It doesn't care at all about reality. So, where does it get its "information"?

Anxiety arrives on the scene with obsolete beliefs. These beliefs are based on what was true at one time, but are no longer true. The basic theme is well known in most psychotherapy circles. The child learns by direct experience that certain things bring pain. Hence, fear. The child learns by direct experience that certain other behaviors bring another kind of pain—punishment (or a threat of punishment which may itself be a punishment) from parenting figures. And these latter behaviors involve what is natural, such as feelings and spontaneous expression of feelings. The child then learns that feeling certain feelings or certain expressions of those feelings brings punishment (pain). By avoiding these feelings or expressions new information, as time goes by, is not gathered and the old contingency is brought along through time. Hence, anxiety.

And that's how anxiety lies. It speaks with a force and certainty as strong as any fear, but it speaks of a danger that only was, and is no more. Anxiety has no regard for historical perspective. This is part of what Freud meant when he said that the neurotic suffers from his memories. And T.S. Eliot used an interesting phrase as he wrote of someone who was "nothing but a set of obsolete responses."

The half-sibs, fear and anxiety, can be recognized one from the other by a special quality which is peculiar to the latter. Anxiety derives this special quality from two factors. First, it is based on the perspective of a child who is threatened to its core by the powerful parent figures. So anxiety is characterized by a feeling of smallness and relative helplessness. Second, the content is anachronistic. Almost as if in a time warp, old situations from a different time and place show up in a current context. (This is a clue to keeping anxiety a close companion. The rule is: to be anxious, assiduously stay in the "there and then.") These two factors give anxiety its power to escalate its warning to the level of certain catastrophe.

Just as fear warns of believed dangers and enhances the process of living, anxiety promises catastrophe based on a lie and diminishes aliveness. The original situations out of which anxiety developed were ones in which parental prohibitions carried a threat and demanded that the child not feel something or that he not express the feeling. This inhibition of feeling and expression is bio-negative, training in deadness.

The journey of intimacy takes one past the familiar and certain landmarks of protocol, manners, and mechanical rituals. Farther on, the traveling companions known as roles find the terrain too unsuitable and drop out. This leaves the person and the companion anxiety. The struggle is between the person who wants to be known by showing who he or she is, feelings and expressions of feelings, and the companion anxiety who shouts warnings of imminent catastrophe. Each time the warning is heeded, a detour is taken which usually leads back to the place where the roles are waiting. Safe in the company of roles, and with anxiety now quiet, one can go on until out of the boredom and loneliness of alienation one returns to the journey.

At some point the traveler may explore a new area of intimacy by telling the other about the companion, anxiety. This might take the form, "I want you to know that I am afraid to let you see me cry." All the while anxiety is shouting threats such as, "Don't let her/him know you are weak, fool. He/she will hurt you like you've never imagined before. Hide, dummy, or you'll really get it." What will it be, another detour to the land where roles are the way to safe, alienated deadness, or straight on into the heartland of intimacy?

If I choose aliveness then I go on in spite of a steadily mounting anxiety to intimacy's sacred ground. There I no longer speak of my anxiety, I simply do what before I only said I was afraid to do. So, I cry before you. In this sacred ground of intimacy, anxiety gives up and waits to meet me and test me later on, another place, another time.

Comment

Martin Margulis

Although I have long been comfortable with the distinction that fear is based on real danger, and anxiety on danger imagined, reading Dr. Smith's article has led me to question whether this distinction is more apparent than real, especially in the realm of the interpersonal. The author contends that anxiety experienced in relationship is a lie based on learned and outdated parental messages which state that it is wrong to feel and worse to share feelings. Fear, on the other hand, is a useful guide which alerts us to real danger and readies us for choice and action.

While I appreciate the validity of the author's interpretation of the function of fear, his fusion of psychoanalytic and behavioral concepts confuses because it does not go to the heart of the matter. The logic of the distinction between the two concepts is circular—only by post hoc analysis can we know that it was fear that was experienced rather than anxiety. A patient recently told me she had discovered that she has a "phobia of heights." She realized this when she became overwhelmed and immobilized when, in order to take a short cut, her husband suggested that they walk across a railroad trestle over a major Maine river. Did she experience anxiety or fear? To an adventurer or a graduate of Outward Bound, she obviously had an anxiety reaction. However, a large proportion of the population would probably react in the manner she did.

In the world of the interpersonal, the distinction between fear and anxiety becomes vaguer. To contend that the aversion to intimacy is based on neurotic fears of punishment for exposure of inner experience has validity but it denies the truly intimate encounter of its essential nature—two beings as process coming together in a venture that has limited conscious predictability. This is what makes in-volvement so attractive and fascinating, yet so frightening. My inner excitement is one of anticipation and reflects a rising creative re-surge-ency. But my craving for this possibility of transformation has too often led me blindly into disappointment, hurt, and self-denial; thus, my excitement easily turns into anxiety. Being truly open means to share one's personal voyage with another in order to enhance one's journey toward wholeness and not in order to receive sustenance from the other.

Beyond the expression of feeling, my vulnerability is expressed in acts of kindness and sensitivity and not just in an unconscious plea for mercy and forgiveness for my acting out. My anxiety can help me assess whether my needs involve self-deception and illusion. I have learned not to dismiss my apprehension but to give it respect and to let it lead me to greater clarity about my relationship to the other.

Although love is blind and instinctual, love-ing involves choice. This choice is based on awareness of the other as well as awareness of one's own needs and their "correctness." Anxiety tempers this process so that relationship can evolve to greater and deeper intimacy based on values more durable than physical satisfaction and infantile dependency—namely, mutual trust, loyalty, tolerance, and respect for the other's uniqueness and individuality as well as the need to nurture one's own evolving toward whole-ness.

RESPONSE BY EDWARD SMITH

Dr. Margulis' response to my discussion of "anxiety—the perverse traveling companion" led me to re-read my material and think further. I recognize the difficulty sometimes of differentiating the experiences of anxiety and fear experientially. The theoretical differentiation is quite clear and useful, but being so clear may set up the expectation that the two will be easily distinguished in experience. Experientially fear and anxiety are very similar. The task is to distinguish the two as best one can. About half way through my discussion I talked about the quality of anxiety by which it can be recognized as different from fear.

The core of the issue, as I see it, is the use of caution based on fear rather than avoidance based on anxiety. The more I avoid, the less I live and grow. But my caution serves to keep me alive, both physically and spiritually, so that there is a me growing.

Chapter 46

Different Now—
If We Want to Be

DAVID ROTHENBERG

As stated in my concepts *Differential Gestalt,* I have three primary values as a psychotherapist.

1. All people, individually and together, are viewed as essentially healthy, intact and complete within themselves.

The traditional pathology model of "mental illness" is rejected in favor of the concept of "undifferentiated mental health."

While identification, assessment and interpretation of origins of stress may be useful, the explicit benefits accrue from similar attention being given to overlooked or obscured aspects of personal strength.

2. All people are viewed as being simultaneously thinking and feeling and behaving at all times.

The predominance in either patient or psychotherapist of one of these personal aspects at any given time shall not preclude the ongoing function and growth of any other aspect.

Only by the recognition of all three aspects can there be utilization of all the available resources. It is critical to be analytic (cognitive) and affective (humanistic) and behavioral in my perceptions and responses to preclude confining my patients to any limited singular approach.

3. All people are viewed as having all three aspects of themselves available at all times and can select from their own "universe of choices" their personal perceptions and responses to life's experiences.

This primary value validates each person's freedom and responsibility for whatever they choose to think, feel or do.

Thus, the bondage of past experience or present disabilities may be given new values which meet current requirements for equilibrium and growth.

I hope the people who work with me will validate for themselves the value of 1) focusing upon their strengths as well as their stresses, 2) utilizing all of their resources of thought, feeling and behavior, and 3) experiencing their freedom and responsibilities to create their own unique states of being.

Further, it is my hope and commitment as a psychotherapist to be simplistic, vigorous and proximate enough to enable the people who work with me to accept that they can be different NOW, if they want to be.

Chapter 47

Only Our Perspectives Vary

HERBERT S. ROTH

O f course we live in a time of social cataclysm—and thus it has been since creation. Only shifting perspectives—of time, of distance, of immediate involvement—define events as exciting emergence or as explosion, as change rather than chaos, as evolution rather than revolution. The cataclysmic events of society may well be macrocosmic parallels to the explosions so vividly confronted in psychotherapy—joyous laughter, tears of anguish, sneezes, orgasms, the burps and farts of life being lived.

Perls defined personality as the interface between changing self and conservative society, and society itself is the always fluid edge between now and history. . . only our perspectives vary. Sometimes, after a heavy day at the office, I like to relax with science fiction—it seems so refreshingly real. So much for my own perspective!

My office, my practice, my home, my life are cluttered with past mementos, present playthings, future projects. Therapy may evoke an old folk song (a guitar is always close at hand) or rehearsal on video tape. And I feel great when I'm in on the process of changing an "oh, woe!" to an "oh, wow!" Cataclysm might be holocaust, and it might be opportunity, and I'm not yet godlike enough to know the difference in advance. I try, for myself and for the folks I work with, to steer some sort of course between the dangerous should have's and ought to's, and cope and hope for the best with what is.

Chapter 48

Personal Growth and Social Influence

EDWARD SMITH

I am both concerned and excited by the social changes which I observe and experience. I am concerned about the dehumanizing forces and the social/political happenings which threaten my safety and the safety of those I love. I am excited at the rearrangement of traditional roles and system in ways which reflect an increasing respect for personhood and the actualization of that personhood. I am most centered when I view and experience the happenings as challenges—challenges to my awareness, my openness to experiencing, my daring to express my feelings, my ability to take effective action. I lose that centeredness when I view the changes through a template of passivity, seeing the happenings as always curses or blessings upon me.

My power to influence social change resides in my person and the effect of my person on others through intimate contacting.

In terms of my person, I can choose toward these experiences which hold likelihood for my growth in the direction of greater wholeness. The important thing, as Don Juan told Carlos (Castaneda), is to pick some path, any path, as long as it has heart, and stick with it. As long as the path has heart for me, I grow by following it. As I pursue my path of growth, I contribute in some measure to the level of positive energy in the world. By raising my personal consciousness I help to raise the societal consciousness.

I influence most powerfully through intimate contacting. I have little or no power at a distance. As I allow myself fuller awareness and more focused excitement in the presence of another, I serve as a powerful model on contacting, as well as a more knowing observer and guide to that person in learning to make need-satisfying, validating contact. I can facilitate another's movement only into those regions where I have been. So, I serve as model and as facilitator. The potential is within and needs only to be adequately supported in its expression.

My path of growth incorporates personal therapy, Aikido, Hatha Yoga, T'ai Chi Ch'uan, and running (with a Zen attitude). My view of the world draws heavily from Gestalt therapy, especially the Zen and Existential underpinnings. My way of doing therapy is primarily Gestalt and Psychomotor. I live this path in the context of a wife and two children.

Of these paths of growth, Aikido is newest to me. Since Aikado I have come to a new perspective: If I am attacked, my attacker is disrupting the harmony of the universe with his aggression. If I remain passive and allow myself to be injured, I both sustain harm (which I do not want) and allow my attacker to become an injurer, a person out of harmony. Out of my respect for my own being and my respect for his being, I can stop the aggression. In Aikido it is just to use only enough assertion to stop the attack, and not to inflict unnecessary injury. I am living the principle now. I have become more assertive and less aggressive, and act more often from a position of harmony rather than from a position of fear.

All I can really do is work on my own consciousness and be open to sharing it.

Chapter 49

On Grandparently Love

JOSEPH C. ZINKER

Creative therapy is a loving encounter between therapist and client.

In the creative process, as in falling in love, we contact our sweetness, longing, powerful intention and profound thoughtfulness. Arthur Rubinstein said, "Playing the piano is like making love, it fills me completely with joy."

Authentic love for another is experienced as ecstasy in the very being of the other, as rejoicing in the loved one's very existence. It is non-manipulative, non-clinging, non-demanding. We let the other be. We do not wish to violate his unique human integrity. The "purest" kind of love (pure, not in the puritanical sense of being clean, but in the sense of prerequisite clarity of rejoicing in the other's being) involves the total experience of the internal tension or energy which is part of one's responsiveness to the loved one.

Thus, we can speak of love as a kind of creative tension. "Staying with" this tension and letting it permeate one's whole being is an enormously difficult task to accomplish, particularly since our society has a tendency to sell canned pleasure for immediate satisfaction.

My love for the client is agapeic—more a feeling of goodwill toward humanity than a romantic, sentimental or possessive love. I seek my client's good, whether I like him or not. Agape love for me is thoughtful, prudent, just, benevolent, gracious. The term "brotherly love" has been used in this relation. My own image is of "grandparently love." Unlike a parent who directs his children passionately and sometimes egotistically, my grandparent asks for nothing, yet takes pleasure in learning, observing, and understanding the life experience of another just as it is. When I experience my love passionately, as a parent, I am leery of losing my perspective and objectivity in clearly perceiving my client.

Grandparently love from me, the counsellor, engenders trust. Because the therapeutic process often deals with the most vulnerable parts of the person, trust must always be there for both parties to allow the unfolding of their feelings. It is this "love" in all its forms, which lubricates the creative process between client and therapist.

Yet one does not have to love someone to respectfully attend to that person. As Martin Buber put it, "One cannot command that one *feel* love for a person, but only that one deal lovingly with him" (1962). And so must the therapist act lovingly with his client.

When I am there for the other
a quietness flows within.
a sweet stillness.
I am engrossed in prayer,
witnessing another life unfolding.
I am an ancient woman
weaving cloth
    for a grandchild.

(May 12, 1975)

The experience of feeling loved is one of acute receptivity, of taking in the gift of the other. It necessitates readiness to let the other person penetrate one's deepest stratum; it requires openness and lack of defensiveness and suspiciousness that the loving person will be injurious. In the experience of letting the other person love us, we willingly take the risk of being hurt. The fact that the loving other has the power to hurt (to reject) and chooses not to, gives the experience a sense of magnetism.

When we feel totally loved by someone who really "matters," the ecstatic receptive experience makes us feel beautiful, perfect, graceful, profound and wise (Maslow, 1962). *Our* deepest, most profound stirrings of self-appreciation, self-love and self-knowledge surface in the presence of the person whom we experience as totally accepting. It is as though we say, "When I know your total acceptance, then I can show you my softest, most penetrable, delicate, beautiful and vulnerable self" (Rogers, 1961).

My clients' "love" for me varies with their stages of development as well as with each person's specific life circumstances. Often the person projects ghosts of his past on me: I am seen as the critical or loving parent, the sadistic villain, the seducer, the teaser, the wise old man, the Christ-Rabbi, a sex object, a potential lover or spouse. As Freud pointed out long ago, psychotherapy is in some ways a working out of the client's perception of the therapist.

At a higher level of development the client can appreciate and love me in the same grandparently way in which I strive to experience him. At the most advanced levels of the relationship, both people take turns grandparenting; each uses his individual competence to enhance the life of the other. Said Martin Buber, "When a man is singing and cannot lift his voice, and another comes and sings with him, another who can lift his voice, the first will be able to lift his voice too. That is the secret of the bond between spirits" (1962).

REFERENCES

Buber, M. *Ten rungs: Hasidic sayings.* New York: Shocken Books, 1962.
Maslow, A. *Toward a psychology of being.* Princeton, NJ: D. Van Nostrand Co. Inc., 1962.
Rogers, C. *On becoming a person.* Boston: Houghton, Mifflin, 1961.

Chapter 50

My Unconscious Takes Care of Me— The Taste of Two Strawberries

VINCENT O'CONNELL

In a very subtle way, hard to describe, I am no less anxious now than I was hitherto, before I ever got into psychotherapy in 1946.

The one thing that's different, except for my age and the growing, is that now "*i*" got some kind of handle on that miserable bastard who makes "me" anxious and gives "me" anxiety feelings. Don't knock it until you get here. It ain't exactly easy to come by, at least for me—to get to this place where I live with my anxieties, honor them, bear them, and keep breathing. Mark Stern calls that *recycling* anxiety and I call it *processing* my anxiety, and it's only a difference in temperament and in terms. I prefer Mark's term for the hydraulic downhill dynamic gut-felt description of the work involved in doing the work. I think I'm going to take the word *recycling* into my vocabulary now.

I used to think I would get the good fortune to reach the place where there was/is awareness and no anxiety. And I reached that place, *mirabile dictu*. That's heaven and/or close to the garden where all things are well and everything's going to turn out alright. Jesus.

And then, you know what? What? There I am in the garden and I begin to have these "anxiety feelings" again. . . . Jesus. . . and well, what I

299

figured out is that even in perfection, even in heaven, I still seem to be hauling my neurosis along, and that's all there is to it. Simple as that. "*Ting-a ling*," Kurt Vonnegut says.

I've had dozens of anxiety attacks and so far I ain't died from any of them. I got a sturdy heart that keeps pumping and breathing and "my" heart has learned to love—which helps me a lot at those moments of acute anxiety and doubt. So I now have a grasp (a contact) with that mother who "pushes" me yet again into the egoless state where all is promising and nothing is hopeless. And when I come back, here I am on square one and what else is new and wonderful. Etc.

And then, exactly at the moment, the "anxiety" really starts. Jesus, not again. And I just keep breathing, praying, do my meditations, and listening as best I can to what my unconscious is trying to tell me, now, here, *this* time around.

Brother/sister, that's what I call *recycling* my here-now anxiety. And if you can come up with another description, please to share it/you with me, for I ain't no further along now than I was then, years ago, and dear Jesus, dear sweet Jesus, "take *this* cup from me." Here-and-now. Soon as possible. AMEN.

Fritz Perls and I had many discussions about anxiety: what it is, how to deal therapeutically with the various and many anxiety feelings. What happens when you do this or/and that. Fritz believed, and I do still, that the client had to have *some* anxiety in the first place to get into therapy. If he or she doesn't, then our job is to stay put and wait for the moment where we can see the client's response to the here-and-now and then ask: "How is your breathing?" He was one of the most capable persons in that regard too. Mostly, I don't make people anxious and just listen to what's happening here-and-now with I and Thou. And then I come in and try out what my unconscious and conscious is telling me here-and-now. Fritz said, "Vin, I make a piece of art or I make a mess." Clients are very forgiving if I make a mess and admit it. (And the "cleanup" is part of the therapy.)

Fritz and I used to discuss our cases and one day he came back again to Columbus, Ohio, puzzled by something. When I asked him, he said, "What do you do with an obsessional patient who turns his anxiety into depression?" And it so happened, I too had such a patient, and I was not only puzzled, admitting I didn't know what to do now, I was also becoming more and more anxious and wishing the client would quit me and go to someone else. That is what I call a come-uppance, and as far as the anxiety level is concerned, it's work—for me. That's my unconscious talking, and I trust him/her, here-and-now. There is a time to say: "No, that's as far as I dare go." And Fritz taught me that too. When I make a mess I admit it and then clean it up. (That's therapy for me.) Shalom.

The taste of two strawberries for me is when I am open/available to the client and myself, and whatever I am here-and-now—granted respect and the certain limitations that surround me and delimit this (our/my) ongoing here-and-now. It's a place of peace, of shalom, of the sound of two hands clapping, and the songs of birds singing. And the sweat and work that goes into it too. Odd things: Once you/I get into the sound of one hand clapping and the taste of one strawberry, you/I becomes more acute and there we are here-and-now and as I am age 68, still trying to figure it all out and praying', still I wouldn't have it any other way. And thank God for the journey and the journeying.

AFTERTHOUGHTS AND POSTSCRIPTS

Just imagine for a moment the place where there are these beautiful books in Hebrew, Greek, Muslim, Latin, and Sanskrit and Gaelic and another unknown language. . . and there is all this eternity to hold there in your/my hands and to learn to read them. . . and they are so beautiful and full of love that you/I bliss out over and over again. That's how I "died" when I had my operation.

Chapter 51

On Anxiety, Functions, and Re-Functions

EDWARD W.L. SMITH

In the Spring 1979 (Vol. 15, No. 1) issue of *VOICES* I wrote about anxiety as a "perverse traveling companion" on our journeys into intimacy. I suggested that anxiety is the perverse half-sib of fear in that fear protects us from real dangers, but anxiety promises protection from that which is no longer a danger, while leading us to believe that the historical danger is still present. As uncomfortable as anxiety may be, one can come to endure and even embrace it, if one becomes familiar enough with it. Perhaps it is this embracing of the familiar, in spite of discomfort or pain, which is the *re*-function of anxiety. I offer a poetic statement of the dynamics of anxiety (from a Gestalt therapy perspective) for your consideration and reaction.

ANXIETUDE

Excitement growing!
Not enough support.
Imagine the worst.
Gasp! Don't breathe!
Anxiety, my old friend.

Chapter 52

A Matter of Choice

JOSEPH C. ZINKER

To this day I don't feel friendly with my past anxieties... or with my present ones for that matter. For the most part, serious old anxieties and anxiety episodes have been replaced by my stronger sense of competence and a greater interest in being fully with people. I allow myself the pleasure of full arousal, attending to the ebb and flow of my energy.

My anxiety has been replaced by episodes of anguish and pain related to illness and hurts in my family and among friends. I suffer existential angst. I suffer every time I enslave myself to limiting relationships or narrow monolithic ideas. I can carry this suffering more gracefully than the old anxieties mostly because I have greater awareness. I *choose* to examine my life critically, with a consequent sense of compassion, regret, shame, or sense of celebration.

I am not choosing between dog shit and horse shit. There is a clear qualitative difference between old anxieties and present aware suffering, and I choose the latter.

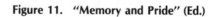

"AND THEY ARE ALWAYS MAKING
INDECENT PROPOSALS TO ME!"

Figure 11. "Memory and Pride" (Ed.)

Part V
Criticism
and Rejoinders

"...BUT IT'S PART OF MY THERAPY!"

Figure 12.   "Responsibility" (Ed.)

Chapter 53

Cognitive Aspects of Abreactive Therapy

ALBERT ELLIS

Abreactive therapy has come to the fore again, after years of relative neglect. Many recent articles describe and endorse, and a few of them present positive research findings on, abreactive methods. Although these papers support a wide variety of evocative, confrontational, experiential, verbal, physical, and other techniques of catharsis and abreaction, they all claim good results with certain types of clients. Granting that devotees of some of these techniques may be overenthusiastic proponents of their own and related theories, it is reasonable to assume that the obtained results have some degree of validity.

The question arises: *How* does abreactive therapy work, if indeed it does? The traditional answer to this question has generally been that release of unacknowledged, blocked, or repressed emotion is *itself* curative; and, by extension, when clients inhibit or repress their strong feelings and physiological concomitants of these feelings (such as their sexual desires and actions), they create dysfunctional energy constrictions and muscular armorings, and that when these constrictions and armorings are released (especially by breathing, kicking, yelling, and other physical exercises) psychic blockings are automatically released, along with the physiological rigidities, and emotional change and cure occurs.

This traditional answer to why abreaction helps inhibited clients may well be partly true; but it is my hypothesis that it is mainly false. I take the position that although humans are basically hedonically oriented animals who are biologically as well as sociologically prone to think and feel in certain common ways, and although they therefore had better not ignore

307

the "natural"—or as Maslow (1954) termed it, the "instinctoid"—urges of their bodies, they are uniquely and primarily motivated by their cognitively oriented values, goals, purposes, ideals, and philosophies (Ellis, 1962, 1971, 1972, 1973). I agree, in this respect, with the basic teachings of other cognitive therapists, such as Adler (1927), Berne (1972), Kelly (1955), Phillips (1956), Rotter (1954), and Thorne (1961).

My hypothesis is, consequently, that emotional disturbance is largely caused by unrealistic, absolutistic, and irrational thinking, and that when cathartic and abreactive therapies work, they are effective because they help clients to consciously or unconsciously change their self-defeating cognitions. I have previously tried to show that there is a powerful cognitive element in experiential and relationship therapy that practitioners in these areas tend to ignore (Ellis, 1970). I shall now attempt to do the same thing for several recent articles favoring abreactive therapies.

GESTALT THERAPY

Perls (1969) indicates, gestalt therapy is a verbal and physical approach to abreaction. Brown (1973) notes that

> When the gestalt therapist detects some incongruity of behavior between a client's perceptual foreground and his sensory-motor-feeling background, he will ask his client to consciously turn his or her foreground awareness upon this bodily mannerism which expresses some internal gap of self-awareness. For instance, if a client has his or her hands placed on some part of the body and is exerting considerable energy touching it, in all probability the hands are placed there because of some unaware neuro-muscular tensions. This bodily tension bespeaks the existence of a corresponding psychic tension which may be tantamount to rigidity of awareness. (pp. 104–105)

Note here that gestalt therapists are clearly cognitive, in that (1) they *detect* some incongruity of behavior between the clients' perceptual foreground and their sensory-motor-feeling background; (2) they *hypothesize* that the clients have several needs (or, more accurately, strong desires) pressing for awareness; (3) they *theorize* that the clients' abreactive experiences in therapy will form a complex sequence of perceptual gestalts each characterized by a unique constellation of sensory-motor-affective elements; (4) they *assume* that as the clients' experiential perceptual gestalten are clearly formed into a distinct patterning of progressive differentiation and becoming, these disturbed individuals will become emotionally healthy and self-actualizing; (5) they *look for* incongruities of behavior between their clients' perceptual foreground and sensory-motor-feeling background and *direct* them to consciously turn their foreground awareness upon their bodily mannerisms which the therapists *postulate* are expressions of some internal gap of self-awareness; (6) they *believe* the clients' bodily tensions bespeak the existence of corresponding psychic tensions which are tantamount to rigidity of awareness; (7) they *conjecture* that awareness by clients of their perceptions, feelings, and bodily processes will itself (without any added cognitive restructuring) lead to significant personality change; (8) they *choose* one set of gestalt techniques for an individual client and another set for a different individual, and in the process they presumably *diagnose* what kind of a client they are treating.

In the course of these highly cognitive assumptions and procedures, gestalt therapists largely help their clients to become *aware* of hidden "needs" (that is, *thoughts*, actions, and feelings); to *differentiate* the patterns of their behaviors; to *reflect* on the validity of their shoulds, their top-dog, bottom-dog, and other self-defeating philosophies; and to *decide* what their own real goals are and to follow these, rather than arbitrary societally-imposed, goals. In the illustration given by Brown, the client probably thinks along the following lines when turning his or her awareness upon a bodily mannerism that was previously out of awareness: "Oh! I notice that I am much more neuromuscularly tense than I previously thought I was. How fascinating! This may well mean that I really am anxious about what the therapist and the people in the group here think of me. If so, I am probably demanding that I be top dog and that they all worship me. How silly! I think I can accept myself even if I'm not top dog. What is more, I don't *have* to hide my anxiety from myself or others. I think I'll let myself feel anxious for a awhile and *still* think I'm okay. Yes, I think I will do that. See how good I can feel about myself, even when I'm anxious! Isn't it good to be honest about this!"

If I am correct about the overt and covert cognitions of the therapist and the client in the course of gestalt therapy, this procedure, for all its seeming abreactive, dramatic, and physical qualities, is perhaps, at bottom, ninety per cent or more cognitive.

*   *   *

DISCUSSION

Several methods of abreactive therapy, ranging from physical and nonverbal to imaginative and verbal techniques, are reviewed and analyzed. It would appear that all of them are based on distinctly cognitive theories of diagnosis and psychotherapy that are firmly held by the therapists who employ them; and that in their employment these therapists are frequently directive, planful, and otherwise overtly or covertly cognitive. It would also seem that the clients who undergo these forms of psychological treatment importantly reflect on, make conclusions about, and decide to act on the information about the past and the present that arises out of their cathartic-abreactive experiences. If it were not for this highly cognitive aspect of emotional experiencing and re-experiencing, it is dubious that any notable personality change would occur in clients. Because abreaction of feeling is itself so dramatic, so intense, and so focussed upon when it is occurring, and because cognitive and behavioral changes so frequently ensue almost immediately after such experience, there is a tendency for us to cavalierly assume that the sudden release of unacknowledged, blocked, or repressed emotion is itself curative; that it mobilizes some powerful, almost magical energy force that works reparative miracles. This is as unlikely as the notion that emotion itself springs directly from experiences (or from prior emotion), without any cognitive mediational processes. Literally scores of recent experiments have shown otherwise: that human behavior and emotion can be drastically changed when the individual's ideas, attitudes, or philosophies are deliberately manipulated. I would suggest a series of similar experiments designed to test the hypothesis that when significant behavioral and attitudinal changes occur subsequent to abreaction, cognitive mediation is almost always importantly and crucially present.

REFERENCES

Adler, A. *Understanding of human nature.* New York: Greenberg, 1927.

Bean, O. *Me and the orgone.* New York: Avon, 1973.

Berne, E. *What do you say after you say hello?* New York: Grove Press, 1972.

Brown, M. The new body psychotherapies. *Psychotherapy: Theory, Research and Practice, 10,* 1973, 98–116.

Ellis, A. *Reason and emotion in psychotherapy.* New York: Lyle Stuart, 1962.

Ellis, A. The cognitive element in experiential and relationship psychotherapy. *Existential Psychiatry, 28,* 1970, 35–52.

Ellis, A. *Growth through reason.* Palo Alto: Science and Behavior Books, 1971.

Ellis, A. Psychotherapy and the value of a human being. In *Value and valuation: Axiological studies in honor of Robert S. Hartman,* J.W. David, Ed. Knoxville: University of Tennessee Press, 1972, pp. 117–139.

Ellis, A. Helping people get better rather than merely feel better. *Rational Living,* 7(2), 1972, 2–9.

Ellis, A. *Humanistic psychotherapy: The rational-emotive approach.* New York: Julian Press, 1973.

Janov, A. *The primal scream.* New York: Putnam's, 1970.

Karle, W., Corriere, R., & Hart, J. Psychophysiological changes in abreactive therapy—Study 1: Primal Therapy. *Psychotherapy: Theory, Research and Practice, 10,* 1973, 123–130.

Kelly, G. *The psychology of personal constructs.* New York: Norton, 1955.

Lowen, A. *The betrayal of the body.* New York: Macmillan, 1967.

Malamud, D. Self-confrontation methods in psychotherapy. *Psychotherapy: Theory, Research and Practice, 10,* 1973, 123–130.

Malleson, N. Panic and phobia. A possible method of treatment. *Lancet, 1,* 1959, 225–227.

Maslow, A.H. *Motivation and personality.* New York: Harper, 1954, 1973.

Perls, F.S. *Gestalt therapy verbatim.* Lafayette, CA: Real People Press, 1969.

Phillips, E.L. *Psychotherapy.* Englewood Cliffs, NJ: Prentice-Hall, 1956.

Reich, W. *The function of the orgasm.* New York: Orgone Institute Press, 1942.

Rotter, J.B. *Social learning and clinical psychology.* New York: Prentice-Hall, 1954.

Shorr, J.E. Imagine, in what part of your body your mother resides? *Psychotherapy: Theory, Research and Practice, 10,* 1973, 131, 134.

Stampfl, P.G., & Levis, D.J. Essentials of implosive therapy. *Journal of Abnormal Psychology, 72,* 1967, 496–503.

Thorne, F.C. *Personality: A clinical eclectic view.* Brandon, VT: Journal of Clinical Psychology, 1961.

Wolpe, J. *Psychotherapy of reciprocal inhibition.* Stanford: Stanford University Press, 1958.

Chapter 54

Egotism in Gestalt Therapy: The Next Boundary

J. RANDOLPH BURNHAM

I have been studying Gestalt Therapy for the last ten years, and for the last five years I have felt comfortable enough to call myself a Gestalt therapist. I received my introduction to Gestalt Therapy in a workshop with Laura Perls in 1971. My initial training was at the Gestalt Institute of Cleveland's intensive program (1976–1977) and since 1978 I have continued my training with Isadore From.

While the self-appointed label of Gestalt therapist finally sits comfortably with me, periodically I find myself needing to explain my understanding of Gestalt Therapy to patients and colleagues. Put simply, I find great ignorance and misunderstanding of Gestalt Therapy. Out of ignorance, colleagues accuse Gestalt Therapy of being irresponsible: uncommitted; unconcerned with closeness, tenderness, love, warmth, and softness. Out of misunderstanding, the general public accuses us of being uncaring, harsh, bombastic, and technique oriented. I am very disturbed by these comments and I disagree with them.

My understanding of the range, depth, and contribution of Gestalt Therapy has been enhanced by my training with Isadore From and by my involvement with the New York Institute for Gestalt Therapy. Although Joseph Zinker (1973, 1975) has already voiced opinions similar to mine of Gestalt Therapy, my experience leads me to believe that some of Dr. Zinker's notions need to be stressed again, this time from my perspective.

312

Many of the distortions surrounding Gestalt Therapy are the result of imbuing Frederick Perls' later writings, demonstrations, and proselytizing with too much importance. Any serious person wishing to understand Gestalt Therapy, or conversely, to challenge its philosophical basis cannot do so without a thorough reading and understanding of Perls' (1947) earlier work, *Ego, Hunger and Aggression,* and the second part of *Gestalt Therapy* by Perls, Hefferline, and Goodman (1951). The unfortunate overemphasis on Perls' later work is best exemplified by the popularity of the "Gestalt Prayer." The prayer itself is embarrassingly simplistic and insipid. Nonetheless, its bastardization of "I do my thing and you do your thing" into "I do my thing and to hell with you" is a crude misinterpretation of Gestalt Therapy, though it is probably a fair interpretation of some of Frederick Perls' later work and life.

While Fritz Perls, by his own admission, was the rediscoverer of Gestalt, he is not, was not, and never will be Gestalt Therapy. Yet his magnificent clinical skill, synthesizing genius, and forceful presence has had a profound effect on the public image of Gestalt Therapy. There is some question as to just what Fritz was about in the last five years of his life. Guru? Dirty old man? Ego tripper? Proselytizer? Popularizer? Clinical master? Creative genius, creating and finally receiving the glory and recognition he had sought for so long? Yes! Gestalt therapist? I have my doubts. The embodiment of Gestalt Therapy? Certainly not!

In discussing Freudian technique, Fritz once said:

Freud had a deep phobia. He was embarrassed to look into anybody's face or to be stared at, so he avoided the situation by putting the patient on a couch and sitting behind him. Soon this symptom became standard procedure. (Perls, 1971, p. 37)

Although there is great question whether this was the case with Freud, I see a similar process of the founder's symptoms becoming dogma in the public image of Gestalt and within the Gestalt movement.

Using Perls' own evaluation of Freud, one could say that Perls himself had a deep phobia. He was afraid of ongoing, long-term, warm, close, soft, loving commitment. He was counterphobic dependent. To avoid long-term, touching situations, he did short-term workshops; he loved and left; he was hard, frustrating, and cold. He refused to commit himself in a warm, soft, loving, *ongoing* manner. (Parenthetically, what I have said about Frederick Perls is the opposite of my experience with Isadore From and Laura Perls.) In Gestalt terms, Frederick Perls was an egotist, and the disturbance of egotism has started to be erroneously established as the standard of Gestalt Therapy.

Egotism in Gestalt Therapy, like all neurotic manifestations, is a disturbance at the contact boundary. It is the attempt to experience the contact boundary as fixed. The egotist can include only the known, self-aware experience. In egotism, experiencing any compelling interest in the other or the new is anxious making, and thus the egotist cannot risk the prospect of genuine confluence.

The egotist is aware of the boundary yet is unwilling/unable to allow interest in the other to go beyond that boundary to the extent that s/he experiences the loss of his or her boundary. The egotist can acknowledge the other and yet cannot allow that acknowledgment to develop into an interest in and understanding of the differences. A genuine We-ness is not experienced. Clinically, the egotist's language contains clear I's, You's, and It's, yet We is conspicuous by its absence. Egotism, then, is an overidentification with one's individuality and separateness, and is a neurotic attempt to maintain that known boundary. As Goodman (Perls, et al, 1951) puts it, "Neurotically, egotism is a kind of confluence with the deliberate awareness and an attempted annihilation of the uncontrollable and surprising" (p. 456). In this context, egotism in Gestalt Therapy is like the transference-neurosis "cure" in psychoanalytic therapy. Egotism is a stage of and a by-product of Gestalt psychotherapy.

When the symptoms disappear and the transference neurosis remains, a serious analyst will push on to analyze the transference. Similarly, a competent Gestalt therapist knows that while egotism is an important and necessary step in therapy, s/he also acknowledges that there is still more to be done. This task, like dealing with the transference neurosis, is not easy. The reasons for the difficulty are many and this paper allows me only to make some limited, tentative statements.

Patients search out psychotherapy because they are experiencing some form of neurotic pain, and because their psychological survival is experienced as threatened. In Gestalt Therapy, we view this "pain" as being a function of disturbances at the contact boundary. We, like all psychotherapists, claim that the cure is greater self-awareness. Our focus is upon assisting the patient with the aware use of the contact-making ego functions of *identification* (this is for me) and *alienation* (this is not for me). Thus, broadly defined, Gestalt Therapy is a therapy of the ego.

At our best, we work with a patient to enhance and expand self-awareness by attending to how, unawares, the patient disturbs his or her contact-making functions. As a by-product of this attention, one becomes interested in one's boundary-making process. This experience of greater self-awareness is coupled with a lessening of "pain" as well as a diminishing of the threat to psychological survival. These two "pleasant" experiences are tied to an increased involvement with the ego function, and so it is relatively late in any successful Gestalt Therapy that an overidentification with the "I" develops. The "I" and the boundary of the "I" become the most important subjects to the patient, in short, egotism. This over-interest in self-awareness is now the new therapeutic problem. In Gestalt Therapy it is at this point, and not until this point, that the focus of the therapist shifts from assisting in the patient's survival to helping the patient grow. As long as one is overly concerned with the "I" to the exclusion of the other, or that which is new in the environment, one cannot grow or thrive. Egotism too has limits, though they are less apparent and, for most patients, less painful.

This new symptom of egotism, one impossible for Frederick Perls to address because of his own egotism, is now, in certain circles, being viewed as the product of a successful Gestalt Therapy. More troubling still is the possibility of Frederick Perls' dramatic, egotistical style being viewed as standard Gestalt procedure. The unfortunate misinterpretation of Fritz's tendency to work in his egotistical manner is a denial of the committed, working-through process in Gestalt psychotherapy. Perls was able to open people up to their ongoing process very powerfully and quickly. His workshop and demonstration films are clear evidence of this skill. As a rule, he did not stay with these people on an ongoing basis, helping them to take the small steps of integration which any well-trained Gestalt therapist considers the real guts and work of Gestalt Therapy. This stress upon the "little-bit-at-a-time, small-bites" process is an existential/behavioral definition of responsibility and caring.

As I understand Perls' earlier writings and work, particularly the second half of *Gestalt Therapy* (Perls' manuscript rewritten and expanded by Paul Goodman), the stress and style is devoted to making explicit the notion that therapy and assimilation are a slow, incremental process. Frederick Perls' later work, public statements, and the media interpretation of this data leave the impression that Gestalt Therapy is not an ongoing incremental process. The legacy Fritz left Gestalt Therapy is visibility and popularity. It has been Laura Perls, Isadore From, and others who have carried forward the philosophy of Gestalt Therapy as a method to help us develop our humanness along all our polarities: responsible as well as irresponsible, soft and loving as well as hard and uncaring. Walter Kempler (1973) seems to be making a similar statement when he writes:

> Fritz was a specialist. His genius rested in his ability to maintain his separateness, and revealed itself in the skillfulness with which he helped others to gain their needed separateness. But when it came to union—the other side of the spinning coin of life—he either opposed it or was helpless. Consequently, he attracted mostly those who struggle for separateness and those who needed comfort in their stuck separateness. As a result, the Gestalt movement is temporarily out of balance with too much emphasis on "I am I" and not nearly

enough appreciation for the equally necessary and difficult struggle for union. Although the best preparation for union is the successful separation, it is not enough for the therapist to stop his work at that point. Neither separateness nor union is the goal of the therapeutic process, but rather the exhortation of the endless and often painful undulation between them. (p.14)

It would be a shame if Gestalt's fullness is lost due to a misinterpretation and overstressing of Frederick Perls' neurotic symptoms and stylistic idiosyncrasies.

REFERENCES

Kempler, W. *Principles of Gestalt family therapy.* Kempler Press, 1973.

Perls, F. *Ego, hunger, and aggression.* New York: Vintage Books, 1947.

Perls, F. Four lectures. In *Gestalt therapy now.* J. Fagan & I. Shepherd, Eds. New York: Harper & Row, 1971.

Perls, F., Hefferline, R.F., & Goodman, P. *Gestalt therapy.* New York: Julian Press, 1951.

Zinker, J. On loving encounters: A phenomenological view. In *Gestalt therapy primer.* Stephenson, Ed. Springfield, IL: Charles C. Thomas, 1975.

Zinker, J. Winter 1973/74, Gestalt therapy is permission to be creative. *VOICES*, 9(4), p. 75.

Chapter 55

The Issue of Cult Identity

MONROE GOTTSEGEN
AND
GLORIA BEHAR GOTTSEGEN

One approach to the problem of countertransferential cult identity and its destructive effect on psychotherapy is to examine a few of the ways professional identity factors find expression in the ongoing session. There is nothing new in observing that the patient is experienced not only through the person of the therapist but through the filter of his professional imago as well. The therapist has conscious and frequently unconscious ties to his training institute and his supervisors. We believe that the consequence of such role identification can be detrimental to patient growth. In developing a professional identity, one may not only learn what supervisors and training institutes teach, but uncritically internalize the school or cult orientation so that a learned piece of information becomes an ordained truth; a founding tenet of the school, an orthodoxy of practice. In short, the professional imago itself has endemic negative procrustean potentials which, when expressed in the work, can be viewed as a defense against enhancement of a more encompassing understanding of the patient.

This cult identity may make its appearance in three forms: 1) structural rigidities in conducting the work which then predetermine patient response, with the accompanying refusal to alter the structure whether or not it be useful for the patient's progress, 2) data insensitivity: a perceptual blindness to certain patient data that would require a therapist response that is different from the orthodox, preprogrammed response, and 3) in-session therapist response to patient behaviors. The characteristic defensive

317

nature of the therapist may merge with the training school orthodoxy to become a cult identity. The result is that the therapist will tend to deny, mis-hear, or punish the patient's communication, communication which, if handled in a non-compulsive manner, might lead to an undoing of resistance and progress toward growth.

We know that data are gathered in different forms dependent upon the method of treatment. For example, in psychodrama, the patient acts out historical data before a group of people, some of whom he may or may not know. He does this as if the event or incident were *now taking place* and uses surrogates from the group who approximate the characteristics of the actual personages from his life drama. The structure through which this data emerges is interactive, interpersonal. The data is alive, energized; the drama is intense; ego and feeling are mobilized; the person is fully immersed. This implicit theory of psychodramatic cure is that the past, re-experienced fully by the person, leads to new resolutions of old conflicts. This is a Freudian position in an operational sense in that one gains freedom from neurosis by re-experiencing the past. With that, the past is put away, so that the person can live in the present. This is abreaction via the "as if" drama.

If the method is couch work or psychoanalysis, stimulus-deprivation methods cause the patient to regress, eliciting pathologies from the past so that they can be brought to the patient's conscious mind through another pseudo-drama, the transference neurosis, with the hope that the patient will put the pathologies aside, resolving old conflicts. Hopefully, he can then live comfortably in the present. No body work is involved. There are no interactive role pressures from others. There is no exhibitionistic, group-pressuring structure. Data is pure, not a role-doctored old tape, reorchestrated and rearranged for concert hall presentation before an admiring throng. There is nothing in couch work to prod affective display beyond the patient's need system itself. Abreaction is nevertheless encouraged, and the goals are the same. This is classical Freudian method.

Hypnotherapy, Bioenergetics and Primal therapy are, in essence, neo-Freudian methods. Again, there is a loss of distance from the immediate, leading to a regressive state, these methods using altered states of patient consciousness. It is only the induction methods that are different. Again, the results are that the patient abreactively re-experiences the past, dialoging with his imagoes in order to put them away, or refashioning them through ego readaptations.

Hypnotherapy requires passive cooperation with an inductor. Bioenergetics uses physical pathways, while Primal method is largely a do-it-yourself regression experience through the guidance of a mediator, coupled with the passive support of others whose presence as a group encourages regression. In all these instances, the emerging data is reasonably pure, while the aim, conflict resolution, remains as it does in the earlier mentioned methods.

Gestalt method involves an exhibitionistic performance before a group utilizing preconscious data for the most part. The point is to work through, in a one-person psychodrama, both ego-dystonic and ego-syntonic defenses. Here, the goal is not to re-experience history, making it vital, as in neo-Freudian methods, but to reclaim aspects of the dissociated person, forcing a disequilibrium in the ego and a resulting reintegration at the point of the defensive breakdown. This method is not abreactive, yet includes ego reorganization in its method, forcing rebuilding of new adaptations as it dissolves old defenses. It is the least Freudian of the above methods in that it substitutes group pressure for transference neurosis while encouraging an artificial dependency based on the therapist's willingness to shame and embarrass the patient into compliance. The attack on the patient's self-respect has the effect of undoing resistance. The therapist's extending influence over the patient in the Gestalt method violates the Freudian spirit in four essential ways: 1) aggressive behavior on the part of the therapist toward the patient is considered appropriate in the service of undoing resistance; 2) all dream symbols are always assumed to contain major elements of disowned self and the patient is required to project onto each of them as a way of ferreting out unconscious content; 3) transference-countertransference phenomena are considered nuisances to be discarded; and 4) resistant patients who do not want to give up their resistances are asked to leave the therapy situation.

Behavior therapy, in its purest sense, functions on the premise that one need not know the past in any form, to put it away. If one desensitizes areas of anxiety, the patient re-experiences himself and makes room in his person for new ways of functioning. This is the clearest example of a non-Freudian method.

Transpersonal analysis opens new avenues in the person and forces the ego to stretch itself to include these new parts of the person. In this way, the past yields to a brighter present. It is not conflict bound and implicitly does not require conflict resolution as a precursor for growth.

We could go on. The data is selectively and differently shaped as a consequence of the action modality required by the method. Each of the catalytic methods requires a different motivating ingredient to push through the patient's resistance. Some of these motivational ingredients are structure bound, e.g. group approbation in one approach, the possibility of shame-faced failure before others in another approach, a sense of personal failure, guilt, in a third approach, etc. Generally, it is easier to feel data when you act it than when you are talking to the wall, so that affective experiences occur more readily in full body involvement than in part involvement or in talk modalities. It should be clear that if an obsessional patient shows no feeling when he is urged to obsess freely while talking to the wall, it might be better that he act out, or scream out his feelings, rather than being told he is resisting, i.e. "bad." We would have to conclude that it is the method and the therapist's compulsive persistence at it, that is resisting, not the patient. If, for example, the hysterical patient loves Reichian body work, or psychodrama, or Gestalt work but makes no life changes, we can only guess that there is too much "as if" drama and not enough "real" drama for the person to be able to find himself beneath his act. Character defenses have not been shown to yield following a swim in the pool of primal pain. Some pathologies are better untouched by some methods than by others. How can one deal with a grandiosity, hysterically expressed, before an applauding group? It is a problem that would seldom even arise in the method-acting school of therapy. There, the very method supports pathology.

A therapist not overly tied to his professional cult identification should have the professional skill to either apply other methods or send his patients to practitioners of these other methods when his patients run into methodological limitations. Unfortunately, this seldom happens. And more shockingly, the therapist is too frequently unaware that difficulties in treatment may be his failure and not the patient's. To this extent, he can be said to have been so "mind controlled" by his training indoctrination that he cannot separate his own orientation from his cult-dominated, training bias. He may be so involved in shoring up the pillars of cult identification that he would prefer to blame himself or the patient rather than admit to the limitations of his approach.

Responses

Edward W.L. Smith

I don't like cults, for me. I have been involved in varying degrees with several cults and have come to not like how I feel when I realize that I am part of a cult. The feeling I have is disgust, a sad disgust at the recognition of the myopic focusing of energy which I do, and I believe anyone does, when caught up in a cult. Being in such a position leads to a diminishing of me, a closing out of those possibilities which lie outside the realm of options delimited by that cult.

Coming from this position, I read the Gottsegen's article with interest and agreement. That is, I agree with their thesis that a therapist may internalize a cult orientation in his training, leading to a rigid orthodoxy which seriously limits that therapist's effectiveness. Their discussion of the forms in which cult identity may appear in therapy was stimulating for me.

When I read the section on Gestalt therapy, I felt uneasy. My discomfort was in response to the reminder of the existence of a Gestalt cult and the misunderstandings of the Gestalt approach which are perpetrated by the cult. I disagree with several of the points which the Gottsegens mention about what they term "Gestalt method." What they describe is an approximation of the Gestalt cult. The Gestalt approach is quite different.

These are my disagreements with the Gottsegens' description of the Gestalt method. First, they identify the Gestalt method as "an exhibitionistic performance before a group." Gestalt work is neither necessarily exhibitionistic, nor necessarily done in a group setting. Good Gestalt work, as any good therapy work, is not exhibitionistic. There are many Gestalt therapists doing individual work in a one-to-one setting.

Second, the Gottsegens say that the Gestalt goal is not to "re-experience history, making it vital." This statement is inconsistent with the phenomenon of the incomplete gestalt, the unfinished business which must be finished in order for the person to experience the here-and-now, free from shadows from the past. A major focus of Gestalt therapy is the vital, psychodramatic finishing of unfinished aspects of one's history. Third, the method, contrary to the Gottsegens' suggestion, can be highly abreactive. The point where this is most obvious is in the "impasse phenomenon" which F. Perls discusses in detail in several places in his works. (For a summary of Perls' understanding of the impasse phenomenon and its connection with Reichian theory see Smith, 1975.)

Fourth, the Gottsegens imply that what makes Gestalt therapy go is "group pressure," "an artificial dependency based on the therapist's willingness to shame and embarrass the patient into compliance," and "attack on the patient's self-respect." Wow! That's hazing, not therapy. F. Perls was very clear in stating that the relationship between therapist and patient was that of I and Thou, following Buber (Levitsky & Perls, 1970). The therapist's tools are support and frustration; support of authentic expressions of the patient's person and frustration of non-authentic or manipulative expressions (Perls, 1973). This position is far from attacking the patient's self-respect!

And fifth, the Gottsegens state that the "therapist's extending influence over the patient in the Gestalt method violates the Freudian spirit." I find that an interesting, if not quaint statement. The essential ways of this violation, which they go on to delineate, are all overstated.

There is a Gestalt cult. And those who participate in it have adopted a jargon-ridden, procrustean approach to therapy, mistaking the words and techniques for the essence. The cult is kept alive by the introjection of things done or said by Gestalt "masters," especially F. Perls. George Brown (1974) has offered an interesting perspective on the cult by suggesting that

F. Perls' particular style of Gestalt therapy was not only an expression of his person, but an emphasis of his hard, frustrating side because of the particular kind of people he most often worked with in settings such as Esalen. Any therapist's views of therapy become biased by virtue of the restricted population with which he works. So, as F. Perls moved toward the workshop format in settings such as Esalen, his therapy style and theorizing reflected his experiences with the kinds of people who came to those settings. The highly creative and effective interventions which he made with those people in those settings cannot be mechanically borrowed by a different therapist/person or used with a different group of patients without loss of essence. And it is just such a mechanical, technical shift that characterizes the Gestalt cult.

F. Perls (1969) spoke against the cult saying, "One of the objections I have against anyone calling himself a Gestalt therapist is that he uses technique. A technique is a gimmick." ". . . the sad fact is that this jazzing-up more often becomes a dangerous substitute activity, another phony therapy that 'prevents' growth" (p. 1). And in *The Gestalt Approach and Eye Witness to Therapy* (1973) it is stated that F. Perls hoped his films and books would help people to understand the Gestalt process, rather than see it as enigmatic or miraculous, in short, to "de-mystify the cult of Fritz Perls."

So, what is Gestalt therapy if it is not the cult, the rigid, narrow approach described by the Gottsegens? Jim Dublin (1976) distinguished clearly between Gestalt therapy, Existential-Gestalt therapy, and "Perls-ism" or the particular style of doing Gestalt therapy which was an expression of the "person" of F. Perls. His style of Gestalt therapy, or "Perls-ism" is amply publicly available to view through his several books and films.

One perspective on what Gestalt therapy is is given by the Polsters (1973). They suggest that the foundations of Gestalt therapy are the recognition that power is in the present (here-and-now perspective), experience counts most (important learning is first-hand, through one's own senses), the therapist is his own instrument (beyond technique), and therapy is too good to be limited to the sick (therapy is for growth, actualization, not just for cure of pathology). A therapy approach which incorporates these four fundamentals is, then, Gestalt therapy.

Irma Shepherd (1976) has emphasized that open-endedness is a basic assumption in the Gestalt approach. By this she means that personality is a constant interaction and integration of a number of functions (perceptual, physiological, cognitive) in relationship to the environment. This is a view of reality as process. Another basic assumption is that therapy requires the full participation of the therapist. The therapist experiences excitement as he/she makes contact, leading to a new experience (Gestalt). An aspect of the therapist's full participation is the use of his creativity or awareness in facilitating the process by enhancing experience. In addition Shepherd sees the Gestalt view as an ecological one, "man-as-part-of-nature," a view based on "energy." She quotes one of F. Perls' definitions of Gestalt therapy as "I and Thou, here and now." Shepherd sees the Gestalt approach as based in these assumptions, constantly evolving as it integrates concepts and techniques from other approaches which are consistent with its assumptions.

In commenting on the new directions in Gestalt therapy Laura Perls (1976) suggests its essence as involving focus on the awareness continuum, the contact boundary, and support. She emphasizes that every Gestalt therapist develops his own style within this essence.

These views of what Gestalt therapy is, by the Polsters, Shepherd, and L. Perls, are illustrations of how the masters' views do not support cultism.

My own view is that the Gestalt approach involves a philosophical position, a theory of personality, and a therapeutic style. The philosophical position is basically existential, with emphasis on personal responsibility, choice, and the I-Thou relationship. In addition, there is the Taoist-Zen flavor of "slowing down" and "getting in harmony with nature." This is a valuing of awareness and experience of "what is," with the knowing that paradoxically I only change as I accept and experience more fully who I am. The goal is the realization of my true nature, and this does not come through thinking, but through allowing my natural experiential process to flow. The personality theory of the Gestalt approach is a holistic one, viewing the person as flowing through homeostatic need cycles (or contact/ withdrawal cycles), with the all-encompassing need being self-actualization. The therapeutic style is phenomenological, focusing on facilitation of the patient's awareness in the here-and-now. Techniques are created which enhance the patient's experience and allow a psychodramatic living out of his process as defined by the "wisdom of his organism." (I can't adequately discuss these concepts in this short paper. I have, however, written at length about these ideas in "The Roots of Gestalt Therapy," 1976).

I consider this blend of existential and Zen philosophy, this organismic personality theory, and this phenomenological experiential style of working to be the necessary and sufficient conditions to define the Gestalt approach. I don't define the Gestalt approach by techniques. The Gestalt approach is given life by the "person" of the particular therapist. Therefore, there are many styles of Gestalt therapy, each reflecting the "person" of that therapist/artist. With an appreciation of this, I have no wish to "cultivate" Gestalt therapy.

REFERENCES

Brown, G. The farther reaches of Gestalt therapy. *Synthesis, 1*(1), 1974, 25–41.
Dublin, J. Gestalt therapy, Existential-Gesalt therapy and/versus "Perls-ism." In *The growing edge of Gestalt therapy*. E. Smith, Ed. New York: Brunner Mazel, 1976.

Levitsky, A., & Perls, F. The rules and games of Gestalt therapy. In *Gestalt therapy now*. J. Fagan and I. Shepherd, Eds. Palo Alto: Science and Behavior Books, 1970.

Perls. F. *The Gestalt approach and eye witness to therapy*. Palo Alto: Science and Behavior Books, 1973.

Perls, F. *Gestalt therapy verbatim*. Moab, UT: Real People Press, 1969.

Perls, L. Comments on the new directions. In *The growing edge of Gestalt therapy*. E. Smith, Ed. New York: Brunner/Mazel, 1976.

Polster, E. and Polster, M. *Gestalt therapy integrated*. New York: Brunner/Mazel, 1973.

Shepherd, I. Gestalt therapy as an open-ended system. In *The growing edge of Gestalt therapy*, E. Smith, Ed. New York: Brunner/Mazel, 1976.

Smith, E. The role of early Reichian theory in the development of Gestalt therapy. *Psychotherapy: Theory, Research, and Practice*, *12*(3), 1975, 268–272.

Smith, E. The roots of Gestalt therapy. In *The growing edge of Gestalt therapy*. E. Smith, Ed. New York: Brunner/Mazel, 1976.

James S. Simkin

My initial response to the Gottsegens' paper was remembering the story of the man walking around with a banana in his ear. Someone seeing him said, "Hey mister, you have a banana in your ear!" His response was, "I'm sorry, I can't hear you, I have a banana in my ear!" My fantasy is that the Gottsegens have a Freudian blindfold which they wear over their eyes.

It is possible that they may have seen a demonstration of Gestalt therapy. However, their distortions of what Gestalt therapy is are so gross that I am convinced that if they have ever been exposed to Gestalt therapy they were not only blindfolded but also deaf.

To briefly rebut some of their claims: "Gestalt method involves an exhibitionistic performance before a group. . . ." In close to 25 years of practicing Gestalt therapy the majority of patients I have seen have been in individual therapy. And of the several scores of Gestalt therapists I have trained over the past decade, the majority also do a considerable amount of individual work along with group and workshop styles.

Any therapists willing to shame and embarrass his patient into compliance is simply not practicing Gestalt therapy. Using group pressure is emotional blackmail and violates both the spirit and the letter of Gestalt therapy.

I agree with the Gottsegens that Gestalt therapists "violate the Freudian spirit" by actively intervening "in the service of undoing resistance." Patients are asked to *be* various parts of their dreams, *not* to project onto them; transference-countertransference phenomena *are* dealt with (not enhanced as in some systems) and certainly not discarded; and *of course* patients who do not want to give up their resistance do not want to give up their resistance.

Monroe and Gloria Gottsegen—please take your paper seriously and read and reread the first paragraph until you understand it.

Chapter 56

Book Reviews

FRITZ PERLS: HERE AND NOW by Jack Gaines. Millbrae, CA: Celestial Arts, 1979, pp. xiii + 440. $12.95.

Fritz Perls: Here and Now is a prodigious effort by Jack Gaines, augmented by amusing and deft drawings by Russ Youngren, to record the life of Fritz Perls, who attracted gossip like nostrils draw air. Gaines provides the reader with his sensitive management of personal interviews with an astonishingly large number of people, all powerfully affected by Fritz. It is evident that he was so "figural," as his theory would put it, that people remember vignettes concerning him with great clarity and just love to talk about him, ironic considering Fritz's well-known scorn for gossip. Many of these reports are nuggets of personal contact; they are joyous, grateful, aggrieved, worshipful, sad, demonic, political, most of them touching and revealing. Others are mundane and familiar, merely a reminder that in his fishbowl existence, Fritz was fair game for everybody's commentary.

These reports give a considerable base for illumination but no integrating perspective. Gaines leaves the reader, instead, to plumb for the sense in Fritz's mysterious nature. The sources of his legendry, the paradoxes of his existence, the relationship of his day-to-day interests to his therapeutic artistry are laid out only in raw detail. This verbatim style may be one legacy of Fritz's own simplistic isolation of experience from meaning. He so frequently emphasized his belief that experience speaks for itself that it is easy to ignore the tight unity and meaningfulness of the work he exhibited in his many movies and in his taped sessions in *Gestalt Therapy Verbatim.* There is no waste and there is always a personal message. Jack Gaines, using the verbatim technique, has also managed to transcend some of the verbatim limits by composing, through these reports, an almost narrative account of Fritz's life, a sequence of episodes which leads the reader compellingly, as a storyteller would, through surprising, then inevitable events. Fritz's death, instead of being merely foretold by our actual knowledge, is fresh as though he still might have survived. When he doesn't, it is a sad time, a culmination of foreboding out of recognitions of Fritz's courage to do what he must, his dependency on others to take care of him, his fixedness of character, and the ultimate power of the inevitable.

The book is compendious, too much so for my taste. However, whenever I began to feel the tediousness of report after report, I was gratefully revived by some new report which gave a novel or wise perspective on Fritz. I was especially moved by the Israel episodes which stretched the sense of Fritz furthest beyond his public image. In Israel he seemed like a ghostly spirit, living a haunted and haunting existence. He was like a wind through time in his mystical presence which contrasted with his very sensual, stubborn, and explosive qualities. The interviews with the Hillels were especially revealing of this rhythm. He studied painting with Ishaiah Hillel and lived in Ishaiah and Sarah's house. Ishaiah and Fritz did not talk much but Fritz once said to him, "Hillel, you have to go back to writing. But before you start, see that you have a writing place with a key and lock so that your wife won't put her hands on it." Hillel says, "When I think of that now, my head is bursting. I am a literary man more than a painter, but I didn't tell him I was a writer. I had stopped writing because of her but nobody in the world knew that; *nobody in the world.*" Sarah, who fed Fritz with warm hospitality, noted he was in and out for varying periods during several months when he suddenly disappeared. Ishaiah tells more about the end of the relationship. He and Sarah had given Fritz a reading lamp, which Fritz apparently installed improperly and the lamp gave him a shock when he was in bed with a woman. Fritz, the next day, said to Ishaiah, "I did not know your wife was a swine like you." Ishaiah was so irate he told him on the spot to pack his things and if he weren't out in an hour, he would break his neck. Ishaiah then went up to his bed, feeling shattered. Fritz soon came up, put his hand on Ishaiah's knee and said in a very soft voice, "Are you feeling well, Hillel?" Ishaiah didn't answer him and Fritz kissed him on the forehead and just left the village. Then, about a half year later, as Ishaiah says, "he came one day as if nothing had happened between us to have my opinion of the paintings he made in Eilat."

Gaines' interviews tell us a lot about the sources of Fritz's power in his personal relationship and in his therapy. As one of many possible examples, Fritz is revealed as a master of articulation. His language was very colorful, as Arthur Ceppos, his publisher at Julian Press, says, and it was also very simple. This combination of simplicity and color is evident in all conversations remembered in his book. For example, when he was hospitalized shortly before his surgery and death he was faced by his doctor with a risky decision about surgery, involving highly complex considerations for and against. All he said, in a soft John Wayne style, was "We go. We operate." He was a man plainly impatient with complexity; he was hospitable only to simplicity. This style created high focus, high intensity, and high clarity, which gave him great personal impact. These qualities normally have an insistent ring but Fritz, on the contrary, always left space around what he said so that his words resonated, as in a song or in a breath. This gave his words a soft specificity rather than a dictatorial imperative. For therapy, his articulatory color and his narrowing of focus created remarkably powerful leverage where the malaise created by complexity and obfuscation had reduced people to bromidic existence. People were usually very moved and would readily follow his suggestions, especially in therapy, with great trust and creativity. However, his need for simple focus left out a lot which could not be readily framed. The words, *if, but, however,* for example, though commonly used for obfuscation, *do* reflect genuine human concerns, as would be evident for many people facing life-threatening surgery.

Looking at another aspect of his special combination of simplicity and high focus, it becomes evident that Fritz and many of his followers did not distinguish well between what was Fritz and what was gestalt therapy. He was both the spotlight, inspiring magnificent revelations, as this book amply details, and the spotlighted, the performer presenting the magician's act, but not his secrets. He showed the rabbit around but he kept it himself. The methodological principles he abundantly communicated were, in themselves, sufficient to unveil the secrets beyond the man himself, but the spell he cast with his personal legerdemain often distracted people from these illuminating guidelines into believing that only by trying to be Fritz could they do what he did.

Fritz had many facets, of course. As Jack Gaines says, "He was a tramp, a gentleman, a poet, a dreamer, and a lonely fellow." He was also a storyteller, a chess player, a man of unusual élan. He could smell out hilarity and loved it. He was profoundly moved by people with spunk. He was a caricaturized lothario. He could be a neighborhood crank. He might erupt with rageful tyranny, as though he were in seizure. It is no wonder, given his own range, that his work frequently centered around the polarities in people, the seemingly irreconcilable aspects of a person which war with each other and reduce the liveliness of the whole person. Fritz, however, did not himself seem to care about making these reconciliations. He was as he was at the moment, made no apologies for any limited aspect of his total range, and was willing to take the consequences of any of these aspects as though they were the whole of him. Though not impelled to reconcile these multilateral aspects of his nature, he did not disregard them either, seeming quite confident that whatever he was *now* was not what he would be at another time. He did not allow prejudicial conclusion-jumping concerning him to thwart him but he, also, lost whatever security could exist in the personal unity which an integrating identity might provide.

Consequently, when in the great loneliness which was often his lot, he would be more tormented, I imagine, than if he could have simultaneously recognized his belovedness. His contacts included innumerable moments of great beauty, as they are described by people in this book, but they would readily fade to be replaced by some new experience. Simultaneity among the disparate experiences of life seemed to be too much for him to handle. This heightened his clarity about the single event and, of course, exemplified the perhaps too pure reality of the existential man he prided himself in being. He lived a life of experiment, not just coincidentally a central concept in gestalt methodology. Experiment, as used in gestalt therapy, is greatly stylized experience and is thus often more graphic and pointed than the unframed life. But simplified clarity, of course, though at the root of gestalt therapy, will never save anyone from contending in everyday life with ineffable incongruities. Fritz often referred to incongruities as phony, as for example, when a person spoke in fixed smile when sadness was evident in the background. He himself wiped incongruity from his manifest concerns as well as anybody I have known. He fought a tough battle against all the compounding and confounding elements in his life and frequently believed he had indeed restored simplicity to life itself. He did make remarkable contributions to this perpetual human quest. His role as savior from incongruity brought him great fascination and renown, but incongruously, a very narrow frame of reference to live in.

In spite of the marvelous range of experiences presented in this book there are two important developments missing. First, there is little here about Fritz's peer relationships in New York, which would include people like Paul Goodman, Isadore From, Paul Weisz, and Elliot Shapiro. He had immense communion with these people whose views were powerful and who surely had an important place in his development. In fact, in the Perls, Hefferline, and Goodman book, *Gestalt Therapy*, it is difficult to distinguish between what came from Fritz and what came from Paul Goodman.

The second gap is the complete absence of Fritz's relationship to the Gestalt Institute of Cleveland, where Fritz accomplished his greatest early breakthrough in getting across his message beyond his peers in New York. He came in 1953 and worked with a highly trained group of people right up to the years before his death. How it could happen that those early New York peers and the mid-country ascendancy of Cleveland could be overlooked is a mystery which I believe bears some connection not only to a possible oversight by Jack Gaines, but also to Fritz's negation of his roots. Many people appreciate the newly realized magnetism of the present, but he got caught in it. He was a most masterful architect of the present in the field of psychotherapy, but he couldn't escape from his own special creation. He became a prisoner in the magnificent house he himself built.

ERVING POLSTER

Fritz Perls Here and Now is collected (not written) for the Fritz cult. Many of the contributors of the reminiscences it is composed of were or are members of that cult. Some of them seem to have been stunned by his death. How else to explain the petty quarrels over who really loved Perls and whom he really loved that are occasionally recorded here?

Jack Gaines, though he had never met Perls, has with this collection become the current celebrant of the Fritz cult. The volume consists mostly of taped statements by people who hadn't suffered Gaines' misfortune— not to have met Perls—and who were ready to reminisce, praise, sometimes carp, and in many cases gossip. Perhaps this is Gaines' vicarious meeting, but he has made no effort to sift fact from fiction.

Many of the tales of which this volume consists seem to be pseudo-religious, of the "I was saved" variety. Even the tales of flagellation by Perls are mostly converted into tests of faith meant for the sufferer's well-being. Of course there are miracles and revelations, which remain so because explanation is never required. The liturgy importantly resembles scatology—diagnosis by means of the faeces—as is suggested by the frequent appearance in the testimonials of the phrases "chicken shit" and "bull shit."

Along with Laura Perls in Ego, Hunger and Aggression and with Paul Goodman in Gestalt Therapy, Friedrich Perls made a major contribution to psychotherapy. It is in these books that the concept of the contact boundary—the concept that differentiated Gestalt therapy radically from earlier therapies—was developed. Revealingly enough, "contact boundary" is not even mentioned in Fritz Perls Here and Now. A serious and adequate biography of the life and assessment of the work of Friedrich Perls has yet to be done (giving him back his real name and dropping the "Fritz" might be a first step). Will Gresham's law prevail and the bad drive out the good? Fritz Perls Here and Now should not be allowed to do that.

ISADORE FROM

Chapter 57

The Importance of Fritz Perls Having Been

JOEN FAGAN

PRACTICE: When Fritz was "on" (and I refer to his films for validation of what I say), he was the most exciting therapist who ever lived. His
was the unique ability to pierce down into a person and grasp what was
most basically awry: where grief, fury, death lay deeply hidden; to specify
the arena where the battle could emerge and be fought; to limn the two
opponents; and, with precision and grace, to direct the battle. The struggle, achingly agonizing, sometimes seeming to last through eternities,
sometimes finished with breathtaking rapidity. The surrender—to life, to
wholeness, to forgiveness, release, tenderness, joy, beauty. Faces now
transformed, movement fluid, existence radiant and open. Onlookers engrossed, moved, purified, released. The possibilities of being godlike re-
affirmed: satori, grace, perfectability existing in this moment.

PREACHINGS: *Listen to yourself, the stirrings, the movements inside;
not to the words in your head: other people's words, your parents' words,
society's words, cold, critical, directing words. Be aware of you, where
you are, what you're doing; not the shoulds, the commands, the expectations. Keep your own eyes and ears, don't give them away and blind and
deafen yourself. Don't give your self away. Acknowledge what is yours.
Hear the important messages inside you. Do you really need others' approval? See—without it, you still breathe, still move. Breathe, move, look,
listen, see. Move into yourself, your body. Move into direct contact with*

331

others. (Not into words, not into expectations.) Move into movement, into excitement, into nature, into flow, into relaxation. Let it all in, all the richness, the fullness. Live rich. Live full. Let it out, empty yourself. Let go. Find your emptiness, suffer your emptiness, enjoy your emptiness, fill your emptiness. Find your resources. Let go; hold on. Leave; come back. Push; let go. Let go now. Flow. Leave the games, the roles as empty skins behind. Step out in nakedness, freedom. Find your rhythm; find your base; find your support. Support yourself. Reach out. Dare. Risk. Discover. Enjoy. Go freely into the now. Where else can you be but here? Who else can you be but you? You here now is enough. Be here. Be now. Be you.

PERSON: Fritz incorporated vitality[1], directness, hedonism[2], a passionate involvement with life, self-responsiveness, sophistication, holism[3]. A poet, artist, dabbler, trend-spotter[4], inventor of forms[5]. His own man[6]. A trouble-maker, rogue, buffoon, wandering Jew[7], dirty old man[8]. Impolite[9], disruptive, colorful, amoral, self-aggrandizing, lonely[10], disdainful[11], demanding, engaging. A genius[12]. A destructuring[13] and creating man. □

---

[1] A young man after watching Fritz dance one evening at Nepenthe: "Sir, I hope when I'm as old as you are, I'll be as young as you are now."

[2] Fritz enjoyed all pleasures; of surroundings, food and wine, body comforts, arts, music, philosophy, Zen-religion. All amenities.

[3] The kibbutz in Canada was Fritz' effort at creating an environment where therapy-growing-developing-living would be of all one piece. Few therapists have had the temerity to make so visible their therapy.

[4] Fritz was one of the first "big names" to become associated with Esalen and to live there. He was also one of the first to leave, with real regret, but with recognition of the shift of some part of the growth movement to the easy turn-on, instant intimacy, and a developing air of cultism.

[5] The autobiography, *Garbage Pail*, was Fritz' way of inventing a form of writing that fit and facilitated him; a mixture of free association, control, confession, theory, fact, fantasy, all personalized, all flowing through awareness.

[6] In Los Angeles in 1964, the Association of Humanistic Psychology, a young, undistinguished organization was being attended by several hundred people, with vague hopes of finding something there. The program called for them to be divided into groups of 10 or 12, each with a leader, to discuss purposes, types of meetings, organizational structure. The groups duly and dully met an hour, and reconvened, with the representatives reporting back the deliberations and advice. After several deadening reports, a dazed young man came up and, very uncertain as to exactly what had happened, said, "I just had a very strange and wonderful experience. Our group leader was Dr. Perls, and he began by asking if anyone had a dream he wanted to work on, and I said I did so...." Instead, of talking about providing workshop experience, Fritz had provided one.

[7] Fritz' statement, chilling in its impact: "I left Germany in 1933; I left South Africa in 1948; I left the United States in 1969."

[8] Several women have spoken to me of their real appreciation of Fritz' ability as a lover; others have spoken with anger of seduction attempts when they were vulnerable.

[9] There are many anecdotes of Fritz' varied ways of indicating forcefully his dislike of boorish speakers, dull meetings, and routinely conventional or game-playing initial contacts with people.

¹⁰ The paradox of most therapists—that they can produce growth and joy in others more easily than they experience these in themselves. Fritz: "I don't really like myself very much."

¹¹ His last words in life to the nurse trying to get him to lie down, "Don't tell me what to do."

¹² Fritz left a legacy of therapy technology, on paper, on film, in those who had studied with him. No one else has given therapists such clear permission to be powerful.

¹³ Fritz: "I am astonished at my extremes of meanness and compassion."

Figure 13. "Confrontation" (Ed.)

Index